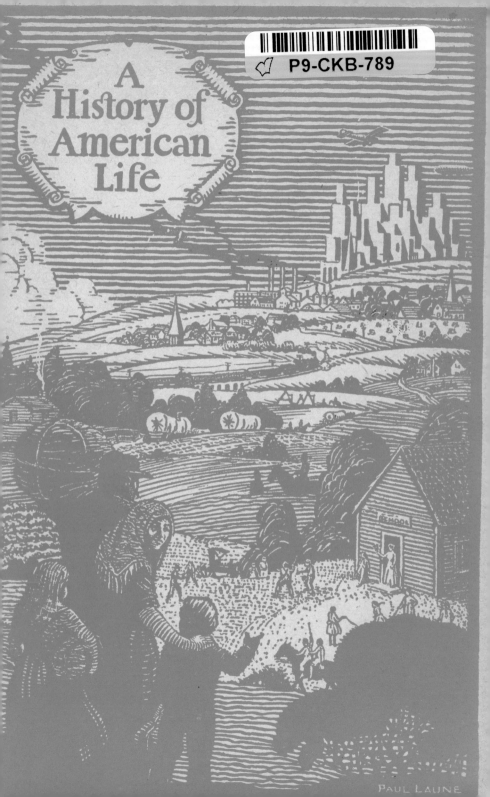

A
History of
American
Life

P9-CKB-789

PAUL LAUNE

A HISTORY OF AMERICAN LIFE

IN
Twelve Volumes

ARTHUR M. SCHLESINGER
DIXON RYAN FOX
Editors

CARL BECKER
Consulting Editor

A HISTORY OF AMERICAN LIFE

Noah Webster,
Who desired his country to be independent in every concern

A HISTORY OF AMERICAN LIFE
Volume V

THE COMPLETION OF INDEPENDENCE
1790-1830

BY

JOHN ALLEN KROUT
PROFESSOR OF HISTORY, COLUMBIA UNIVERSITY

AND

DIXON RYAN FOX
PRESIDENT OF UNION COLLEGE

New York
THE MACMILLAN COMPANY
1944

History

47779

MAR 2 0 1945

Americans, unshackle your minds, and act like independent beings. . . . You have now an interest of your own to augment and defend: You have an empire to raise and support by your exertions, and a national character to establish and extend by your wisdom and virtues. To effect these great objects, it is necessary to frame a liberal plan of policy, and build it on a broad system of education. Before this system can be formed and embraced, the Americans must believe, and act from the belief, that it is dishonorable to waste life in mimicking the follies of other nations and basking in the sunshine of foreign glory.

NOAH WEBSTER, *A Collection of Essays and Fugitive Writings* (Boston, 1790), 36.

A people, into whose minds the thoughts of foreigners are poured perpetually, needs an energy within itself to resist, to modify this mighty influence . . . . The true sovereigns of a country are those who determine its mind, its modes of thinking, its tastes, its principles; and we cannot consent to lodge this sovereignty in the hands of strangers. . . . We need an inward power proportionate to that which is exerted on us, as the means of self-subsistence.

WILLIAM ELLERY CHANNING, "On a National Literature," *Christian Examiner*, VII (1830), 281-282.

CONTENTS

CONTENTS

ILLUSTRATIONS

(By the Editors)

of whom, however, purchased it; and it was finally disposed of by raffle which yielded barely sufficient to pay for paints and canvas." It is now owned by the New York Historical Society.

From a painting (23 in. x 29 in.) by John Lewis Krimmel (1789-1821), in the Pennsylvania Academy of the Fine Arts, Philadelphia, by whose courtesy it is here reproduced. Like Guy (plate i) he was a "carrier" of art from the Old World; he came to America from Germany in 1810 and supported himself chiefly by portrait painting and teaching; he became president of the Association of American Artists shortly before he was drowned in 1821. Because of certain qualities in his group paintings he was called by his contemporaries "the American Hogarth." This canvas was painted about 1812.

The building shown is the water tower (where the City Hall now stands) which was designed and built by Benjamin Henry Latrobe (England, 1764-New Orleans, 1830) in 1799-1800 as part of his water-works system; water was pumped by steam from the Schuylkill and distributed through the city from this Doric marble tower.

The statue in the fountain, as shown in the painting, was by William Rush (1756-1833), America's first notable sculptor. Installed in this little park at the beginning of the century, and called variously "Leda and Swan," "Nymph of the Schuylkill," and "Water-nymph and Bittern," it was cast in bronze in 1854, and after a long sojourn in Fairmount Park is now placed in the Philadelphia Museum of Art. The carving of the statue, with the model demurely chaperoned by Mrs. Rush, is the subject of an historical painting by Thomas Eakins (1844-1916).

From *Picturesque United States of America, 1811, 1812, 1813, Being a Memoir on Paul Svinin . . . with Fifty-two Reproductions of Water Colors in His Own Sketch-Book,* by Avrahm Yarmolinsky (N. Y., 1930), plate 15. Svinin, a Russian diplomatic officer, artist and author, published *A Picturesque Voyage in North America* (St. Petersburg, 1818) in his native language, after returning from twenty months' residence in the United States. A rare copy was discovered in Russia by Dr. Yarmolinsky, of the New York Public Library, who found himself fascinated by six black-and-white illustrations. Extensive inquiry regarding the book and illustrations yielded little, but Dr. Yarmolinsky did discover a good deal about the author. Back in America, Dr. Yarmolinsky fell in with Mr. R. T. H. Halsey, who had in his possession a portfolio of 52 original water-color paintings, apparently the work of a

"Paul Svignine," which an American Red Cross worker had purchased in Paris at the end of the First World War. The six illustrations were promptly recognized as reproductions from this collection; the subjects of the whole 52 were identified only after much consultation. They were then reproduced in the volume named above, but only one in color.

In the present illustration old Christ Church is seen in the background. This is probably the first artistic treatment of American chimney sweeps, appearing here with their master, who is rudely jostling a fashionable beau.

(a) The Hongs of Old Canton. From a painting (25 in. x 35 in.) by an unknown Chinese artist about 1820. It was presented to the Peabody Museum, Salem, Mass., in 1903 by James S. Paine, of Worcester, whose ancestor Russell Sturgis probably acquired it in China about 1834. It is here reproduced by permission of the Peabody Museum.

(b) Ship *Columbia* attacked by Indians in Juan de Fuca Strait. From a drawing by George Davidson, who accompanied the *Columbia* on her second voyage; owned by Dr. E. C. Twombly. It is here reproduced, by permission of the Houghton Mifflin Company, from an illustration in Samuel E. Morison, *Maritime History of Massachusetts* (Boston, 1921), 46.

(a) An advertisement from the *Niagara Journal*, April 13, 1819 (Buffalo Historical Society), announcing the Buffalo-Canandaigua, N. Y., stagecoach line, fare $2.50.

(b) From *A Description of Ithiel Town's Improvement in the Construction of Wood and Iron Bridges* (New Haven, 1821), a small pamphlet setting forth Town's argument for his lattice truss—revealed in the engraving by S. S. Jocelyn (1799-1879)—from whose construction he earned a considerable income. Ithiel Town (1784-1844) studied architecture under Asher Benjamin (1773-1845), won a reputation as a designer of churches from his Center Church and Trinity Church on New Haven Green, and, with his firm, planned public buildings as far away as the capitols in Indianapolis, Ind., Springfield, Ill., and Raleigh, N.C. "He evidently dreamed of an American architecture and an American art, independent and standing on their own feet, and through his magnificent collection of books wished to open to American architects all of the stores of European knowledge, so that with a solidity of foundation they might develop an American architecture for American conditions." Talbot Hamlin, *Greek Revival Architecture in America* (N. Y., 1944), 138.

method. I submitted therefore without enquiry, but it was
a bold experiment on his part on the health of an Octogenarian, worn down by sickness as well as age. successive
coats of thin grout plaistered on the naked head, and kept
there an hour, would have been a severe trial of a young
and hale person. he suffered the plaister also to get so
dry that separation became difficult & even dangerous. he
was obliged to use freely the mallet & chisel to break it into
pieces and get off a piece at a time. these thumps of the
mallet would have been sensible almost to a loggerhead
[turtle]. the family became alarmed, and he confused, till
I was quite exhausted, and there became real danger that the
ears would separate from the head sooner than from the
plaister. I now bid adieu for ever to busts & even portraits." [Knoedler & Co.], *Life Masks of Noted Americans of 1825* (N. Y., 1940), facsimile of complete letter
opposite Plate I.

  From a primitive painting by an unknown artist, about
1800. Owned by Kennedy and Company, New York
City, by whose courtesy the painting is here reproduced
from a photograph taken by the Works Progress Administration when it was exhibited in 1938 at the Museum of
the City of New York.

  From a print (9.8 in. x 7.8 in.) whose subject is fully
identified in the legend. The original appeared in the
Columbian Phenix, and Boston Review, Boston, January,
1800. It was republished by Charles E. Goodspeed in
1903, from a reëngraving on copper by Sidney L. Smith
(1865-1929), a notable American engraver. Our reproduction is from a copy in the I. N. Phelps Stokes Collection in the New York Public Library.
  The state house was largely completed by 1799, from
the plans of Charles Bulfinch (1763-1844), and obviously
has influenced the design of state capitols ever since. The
accompanying account in the *Columbian Phenix* speaks not
only of the state house, and Beacon Hill, but also of "the
monument upon it to the right, in the back ground, the
late Governor Hancock's and the other seats to the left
between the State House and the Charles River, as viewed
from the Mall."

  "Macdonough's Victory on Lake Champlain, and Defeat
of the British Army at Plattsburg by Genl. Macomb,
Septr. 11, 1814. Published 4th July 1816 by B. Tanner
Engraver No. 74, South Eighth Street, Philadelphia.
Printed by Rogers & Esler . . . ." Drawn by Hugh
Reinagle (°1790-1834); line engraving by Benjamin

Tanner (1775-1848).

From copy in Union College. When the engraving
was hung there, the president of the college made the
following remarks:

"When Reinagle did this fine piece in 1816 he was but
twenty-six years old, yet he already had some reputation
as a landscape painter in oils and water colors. But like
most American artists of his time, especially if they did
not specialize in portraits, he had to turn his hand to any
sort of work that would pay for food and lodging. Scene
painting and construction in New York and Philadelphia
theaters was a natural resort, for his family was connected
with the stage, and, for exhibition purposes, he painted a
vast panorama of New York City, furnishing a primitive
kind of entertainment foreshadowing the motion picture.
He was popular and respected, and later was one of the
little band of artists who founded the National Academy
of Design in 1829. For his Champlain drawing, thus
early in his maturity, he was fortunate to secure as an
engraver so competent a man as Benjamin Tanner, or, for
all we know, it was Tanner who solicited Reinagle to
produce a drawing for his purpose. Like the much younger
Reinagle, Tanner had found pictorial art a dubious support
by itself and had made his living mostly in the production
of maps before, in this year of 1816, he turned to engraving bank-notes (doubtless under proper authority) and
later to the publishing of blank cheques and drafts. By the
temporary juncture of these two men of pencil and graving
tool there was produced one of the first really notable works
of native American graphic arts. When published a copy
brought between five and twelve dollars, but I violate no
confidence in saying that one commands a considerably
higher price in 1943. . . .

"So we may leave the Reinagle-Tanner print of the
Battle of Lake Champlain, but not before we take note of
three spry and eager boys clambering over the branches of
the great tree at the right. They may not have realized
just how the issue of the battle would affect their country's
destiny, but they certainly knew that they were seeing a
magnificent show . . . ."

From a water color, one of three in this series, in the
collection of I. N. Phelps Stokes in the New York Public
Library. This Erie Canal series was never published; but
our view is reproduced in I. N. Phelps Stokes and D. C.
Haskell, comps., *American Historical Prints, Early Views
of American Cities* (N. Y., 1933), plate 49b. The artist,
John William Hill, was born in England in 1812 and, at
the age of four, came to America with his father, John
Hill, who was to lead in the field of American aquatint.
J. W. Hill became a famous water-colorist, dealing with

landscape; Stokes regards him as one of the four best
and most prolific New York artists of his time, up to the
middle of the nineteenth century. He drew views of North
American cities from Halifax to Havana, and produced some
of the illustrations for the great New York State Natural
History Survey volumes. He died in 1879.

    Plate No. 7 in Avrahm Yarmolinsky's *Paul Svinin.* See
note for plate iii in the present volume. "The structure
of the *Paragon*," wrote Svinin, "is exceedingly curious.
It is 170 feet long and twenty-eight feet wide. The interior is divided into two sections: one for women, the
other for men. The first consists of two large cabins, one
for sleeping, with sixteen berths and eight sofas, the other
a dining-saloon, furnished with twenty berths and ten sofas.
In addition there is in this section a water-closet and a
pantry. The men's section is also divided into two large
cabins, with 104 berths along the walls, each accommodated
with a soft, clean bed, with shelves for clothes, curtains
and everything necessary for making one's toilet. In the
fore-part of the boat there is a fine cabin for the captain,
offices for the engineer, and servants' quarters. The kitchen
is remarkable both for its cleanliness and its location: all
the cooking and frying is done with the aid of steam, and
every day food is prepared for 150 persons with great
ease . . . ." Svinin tried unsuccessfully to get from Robert
Fulton the Russian rights for the steamboat.

    From an engraving in possession of the Tabernacle
Church, Salem, Mass.; photograph furnished by courtesy
of this church, the Essex Institute and the American Board
of Commissioners for Foreign Missions. The artists who
drew and engraved the picture have not been identified.
The *Panoplist*, February, 1812, has this to say: "Or-
dained on Thursday, the 6th instant, in the Tabernacle in
Salem, the Rev. Messrs. Samuel Newell, Adoniram Judson,
Samuel Nott, Gordon Hall and Luther Rice, to the work of
the gospel ministry, as missionaries to the heathen in Asia.
The ordaining council was composed of the pastors of the
North Congregational Church in Newburyport [Rev. Dr.
Samuel Spring], the Congregational Church in Charlestown
[Rev. Dr. Jedidiah Morse], and the Tabernacle Church in
Salem [Rev. Dr. Samuel Worcester], and delegates from
the same churches; and of the Rev. Dr. [Edward Dorr]
Griffin, pastor of the Park Street Church, Boston, late pro-
fessor at Andover, and the Rev. Dr. [Leonard] Woods,
professor at Andover."
The ordaining clergy may be identified, left to right:
Morse, Griffin, Spring, Woods and Worcester; the candi-

dates: Newell, Judson, Nott, Hall and Rice. The kneeling
lady *may* be Mrs. Ann Haseltine Judson, who had been
married the day before. She, Mrs. Nott (married February 8) and Mrs. Newell (married February 9) sailed for
Calcutta with their respective husbands on February 18
and 19.

Joseph Jacques Ramée (1764-1842), a French émigré,
who had been court architect in Denmark and Mecklenberg-
Schwerin and had designed many palatial houses in Europe,
came to America in 1811 to visit a wealthy friend. In
January, 1813, he was engaged by President Nott of Union
College to plan its new, and third successive, campus in
Schenectady. The end houses, the large front buildings and
the "colonnades" running back at right angles to them
were promptly built, financed by public lotteries. The halls
at the rear were not attempted. The round building was
delayed until the seventies, and then was modified in plan.
The second planned campus was that of Jefferson, providing for the University of Virginia, 1819.
Reproduction from a contemporary painting (21 in. x
66 in.) now in Union College, Schenectady, N. Y., by an
unidentified artist.

From a contemporary engraving by William Cooke,
N. 40 Kirby St., Hatten Gardens, London, reproduced in
Centennial Anniversary Issue, *American Journal of Psy-
chiatry*, 1944 (edited by C. B. Farrar, M.D., Toronto,
Ont.)
The legend over the oval reads: "South Front of the
Pennsylvania Hospital." That below is as follows: "This
Building by the Bounty of Government and of many
private Persons was piously founded for the Relief of the
Sick and Miserable, Anno 1756."
The building was designed by the versatile Samuel
Rhoades (1711-1784) in 1755 so that it could conveniently be built in parts. The T-shaped East Wing (shown
at the left) was completed in 1756, the first floor being
used for men patients and the second for women. When
the West Wing was built in 1796, the mental cases were
installed there; the attic was assigned to "ambulant" patients, while "cells" for active male patients were provided
in the basement. Noisy women patients were lodged in
a detached building. The Central Building (1802) contained a lecture room and clinical facilities. This was the
most complete American hospital before 1830, and its opportunities contributed much to make Philadelphia the
principal center of medical education for that period. The
building still stands.

From [Michael Martin], *Captain Lightfoot, the Last of the New England Highwaymen; a Narrative of His Life and Adventures, with Some Account of the Notorious Captain Thunderbolt,* reprinted by George Francis Dow's Wayside Press (Topsfield, Mass., 1926). The original pamphlet was written by Frederick W. Waldo, a reporter on the Boston *Columbian Centinel,* after interviews with Michael Martin, alias Captain Lightfoot, shortly before his execution in 1821.

This illustration does not appear in any of the ten editions and reprints of the narrative of Martin, or "Lightfoot," published in the first half of the nineteenth century. But, as Dr. Clarence S. Brigham, Director of the American Antiquarian Society, remarks: "Since George Francis Dow compiled and arranged this [1926] edition, I would say that the print is undoubtedly authentic" as a contemporary picture; "he evidently obtained the view of the Portsmouth Gin Shop from some other book, or broadside, and I think it was an American print. Mr. Dow was such a painstaking and accurate student that he would not use an English print" in such a connection.

It is here reproduced by permission of Mrs. Dow.

From *The Book of Games, or a History of Juvenile Sports Practiced at the Kingston Academy* (Phila., 1811), in the collection of Dr. A. W. S. Rosenbach. In this little storybook, a Dr. Benson and his young sons introduce a guest to sundry games and exercises, through narrative and dialogue; by correspondence the quieter sports of their sisters are also described. Our illustrations are slightly smaller than the originals.

View of the city from a point near the Middle, or Picayune, Ferry. From an aquatint (25.3 in. x 16.14 in.) by William J. Bennett (London, 1787?-New York, 1844), after his own painting, based on a sketch by A. Mondelli; published by H. I. [J.] Megary, New York, 1841.

Though our illustration violates the date limits of this volume, its inclusion is thought appropriate as indicating the impressive developments which had begun to attract nation-wide attention about 1830. The outstanding spires, left to right, were St. Patrick's Roman Catholic Church (1837), Presbyterian Church (1834), Methodist Episcopal Church (1836). The large dome in the center marked the Exchange Hotel (1835). The slim round tower and the smaller one below it, at the right of the picture, were on the old Cathedral (still standing).

Bennett, who came to this country in 1816 after two campaigns with the British forces in the Mediterranean,

is best known for his 21 plates on towns, which I. N.
Phelps Stokes, in his *Iconography of Manhattan Island*
(N. Y., 1915-1928), III, 620, calls "the finest collection
of folio views of American cities, etc., in existence."

Our reproduction is from a copy in the Library of
Congress.

EDITORS' FOREWORD

THE title of this volume of the *History of American Life* might better have been put in quotation marks, for the Completion of Independence was more a slogan summing up a strong desire rather than a description of complete accomplishment during the period between 1790 and 1830, or, indeed, for long afterward. At some time since that period—it would be difficult to fix the exact date—the American people became convinced that they had achieved a characteristic culture which, however different, could be compared in generally equal terms with the various cultures of Europe. Certainly in the middle of the twentieth century we Americans are not deeply worried as to whether or not we have a clearly recognized way of life; we know that this American way exists, through the successive contributions of countless forebears. It is one of the great cultural facts with which the whole world reckons, and we are showing that it is worth enormous sacrifice to preserve. If cultural maturity has ceased to be a matter of violent concern, there remains, as we hope always will remain, a patriotic anxiety that America give the best benefits she can in building up the civilization of mankind. It scarcely needs to be said that twentieth-century Americans wholeheartedly reject the Spengler thesis that maturity leads necessarily into decay.

Throughout most of the colonial era there was an acceptance, quite as general, of the fact of cultural immaturity. The First Americans brought parts of Europe with them, and the Provincial Society which succeeded knew full well that most of its civilization was derivative. But, with community experience behind it in time and a rich continent revealed behind it in space, a Revo-

xxi

lutionary Generation successfully demanded the right to plan the future of this new country and set up a political framework under which the plan could go forward.

By 1790 America had both the opportunity and the will to develop a way of her own. Without stretching the biological analogy too far, we may discern a period of yearning adolescence which followed the colonial childhood and merged into the growing maturity of the later decades after 1830. So it looks to us today, though the perspective of the centuries may throw the two score years into relation to a much longer movement.

Certainly the driving ideal of that time was cultural independence. This involved national self-reliance as soon as possible, and that in turn prompted an eager importation of arts and crafts, of institutional modes and economic devices, of literary and professional learning, all to be modified to American use and naturalized on American soil. Political theory and practice was, much of it, distinctly creative in this post-Revolutionary era, and environmental opportunities changed social life away from European precedent. Degrees of maturity were measured by the branching off of specialized callings, with the rapid growth of towns—a development that seemed dramatic to a people long accustomed to simple agriculture. The conquest of inland distances, for the benefit of commerce and communication, was a peculiarly American problem; this generation was the first to see how steadily it could be solved by improved roads, steamboats, canals and finally railroads.

National pride was touched, very consciously touched, by these accomplishments. Every American was loud, perhaps too loud, in praise of what his countrymen were doing. There was a disposition to organize many cultural efforts on a nation-wide scale. After the long and inefficient War of 1812—which most Americans insisted on regarding as a glorious success—it seemed for

a time that strong national controls might be set up in
political affairs. But in nearly all parts of the country
there were deep and sensitive fears impelling toward defense against a distant "tyranny," however strongly supported by a national majority. Home rule was still a
potent cry, just as it had been in the colonial era, and
sectional resistance threatened whenever occasion seemed
to warrant, whether in the Northeast, South or West.
The extension of the settled country brought new sections into being, jealous of their own rights, or, in their
lusty strength, menacing the prestige of the old towns.

Rehearsed in this way, such general statements seem
thin and vaporous abstractions. It has been the effort of
the authors to discover and arrange the evidence that
gives them form, solidity and force. They have brought
much into general American history that was but dimly
apprehended before; many creative personalities, hitherto
undeservedly obscure, have been accorded their proper
place in the national memory; certain American traits
not only have been clearly recognized at the beginning
of the nineteenth century, but have been explained in
terms of American causes. It is to be hoped that provocative statement and generous bibliographical annotation
will lead many a reader to go far beyond the text in the
great adventure of historical inquiry.

A. M. S.

THE COMPLETION OF
INDEPENDENCE
1790–1830

THE COMPLETION
OF INDEPENDENCE

CHAPTER I

THE ATLANTIC PORTS

"No part of the world," observed a London newspaper in 1791, "affords, at this time, a more pleasing prospect to the lovers of mankind than the United States of North America." Novelists dreamed of ideal societies to be created in the untrodden woods. Poets, even when they did not, like Coleridge and Southey, plan to take ship themselves, sang of life beyond the Alleghanies as the most enviable fortune; so it was in the songs of Blake and Byron. Shelley in a lofty passage apostrophized that nation mighty in its youth, the resort of all whom the rulers of men in rage or fear had driven from wasted homes.[1] In the romantic literature of France and Germany, throughout the last years of the eighteenth century, there were echoes of the same faith. Discontented and ambitious men in Europe were thinking of America as a practical personal alternative. This was nothing new, but now in an independent country, especially since the new Constitution had insured good order, there seemed larger possibilities than when American communities had been provinces exploited, with how-

[1] Pococurante, *pseud.*, "On the American States," *The Bee, or Literary Wkly. Intelligencer*, V, 239 (Oct. 26, 1791); Thomas Holcroft, *Anna St. Ives* (London, 1792), V, 78-79; William Blake, *Poetical Works* (Oxford, 1914), 117; Lord Byron, "Don Juan," *Works* (London, 1833), XVII, canto viii, stanzas lx-lxviii; P. B. Shelley, *The Revolt of Islam* (London, 1829), canto xi, stanzas xxii-xxiv.

ever much good will, for the benefit of England. Some, of course, considered a removal to America merely as an exciting adventure, but for most it was a matter of serious calculation. By many an evening candle families discussed the advantages of such an enormous step, aided oftentimes by letters from relatives or friends who had already taken it.[1]

Those who, speaking the truth as they saw it, had been silenced by the heavy hand of government hailed America as the land of freedom. Especially was this true, if they spoke through the printed page. Some of these refugees were of the highest worth, the many-sided Dr. Thomas Cooper, for example, who was to crown a long career of public service in America by becoming president of the College of South Carolina; but there was also a swarm of professional scribblers who were to add little except venom to public discussion in their new home. The fires of religious persecution had died down in the Old World, but here and there the embers flared too brightly for the comfort of the unprivileged, and some of these, like Joseph Priestley and his Unitarian friends, arrived seeking liberty of worship.[2] In New England, with its favored church, there was a stigma in dissent; in some other states only Protestants could hold high office; but religious refugees, like escaping journalists, pinned their faith on the First Amendment to the Constitution as guaranteeing them against molestation, at least by the federal government.

[1] Bernard, Faÿ, *The Revolutionary Spirit in France and America* (N. Y., 1927), chap. iv; J. T. Hatfield and Elfrieda Hochbaum, "Influence of the American Revolution on German Literature," *Americana Germanica*, III, nos. 3-4, *passim*.

[2] South Carolina and Pennsylvania abolished religious test oaths in 1790, Georgia in 1798, New York in 1806, Connecticut in 1818, Virginia in 1830, Delaware in 1831, Massachusetts in 1833, North Carolina in 1835, New Jersey in 1844, and New Hampshire in 1852. E. J. Byrne, "The Religious Issue in National Politics," *Catholic Hist. Rev.;* n. s., VIII, 337. Outside New England these laws had been lightly enforced.

They could see three Roman Catholics sitting in the first Congress and men of all faiths or of none prominent in public life. As the French Revolution succeeded and that in Ireland failed, there were many people who, as we shall see, fled to the United States to save their very lives.

But most of the immigrants were not refugees. They refused compliance not with government but with circumstances, and came to "better themselves" in a land where they could escape their traditional status. They did not fret because their adopted home was deficient in art, letters and science. A place where many could live in comfort, though few could live in luxury, seemed, and was, to them a good place to begin. One could always begin again in America, even again and again. Bankruptcy, which in the fixed society of Europe was the tragic end of a career, might be merely a step in personal education. To acquire enough land on which to build a cottage was a hopeless aim in ninety-nine English parishes out of a hundred.[1] In the United States land, the principal support of life, was not engrossed and assigned by any law of primogeniture, but could be had for a very small accumulation. Indeed, it could be purchased on confidence, that is to say, credit; Americans were always trading in futures. To a European the taxes in the new country seemed ridiculously small, in some places only six or seven shillings to a hundred pounds' value of property.[2] The public debt was smaller in proportion to the wealth and population than

[1] Arthur Young, "An Inquiry into the Propriety of Applying Wastes to the Better Maintenance and Support of the Poor," *Annals of Agriculture*, XXXVI, 505.

[2] Mathew Carey, *Reflections on the Subject of Emigration from Europe* (Phila., 1826), *passim;* Duke de La Rochefoucauld-Liancourt, *Travels through the United States . . . in the Years 1795, 1796, and 1797* (London, 1799), I, 16. Henry Wansey, *An Excursion to the United States . . . in 1794* (Salisbury, Eng., 1798), 176, speaks of a New York gentleman paying a total tax of £6 5s. on property renting for £210.

that of any other civilized country, and it was steadily
decreasing.[1] Outside the few cities, poor rates were
negligible because there were virtually no paupers,
whereas in England many were fed in whole or in part
at the public charge; and the rate to pay for it, before
the eighteenth century had passed, rose to about two
pounds per family the country over and was to rise much
higher.[2] European travelers in America were astonished
to find civilized life without beggars.[3] There was a
general sense of simple plenty.   "In England," wrote
Dr. Cooper, "no man has a right (calculating upon the
common chances) to expect that five or six children
shall all succeed." [4] In the United States that hope was
reasonable.

Some who would have profited by going to America
knew very little about it. Samuel Topliff, traveling in
Europe as late as 1829, had to explain to certain countrymen where America was; others, however, had heard
of it and of President Washington and asked after his
health.[5] Governmental policy at times stood in the
way; for example, English artisans, prior to 1824, were
prohibited from emigrating.[6] In general, European
governments, though willing to see paupers and criminals leave, believed that the loss of a hundred thousand
ordinary emigrants would be as great as that of an army

[1] Tench Coxe, *A View of the United States of America* (Phila., 1794),
chap. xv.
[2] See table in H. de B. Gibbins, *Industry in England* (N. Y., 1897),
422. The authorities estimated the quantum of subsistence at about half
what would be approved today. See Sidney and Beatrice Webb, *English
Local Government: English Poor Law History* (London, 1927-1929),
pt. i, 182.
[3] Jane L. Mesick, *The English Traveller in America, 1785-1835* (Columbia Univ., *Studies in English and Comparative Literature*, 1922), 65.
[4] See Thomas Cooper, *Some Information Respecting America* (London,
1794), 55-56.
[5] Samuel Topliff, *Travels . . . in the Years 1828 and 1829* (Ethel S.
Bolton, ed., Boston, 1906), 198.
[6] 22 George III, c. 60, and 5 George IV, c. 92. Of course some came,
but it was by special favor or by stealth.

the same size.[1] After April, 1792, when the French Revolution widened into a European war, the excitement of arming and marching, to say nothing of conscription and impressment, kept many a European from realizing a larger destiny in America. On this account more than any other, it may be said that there have been few periods in American history when immigration has been so inconsequential as it was between 1790 and 1815. Since official records do not begin until 1820, we must depend on estimates, but apparently the total did not average much more than five or six thousand a year, a number often matched in a single day in the unrestricted immigration before the First World War.[2] Perhaps it was well that American culture could develop for a quarter of a century on colonial foundations without drastic modification from newcomers. Thus it struck firmer roots before the onslaught of the hosts who were to follow in the nineteenth century.

When one reads of the conditions of sea travel, one realizes that it took no little resolution to try the Atlantic crossing. There had been slight improvement during the past half-century.[3] Most immigrants of whatever origin came in British or American boats which were cheaper and faster, as well as dirtier, than the French and German.[4] They were small craft, about one two-hundredth the size of the largest modern liners. The cabin passengers paid twenty-five or thirty pounds, which included the cost of board; but most of the new-

[1] T. W. Page, "Causes of Earlier European Immigration to the United States," Journ. of Polit. Economy, XIX, 691.

[2] See estimates in Adam Seybert, Statistical Annals (Phila., 1818), 29; G. M. Stephenson, History of American Immigration, 1820-1924 (N. Y., 1926), 99; and Max Farrand, "Assimilation," New Republic, IX, 208-210 (Dec. 23, 1916).

[3] See J. T. Adams, Provincial Society, 1690-1763 (A History of American Life, III), 175-177.

[4] T. W. Page, "Transportation of Immigrants and Reception Arrangements in the Nineteenth Century," Journ. of Polit. Economy, XIX, 732.

comers traveled by steerage. Here, for quarters not much better than those of a slaver, the price varied from three to ten pounds, and the passenger was furnished nothing except water and fire, and these sparingly.[1] It was necessary to bring not only bedding but enough food to last from eight to twelve weeks. Contractors leased the space of a ship and crowded in the hapless victims to reap the greatest possible profit. Such conditions led the British government in 1803 to insist that each individual should have a space approximately equal to a four-foot cube.[2] Since the germs of typhus, smallpox and other pestilence lurked in the crannies of these ill-washed hulks, now and then a vessel docked with a story of throwing overboard thirty or forty corpses, a tenth of the list, as the toll of the mysterious "ship fever."

When the immigrant set foot upon the wharf at Philadelphia, New York, Boston or Charleston, he had reason enough to be thankful, but his trials were not all past. Smooth swindlers were waiting at the gangplank, ready to guide him or her, especially if unfamiliar with the English tongue, to evil dens called "labor agencies" where the prey was rifled of precious savings. It was thus that something like the white-slave traffic was begun.[3] To counteract such sharks and lend a sympathetic hand to the bewildered newcomer, the St. An-

[1] S. H. Collins, *Emigrant's Guide . . . to the United States* (4th edn., Hull, Eng., 1830), 66, 80. T. Wolfe Tone, *Autobiography* (R. B. O'Brien, ed., Dublin, 1910), I, 215, says in 1795 that his family of six occupied one stateroom eight feet by six, but the crossing in the steerage was worse. In one case a family of ten occupied four berths and yet could only draw allowance for four. See also Phineas Bond, "Letters" (1791), Am. Hist. Assoc., *Ann. Rep. for 1897*, I, 472-473, 488. Henry Wansey's fare of 40 guineas (*Excursion*, 1) was extraordinarily high even for the best cabin passage.

[2] Page, "Transportation of Immigrants," 783. This British law exacted a ratio of at least five tons to each three passengers. In 1819 Congress provided that American ships must assign five tons for two passengers. M. L. Hansen, *The Atlantic Migration, 1607-1860* (A. M. Schlesinger, ed., Cambridge, 1940), 82-83, 102.

[3] Page, "Transportation of Immigrants," 744-745.

drew's, St. George's and St. Patrick's societies in most of the cities sought to look after the Scots, the English and the Irish, respectively.[1] The Irish, as they became more numerous, depended on the Hibernian and the Shamrock societies in New York, while the Germans, many of whom were skilled artisans, had similar organizations in that city and in Philadelphia.[2] These societies accomplished something, but as the cities grew the perils of the immigrant increased. Nevertheless, the majority got through without disaster, thanks oftentimes to the help of relatives or friends. Many Irishmen landed in Canada in the twenties, when emigration to the colonies was assisted, and then crossed the border into New York and New England. They were more prompt than the others to qualify as citizens, seldom letting more than the necessary two years elapse.[3]

The immigrant of 1790 had before him a country of about a million square miles, running northward from the thirty-first parallel, if Spain would agree to that line, and westward to the Mississippi. The population of four million was roughly divided by the old Mason and Dixon line.[4] Of the southern half three eighths were Negroes, being most numerous actually and relatively in Virginia, which was also the most populous state in the Union. The other half was halved again at the Hudson River. The immigrant, disliking the theory of slavery, was apt to shun the South. Moreover, there was a general impression that only a slaveholder could

[1] Sometimes the societies prosecuted offending ship captains. See Bond, "Letters," 472, 481-482.

[2] N.-Y. Gazette, Jan. 20, 1797.

[3] M. L. Hansen, The Immigrant in American History (A. M. Schlesinger, ed., Cambridge, 1940), 156-160; Stephenson, Immigration, 14, 27-28. The immigration law of 1790 specified two years as preliminary residence.

[4] The census of 1790 gave the total 3,930,000, but since the enumeration was not complete beyond the Alleghanies it was thought that 3,950,000 was a safe estimate. See Jedidiah Morse, American Universal Geography (Boston, 1802), 223.

start advantageously in the South; and the newcomer seldom had sufficient capital to buy either a proper estate or a complement of laborers to work it. Partly for this reason, the South was destined to be outstripped in the growth of population and consequently political power; and, in eventual resentment, there was to come the Civil War.

Neither was New England, though a region of small farmers, inviting to the settlers. It was comparatively crowded and land prices were high, especially when agricultural quality was considered. In the northern reaches there was plenty of open country, it is true, but stories of long and frigid winters deterred the immigrant. The section had been declining in relative importance for over a hundred years, and it was now notorious that people were moving out at a rate of many thousands each year. Massachusetts, Connecticut and Rhode Island began to exhibit the phenomena of an "old country." For example, the census lists showed more women than men because so many of the latter had gone to seek their fortunes elsewhere. For thirty years the population total of Connecticut stood almost still. Not unnaturally the immigrant reasoned that New England was a country for a poor man and his family to leave rather than to enter and settle.[1]

Some, like Brissot de Warville, were champions of the Shenandoah Valley, and others wrote fervently of Kentucky; but the latter region could more easily be settled by native pioneers. Even its warmest partisan admitted that the raw wilderness was no place for an unseasoned European.[2] Indian wars rendered the Northwest for-

---

[1] Oscar Handlin, *Boston's Immigrants, 1790-1865* (*Harvard Hist. Studies*, L), 29-30.

[2] J. P. Brissot de Warville, *New Travels in the United States of America in 1788* (N. Y., 1792), letter iv; Gilbert Imlay, *A Description of the Western Territory of North America* (Dublin, 1793), 149, and *The Emigrants* (London, 1793), I, *passim*.

bidding during the early nineties. Although Anthony Wayne's victory of 1795 so pacified the Ohio country as to make even statehood possible in seven years, the region as a whole had to wait until after the War of 1812 before there was sufficient security to attract great companies of settlers.

At almost any given time since the Revolution some section of the country has especially stirred the imagination of those able to pack their household goods into wagons and start off. At the end of the eighteenth century it was the western parts of New York and Pennsylvania. The northern portion of this area, around the Finger Lakes, had better soil, but the lands along the Susquehanna were nearer to markets. The latter's fertility could not easily be improved, but the former's facilities of transportation could; and New York now began its remarkable rise to the rank of Empire State. In the three decades that followed the first census it quadrupled in population — grew greater by a million — and more than four fifths of this increase occurred in the western lands that had been lately wrested from the Iroquois. Starting with fourth place among the states, slightly ahead of North Carolina, it now gained the lead.[1]

The growth throughout the nation was, of course, largely rural. Urban concentration was a phenomenon of the nineteenth century the world over,[2] but if cities were less important in the older European countries in 1790 than today, this was even more true in a country of abundant land like the United States. Only three

[1] *Spectator* (N. Y.), Jan. 8, 1822. William Winterbotham, *An Historical, Geographical, Commercial, and Philosophical View of the United States* (N. Y., 1796), III, 313, warns against New Jersey on account of the arid and swampy parts, especially the mosquitoes and ague near the latter, and the close settlement and consequently high price of the good land.

[2] A. F. Weber, *The Growth of Cities* (Columbia Univ., *Studies*, XI), 1-19.

per cent of the inhabitants lived in communities of eight thousand and upwards.   Nevertheless, urban life then, perhaps more largely than today, when rural isolation has been broken down by the modern miracles of transportation and communication, formed the substance of American civilization.   It was in the cities that men by mutual imitation changed toward what they considered improvement.   In picturing American social life toward the close of the eighteenth century it is necessary to give the towns far more than three per cent of our attention.

A traveler sailing in toward the peninsula of Boston threaded a careful way past a score of wooded islands into a spacious harbor that could accommodate five hundred ships.   He saw before him a town of eighteen thousand, whose most striking feature was the file of church steeples piercing the green of the treetops.   Learning that two thirds of the sixteen churches were Congregational, he might infer a certain homogeneity in the population.   Later he would find the directory showing a larger proportion of English names than that of any considerable city to the southward and he would be told that they represented old native stock, with rarely a man whose father had been born abroad.   If he had heard of a tradition of public education he would search in vain for any impressive indication of it on the skyline. The seven public schools were rather shabbily housed, and the fact that there were twice as many schools in private hands might suggest that the fruits of the famous law of 1647 were somewhat less than had been expected.[1]

[1] T. P. (Thomas Pemberton), "A Topographical and Historical Description of Boston, 1794," Mass. Hist. Soc., *Colls.*, ser. 1, III, 256-266; *The Boston Directory . . . to Which Is Prefixed a General Description of Boston* (Boston, 1796), 212 ff.; Jedidiah Morse, *The American Geography* (Boston, 1789), 177-178; T. J. Wertenbaker, *The First Americans, 1607-1690* (*A History of American Life*, II), 246.

Boston's commercial enterprise was chiefly advertised by the Long Wharf jutting a third of a mile into the water, though there were nearly eighty others, large and small. Walking its length past the row of buildings lining the side, one came to the old two-story Faneuil Hall Market, redolent of history and fish, and then across the broad expanse called State Street, which led to the red-brick state house still topped by the lion and the unicorn.[1] The European as he followed the narrow, crooked streets, in many of which two men with hands clasped could almost touch the opposing walls,[2] would have especially noticed the wooden houses, commonly painted white and often standing in little grass plots separated by white palings. The pavement, where it existed, consisted of round beach stones. Footways were sometimes marked off by a row of posts and a gutter. On nights when the moon was hidden a few oil lamps were lighted, serving only to make the surrounding darkness more palpable.[3] In general appearance the town had changed little since before the Revolution. Beacon Hill was a high ragged eminence from which one could watch the cows browsing on the common.[4] Charles Bulfinch, though returned from European study, had not yet worked his miracle, which began in 1794 with the construction of the attached brick houses of the Tontine Crescent in Franklin Place. Perhaps it were better to say that the commercial wealth was just beginning to flow into Boston which would

[1] Samuel Breck, *Recollections* (H. E. Scudder, ed., Phila., 1877), 183; H. P. Kidder and F. H. Peabody, "Finance in Boston," Justin Winsor, ed., *Memorial History of Boston* (Boston, 1880-1881), IV, 151; A. E. Brown, *Faneuil Hall and Faneuil Hall Market* (Boston, 1900), chap. xiv.

[2] Anne H. Thwing, *The Crooked & Narrow Streets of the Town of Boston, 1630-1822* (Boston, 1920), 46-47, 116.

[3] S. A. Drake, *Old Landmarks and Historic Personages of Boston* (Boston, 1873), 22; Wansey, *Excursion*, 18-20.

[4] R. M. Lawrence, *Old Park Street and Its Vicinity* (Boston, 1922), 24.

enable Bulfinch and his disciples to rebuild the town in the "federal style" during the next quarter of a century.[1]

The town crier making his way down some street that led to the water — and all streets did — might be jostled by a sailor clad in a broad-brimmed leather hat and short jacket with wide petticoat breeches flapping at the knees. Betokening the other principal interest of the town — the backcountry — might come a farm wife vending tow cloth, linen sheeting, striped flannels or other products of her spinning wheel and loom.[2] In the little shops craftsmen — wigmakers, paper stainers, blockmakers, chandlers and others — made up and sold their own merchandise. There was nothing like the modern factory unless it were one of the larger of the fourteen ropewalks, where men worked together by division of labor, or the duck manufactory in Frog Lane, or possibly the distilleries.[3] Rum stood first among the town's productions, then beer, then paper hangings, loaf sugar, sailcloth, spermaceti and tallow candles, and glass. Mingling with the artisans now and then might be seen a merchant resplendent in braided cocked hat and scarlet cloak and usually attended by a sable Scipio or Cato. Possibly one might catch a glimpse of the governor's carriage clattering down to the state house. There was no more humility in John Hancock's bearing than in his signature, but gout had laid him low and he must ride. Until his death in 1793 he remained the most elegant figure in Boston, especially when in his fine stone mansion his servants bore him, clad in lace and velvet, into

[1] C. A. Place, *Charles Bulfinch, Architect and Citizen* (Boston, 1925), chap. iv; E. B. Greene, *The Revolutionary Generation, 1763-1790* (*A History of American Life*, IV), 396-397.

[2] T. P., "Boston in 1794," 283; W. B. Rice, "The Boot and Shoe Trade," C. M. Depew, ed., *One Hundred Years of American Commerce* (N. Y., 1895), II, 567.

[3] The ropewalks seemed particularly susceptible to fire, half of them burning in 1793. C. D. Wright and H. G. Wadlin, "The Industries of the Last Hundred Years," Winsor, *History of Boston*, IV, 80.

his dining room to preside over a table laid for fifty guests.[1]

Boston was the metropolis not only of Massachusetts but of New England. It was intensely conservative — smallclothes and silver buckles were worn later there than elsewhere — and complacent. Its distinguished citizen George Cabot spoke simply the conviction of the section when he claimed that there was among its people "more wisdom than in any other part of the United States." [2] Except for little Hartford no municipalities existed in New England, even Boston retaining its town government until 1822; but there were more large villages than in any other region. North of Boston in Essex County, Salem, Newburyport, Marblehead, Gloucester and Ipswich, all towns of over four thousand people, were entering upon their great era of commercial prosperity, as was also Portsmouth a little beyond.

Southward around the cape lay Rhode Island, with Newport and Providence slowly recovering from the dislocations of the war. Crossing its border early in 1790 one was not quite sure whether he was still in the United States, as Rhode Island had not yet ratified the new Constitution. Newport's merchants, favoring a stronger federal government, were threatening to secede. Combining with the business men of Providence, who likewise suffered under paper-money laws from which the new federal instrument would relieve them, they secured a majority of two in the legislature for ratification. It was a coup of the two towns, for without doubt the bulk of the people in the state were against it.[3]

[1] *Boston Directory* (1796), 212; T. P., "Boston in 1794," 277-278; M. A. De Wolfe Howe, *Boston, the Place and the People* (N. Y., 1907), 137; H. C. Lodge, *Boston* (London, 1891), 176.

[2] S. E. Morison, *The Maritime History of Massachusetts* (Boston, 1921), 128; Mrs. St. Julien Ravenel, *Life and Times of William Lowndes of South Carolina, 1782-1822* (Boston, 1901), 79.

[3] F. G. Bates, *Rhode Island and the Formation of the Union* (Columbia Univ., *Studies*, X, no. 2), chap. iv.

In both cities the Baptist churches were dominant, and in Providence a college flourished under like auspices, which must have struck most other New Englanders as perverse.[1] The Quaker element was strong in the latter town, as was evidenced by the street names, Benefit, Hope, Friendship, Peace, etc. But there must have been plenty of commercial reckoning on Sovereign, Pound, Shilling and Doubloon streets. These towns, like their northern neighbors, were about to enjoy a great era of trade, especially Providence, with its better inland communications,[2] making possible more and more handsome entertainment in the mansions of the Browns, the Iveses, the Hopkinses and other homes which still linger little changed in their ancient dignity. The Connecticut towns were smaller and less urban than those on the eastern coast. Those beyond the Housatonic felt the influence of a metropolis to the westward.

By 1790 the harbor of New York had become a noble sight, with deep water bringing the largest ships to the very shore line of the city. The thirty thousand people, spread across the tip of Manhattan Island, lived mostly toward the East River side, where the mile of warehouses clearly revealed their chief concern. One scarcely left the wharf before discovering sharp contrasts between this city and Boston. The Dutch background was apparent. Many houses, faced with yellow brick, stood with ends to the street, some gables being stepped up to the weather vanes. In the Dutch Reformed churches, strongest in numbers, the services were held in both languages. The lettered shop signs, which here as elsewhere with the increase of literacy were supplanting the old symbols such as the hat and glove, showed a large

---

[1] C. A. Place, "From Meeting House to Church," *Old Time New England*, XIII (1923), 112, 116-117.

[2] W. B. Weeden, "Industry," William Kirk, ed., *A Modern City: Providence, Rhode Island, and Its Activities* (Chicago, 1909), 78-85.

proportion of Dutch names. But the Dutch and English by no means made up all the population. It was already the most cosmopolitan town in America and almost any European could find fellowship with people of his own nation and tongue. In addition, there were the Negroes, about a ninth of the population, two thirds of whom were still held as slaves.[1]

Gaunt ruins marked the central wards, memorials of the war fire in 1776, and the city was just beginning to lose an appearance of decay and neglect. Churches and houses were rising again, their builders urged by hope that New York would remain the federal capital for some time. The streets were somewhat wider, straighter and better than those in Boston, particularly the Bowery and Broadway, running from the Battery to the Park, the tree-lined portion in front of the new Trinity Church being known as the Mall.[2] The street which led down to the east from this point was beginning to acquire a special character through the presence of two new banks, but it was still a fashionable residential row and in 1790 a spring poet could write:

> In Wall-street oft' I view that beaut'ous form
> Which does my breast with soft emotions warm.[3]

Five markets, highly regulated and famous for their fruit and fish, purveyed the food brought in by cart

[1] Timothy Dwight, *Travels in New-England and New-York* (New Haven, 1821-1822), III, 469-470; Breck, *Recollections*, 90; T. E. V. Smith, *The City of New York in the Year of Washington's Inauguration* (N. Y., 1889), 125; Bureau of the Census, *A Century of Population Growth* (Wash., 1909), 84. Albany was described about 1800 as "indeed Dutch in all its moods and tenses; thoroughly and inveterately Dutch." G. A. Worth, *Random Recollections of Albany* (Albany, 1849), 27.

[2] John Lambert, *Travels through Canada, and the United States* (3rd edn., London, 1816), II, 55-56; Arthur Hornblow, *History of the Theatre in America* (Phila., 1919), I, 152; Frank Monaghan and Marvin Lowenthal, *This Was New York* (Garden City, 1943), 27-45.

[3] Anon., "The Belles of New York," *N.-Y. Mag.*, I (1790), 186.

and sloop.[1] Purchasers had here as well as elsewhere to carry their baskets, for no shop delivered goods until about 1820.

No stranger would have been allowed to overlook the Federal Hall, which Major Pierre Charles L'Enfant had elaborated out of the old municipal building at the head of Broad Street as a home for the new government as long as it should stay.[2] In like anticipation the city was soon clearing away the useless old fort by the Battery and putting a house for the President on its site. These hopes were dashed in the spring of 1790 when the government loaded its paraphernalia into a few wagons and moved to Philadelphia. But the people's spirit was sustained by prosperous times in commerce. After all, New York was still the capital of the state, and Governor George Clinton moved into the Government House, thereby saving the seven hundred and fifty dollars he had paid yearly for renting a house.[3] The citizens set themselves even more ardently to business; nothing would please them more than to surpass in wealth and population the rival city on the Delaware.

Philadelphia, one hundred miles up that broad estuary, was America's principal city. Its forty-two thousand people lived in a great triangle running two and a half miles along the shore with its apex lying back a mile or so on the High Street, which divided it in two. More than a century's experience had proved the practicability of the broad checkerboard which William Penn's engineer had laid out between the Delaware and the Schuylkill, and of which the city now covered about

[1] Oliver Ellsworth found the cost of food 25 per cent higher in New York than in Hartford. R. W. Griswold, *The Republican Court, or American Society in the Days of Washington* (N. Y., 1864), 206.

[2] S. I. Pomerantz, *New York, an American City* (Columbia Univ., Studies, no. 442), 226-237; Smith, *New York*, 40-43; Adams, *Provincial Society*, plate xv, figure b.

[3] Smith, *New York*, 40-50.

Wall and Water Streets, New York, 1797

Fourth of July in Centre Square, Philadelphia, 1812

a third.[1] Most visitors admired the plan, though some affected to think it tiresome in its monotony, regarding the designation of streets by numbers, which was to set a precedent in America, as too great a sacrifice of picturesqueness for mere convenience.[2] The pebble-paved streets, in advance of other cities, were bordered by brick walks, raised to the height of a foot.

The city had a well-marked character. If New York had Dutch names on its signs, here were German in even larger proportion, and church services and public notices in the same language as well. On the street one met Amish, Mennonites and other German sectaries, distinguished by an excessive plainness of dress. Of similar drab habit were the Friends, whose men were long known as "broadbrims" because of their hats, which never came off in deference to any person or place. The women were less somber than their English cousins, but even then there were heartburnings at the restrictions as to color. Their churches or "meetings," set back behind high walls, were the most numerous houses of worship, here as in the near-by countryside.[3]

Quite as characteristic was the arcaded, one-story market running for nearly half a mile up the center of the main street. On Tuesday and Friday evenings a church bell, called in this function the "butter bell," announced the market for next day. At dawn or before came thrifty fathers, and some housewives as well, to buy the meat cuts — its beef, mutton and veal were famous —

[1] The figure given includes the contiguous suburbs. See *Century of Population Growth*, 13, and map opposite page 14. Compare with the original map of Thomas Holme (1625-1695) in E. D. Fite and Archibald Freeman, comps., *A Book of Old Maps* (Cambridge, 1926), 168-171. See also Oliver Hough, "Captain Thomas Holme," *Pa. Mag. of History and Biog.*, XIX, 413-427; XX, 128-131, 248-256.

[2] Lambert, *Travels*, II, 55; anon., "Philadelphia," *Literary Mag. and Am. Register*, VI (1806), 261. La Rochefoucauld-Liancourt called it "one of the most beautiful cities in the world." *Travels*, IV, 91.

[3] See Allan Nevins, *The Emergence of Modern America, 1865-1878* (*A History of American Life*, VIII), plate iii, figure e.

or butter (at 1d. or 2d. a pound) or possibly hay or wood. Though there were other markets in Philadelphia, this was indubitably the greatest in America, and in 1790 High Street, throwing over English traditions, became Market Street in recognition of its importance. Scores, if not hundreds, of American towns founded since this date have named their main thoroughfare in imitation, even though they had no public markets.[1]

One who entered Philadelphia on April 21, 1790, would have witnessed a solemn demonstration. Twenty thousand people, the largest concourse the country had ever known, lined the streets as the bier of Benjamin Franklin was borne to Christ Church yard amidst the tolling of bells and the booming of cannon.[2] The influence of one heroic spirit was never more strikingly illustrated. In the cortege walked the faculty of the college and the members of the American Philosophical Society, both of which he had founded. Near the line of march was the new building of the Library Company, another of his pioneer enterprises, where a niche in the façade awaited his statue. One remembered him, too, in connection with the state house in Chestnut Street, where he had promoted independence, the Confederation and the Constitution. Close by was Carpenters' Hall, the only guild house in America, where he had met with the Second Continental Congress. If on that day in 1790 those who passed by to the funeral thought of these old buildings, they must have realized that their "young" country had already a richly interesting history.

[1] Joseph Jackson, *Market Street, Philadelphia* (Phila., 1918), 2-3, 9; Brissot de Warville, *New Travels*, 133; anon., "Sketch of the Origin and Present State of Philadelphia," *Literary Mag. and Am. Register*, II (1804), 172; W. P. and Julia P. Cutler, *Life, Journals and Correspondence of Rev. Manasseh Cutler* (Cincinnati, 1858), I, 271-272; Greene, *Revolutionary Generation*, 32, 58.

[2] Benjamin Franklin, *Works* (Jared Sparks, ed., Boston, 1856), I, 532-533; Jacob Hiltzheimer, *Extracts from Diary* (J. C. Parsons, ed., Phila., 1893), 161.

At the end of the century old men might have reflected on the changes in the city during fifty years. Very few of the square front gardens remained, and most homes now stood sidewise along the brick walk itself. Gone were the porches with the flanking, high-backed benches where the family had sat in the evening. Houses now had three stories instead of two, and much marble was used in the front walls. The cellars had become basements with good-sized windows, the doorsteps running up to the first floor high above the level of the street and blocking the sidewalks as much as the old cellar hatchways had before them.[1] Except for its regularity of streets, it resembled an English town more than did most others in America.

A few days' journey to the southeast lay Baltimore, an overgrown village of thirteen thousand people, shortly to become a city in 1797. The port grew busier each year because of radiating lines of inland transportation carrying more and more tobacco, flour and other staples. Into the tavern yards at night rolled scores of ponderous, blue, canvas-covered wagons, each with four or six horses soon munching their hay at the rough open mangers. In the morning the loads of whisky and provisions would be delivered at the merchants' doors on Howard Street and then, stocked with groceries and fancy goods, the caravans would start westward into the country. Some houses they passed were brick, but more were of wood, hip-roofed and painted blue, white or yellow, all tight to the street. On the Patapsco River front, wharves and warehouses were rapidly building in 1790, setting a pace which would be followed, except for the war years, during the next three decades, while

---

[1] Anon., "Sketch of Philadelphia," 173-174; anon., "The American Character," *Literary Mag. and Am. Register*, II, 256; Talcott Williams, "Philadelphia," L. P. Powell, ed., *Historic Towns of the Middle States* (N. Y., 1899), 314; L. I. Rhoades, *The Story of Philadelphia* (N. Y., 1900), 149-153.

the Smiths, Buchanans, Swanns and other men of enterprise increased the city's size fivefold.[1]

In strong contrast was Annapolis further down Chesapeake Bay. If the America of 1790 seems in retrospect young, age is relative, and there were already "interesting old towns," distinguished chiefly for the mellow charm of history, to say nothing of those which had died of disappointment and lay crumbling and weedgrown in loneliness. Annapolis was still vigorous, but it had a patrician air about it as though its elegance could not be suddenly rivaled by upstart towns like Baltimore. The state house, one of the handsomest buildings in America with its pillared portico and lofty dome; the governor's mansion, built some sixty years before; the little old treasury building, set up to accommodate the legislature in the seventeenth century; venerable houses of size and character out of keeping with a place of less than two thousand people — all these evidenced an older glory. Fortune had destined it to remain a permanent example of a fine colonial town.[2]

There were other communities in the last years of the eighteenth century which basked in an optimism that time would ruthlessly dispel. An example was Alexandria. "It appears that all the world is after wheat," wrote a citizen in 1789. Grain and flour were ousting tobacco from the region and warehouses constantly increased in number. Exports grew nearly threefold between 1791 and 1796 and held their level while Americans were permitted a precarious access to the ports

[1] Fillmore Norfleet, tr. and ed., "Baltimore as Seen by Moreau de Saint-Méry in 1794," *Maryland Hist. Mag.*, XXXV, 225-230; J. P. Kennedy, *At Home and Abroad* (N. Y., 1872), 167-186.

[2] Winterbotham, *View*, III, 38-39; William Priest, *Travels in the United States* (London, 1802), 17; W. B. Norris, *Annapolis, Its Colonial and Naval Story* (N. Y., 1925), chap. xiii; Sara A. Shafer, "Annapolis," L. P. Powell, ed., *Historic Towns of the Southern States* (N. Y., 1900), 58-63. See also C. C. Jones, jr., *The Dead Towns of Georgia* (Savannah, 1878), 140, 228-229.

of warring Europe, that is to say, until 1807.[1] Norfolk, watching tobacco exports decline, shared the ambition to become a great wheat port, handling also the timber, minerals, hemp and much of the tobacco that Virginia and North Carolina produced.[2] But travelers found Norfolk handicapped, even more than New York or near-by Richmond, by reason of fires set during the late war. Slapped up in hasty wooden buildings, it had the reputation of being one of the most irregular, filthy and ugly towns in Christendom.[3] To the southward there was little town life to be found nearer than Charleston, over three hundred miles away. This was the fourth city in size, but its interests were so interlaced with those of its plantation hinterland that its description may be deferred to a later treatment of the South.

The ports, particularly in the North, were growing rapidly, but it was significant that the state capitals were being moved to the westward. Before 1790, except for Dover, in the little state of Delaware, only two capitals had been situated in the upland country — Richmond and Augusta — in both cases to avoid danger from the British during the Revolution. By 1815, in those original states which had single fixed seats of government, only Massachusetts and Maryland kept their capitals by the sea.[4] All this indicated not only that the inland regions were becoming more populous and accessible by better roads, but also that there was a conviction, which

[1] Fairfax Harrison, *Landmarks of Old Prince William* (Richmond, Va., 1924), 408-410; La Rochefoucauld-Liancourt, *Travels*, II, 339.

[2] T. J. Wertenbaker, *Norfolk, Historic Southern Port* (Durham, 1931), 90-94.

[3] La Rochefoucauld-Liancourt, *Travels*, III, 11.

[4] In Connecticut, Hartford and New Haven shared the government until 1873; likewise Providence and Newport until 1900. Concord became the capital of New Hampshire in 1808, Albany of New York in 1797, Trenton of New Jersey in 1790, Lancaster of Pennsylvania in 1799 (then Harrisburg in 1812). Raleigh was laid out as the capital of North Carolina in 1792, and Columbia as that of South Carolina in 1790.

had found expression in the debates on locating the federal capital, that governments were less safe in the proximity of accumulated wealth, highly organized enterprise and the possibility of mob tyranny. Thus began the peculiar American practice, a triumph of the agricultural interest, of separating the capital from the metropolis.

"In Boston, New York, Philadelphia, and Baltimore," it was remarked at the end of the eighteenth century, "the state of society is much the same as in the large towns of Great Britain, such as Birmingham, Bristol, Liverpool, and Manchester." [1] The similarities were striking. The two groups totaled about the same in population; in outward aspect the towns were much alike and also in scheme of government. Except in Boston, which, as we have seen, retained its town meeting until 1822, those who had property enough to vote elected aldermen and assistant aldermen, just as in England, and these chose the mayor who, apart from his function as a judge, was little more than a figure of ceremonial dignity. [2] There had been few changes by reason of the Revolution, except to put cities directly under the control of state legislators who, being close by and meddlesome, greatly retarded the development of home rule. [3]

Likewise following English precedent, the municipality more closely, or at least more visibly, controlled trade and industry than now. The number of apprentices a master could take was specified by ordinance, and

[1] Cooper, *Some Information*, 48.   He found New York "a perfect counterpart of Liverpool."   Felix de Beaujour spoke of Boston and Baltimore as much like English towns.

[2] The three close corporations by which Philadelphia, Norfolk and Annapolis had been ruled had been abolished after the Revolution.

[3] J. A. Fairlie, *Essays in Municipal Administration* (N. Y., 1908), 62; H. L. McBain, "The Evolution of Types of City Government in the United States," *Natl. Municipal Rev.*, VI (1917), 19-21; W. B. Munro, *Municipal Government and Administration* (N. Y., 1923), I, 92.   In New York the mayor was named by the state council of appointment.

no apprentice could afterward set up near by in competition. A man could open a shop in New York only by becoming a freeman, which entailed a substantial payment. The price and weight of bread loaves were specified by the assize, competition coming only in the quality of the product and the geniality of the service. There were inspectors of various kinds of meats, of flour and of cart wheels, also hay weighers, wood corders and many other officials.[1]

Yet the leading American cities left much to private effort that would later become a community responsibility. In Boston, for example, till 1823 drains were built by private companies when they pleased, and no householder could use them without buying the privilege.[2] Other towns built sewers only a little more promptly, and, whether of wood or brick, they usually were leaky and too small. Boston's streets, during the period of town government, were swept by farmers when they desired the sweepings as fertilizer.[3] New York directed each householder to clean the street in front, but in vain. Pigs ran the thoroughfares of that city till near the middle of the nineteenth century, co-operating in the disposal of refuse. Shortly after 1790 systematic street cleaning as a municipal function began, like nearly every other such improvement, in Philadelphia.[4]

[1] R. B. Morris, "Criminal Conspiracy and Early Labor Combinations in New York," *Polit. Sci. Quar.*, LII, 82-85; Common Council of the City of New York, *Minutes, 1784-1831* (N. Y., 1918), I, 518-519, 522, 528; anon., "Sketch of Philadelphia," 172; Baltimore Town and Jones' Town, *First Records, 1729-1797* (Balt., 1905), 70-108.

[2] Josiah Quincy, *Municipal History of the Town and City of Boston* (Boston, 1852), 119.

[3] *Ibid.*, 69.

[4] James Mease, *A Picture of Philadelphia* (Phila., 1811), 125. In 1789 New York had named a special superintendent to clean streets, with unsatisfactory results. Common Council of New York, *Minutes*, I, 369, 379. Pigs were forbidden in the streets of New York (for example, *ibid.*, I, 251), but they infested them nevertheless. For satirical reference to them, see anon., *Some Very Gentle Touches to Some Very Gentle-men*

All American cities in 1790 obtained their water from wells, rain barrels and cisterns, and some, like Boston, were to have no general system for many decades. In New York the "Tea Water Pump" in Chatham Street had a singular reputation for purity and from it daily were filled large casks mounted on wheels from which water was hawked about from door to door. A few years later Colonel Aaron Burr set up a small piping system run by hand pumps, but nearly half a century was to pass before New York made any adequate provision for this elementary need.[1] Until 1797 Philadelphia relied on public pumps set up in the principal streets at thirty-yard intervals; then this enterprising city began a system which tapped the Schuylkill and forced water by steam pumps through a "subterraneous canal" to a tower in Centre Square, whence it was distributed through bored logs underground.[2] Completed in 1801, it stood as the greatest public work in America, creditable in every way.

One factor in the water problem was the need of an ample supply for fire fighting, but without a proper organization of men this water would have been useless. Though fire companies were not new in 1790, no agreement yet existed as to their responsibilities. In Boston there were mutual companies protecting only the property of their members. Half the fire engines of that city were privately owned.[3] In Philadelphia the insur-

(N. Y., about 1820)—fifteen pictures and verses on this subject; Samuel Woodworth's comedy, *The Forest Rose* (N. Y., 1825) ; and Charles Dickens, *American Notes*, first published 1842 (London, 1913), 72. See also picture of pig and parade at Croton Water celebration in S. E. Morse, *System of Geography* (N. Y., 1844), 23.

[1] Munro, *Municipal Government*, I, 99; C. R. Fish, *The Rise of the Common Man, 1830-1850* (*A History of American Life*, VI), 104. Wansey, *Excursion*, 219, says water from some of the New York pumps gave him "very severe pains in the bowels, from its bad quality."

[2] The tower was a handsome edifice designed by B. H. Latrobe. **Anon.**, "Sketch of Philadelphia," 169-174; Wansey, *Excursion*, 172.

[3] T. P., "Boston in 1794," 268-269.

ance brigades performed a similar service. Only persons who displayed the leaden sign of the company could be sure of help from the fire fighters partially supported by it. In the 1790's, however, protection from fire was evolving from a private to a public function.

Insurance was being more widely introduced and by American companies, which were no longer denied incorporation because of the monopoly once granted to certain British concerns. In 1795 probably no house in Boston was insured; in 1798 several companies were founded and one, the Massachusetts Mutual, succeeded. By this date, however, New York had had one for a decade and Philadelphia had supported a thriving general company since 1792.[1] At the beginning of the new century the American business was so profitable that British companies, older and stronger, reëntered the field, of which until recently they had occupied so large a part.[2]

To a certain extent putting out fires fell under general city business, for the mayor and other officials were supposed to appear and assist. But the chief reliance was the volunteer brigade, compensated only by remission of jury and militia duty, though the superintendents might be salaried. Each member brought a bag to salvage small furnishings, a leather water bucket which could be passed from hand to hand, an ax and a wrench to unscrew rope bedsteads for removal.[3] By 1800 there were scores of hand engines of American manufacture

[1] Marquis James, *The Biography of a Business, 1792-1942: Insurance Company of North America* (N. Y., 1942), 18-24.

[2] Osborne Howes, jr., "The Rise and Progress of Insurance in Boston," Winsor, *History of Boston*, IV, 183; H. H. Hall, "Fire and Marine Insurance," Depew, *American Commerce*, I, 84; Smith, *New York*, 112-113; anon., *The Independence Square Neighborhood* (Phila., 1926), 63-73; J. A. Stevens, *Progress of New York in a Century* (N. Y., 1876), 42. The salvage corps was a vestige of the insurance companies' private war on fires.

[3] S. L. Mitchill, *The Picture of New-York* (N. Y., 1807), 71-72; anon., "Institutions for Extinguishing Fires," *Literary Mag. and Am. Register*, V (1806), 231.

and hose companies carrying fifty-foot lengths of leather hose. By 1830 steam was being brought into requisition.

The professionalization of the policeman proceeded further in these forty years than that of the fireman, though he was never sufficiently differentiated to have a uniform or full-time employment. Neither did he ever patrol in the daytime, for constables or marshals could be called upon if needed.[1] The night watch usually went on duty at ten o'clock. After a day's labor in mill or warehouse the watchman assumed his rattle, lantern, stick and badge and started on his rounds. By patrolling in alternate two-hour periods, between which times he slept, and by crying the hours, trying the doors and helping home the unsteady, he earned his five and a half shillings. Though frequently the butt of jests, he was slowly developing a professional spirit. After 1802 Jacob Hays, a New York police constable of protean disguises, emerged as the first American detective.[2]

The growth of a city naturally implies a changing skyline, but one is apt to take topography for granted. Yet cities often remake the earth as well as build houses on it. In Boston and Charleston, South Carolina, the filling had scarcely begun, but it was to go forward rapidly in the years ahead. New York, on the East River side, was slowly adding land which eventually was to be occupied by thousands of people. At the same time urban communities were taking an interest in street levels, revising them especially for drainage. Unlike European cities they saw increased convenience, here and there, by giving a continuous street a single name. For

---

[1] The first day patrol in New York, for example, was 1837. See Fish, *Rise of the Common Man*, plate xv, figure c, and note on pages xiv-xv.

[2] Pomerantz, *New York*, 297-303; E. H. Savage, *The Boston Watch and Police* (Boston, 1865), 41; James Hardie, *Census of New Buildings* (N. Y., 1824), 41; Fairlie, *Essays*, 86; Munro, *Municipal Government*, II, 98. Timothy Dwight praised the policing of New York, especially in the light of its polyglot population. See his *Travels*, III, 474-475.

example, after the first President in 1789 rode into Boston through Orange, Newbury and Marlborough streets and Cornhill, all virtually one thoroughfare, it was thought appropriate to name it Washington Street. In New York, Pearl, Great Dock, Queen and Magazine streets were consolidated into Pearl Street, while across town Great George Street was absorbed into Broadway.

The old Fresh Water Pond, the "Collect," at the north of New York, was filled in; and similar effort in Boston had by 1821 transformed the Mill Pond at the end of the peninsula into a substantial section of the town.[1] Into the Mill Pond had been dumped a large part of Beacon Hill. Three times that famous eminence was cut down until it finally gave the right setting for Bulfinch's new state house. Similar liberties were taken with Court House Hill in Baltimore.[2]

Since the towns of the young republic resembled those of the mother country in appearance and organization, no English immigrant need feel homesick as he landed on their wharves — not nearly so much, indeed, as if he had only crossed the scant thirty miles of the English Channel. Nevertheless, the imitative phase was passing and there now began quite consciously an evolution which we shall see paralleled in every other phase of social life. The immigrant, heartened by superficial similarities, might well look more deeply into society itself to see how far this transferred culture had been modified by American conditions.

[1] Boston was just beginning to undergo "a transformation as no other great city of the world has ever undergone at the hands of men." Edward Stanwood, "Topography and Landmarks of the Last Hundred Years," Winsor, *History of Boston*, IV, 25; N. B. Shurtleff, *A Topographical and Historical Description of Boston* (3rd edn., Boston, 1891), *passim*. The reclamation of the Back Bay waited until after the Civil War. See A. M. Schlesinger, *The Rise of the City, 1878-1898* (*A History of American Life*, X), 85.

[2] J. P. Kennedy, "Baltimore Long Ago," in his *At Home and Abroad*, 177-180.

CHAPTER II

REPUBLICAN ARISTOCRATS

THOUGH the European aristocratic tradition in American life had been weakened by the philosophy of the Revolution, the rapid accumulation of wealth and the institution of a more vigorous federal government were factors strengthening it again. The state and national constitutions had proclaimed that all men were equal before the law, but not necessarily in political privilege. Whether the new nation should favor or forbid a social stratification was as yet quite undecided.

When it is remembered that in every other country throughout Christendom certain families enjoyed the distinction of honorific titles, it is not surprising that their American counterparts in the reorganized society of 1790 felt a secret envy. But American custom had long opposed such marks of privilege, and most of the constitutions explicitly forbade titles of nobility. The European tradition of aristocracy managed to persist in America, but it was challenged by 1800 and deposed, at least politically, by 1830.[1] Hereditary privilege and the engrossment of opportunity proved impossible in a country where every ambitious man had so many chances to begin life anew. Sometimes it was the lure of a Western farm, more often the possibilities of a new business, that prevented free Americans from falling into a permanently unprivileged class. Foreign visitors who said that money alone counted in the United States spoke with some exaggeration, but money did mature into prestige

[1] The extension of political privileges is graphically presented in C. L. and Elizabeth H. Lord, *Historical Atlas of the United States* (N. Y., 1944), 54-55.

faster here than in most places. Rank and birth, as assets, could not be carried to a poorer market than America.[1]

In the cities there were no well-marked "quarters." Usually shopkeepers and even many wealthy wholesalers lived over their stores or behind them, and most professional men received their clients in their homes.[2] Nevertheless, there were some mansions belonging to those generally admitted to be "the quality." From their windows on winter evenings streamed the light of many candles and the sound of flute and violin, and gaily painted carriages, with liveried coachmen, clattered over the cobbles to their doors.

At the top of the social scale were the well-to-do merchant-shipping families, especially those who had taken the right side during the Revolution, together with their lawyers, and at a little economic (and therefore social) distance, their physicians. Next came the rich newcomers who had moved in from the country during the war or afterward, a class of great importance in Boston — the Prescotts, Lees, Cabots, Lowells and others — who, it was said, had bought the property of exiled Tories at bargain prices.[3] Then followed the self-made business men, whose rise from humbler circumstances the community could still remember.

Many of these families had broad-lawned suburban

[1] William Winterbotham, *An Historical, Geographical, Commercial, and Philosophical View of the American United States* (London, 1795), III, 298; F. M. Bayard, *Voyage dans l'Intérieur des États-Unis* (C. H. Sherrill, tr., Paris, 1797), 47. For the passing of the aristocrats, see Dixon Wecter, *The Saga of American Society* (N. Y., 1937), chap. iii.

[2] T. E. V. Smith, *The City of New York in the Year of Washington's Inauguration* (N. Y., 1889), 32; H. M. Lippincott, *Early Philadelphia* (Phila., 1919), 76; Mrs. St. Julien Ravenel, *Charleston, the Place and the People* (N. Y., 1906), 405-406; anon., *The Congregation "Beth Elohim"* (Charleston, 1883), 9. The New York post office was in the home of the postmaster until 1827.

[3] H. C. Lodge, *Boston* (London, 1891), 167; R. A. East, *Business Enterprise in the American Revolutionary Era* (Columbia Univ., Studies, no. 439), chaps. iii, ix.

houses for the hot months, especially on Manhattan Island and beside the Schuylkill, which without achieving a baronial dignity compared well with the lesser manor houses of the old country. But by the first years of the nineteenth century such families were discovering the watering place as a summer resort. In 1789 Saratoga Springs consisted of three log cabins hidden in a wilderness; then a dissertation published by a New York doctor in 1793 began the widespread advertisement of the virtues of the waters, and soon a number of hotels were built.[1] By 1809, we are assured, "invalids of fashion and opulence" could find at near-by Ballston every luxury they desired.[2] Originally a resort of the stricken, it had developed facilities for recreation and become a center of elegant leisure. In the phrase of Washington Irving's *Salmagundi Papers,* Southern ladies arrived, each with the annual produce of a rice plantation in her costume, and encountered an occasional competitor from Salem wrapped in the net proceeds of a cargo of whale oil.[3]

Though other springs in the state came into vogue,[4] they were soon rivaled by those in Virginia. Berkeley Springs could show the airs and graces of fashion as well as cure neuralgia, while the White Sulphur Springs were described in 1817 as a backwoods therapeutic resort as yet without a drawing-room. Far to the west at Olympia, "the Bath of Kentucky," cards, billiards and

---

[1] W. L. Stone, *Reminiscences of Saratoga* (N. Y., 1880), 22-31; Valentine Seaman, *Dissertation on the Mineral Waters of Saratoga* (N. Y., 1793); J. H. French, *Gazetteer of New York State* (Syracuse, 1860), 591-592.

[2] Valentine Seaman, "An Examination of the Account of Ballston Waters," *Medical Repository,* XI (1807-1808), 254; review of Seaman's *Dissertation on the Mineral Waters of Saratoga, ibid.,* XIII (1809-1810), 58.

[3] Sixteenth paper (Oct. 15, 1807).

[4] See Robert Munro, *A Description of the Genesee Country* (N. Y., 1804), for a description of the Clifton Springs and "those near the head of the river, on top of which floats Seneca oil [petroleum]."

horses supplemented the attractions of the waters.[1] As
early as 1790 valetudinarians from the Southern states
and the West Indies were being solicited to summer at
Rockaway, where sea bathing might cleanse and brace
the body against debility. The watering place was the
first theater of conspicuous leisure in America.[2] In a
land where work was generally praised, idleness could be
justified only by the affectation of ill health. It was
not until the twenties that summer leisure in itself became respectable, but then, as ever since, the men for the
most part enjoyed it vicariously through their wives and
daughters.[3]

The snobbishness of the fashionable circles in the cities
was doubtless a little cruel, though it pales beside the
real thing as portrayed by Thackeray. At the Philadelphia dinner parties of the dazzling Mrs. William
Bingham one might hear oaths and stories of a more or
less delicate naughtiness, echoing the banter of modish
tables in Mayfair or in the old Faubourg St. Germain. A
Bostonian like H. G. Otis, or a French puritan like Brissot de Warville, might be startled by the generous revelation of the female form in the salons of New York
and Philadelphia. But these coteries were useful in con-
serving the arts of deportment which otherwise might
easily have been forgotten.[4] They and their imitators

[1] J. K. Paulding, *Letters from the South by a Northern Man* (N. Y.,
1817), II, 237. The hot springs near Harrisonburgh were discovered in
1804. See *Winchester Independent Register*, Nov. 20, 1804, and John
Baltzell, *Essay on the Mineral Prospects of the Sweet Springs of Virginia*
(Balt., 1802).

[2] R. H. Gabriel, *The Evolution of Long Island* (New Haven, 1921),
172-173.

[3] C. R. Fish, *The Rise of the Common Man, 1830-1850* (*A History
of American Life*, VI), plate iii, figure b, and note on page x.

[4] S. E. Morison, *Harrison Gray Otis* (Boston, 1915), I, 135, 137;
J. P. Brissot de Warville, *New Travels in the United States of America*
(London, 1794), 95. For pictures of "The Social Background," see
the chapter so entitled in C. G. Bowers, *Jefferson and Hamilton* (Boston,
1925), and Edith T. Sale, *Old Time Belles and Cavaliers* (Phila., 1912),
99-171.

studied Lord Chesterfield, whose writings had been reprinted in America several times before 1790 and
formed the central canon of etiquette for more than half
a century. Though the polished meanness of the noble
earl was plentifully satirized, it was a matter of personal
interest to many Americans to learn that eating principally with a knife, using a fork to pick one's teeth,
and raking the mouth with a finger, were to be
deprecated.[1]

In some particulars standards of polite behavior differed from those in England, notably in the use of
tobacco. "No gentleman in Europe ever smokes except
by way of a frolic," the reader was told. William Pinkney, sent across in 1800 on a diplomatic mission, had
to puff his cigars furtively behind the closed doors of
his London apartment so as not to prejudice his reputation.[2] The Spanish cigar, introduced into the United
States shortly before 1790, gained vogue rapidly despite
warnings from some physicians. About fifteen years
later Americans were annually importing a hundred and
forty thousand dollars' worth.[3] No one lost caste, even
in the cities, by the public chewing of tobacco, though a
writer on *Clerical Manners* questioned the propriety of
spitting in church.[4] With cigars, after the ladies had left

[1] For example, Lord Chesterfield, *Letters to His Son* (N. Y., 1775);
anon., *Principles of Politeness* (New Haven, 1789); anon., *The American
Chesterfield* (Phila., 1827); Alfred Howard, ed., *The Beauties of Chesterfield* (Boston, 1828); the character of "Dimple" in Royall Tyler, *The
Contrast* (N. Y., 1787).

[2] Anon., *American Chesterfield*, 202; William Pinkney, *The Life of
William Pinkney* (N. Y., 1853), 35.

[3] *Medical Repository*, XI, 329. J. T. Scharf, *Chronicles of Baltimore*
(Balt., 1878), 267-268, and J. F. Watson, *Annals of Philadelphia*
(Phila., 1857), are wrong in believing that cigars were first smoked in
American streets to ward off yellow fever. Brissot de Warville mentions
them in New York in 1787 (*New Travels*, 87). See Benjamin Waterhouse, *Cautions to Young Persons . . . Shewing the Evil Tendency of
the Use of Tobacco upon Young Persons* (Cambridge, 1805).

[4] Samuel Miller, *Letters on Clerical Manners and Habits* (N. Y.,
1827), 83.

the dinner table, came the best port, madeira and brandy that the host could furnish. Almost no American at the end of the eighteenth century scrupled a moderate amount of good liquor, even among the "middle class." [1]

The gentleman of 1790 could still evidence his status by his dress. In all the coastal towns he followed the same fashions, imported like his manners. Traveling Frenchmen recognized the Paris modes of two years back slightly modified by a year's sojourn in London. [2] For design the well-dressed found mere pictures insufficient and had dolls sent across to display the latest conceits. [3] People bought imported clothes partly under the impression that goods worth sending three thousand miles were probably better than home products, and partly because they actually saw superiorities in articles fashioned in the European tradition of highly specialized skill; but to a large degree, especially with respect to style, their purchases reflected mere colonialism. "Many *hats*," said Professor Adam Seybert in 1809, "are annually fabricated in the United States, and *labelled* as of English manufacture, which would not be worn if this harmless deception were not practised . . . ." [4] Such deference aroused the boundless scorn of nationalists like Noah Webster, who wanted to complete our independence. [5]

Though American gentlemen had far less exemption

[1] Between 1790 and 1794 the importation of wine increased from about 3½ million gallons to 5½ million, whether from the larger prosperity of the country or from the coming of French merchant-importers. Duke de La Rochefoucauld-Liancourt, *Travels through the United States . . . in the Years 1795, 1796, and 1797* (London, 1799), II, 570.

[2] C. F. Volney, *A View of the Soil and Climate of the United States of America* (C. B. Brown, tr., Phila., 1804), 223-224; David Ramsay, *The History of South-Carolina* (Charleston, 1809), II, 409.

[3] J. D. Schoepf, *Travels in the Confederation, 1783-1784* (A. J. Morrison, ed., Phila., 1911), I, 110.

[4] Adam Seybert, *An Oration . . . at the Meeting of the Manufacturers and Mechanics of the City of Philadelphia* (Phila., 1809), 14.

[5] Noah Webster, *A Collection of Essays and Fugitive Writings* (Boston, 1790), 91.

from labor than those whose styles they imitated, they too paraded color as a badge of class.   Scarlet coats lined the aisles of the Brattle Street Church in Boston as well as the theater boxes in New York.   It was a day when gentlemen, if occasion suited, let themselves into their white, close-fitting doeskin breeches by stepping from a little platform to which the fragile articles were attached by hooks.[1]   Swords had disappeared from civil dress, but sword canes were popular with the buckish,[2] a transition to the more peaceful walking stick that still advertises the hand without employment.   Wigs were giving way except among the clergy, but the gentleman wore his hair long, even if not powdered, and tied it in a queue.   Of the fifty-six members of the New York legislature in 1798, all but five were so depicted.[3]   That this style was expensive — a hairdresser in Philadelphia cost twenty-two shillings a month [4] — made some cherish it the longer as evidence of their social standing.

Suddenly all this was challenged.   Startled into fear by the rise of the workers, the Paris *beau monde* disguised itself in workmen's pantaloons by way of protective coloring.   The new fashion spread, partly by the authority of the place of its origin and partly because it symbolized an equalitarian tendency which was to be widely accepted, with acclaim or with resignation. When the government lists in 1804 revealed that two patents had been granted for galluses to hold up trousers, another step in the history of democracy was registered.[5]   Irreconcilable old gentlemen refused to give

[1] Alice M. Earle, *Two Centuries of Costume in America* (N. Y., 1903), II, 408-409.

[2] V. L. Collins, *President Witherspoon* (Princeton, 1925), II, 154.

[3] See illustrations inserted between pages 1023 and 1024 in E. B. O'Callaghan, ed., *The Documentary History of the State of New-York* (Albany, 1849-1851), IV.

[4] Brissot de Warville, *New Travels*, 133.

[5] M. D. Leggett, comp., *Subject Matter Index of Patents for Inventions* (Wash., 1874), 1503.   The old form of the word was "gallows."

up the traditional costume even in the thirties, but James
Monroe was the last President to wear smallclothes, silk
stockings, silver buckles and a queue.[1]

Women's fashions underwent a like reaction toward
simplicity, a reflection of the Romantic movement. The
mountainous headdress reared on wire cage and cushions
and harnessed together with streamers now gave way as
girls clipped their tresses almost to the scalp, heavily
pomading the short ends about the face. "At the assembly," wrote a miss of 1798, "I was quite ashamed of
my head, for nobody has long hair." [2] New light muslin dresses cut low and sleeveless and draping naturally
over the figure aroused criticism as being ridiculous imitations unsuited to winter weather; the consequent exposure to the night air was certain to lead to consumption. A poet admonished the wearers:

> Full many a beauty blasted in her bloom,
> This stripping mania hurries to the tomb . . . .[3]

Moreover, they were shrouded from head to foot in com-
bustibles, a disadvantage in those days of open hearths
and candles.[4] Something, though not much, was also
said about immodesty.

The new style also had its enthusiastic advocates,
who rejoiced to see the old whalebones and heavy petti-
coats yield to simpler garments, whereby the muscles had
free play and beauty could be "ascertained by the un-

---

[1] D. C. Gilman, *James Monroe in His Relations to the Public Service*
(J. T. Morse, ed., *American Statesmen;* Boston, 1883), 182. Noah
Webster was one such incorrigible conservative.

[2] Eliza S. Bowne, *A Girl's Life Eighty Years Ago* (N. Y., 1887), 23.
On the older headdress, see Abbé Robin, *New Travels through North
America* (Phila., 1783), 14. The transition back to long hair was eased
by wigs and turbans.

[3] T. G. Fessenden, *The Ladies Monitor* (Bellows Falls, Vt., 1818), 65.

[4] Anon., "Hints Respecting Women and Children's Clothes Catching
Fire," *Literary Mag. and Am. Register,* IV (1805), 95.

equivocal testimonies of symmetry and nature." [1] But a fashion never survives simply because it is hygienic, cheap, comfortable or graceful. The conservatives who sighed for the return of silks and stuffs were to see them all again with the passing of a few more years. By the middle of the second decade of the nineteenth century the style was veering back. Soon the doctors were again inveighing against stays, busks and stomach boards, and a new generation of conservatives spoke pensively of the good old days of muslin. [2]

Perfection in the amenities of urbane society requires study and, by implication, models. Suddenly in the early 1790's the explosions in revolutionary Europe threw the most perfect patterns into American coastal towns. If in times past refugees had fled to escape the exactions of an aristocracy, now came aristocrats fleeing the fury of the mob. The rebellion in Santo Domingo, begun in 1791 by Negroes in the interest of liberty, fraternity and equality, sent thousands of French colonists to American shores. Probably Baltimore was affected most by the coming of fifteen hundred in a single month, notwithstanding the larger numbers of French who later landed at New York and Philadelphia. Accustomed to luxury and refinement, many of them arrived with scarcely more than the clothes they wore and a meager English word or two to ask for shelter. Congress, with fine disdain of constitutional limitation, voted fifteen thousand dollars, and states followed this example. Clothing, furniture and tools were given, and whole families were taken as guests into American homes for as long as two years. Important precedents were set when public subscription built up funds to be administered by committees. A grateful exile reckoned that from this source alone came nearly a quarter of a million

[1] Anon., "Picture of London," *ibid.,* II (1804), 283.
[2] *Boston Medical Intelligencer,* July 5, 1825; April 18, 1826.

dollars.[1]   Hospitality was more severely tested by the
shiploads of French royalists who a few years later saved
their lives but not their property by emigrating from
a homeland enveloped in the Terror. The total number has been estimated all the way from ten to twenty-
five thousand.[2]

Among them were many of great distinction.[3]   Louis
Philippe, who later would be king, taught French in a
suburb of New York, or entertained at dinner a few
guests seated on his straw bed over a Philadelphia barroom.   The Duke de La Rochefoucauld-Liancourt,
lately the liberal leader of the French nobility with over
half a million francs a year, boarded with a barber, but
was obliged for want of extra pence to shave himself.
The Vicomte de Noailles, who had been richer than the
Duke, was now beginning another fortune in two furnished rooms as he cast up the accounts of his Pennsylvania tract, appropriately named Asylum, where were
"sundry ci-devant French Barons, Counts & Marquises,
employed in the Labors of Agriculture." [4]   A French
admiral worked as journeyman to a Baltimore potter,
while a marquis set up as a Philadelphia whitesmith.
Some, like Count Talleyrand, were in better circumstances; and some, like Chateaubriand, Volney and
young Jerome Bonaparte, can hardly be classed as
refugees.

But peace and security in Europe were long delayed,

---

[1] La Rochefoucauld-Liancourt, *Travels,* III, 33-35; Moreau de Saint-
Méry, *Voyage aux États-Unis de l'Amérique* (New Haven, 1913), 55;
Daily Advertiser (N. Y.), July 15, Aug. 7, 1793; Frances S. Childs.
French Refugee Life in the United States, 1790-1800 (Balt., 1940),
84-90.

[2] H. M. Jones, *America and French Culture* (Chapel Hill, 1927), 134.

[3] A number were elected members of the American Philosophical Society.   J. G. Rosengarten, "Moreau de Saint Méry and His French
Friends in the American Philosophical Society," Am. Philos. Soc., *Proceeds.,* L, 168-178.

[4] Charles Nisbet to Charles Warren, May 18, 1797, Nisbet MSS. (New
York Public Library).

and others came evading one oppression or another: Du Pont de Nemours in 1799 and the Napoleonic exiles after 1814. Of this last group Joseph Bonaparte, the Count de Chaumont and Marshal Grouchy may stand as examples.[1] "Have we not jostled ex-kings and ex-empresses and ex-nobles in Broadway;" asked a reminiscent writer with a trace of extravagance, "trod on the toes of exotic naturalists, Waterloo marshals, and great foreign academicians . . . and seen more heroes and generals all over town than would fill a new Iliad?"[2]

Some gained a livelihood by teaching their culture to any who could pay, instructing in the arts of dancing, music and French conversation. But much of the French influence was less direct, though not less effective.[3] The nine or ten French newspapers maintained for the *émigrés* doubtless found some native readers who desired to increase acquaintance with the language.[4] French books were to be had more easily at such establishments as that set up by Moreau de Saint-Méry.[5] The exiles sponsored numerous concerts and the first rendering of opera in a foreign language.[6] Certain merchants, like Stephen Jumel, made fortunes by importing French merchandise, mostly articles of luxury, such as wines, fine fabrics, jewelry, gold watches and gilt frames for mirrors and pictures.[7] With the refugees also came

[1] S. G. Goodrich, *Recollections of a Lifetime* (N. Y., 1857), II, 61-62; Childs, *French Refugee Life*, 31-61; J. S. Reeves, *The Napoleonic Exiles in America* (Johns Hopkins Univ., *Studies*, XXIII, nos. 9-10); Jones, *America and French Culture*, passim. Louis Philippe's two brothers were with him.

[2] G. C. Verplanck, W. C. Bryant and R. C. Sands, *Miscellanies* (N. Y., 1833), II, 317.

[3] John Davis, *Travels of Four Years and a Half in the United States of America* (London, 1803), 322-323.

[4] The *Courrier des États-Unis*, still flourishing, was founded in 1828.

[5] Moreau de Saint-Méry, *Voyage*, introduction.

[6] O. G. Sonneck, *Early Concert in America* (Leipzig, 1907), 188, 227.

[7] On French importers who became rich, see J. A. Scoville (Walter Barrett, *pseud.*), *Old Merchants of New York* (N. Y., 1885), V, 351-

French cooks.   These had been known before, but never a great artist like Brillat-Savarin, who later recorded his American experiences in his *Physiologie du Goût*. Vegetables began to find a larger place on American menus, some like artichokes and okra appearing for the first time; yeast commenced to supplant the old dough-leaven previously in general use; and confectioners and caterers wrought miracles in pastry, ices and blancmange. The word restaurant was naturalized.   By the early thirties a competent observer could say that "American cookery has somewhat engrafted the French upon the English." [1]

The French Revolution accounted, too, for another group of immigrants, who though small in number were not without influence.   Irish nationalist leaders, desperate in discouragement, had emigrated from time to time to the French West Indies or to France itself.   But French soil was none too safe when the Terror triumphed, and these "wild geese" now took their flight to the American continent, especially to the Southern towns.   The failure of the United Irishmen's final stroke started many more, one ship landing at Norfolk in 1798 with over four hundred such passengers, mostly persons of property.   Some, like the leading French refugees, returned home when political skies cleared, but others stayed to win high places in their professions.[2]   Like the French,

353, and Abraham Ritter, *Philadelphia Merchants* (Phila., 1860), 23, 71, 108, 198.   The greatest of them, Stephen Girard, came before the *émigrés*.

[1] Francis Lieber, *The Stranger in America* (N. Y., 1835), I, 226, cited in Jones's account in *America and French Culture*, 300-309.   See also Fernand Baldensperger, "Le séjour de Brillat-Savarin aux états unis," *Revue de Littérature Comparée*, II, 94-95.

[2] For example, Thomas Addis Emmett and William Sampson, the lawyers, William J. MacNevin, the physician, Robert Adrain, professor of mathematics at Columbia, and Bernard MacMahon, the Philadelphia horticulturist.   Harmon Blennerhassett's island mansion on the Ohio was the scene of Burr's scheme for empire.   Like the Frenchmen, they sometimes taught dancing.   See M. M. Bagg, *Pioneers of Utica* (Utica, 1877), 137-142, 376-379.   Some went first to Newfoundland, where they unsuc-

too, as a whole they added prestige to the Catholic Church. Unlike them, the Irish found an important function as interpreters between their peasant compatriots, who soon began to arrive in great numbers, and the older Americans.

European *émigrés* and travelers were surprised to see how generally respectable in the United States was ordinary labor: for example, how many cultivated women did their own work. Americans took pride in the fact. "No country of the same wealth, intelligence and civilization," remarked Tench Coxe, the economist, "has so few *menial* servants (strictly speaking) in the families of persons of the greatest property." This was a result, at least in part, of the dearth of available servants. The competition in America was not for the place, but for the service.[1] It was to meet this condition that the early settlers had introduced Negro slavery. This, of course, remained the dominant labor system of the South, but it was disappearing elsewhere.

Only one out of fourteen slaves, according to the first census, was held north of Maryland and Delaware. Vermont, Massachusetts and New Hampshire had forbidden slavery in their constitutions and one by one other Northern states followed with laws for gradual freedom.[2] The institution had been strongest in New York, but there, as elsewhere in the North, the movement for emancipation aroused little controversy and was largely carried through by the slave owners them-

cessfully tried raising a rebellion. For a general account, see E. O. Condon, "Irish Immigration to the United States after 1790," Am. Irish Hist. Soc., *Journ.*, IV, 84-89.

[1] Tench Coxe, *A View of the United States of America* (Phila., 1794), 441; Timothy Dwight, *Travels in New-England and New-York* (New Haven, 1821-1822), IV, 349.

[2] Pennsylvania in 1780, Rhode Island and Connecticut in 1784, New York in 1799 and New Jersey in 1804. See L. D. Turner, "Anti-Slavery Sentiment in American Literature," *Journ. of Negro History*, XIV, 371 ff., and E. B. Greene, *The Revolutionary Generation, 1763-1790* (*A History of American Life*, IV), 288, 322-323.

Street Scene, Philadelphia

selves or those connected with them. Most of the Negroes, especially the older ones, remained in the households of their former masters, following the family to church and celebrating their old "Pinkster" holiday after the final date of 1827 just as before, hardly conscious that their legal status had changed. In New Jersey the process was likewise slow and peaceful, a few remaining in bondage until after 1860.[1] Pennsylvania was called the paradise of the blacks.[2] Except for an occasional outbreak, such as that at York in 1793, the relations were certainly as friendly as in the states to the east, and the Negroes for the most part continued in domestic service.[3]

Older even than slavery as an American means of regimenting labor was the system of indenturing immigrants. This, too, was rapidly passing, but by force of circumstances rather than by law. The reduction of immigration was partly responsible. The Revolutionary philosophy, too, had done its work and made the unfree white man seem an anomaly. The system lingered longest in Pennsylvania, but there the last act to govern such contracts was passed in 1818 and no trace of the practice has been found after 1831. The system had disappeared in Maryland and New Jersey a little before.[4]

[1] Samuel McKee, jr., *Labor in Colonial New York* (Columbia Univ., Studies, no. 410), 173-176; D. R. Fox, "The Negro Vote in Old New York," *Polit. Sci. Quar.*, XXXII, 252-275; C. F. Hoffman, *The Pioneers of New York* (N. Y., 1848), 30-33. There were 21,000 slaves in New York and 12,000 in New Jersey in 1790. H. S. Cooley, *A Study of Slavery in New Jersey* (Johns Hopkins Univ., Studies, XIV, nos. ix-x), 19, 26, 30-31; A. Q. Keasby, "Slavery in New Jersey," N. J. Hist. Soc., Proceeds., ser. 3, IV, 90-96; V, 12-19, 79-85.

[2] Samuel Breck, *Recollections* (H. E. Scudder, ed., Phila., 1877), 107.

[3] When they left service it was thought their character deteriorated. E. R. Turner, *The Negro in Pennsylvania* (Wash., 1910), 129, 135, 145, 152.

[4] English ships had been forbidden to carry indentured servants in 1785, but the act was ill enforced. C. A. Herrick, *White Servitude in Pennsyl-*

Another source of household labor, though in no great quantity, was the bound apprentice, whose origins date back to the days of Queen Elizabeth. In the Southern states, where slavery tended to suggest protection for the white, it was usually required that a pauper child apprenticed by the authorities to a master must be taught a trade; but in the North a provision for "other useful employment" legally made a household drudge out of an orphan girl throughout most of the nineteenth century.[1] Philanthropic women, especially in New England, organized "female asylums," where orphans dressed in neat blue uniforms were schooled up to the age of ten, after which they were bound out to pious families for a period of eight years.[2] But the pretentious homes in the Northern towns depended for the most part on free servants, black or, more generally, white.

Human service seemed a major necessity to those of that generation who lived at all spaciously, for the household was a far more extensive enterprise than it is today. Although well-to-do urban dwellers relied upon shops much more than those isolated in the country, even in town houses there was likely to be a spinning room; and soap, candles, carpets and other furnishings were largely made at home. When Mrs. Adams moved

vania (Phila., 1926), 254, 266; Phineas Bond, "Letters," Am. Hist. Assoc., Ann. Rep. for 1897, 455. The traffic in indentured servants never recovered from the effects of the depression of 1818-1819; see M. L. Hansen, The Atlantic Migration, 1607-1860 (A. M. Schlesinger, ed., Cambridge, 1940), 105.

[1] Elizabeth L. Otey, The Beginnings of Child Labor Legislation in Certain States (U. S. Bur. of Labor, Report on Condition of Woman and Child Wage-Earners in the United States, Wash., 1910-1913, VI), 19-20, 50; Allan Nevins, The Emergence of Modern America, 1865-1878 (A History of American Life, VIII), 329.

[2] Joseph Eckley, Discourse Delivered before the Members of the Boston Female Asylum (Boston, 1802), 2, 13-14; Providence Female Asylum, Charter and Constitution (Providence, 1802); Abiel Abbot, Sermon before the Portsmouth Female Asylum (Portsmouth, 1807); Dwight, Travels, III, 464; Moses Stuart, Sermon before the Female Charitable Society (Andover, 1815), 18-19, 23, 25.

into the new "President's House" in Washington she
required thirty servants. The great East Room, for
example, called for a hundred and eighty lights. Each
candle had to be made by hand, which was a considerable operation, for an ordinary recipe required
twenty-five pounds of tallow.[1] Someone must pump
the water by hand and carry it to all the bedrooms.
Someone must carry the oak and hickory to feed the big
voracious fireplaces on which depended the achievement
of a tolerable temperature; someone must carry out the
ashes; someone must be ready with a cloth to wipe
away the dust that flew from the hearth about the
room.

The hearth presented other serious service problems.
The women must keep the space between the backlog
and the forestick well filled with burning small-wood.
A generation accustomed to aluminum utensils would
quail before the challenge of brass and copper pots
and heavy iron pans and kettles, which had to be set
on trivets or lifted to the sooty pothooks and notched
trammels hanging from the crane or the less accessible
crossbar bridging the chimney above the fire. There
were spits to turn and innumerable racks and grills to
keep in order. The transition to the box stove, especially that burning coal, which was well under way
by 1830, was an important step in the emancipation of
women, and not alone in lightening the drudgery of
cooking. It became possible to heat rooms and not
merely an area about the hearth, even to warm considerable portions of the house, a development to be com-

[1] The whole recipe is as follows: Dissolve 25 lbs. of beef tallow in a
copper or brass vessel, adding 20 lbs. of water. With this mix 1½
qts. of brandy, 5 oz. of cream of tartar, 5 oz. of sal ammoniac; 5 oz. of
salt of tartar, 2 oz. of dry, clean potash. Cake and then cut up into slivers
to whiten in the air. Make wicks of the best cotton; steep these in wine
and wax them. Then pour the heated tallow on them in the moulds.
From J. B. Bordley, *Essays and Notes on Husbandry and Rural Affairs*
(Phila., 1799), 469-470.

pleted a half-century later with the furnace.[1] Few phenomena at the beginning of the nineteenth century seem
more impressive to the modern reader than the immense
effort which women had to make to "keep house." Little
leisure existed for self-cultivation unless the housewife
could call upon a servant.

Large establishments maintained rather imposing
retinues.   When Washington set up as President in New
York he had eighteen house servants, seven of them
slaves and the others white.   Five of the latter received
seven dollars a month each, besides liveries costing
twenty-nine dollars each; three women were content
with five dollars; a housekeeper with eight, a valet with
thirteen and a half, and a steward with twenty-five.
Jefferson, living more simply as secretary of state in
Philadelphia, had six menials.[2]   The President's wage
scale was about normal, though in New England, where
the willing hands of spinster aunts and daughters reduced the need for domestics, a dollar a week was usually
considered sufficient.[3]   But the servant was coming to
demand something besides money—a distinctly higher
social status than his class had enjoyed before.

With the passing of the indenture the social chasm
narrowed.   The first stage in the history of domestic
service had closed and the second, a democratic period,
opened, to be followed in the fifties by a third, when
with new immigration the advent of large numbers of

[1] Anon., *The Experienced American Housekeeper* (N. Y., 1823), for
recipes calling for the stove; *Medical Repository* IX (1905-1906),
96-97; Jeremiah Dwyer, "Stoves and Heating Apparatus," C. M. Depew,
ed., *One Hundred Years of American Commerce* (N. Y., 1895), II,
327; Edward Parrish, "Historical Memoirs of the Philadelphia College of
Pharmacy," *Am. Journ. of Pharmacy*, XLI, 107; Fish, *Rise of the Common Man*, 98-99.

[2] W. E. Woodward, *George Washington, the Image and the Man* (N.
Y., 1926), 433; Anne H. Wharton, *Salons, Colonial and Republican*
(Phila., 1900), 109.

[3] A. W. Calhoun, *A Social History of the American Family* (Cleveland, 1917-1919), II, 147.

servants speaking English with difficulty, if at all, somewhat restored the distance familiar in the eighteenth century. But the phenomenon of the contented intelligent servant, so constantly encountered in the Old World, was rare indeed. English menials who crossed the sea were lonesome for like-minded company. Few American women and fewer men studied to perfect themselves in domestic service as a permanent calling, because, in contrast with England, there were openings to so many other occupations which led one higher.

The difficulty of hiring or cajoling women into this permanent status increased about 1807, when to the opportunities held out by the farming bachelor in search of a partner were added those offered by the manufacturer, especially in the textile mill.[1] But machines for spinning and weaving, while they lured away the servants, at the same time made them less necessary in the household. There was no similar industrialization of cooking. By 1830, it is true, François Appert's principles of sealing under heat, discovered in 1795, were known in New York and Boston, and in 1825 two men had been granted patents for preserving salmon, lobsters and oysters in sealed containers; but the great American canning industry, with its prepared soups, meats, vegetables and fruits, was to come many years later.[2]

[1] For attempts to entice servants into permanent tenure, see Society for the Encouragement of Faithful Domestics, *Constitution* (Phila., 1829), and Society for the Encouragement of Faithful Domestic Servants, *Annual Report* (N. Y., 1826).

[2] On Appert, who is variously cited as François, Nicolas or Charles, the best account in English is by Katherine G. Bitting in anon., ed., *A Complete Course in Canning* (Balt., 1924), 9-22. Ezra Daggett and Thomas Kensett, the patentees mentioned above, who had probably picked up the technique in England, started canning in New York in 1819. William Underwood and Charles Mitchell began in Boston in 1820, the Underwood firm still existing. G. C. Butz, *Canning of Fruits and Vegetables* (Pa. Dept. of Agr., *Bull.*, no. 91), 11-12; Florence R. Corbett, *Canned Foods* (Teachers College, Columbia Univ., *Technical Educ. Bull.*, no. 18) 3.

The housewife finding help hard to get, and being unable as yet to bring home a dinner half-prepared from the shops, succumbed more and more to the seductions of the boarding house.   There were said to be three hundred and thirty such establishments in New York in 1789.[1]   The boarding house developed into the residence hotel, though in later times a reaction occurred, wholesome as far as it went, to the small housekeeping flat where maids were scarcely needed or, as was the case with larger apartments, cut to a minimum.[2]   It may be hazarded that with all the increase in wealth since 1800 the proportion of American families employing domestic service was as great then as it is today.

[1] Hiram Hitchcock, "The Hotels of America," Depew, *American Commerce*, I, 150.
[2] Nevins, *Emergence of Modern America*, 208.

CHAPTER III

THE BUSINESS SCENE

IN the last decade of the eighteenth century business men had every reason to be hopeful. By natural reaction, if nothing else, a growing confidence had succeeded the distrust and stringency of 1786 and 1787. Washington was quick to realize that the new government would be praised for many blessings which were really flowing from the industry and frugality of a people struggling against hard times.[1] But the new government did make its own contribution toward the restoration of public and individual credit; and the president of Princeton correctly assumed that because of it "millions that had been lying dead in the hands of their possessors were suddenly revivified and brought into active and extensive operation."[2] The business classes—creditors, merchants, shippers, land speculators—who had been particularly zealous in carrying through the Constitution, felt well satisfied. Optimism was being coined in every countinghouse. Travelers characterized America as the land of speculation; in its short, familiar form of "spec" the word was on nearly every lip.[3]

The two centuries of Anglo-American history since Jamestown, broadly speaking, had been a record of speculative exploitation. Many a career had been made in

[1] Washington to Lafayette, June 18, 1788. George Washington, *Writings* (Jared Sparks, ed., Boston, 1834-1837), IX, 382.

[2] S. S. Smith, *The Divine Goodness to the United States of America* (Phila., 1795).

[3] John Phillips, *General History of Inland Navigation* (London, 1792), 355; William Priest, *Travels in the United States* (London, 1802), 132; William Faux, *Memorable Days in America, 1818-1820* (R. G. Thwaites, ed., *Early Western Travels, 1748-1846*, Cleveland, 1904-1907, XI-XII), I, 62.

the narrower sense, but the great event which stirred up widespread speculation was the establishment of the funding system. Under the new Constitution the secretary of the treasury, Alexander Hamilton, in January, 1790, brought forth a plan intended to restore and fortify the nation's credit and incidentally to ally the business interests more closely with the government. Everyone admitted that the nearly twelve million dollars owed abroad should be paid in full, but the secretary, following his double purpose, proposed also an eventual full payment of the forty-two million owed to domestic creditors. His supporters in Congress finally bore down all opposition and put it through. When Hamilton then boldly suggested the national assumption of state debts, quick objection arose from local patriots who foresaw the overwhelming prestige that the federal government would gain with the creditor class. More practical were the arguments advanced by commonwealths like New Hampshire and Maryland which, untouched by military invasion, had little debt to pay, and by those like Virginia, which had already retired their obligations. After acrimonious debate, and finally a quiet bargain for Virginia's support by which the federal capital was to be located on the Potomac, this proposal likewise passed.

As a further measure Hamilton designed a national bank. This institution would take care of the public funds, put them at the temporary disposal of private business when not in use, through loans of redeemable paper money, and, again, enlist the commercial classes in support of the government. There were plenty of scruples respecting an agency apparently not contemplated in the Constitution, but the indomitable secretary and his phalanx of congressional leaders registered this victory as well.[1]

[1] C. A. Beard, *Economic Origins of Jeffersonian Democracy* (N. Y., 1915), 132-164.

While these measures dragged on in debate, the price of federal and state securities in the leading cities fluctuated violently with each rumor of the trend of sentiment in Congress. As soon as it seemed clear that the paper would be redeemed at par, sharp traders filled their saddlebags with coin and, racing into the backcountry, purchased all they could at the prevailing prices before the news arrived. Others, chartering swift sailing boats, reaped a fortune in the Southern states.[1] Profits were tremendous. Patrick Henry, who the year before had purchased state paper at two shillings in the pound, sold it now at twenty-seven.[2] In the interior counties of North Carolina, where information circulated slowly, securities were bought at seventy-five-per-cent discount. Had the owners instead of the traders received the par price, they might have developed a strong attachment to the Federalist party; instead they developed deep resentment.[3]

When on July 4, 1791, the subscription books of the new Bank of the United States were formally opened, the capital was promptly oversubscribed by a fifth. Confidence in its success sent its stock well above par and for several years it enjoyed an almost dangerous popularity.[4] Yet in this respect it was by no means singular. Only four banks had preceded it, but by the end of 1793

[1] Timothy Dwight, *Travels in New-England and New-York* (New Haven, 1821-1822), I, 219-230; T. H. Benton, ed., *Abridgment of the Debates of Congress* (N. Y., 1857-1861), I, 198; Richard Hildreth, *The History of the United States of America* (N. Y., 1851-1852), IV, 158 ff.

[2] Memorandum by Thomas Jefferson, *Historical Magazine*, n.s., II, no. 2, 93. Henry had acquired the paper expecting to use it in purchasing land.

[3] John Steele, *Papers* (H. M. Wagstaff, ed., Raleigh, 1924), I, 57-58; William Barry to James Hogg, *James Sprunt Hist. Monographs*, no. 3, 85-88.

[4] Alexander Hamilton, *Works* (J. C. Hamilton, ed., N. Y., 1850-1851), V, 474-475; J. T. Holdsworth, *The First Bank of the United States* (Phila., 1911), 22-25; J. O. Wettereau, "New Light on the First Bank of the United States," *Pa. Mag. of History and Biog.*, LXI, 263 ff.

a score existed.   Active speculation occurred in the stock
of all, and with the profits reported — the Massachusetts Bank paid twenty per cent a year — there developed, at least in New York, a veritable "bancomania"
during 1792.[1] Of course, there were voices raised against
these privileged institutions.   On the one hand small
farmers believed a money monopoly would be exacting
toward its debtors and, on the other, certain political
scientists like John Adams feared banks on historical
grounds.[2]

But banks satisfied a real need.   British credit, upon
which previous generations of business men had relied,
was temporarily curtailed.   At the same time trading
profits were providing a reservoir of capital which must
be properly administered.   The value of the pound,
however, differed widely through the country.   In South
Carolina it approximated sterling, in New York it rated
at about half as much, and elsewhere it varied between
the two extremes.   Merchants dealing at a distance preferred hard money, but for this they had to depend on
chance cash surpluses from the West Indies and other
foreign ports.   Consequently, banks that could issue dollar notes based on miscellaneous wealth on hand were
immensely convenient.   By 1802 bank vaults had some
twenty-three million representing notes outstanding;
and currency listed with the dollar sign, the modified
monogram of the initials U. S., was growing common.[3]

[1] J. S. Davis, *Essays in the Earlier History of American Corporations*
(*Harvard Econ. Studies*, XVI), II, 66, 81, app. B; H. W. Domett,
comp., *A History of the Bank of New York* (N. Y., 1884), 44.

[2] William Manning, *The Key of Libberty* [1798] (S. E. Morison, ed.,
Billerica, Mass., 1922), 25-26; *Columbian Centinel* (Boston), April 11,
1791; A. O. Eliason, *The Rise of Commercial Banking in the United
States* (Minneapolis, 1901), 25-29; John Adams, *Works* (C. F. Adams,
ed., Boston, 1850-1856), X, 375.

[3] Alexander Baring, *Inquiries into the Orders in Council* (London,
1808), 55; Eliason, *Commercial Banking*, 29.

Other corporate enterprises were also developing. Starting in 1790 with twenty-six the number doubled within a decade. North Carolina in 1795 and Massachusetts in 1799 took the lead in passing general statutes under which certain kinds of corporations could be set up, thus making unnecessary the political maneuvering for special acts. Other states extended the scope of such legislation, New York, for example, in 1811.[1] No longer did the small investor have to content himself with loaning on real estate or taking a share in a ship, and no longer did the wealthy perforce go into business themselves.[2] The states not infrequently subscribed for shares of the public-utility companies they had created, and hence needed to engage in more borrowing. What with the active demand for state and federal stocks, as government bonds were then generally called, and the multiplication of banks and insurance companies, it was not surprising that a money market should come into being.

For several decades after 1790 business finance centered chiefly in Philadelphia. Unlike New York it had been little disturbed by British occupation, and now the federal government was established there for ten years. Philadelphia led New York in imports until 1796 and in exports until 1797, but its primacy in domestic trade lasted longer. The first two American banks had been set up in the Pennsylvania metropolis and now, in securing the main offices of the Bank of the United States,

[1] These early laws were permissive rather than regulatory. E. S. Baldwin, "American Business Corporations," *Am. Hist. Rev.*, VIII, 465; Davis, *Essays*, II, 16. The increase in corporations between 1790 and 1800 was as follows: insurance companies, from 3 to 30; canal, 14 to 60; bridge, 3 to 70; turnpike, 0 to 72; water, 0 to 29; manufacturing, 2 to 6; miscellaneous, 4 to 4. *Ibid.*, II, app. B.

[2] In 1828 New York made limited liability of the stockholder a feature of the corporate charter. C. M. Haar, "Legislative Regulation of New York Industrial Corporations," *N. Y. History*, XXVI, 195-196.

the city capped a financial prestige which it would yield but slowly.[1]

New York was frankly envious. Its merchants traded as actively as any in securities. In May, 1792, to meet the menacing competition of auctioneers, about two dozen merchant-brokers, firms and individuals, agreed to deal by preference with one another and to sell on a commission of less than one fourth of one per cent, an understanding which persisted until a formal constitution was drawn up a quarter-century later. On pleasant afternoons at "high 'change hour," according to tradition, they came together in the shade of a huge buttonwood tree on Wall Street near the two banks and bought and sold securities. In 1794 more convenient quarters were found in the new Tontine Coffee House farther down the street.[2]

By the middle twenties the New York stock exchange had distanced that established in 1800 at Philadelphia, though in all large towns there were minor markets, and country storekeepers also acted as agents in this commerce. Industrial stocks were not quoted until nearly 1830, for such enterprises usually represented a modest neighborly coöperation. The daily total of sales even in New York was low, averaging about a hundred shares until the great expansion in that year.[3] Yet foundations had been laid for the immense growth of this institution during the next half-century. As the American banker emerged from the general business man, so the stockbroker also grew more important. "Stockjobbing," wrote a member of the firm of Brown Brothers in 1820, "is a trade of itself and only suits those that make a

[1] R. A. East, *Business Enterprise in the American Revolutionary Era* (Columbia Univ., *Studies*, no. 439), chap. xiii; Margaret G. Myers, *The New York Money Market* (N. Y., 1931), I, 3-9.
[2] Martha J. Lamb, *Wall Street and Its History* (N. Y., 1883), 72; L. H. Jenks, *The Migration of British Capital* (N. Y., 1927), 65-66.
[3] Myers, *New York Money Market*, I, chap. ii.

trade of it."[1] The bulls and bears of Threadneedle Street now had their American counterparts.[2]

But during the decades following the Revolution the merchandising of land was a more important factor in American business than the trading in securities. Many a rich man could have said with Timothy Pickering, "All I am now worth was gained by speculation in land."[3] and many a fortune eventually suffered the same sad fate as his. The census of 1790 had outrun the most hopeful estimates. Robert Morris, recalling Franklin's computations, assured foreign investors that the population would double every twenty years, that fifty thousand young people were moving westward annually and hence that every dollar invested in American land would yield unprecedented profits. "The country," he wrote, "is rushing into wealth and importance faster than ever was expected by the most sanguine."[4] Such men, even the great wholesalers who did not sell to individual settlers, looked upon themselves as forwarders, not obstacles to progress, playing grand rôles as architects of empire.[5] Those who bought up soldiers' land warrants, sometimes as low as five cents on the dollar, could hardly have been moved by idealism, though it was considered a respectable kind of trade followed by reputable men. Washington bought such scrip and a Columbia professor gained enough from it to retire from his chair.[6]

[1] J. C. Brown, *One Hundred Years of Merchant Banking* (N. Y., 1909), 69.

[2] These terms had come into use about the time the London Trading Association took up its quarters in that street in 1773.

[3] Octavius Pickering and C. W. Upham, *The Life of Timothy Pickering* (Boston, 1867-1873), III, 296.

[4] E. P. Oberholtzer, *Robert Morris, Patriot and Financier* (N. Y., 1903), 315-316.

[5] The large land companies of this period were voluntary associations in which the organization and methods of modern corporate management were tested, often without benefit of incorporation. Shaw Livermore, *Early American Land Companies* (N. Y., 1939), 7-8.

[6] W. E. Woodward, *George Washington, the Image and the Man* (N. Y., 1926), 392. See also article on J. D. Gros in *Appletons' Cy-*

In the East the largest purchases of wild lands were made from states; in trans-Appalachia, from the federal government.   During the early 1790's Massachusetts disposed of three million acres in central Maine to Henry Knox, the secretary of war, and William Duer, the assistant secretary of the treasury, at twenty-one cents per acre.   It had recently sold to Oliver Phelps and Nathaniel Gorham for a hundred thousand dollars the six million acres which it had retained in western New York by interstate agreement.[1]   At the same time New York itself was selling parcels almost as princely in extent, notably the nearly four million acres in the northern ranges obtained by Alexander Macomb and associates for about eight cents per acre, in addition to his previous purchases along the St. Lawrence.[2]   Thirty-five partners bought from Connecticut in 1795 nearly all of her Western Reserve in Ohio for $1,200,000.[3]

Flushed with confidence, sober men of business risked all they could borrow, in lands whose character they knew only by hearsay.   James Wilson, gowned and periwigged as a justice of the federal Supreme Court, may now and then have lost the thread of some prosy argument as his mind strayed to the fair prospect of his domain beyond the Alleghanies or his million acres in the

clopædia of American Biography (N. Y., 1887-1901), III, 5, and Daniel Agnew, *History of Pennsylvania, North of the Ohio and West of the Allegheny River* (Phila., 1887), 28.

[1] In the arrangement of 1786 Massachusetts satisfied her old charter claims by keeping the preëmption rights, that is, the right to acquire land proprietorship from the Indians from Lake Seneca to Lake Erie, while New York was acknowledged to have political jurisdiction over the territory.   Massachusetts sold two million acres of Maine land to Henry Jackson and Royal Flint at ten cents an acre.   Davis, *Essays*, I, 268-269.

[2] E. A. Werner, comp., *Civil List and Constitutional History of New York* (Albany, 1886), 239; Gates Curtis, *Our County and Its People: a Memorial History of St. Lawrence County, N. Y.* (Syracuse, 1894), 82-85; E. B. O'Callaghan, ed., *The Documentary History of the State of New-York* (Albany, 1849-1851), III, 1069-1083.

[3] B. A. Hinsdale, *The Old Northwest* (N. Y., 1888), 370 ff.

Creek country.[1] His friend, John Nicholson, comptroller of Pennsylvania, had acquired an area in the western part of his state nearly equal to that of Connecticut and Rhode Island.[2] Rufus King, James Duane, John Jay, Stephen Van Rensselaer and other prominent public men of New York were also involved in the business. Alexander Hamilton, bent on establishing a family fortune, invested all his surplus earnings in wild lands near Lake Ontario, while Gouverneur Morris purchased heavily not only in the St. Lawrence region, where the towns of Gouverneur and Morristown remain as monuments, but also in the Western wilderness. For the lord of Morrisania mere countinghouse speculations were not enough. By shadowed trail and birch canoe he made his way time and again along the Mohawk Valley and slowly westward to Niagara or into Canada.[3]

But it was another Morris, the senator from Pennsylvania, who most dazzled his contemporaries in this trade. In the nineties Robert Morris strained his ample credit in land deals through seven states. His most ambitious ventures were in the Genesee country of New York, twelve hundred thousand acres of which he sold to Sir William Pulteney, an Englishman, at a profit of a hundred thousand dollars. The famous "Holland Purchase," [4] comprising three and a half million acres,

[1] P. D. Evans, *The Holland Land Company* (Buffalo Hist. Soc., *Publs.*, XXVIII), 24; C. H. Haskins, "The Yazoo Land Companies," Am. Hist. Assoc., *Papers*, V, 47.

[2] Emily C. Blackman, *History of Susquehannah County, Pa.* (Phila., 1873), 486; A. C. Clark, "James Greenleaf," Columbia Hist. Soc., *Records*, VI, 217.

[3] J. C. Churchill, *Landmarks of Oswego County* (Syracuse, 1895), 13; Gouverneur Morris, *Diary and Letters* (A. C. Morris, ed., N. Y., 1888), II, 459; Rufus King, *Life and Correspondence* (C. R. King, ed., N. Y., 1894-1900), IV, 404. For other well-known New York speculators, see D. R. Fox, *The Decline of Aristocracy in the Politics of New York* (Columbia Univ., *Studies*, LXXXVI), chap. iv.

[4] W. G. Sumner, *The Financier and Finances of the American Revolution* (N. Y., 1891), II, chap. xxxiii; *Observations on the North Amer-*

went to Van Staphorst and other Dutch bankers. But peddling principalities to customers in Amsterdam and London did not exhaust Morris's interest in the land trade, to say nothing of his government six-per-cents, his bank stocks and his miscellaneous investments in improvement projects. With two partners he headed a syndicate which bought six thousand lots, half the number the government owned in the projected federal city of Washington, on the Potomac.[1]

Since land speculators frequently dealt with state legislatures, their negotiations afforded abundant opportunity for politics, often involving the use of private friendship as a channel to special favors and, in some cases, raw bribery. The most monstrous scandal concerned Georgia where it developed that the legislature in 1795 in granting great tracts to the Yazoo companies, mostly at a cent and a half an acre, had shared in their profits. After the grant had been rescinded and Georgia had ceded its Western lands to the United States in 1802, all who said they had purchased Yazoo "rights" in good faith descended upon Congress and, though opposed by purists like John Randolph of Roanoke, their claims were finally compromised in 1814, the one year Randolph was absent from his seat.[2]

Millions of acres passed under the auctioneer's hammer in American cities, but it was faith in the European market which inspired the boldest speculations. Vainly

ican *Land Company* (London, 1796), 56; Thomas Morris, "Narrative," *Hist. Mag.*, ser. 2, V, 370-377; Orsamus Turner, *History of the Pioneer Settlement of Phelps and Gorham's Purchase* (Rochester, 1851); Evans, *Holland Land Company*, chap. i.

[1] W. B. Bryan, *History of the National Capital* (N. Y., 1914), I, chap. ix.

[2] R. G. Harper, *Case of the Georgia Sales on the Mississippi* (Phila., 1799), *passim*; Abraham Bishop, *Georgia Speculation Unveiled* (Hartford, 1797), I, *passim*; Haskins, "Yazoo Land Companies," *passim*; W. B. Stevens, *History of Georgia* (Phila., 1859), II, 479-489. See also Sally S. Wood, *Dorval, or the Speculator* (Portsmouth, N. H., 1801), 68-69, 94.

did Phineas Bond, the British consul at Philadelphia, warn his countrymen against investing money in America, and point out the risks of Indian wars, defective titles, misrepresentation and adverse laws. In every state except Pennsylvania the alien was forbidden to hold land directly, and there was always danger that the subterfuge of trusteeship would be prevented by new legislation.[1] By 1794 Joseph Fauchet, the French minister, was issuing like bulletins to his compatriots,[2] but this was tardy counsel for investors in the Scioto scheme which Joel Barlow had promoted in Paris for William Duer and Company.[3] Barlow's fancy had pictured crops of wheat running from sixty to eighty bushels an acre, to say nothing of eighty-pound fish and other prodigies. The five hundred emigrants, reaching the Ohio wilderness in 1789, had found a palisaded row of cabins rather than a provincial city. They celebrated their arrival with a ball to keep up their courage, but courage could not stave off tragedy and, for the most part, they starved or scattered into oblivion.[4] The French refugees who settled on Duer's tract in Maine had scarcely better fortune. There was many a heartbreaking failure in premature attempts to take civilization to the backwoods, but speculators who must have guessed the consequences broke hearts without scruple.

The European reservoirs of capital and population on which the speculators had counted were soon shut off by reason of various developments. The long series of Continental wars beginning in 1792 caused every

[1] Phineas Bond, "Letters," Am. Hist. Assoc., *Ann. Rep. for 1897*, I, 472, 482-483, 536-537; Evans, *Holland Land Company*, 203.

[2] Sumner, *Financier and Finances*, II, 26.

[3] Joseph Dorfman, "Joel Barlow: Trafficker in Trade and Letters," *Polit. Sci. Quar.*, LIX, 83 ff.

[4] T. T. Belote, *The Scioto Speculation and the French Settlement at Gallipolis* (Univ. of Cincinnati, *University Studies*, ser. 2, III, no. 3), *passim*; W. B. Sibley, *The French Five Hundred* (Gallipolis, Ohio, 1901), 11-118.

available gold piece to go into government bonds and taxes and sent every available man to the battlefield. A little later Aaron Burr, caught in a falling market, persuaded New York to permit aliens to own and sell land, but this availed little when Europeans did not wish to buy.[1] General Arthur St. Clair's defeat by the Ohio Indians likewise discouraged speculation farther west. But there were other reasons for caution in 1792. Credit had been injudiciously stretched in most commercial fields. William Duer, after selling his vast Maine holdings to Senator William Bingham and frantically borrowing at ruinous rates, still could not meet his notes and had to make an assignment. In the apprehensive poise of business this threw the city of New York into its first panic. "No place was ever in such a state of distress as this . . . ," wrote one in the midst of it. "It is expected that before Saturday upwards of Forty persons of considerable Note will stop."[2] Yet the depression lasted but a few months. Property increased as a whole, though the nineties were strewn with individual failures.[3]

The commercial records of the period evidence the relations of government to business. The new Constitution, making control of commerce a federal and not a state concern, immensely benefited the merchants. Since regulations now were uniform, imports could be landed at the best market rather than digressing to find the most favorable port rules and tariff duties. Treaties could be negotiated, such as that obtained by John Jay with England in 1794, which, to the disgust of Lord Sheffield and other jealous English publicists, accorded the United States a status equaling that of any other nation in Brit-

[1] Evans, *Holland Land Company*, 204.
[2] Henry Knox Papers, quoted in Edward Channing, *A History of the United States* (N. Y., 1905-1925), IV, 104 n.
[3] Davis, *Essays*, I, chap. iv.

ish harbors. Concessions were likewise secured from Spain in 1795 and from France in 1800. Congress early passed a navigation act granting for ordinary goods brought in American ships a customs discount of a tenth and for teas a third; and by a law of 1791 even these collections were postponed until the sales were actually made at the warehouse. Vessels built and owned in the United States paid only an eighth as much in tonnage duties as their foreign rivals entering American ports.[1]

Many British firms had branches in the larger Atlantic cities and others maintained factors who served the same purpose.[2] The old commerce with the British West Indies was forbidden to the new nation, an exclusion virtually continued under the Jay treaty; but with prices of American stores and lumber twice as high in the British islands as in the French, which could buy freely from New England ships, smuggling flourished there. Much clandestine trade was carried on by way of the Dutch island of St. Eustatius. The British governors were authorized to open their ports to Americans in case of famines or hurricanes, which, judged by reports, grew in frequency. An American ship could also be admitted if in distress from the loss of a mast or a rift in its side, and according to Lord Nelson, who had tried to enforce the navigation laws in West Indian waters, some Yankee skippers would "swear through a nine inch plank" to the existence of such an alleged emergency.[3]

Two thirds of the trade of the United States in 1790 continued with the erstwhile mother country and her possessions, the great bulk with the former. Bread-

[1] E. R. Johnson and others, *History of Domestic and Foreign Commerce of the United States* (Carnegie Inst., *Publs.*, no. 215 A), II, 16-19; S. E. Morison, *The Maritime History of Massachusetts* (Boston, 1921), chap. xii, 173, 203.

[2] N. S. Buck, *The Development of the Organisation of Anglo-American Trade* (New Haven, 1925), 114-115.

[3] H. N. Nelson, *The Dispatches and Letters of Vice-Admiral, Lord Viscount Nelson* (N. H. Nicolas, ed., London, 1845), I, 129-130.

stuffs formed the leading exports. In 1792, when the total reached near to twenty million dollars, these accounted for more than a third. Next in order came tobacco, rice, wood products, fish and salt meat, and about four millions' worth of miscellaneous items.[1] Though manufactured wares were imported largely from British mills, the Americans traded actively with Germany and Holland for linen and metal goods, with Göteborg and St. Petersburg for iron, duck and hemp, with southern Europe for wines, dried fruits, lead and salt, and with Spanish America for bullion and coin, hides, coffee and indigo.[2]

Trade was not highly concentrated in a few ports. On many a village wharf there was a bustling, profitable business day after day. River towns like Albany and Middletown sent ships to the West Indies and to Europe. Eighteen of the twenty-three states and territories in 1812 were represented in the tonnage. But, of course, the coast cities figured principally in sea-borne commerce as they did in other business. Baltimore carried on a growing trade with South America, contraband at first but legal after the Spanish colonies revolted.[3] Philadelphia and New York handled about a third of the entire commerce of the country, the former in the early nineties having twice the total of the latter. But by 1800, as we have seen, Pennsylvania had fallen behind New York and by 1810 behind Massachusetts as well. In 1805, when American shipping reached a million tons, half of it was owned in New England.[4]

When England joined the coalition against revolu-

[1] Timothy Pitkin, *A Statistical View of the Commerce of the United States* (New Haven, 1835), 167.

[2] Johnson and others, *Commerce*, II, 6, 23, 24; Pitkin, *Statistical View, passim.*

[3] F. R. Rutter, *South American Trade of Baltimore* (Johns Hopkins Univ., *Studies*, XV, no. 9), 10-11.

[4] Thomas Cooper, *Some Information Respecting America* (London, 1794), 16, and notes of Johnson and others, *Commerce*, II, 22.

tionary France in 1793, the United States found itself
the only important trading neutral in the world. French
and Dutch merchant flags virtually disappeared from the
seas, and Spain was content to receive the specie and
bullion from its colonies at the convenience of Yankee
merchant captains.[1] Americans likewise carried goods
from the French West Indies to the ports of France
itself, military need having abrogated the old ban against
this trade enforced in time of peace. As long ago as
1756 Great Britain had declared such a change of trade
regulations to be contrary to international law, but
Americans regarded England's dictum simply as an ob-
stacle to be circumvented by shrewd expedient. The
favorite device was to take a cargo, laden in some French
West Indian port, to an American customhouse, enter
it and then transship it as American goods to France, a
substantial part of the duties having been refunded.
Under the threat of war in 1794 Great Britain somewhat abated the seizure of vessels in this trade.[2] Nevertheless, French and British privateers, despite treaties and
agreements, stretched every point to make prizes of
American ships. Between 1803 and 1807 the losses rose
to about two hundred ships a year. Even Denmark and
Naples practised their tiny navies on United States merchantmen.[3]

With France and England at each other's throats the

[1] J. B. McMaster, *A History of the People of the United States* (N. Y.,
1883-1913), III, 225. The prosperity of Connecticut merchants is
stressed in Margaret E. Martin, *Merchants and Trade of the Connecticut
River Valley, 1750-1820* (Smith College, *Studies*, XXIV), 61-65.

[2] In the case of the *Polly* (1800) the British admiralty court allowed
the broken voyage, but in that of the *Essex* (1805) a higher court insisted that such voyages were continuous. Even then, by landing the
same goods at more than one American port, the issue seemed to be
changed and the trade proceeded under this elaborate subterfuge. It was
vigorously harried after the British order in council in 1806, designed
to stop the "frauds of the neutral flag," and largely ceased in 1807, when
the French West Indies, for the most part, fell into the hands of the
British.

[3] Johnson and others, *Commerce*, II, 30.

life of the neutral trade, dodging here and there between them, was bound to be active and dangerous. Any day at sea a shipmaster might be halted by an unexpected shot across his bow and be forced to yield to a brig-of-war.[1] "We are neutral only in name," wrote Stephen Girard, "for our ships are not only stopped and plundered daily, but even run the risk of being taken into the ports of these despots, who while observing legal forms, rob us of our cargoes."[2] Nevertheless, it was by just such trade, with final prices properly adjusted, that he became the richest man in the United States.

Some great merchant fortunes of the day were founded on adventures which in retrospect seem even more romantic. The China trade, which had begun with the voyage of the *Empress of China* in 1784, was of this nature.[3] New Englanders eagerly prosecuted this far commerce in the hope that it would offset the losses suffered because of exclusion from the British West Indies. The *Astrea*, belonging to Elias Hasket Derby of Salem, first showed the Stars and Stripes at Manila in 1796. A Salem vessel, the *Salley*, was the first to trade at Batavia about the latter date, and three years earlier the *Rajah* had made its way to Sumatra. In 1798 a ship from the same port putting in at Mocha astonished the Arabs as if it were a visitor from another planet and, loading with coffee and then circumnavigating Africa, made a staggering fortune in the home market. A Salem captain, Jonathan Carnes, hearing that pepper grew wild on certain slopes of Sumatra, guessed his way along those treacherous, unmapped shores, keeping a keen eye against the hostile islanders, and took back a cargo to multiply

---

[1] "Essex County Vessels Captured by Foreign Powers, 1793-1813," Essex Inst., *Hist. Colls.*, LVIII, 280-281; LIX, 25-32.
[2] J. B. McMaster, *The Life and Times of Stephen Girard* (Phila., 1918), I, 258-259.
[3] See E. B. Greene, *The Revolutionary Generation, 1763-1790* (A History of American Life, IV), 350-351.

the ship's investment eightfold. By 1800 the harbors
of the Malay archipelago were as familiar to Salem shipowners as Danvers River.[1]

Only a Conrad could do justice to these sea dogs of
old Salem as they fought with swarthy pirates, chaf-
fered on ancient Oriental quays with sleek, brown-
skinned natives and beat their way up the Chinese river
Pearl to the Pagoda anchorage at Whampoa. Mingling
with the castle-ships of the British East India Company,
brushed by swarms of little craft gay with bells and lan-
terns, visited by the ceremonious, silk-robed *hoppo* come
to measure the ship for port fees, coping everywhere
with elaborate formalities, preposterous rules and inter-
minable graft, the Yankee lads found a new world, fascinating as well as profitable.[2] Despite exorbitant fees and
irritating delays — landing and loading took four or five
months and the whole voyage lasted at least a year and a
half — a total gain of a hundred per cent was highly
satisfactory.[3] The merchants of Massachusetts and New
York absorbed most of the profits, but those of Philadelphia, Providence and other ports also played a part.

The traders to Canton were importers. They hoped
to build their fortune on sales of Oriental goods in America and Europe rather than on sales of American goods
in the Orient. China was a particularly poor market
for American products, for the Celestials stubbornly refused to want the things Americans made and grew.[4]
The one exception was the ginseng plant. Few delu-
sions in the history of medicine are more astonishing

[1] W. B. Weeden, *Economic and Social History of New England* (Boston, 1890), II, 820-826; Morison, *Maritime History*, 91.

[2] Tyler Dennett, *Americans in Eastern Asia* (N. Y., 1922), 58; F. R.
Dulles, *The Old China Trade* (Boston, 1930), chaps. i-ii.

[3] R. E. Peabody, *The Log of the Grand Turks* (Boston, 1926), 74-
102; Samuel Shaw, *Journals* (Josiah Quincy, ed., Boston, 1847), 176;
W. C. Hunter, *The "Fan Kwae" at Canton before Treaty Days* (London, 1882), *passim*.

[4] Johnson and others, *Commerce*, II, 26.

than the almost miraculous curative value which the Chinese have ascribed to this inert root.   An American variety throve in northern New York and New England, and considerable numbers, including children and Mohegan Indians, roamed the woods to gather it for the Oriental trade.[1]   But in time the market became glutted and prices fell.   Merchants were confident that, if some staple could be found with good exchange value in China, profits could be pyramided.   It was the Bostonians who found it.   On the ninth day of August, 1790, a sail of extraordinary interest pushed up to a Boston wharf: the first American ship to circumnavigate the earth.   Among the countinghouses, however, its three-year voyage meant more than a noble feat of navigation, for this expedition had fully realized a high commercial hope.   In a year's trade on Nootka Sound the *Columbia* had gathered a cargo of sea-otter peltry; then, traversing the Pacific, had exchanged it for tea; and now, after its long passage by the Cape of Good Hope, had reported home.[2]   As Captain Robert Gray and his officers marched to the governor's house, along with a human trophy, a Sandwich Islander gorgeous in many-colored feathers, certain merchants realized that a new road to fortune had been mapped.   James and Thomas H. Perkins fitted out the *Hope,* the first of thirty of their ships to make the globe-encircling voyage.[3]   When two years later Captain Gray discovered the river which he named after his ship, the seventeen-year-old fifth mate John Boit re-

[1] Colonists had sold the root to agents of the East India Company for many years.   The *Empress of China* had carried thirty tons of it.   Dulles, *China Trade,* 6; D. M. Humphreys, *A Poem on Industry* (Phila., 1794), 9.

[2] Robert Haswell, "Journals," H. H. Bancroft, *History of the Northwest Coast* (San Francisco, 1886), I, 703 ff.; E. G. Porter, "The Ship *Columbia* and the Discovery of Oregon," *New England Mag.,* n.s., VI (1892), 472 ff.

[3] Anon., "Commercial Sketch of Boston," *Merchants' Mag. and Commercial Rev.,* I (1839), 132.

The Hongs of Old Canton

Ship "Columbia" Attacked by Indians

On Pacific Shores

marked, "This River in my opinion, wou'd be a fine place for to set up a *Factory*." [1] It was a prophecy of the Pacific Northwest.

During these same years John Jacob Astor, after briefly peddling petty merchandise in New York, struck into the woods up-state and built up a fur traffic that reached well into Canada and the West. At the opening of the nineteenth century, with a fortune of a quarter of a million dollars, he entered the Northwest-Canton commerce, founding the American Fur Company in 1808 and two years later the Pacific Fur Company. He planned to establish a trading colony, Astoria, at the mouth of the Columbia, thus forestalling the English companies and incidentally strengthening America's claim to a great domain. But a fatal Indian onslaught on the first ship he sent, the reported hardships of the overland party and especially the outbreak of war with England about a year later combined to ruin the project. [2] Nevertheless, the Astorians and other Northwest traders had stirred up interest in the Oregon country among American statesmen. Otherwise it would have passed smoothly and easily into the permanent hold of Canada.

What this contact with the Orient meant to American culture it is hard to say. It must have stirred the fancy to see advertisements of Chinese merchants in New England newspapers. [3] Certain objects of art were scattered here and there among private families — notably fine porcelains, images, screens, wall hangings, ivory and lacquer fans and boxes. The East India Marine Society of Salem brought back an astonishing range of

[1] John Boit, "Remarks on the Ship *Columbia's* Voyage," Mass. Hist. Soc., *Proceeds.*, LIII, 248.

[2] Washington Irving, *Astoria* (Phila., 1836), I, chaps. ix-xi; K. W. Porter, *John Jacob Astor, Business Man* (Cambridge, 1931), I, chap. vii; Stella M. Drumm, "More about Astoria," Oregon Hist. Soc., *Quar.*, XXIV, 4.

[3] Sydney and Marjorie Greenbie, *Gold of Ophir* (Garden City, 1925), 80; P. C. Kuo, "Canton and Salem," *New England Quar.*, III, 420-441.

treasure for their museum, from beautiful Calcutta shawls to a huge wooden idol that once had stood alone in a Sandwich Island desert.[1] Moreover, ginghams, nankeens and crêpe de Chine newly enriched the Yankee lady's costume; and strange weapons, ornaments and musical instruments aroused the curiosity of village Puritans. Whittier, Emerson and others, a little later, asked questions about Indian philosophy.[2] Yet presumably the greatest gains were in the wealth thus brought to sustain the native culture of America and in the new contribution to the prestige of the merchant marine.

The American merchant in 1790 little realized that in time, as a growing self-sufficiency reduced the need of oversea exchange, he would be overshadowed by the manufacturer, who would capture not only his superior prestige but also to some extent his profits. In most important lines manufacturing was a phase of farm work rather than a separate enterprise. Household industry, the most primitive form, ruled in making textiles — woolen, linen, as well as some cotton from the offshore southern islands — though even in this it was supplanted here and there by the so-called domestic system, under which a contractor brought material to the farmhouse door and called later to claim the completed articles. In the towns the handicraftsman with his dark buckskin breeches and his well-greased leather apron was a familiar sight.

The master of the shop might have apprentices who for a term of from four to seven years would be members of his family, acquiring by tutelage and practice full knowledge of the craft. Theoretically this was an ideal scheme of vocational training, and it helped build a tradition of fine workmanship in the days before human

[1] T. W. Higginson, *Travellers and Outlaws* (Boston, 1889), chap. i.
[2] A. E. Christy, "Orientalism in New England: Whittier," *Am. Lit.*, I, 372-392.

skill was superseded by mechanical contrivance; but it
had its drawbacks. The inelastic term handicapped the
bright boy, and the master's undefined control led oftentimes to exploitation. To qualify as a chair maker or
a pewterer the apprentice might have to tend the horses,
assist the women with the chores and lend a hand at the
harvest, in short, take the place of a hired man.[1] When
at last he graduated journeyman, with two suits of
clothes and the handful of silver agreed upon in his indenture, he still might not be a skillful craftsman. By
hiring out where he could, he completed his education
and, if prudent, saved his money till he could set up his
own shop. "It is a singular fact in the history of the
mechanical arts in this country," wrote Benjamin Rush,
"that the same arts seldom descend from father to son.
Such are the profits of even the humblest of them, that
the sons of mechanics generally rise from the lower to the
more respectable occupations; and thus their families
generally ascend to the first ranks in society among us."[2]

Manufacturing in America faced substantial obstacles,
especially in competition with low-priced importations.
Long custom called for European trade names even in
the coarsest wares. There was comparatively little mobile capital to undertake experiments. Difficulties of
distribution precluded the economies of large-scale manufacture or specialization. Moreover, labor was a more
important factor in production then than now, and the
laborer's day commanded a dollar in many places North
and South, a rate unmatched in any other country.[3]
According to one writer, the high cost of labor, occasioned by the opportunities of farm ownership, obliged

[1] P. H. Douglas, *American Apprenticeship and Industrial Education*
(Columbia Univ., *Studies*, XCV, no. 2), 51.
[2] Benjamin Rush, *Essays, Literary, Moral & Philosophical* (Phila.,
1798), 198.
[3] Henry Wansey, *An Excursion to the United States . . . in 1794*
(Salisbury, Eng., 1798), 208.

manufacturers "to sell their clumsy imitations at a higher price than the elegant imported originals would cost." [1] Yet there were some offsetting advantages: low taxes, an expanding market, many natural resources in abundance, and a versatility of competence in the hands. Three thousand miles of ocean, every mile of which had helped toward political independence, also helped toward economic self-sufficiency. The long voyage, said Tench Coxe, amounted to a bounty of twenty-five per cent. The people were growing so rapidly in substance as well as in numbers that demand outran the importations. [2]

The new federal administration smiled encouragement upon American manufactures. On inauguration day the President wore a suit of homespun broadcloth which General Knox had procured for him at the mill established the year before at Hartford. "I hope," said Washington, "it will not be a great while before it will be unfashionable for a gentleman to appear in any other dress." [3] Secretary Hamilton, cherishing the ideal of a self-reliant nation, put before Congress on December 5, 1791, his "Report on Manufactures," the holy writ of protectionism from that day to this. But the agricultural interest, apprehensive lest bounties and customs duties raise prices, and the commercial interest, which feared a decrease in imports, easily combined to defeat the plan. The first tariff, averaging eight per cent, was generally designed for revenue only. Nevertheless, the subject had been widely discussed, and societies to encourage manufacturing existed in the chief towns. Some

[1] Anon., "An Account of the City of Washington," *Literary Mag. and Am. Register*, IV (1805), 136.
[2] Tench Coxe, *A View of the United States of America* (Phila., 1794), 25; V. S. Clark, *History of Manufactures in the United States, 1607-1860* (Carnegie Inst., Publs., no. 215 B), 245-246.
[3] See P. L. Ford, *The True George Washington* (Phila., 1896), 189-190. Possibly he felt relieved, however, to step into his imported grogram silk evening clothes which he wore at the inauguration ball. These are still preserved in the Headquarters building at Morristown, N. J.

even acted as partnerships in organizing industry.[1] The most famous and ambitious venture was that of the Society for Establishing Useful Manufactures promoted in 1790 by Secretary Hamilton. The company set up the town of Paterson at the falls of the Passaic, spent much money blowing rocks, digging a canal, erecting buildings and organizing a cotton company, but finally dissolved with almost total loss.[2] States sometimes loaned money to manufacturing enterprises, or granted exemptions from taxation and from militia service for their employees.[3]

Here and there a town specialized in some industry, though without a common organization. Reading, Pennsylvania, and Danbury, Connecticut, were famous for wool hats; Lynn, Massachusetts, in the middle nineties was already producing three hundred thousand pairs of shoes in a year; Pittsburgh, in the West, was improving on the muddy poured glass that had had to serve those who could not buy in the European market. The iron trade, of course, was concentrated near the mines, particularly in Virginia and Pennsylvania.[4] In the Waterbury region of the Naugatuck Valley clocks were made in many a small shop. Eli Terry, in 1793, was a typical clockmaker, sawing and filing the parts out of hard wood and then on horseback peddling the finished product through the country. Later he went in for quantity

[1] T. E. V. Smith, *The City of New York in the Year of Washington's Inauguration* (N. Y., 1889), 108-109.

[2] Davis, *Essays*, I, 349-427; Alexander Hamilton, *Industrial and Commercial Correspondence* (A. H. Cole, ed., Business Hist. Soc., *Studies*, I), pt. iv.

[3] Coxe, *View*, 278-279; F. L. Humphreys, *Life and Times of David Humphreys* (N. Y., 1917), II, 373.

[4] Anon., "Memorandums Made on a Journey through Part of Pennsylvania," *Literary Mag. and Am. Register*, I (1803-1804), 170; Felix de Beaujour, *Sketch of the United States . . . from 1800 to 1810* (William Walton, tr., London, 1814), 90, 92, 93; Coxe, *View*, 141-142; Malcolm Keir, *The Epic of Industry* (R. H. Gabriel, ed., *Pageant of America*, New Haven, 1925-1929, V), 273.

production with the help of Seth Thomas and others. Simon Willard's "banjo" clock was a Yankee invention winning a well-deserved popularity. Peddlers carried these Connecticut clocks clear to the Gulf and the Mississippi. The spinster no longer had to turn the hour-glass, and the farmer's wife knew when to blow the dinner horn without depending solely on an inner admonition or on the sun mark set in the kitchen floor.[1]

Most manufactures were of modest size. The fifty paper mills in Pennsylvania in the early nineties represented an average investment of about five thousand dollars and together employed from one hundred and fifty to two hundred hands, or three or four each.[2] Few textile shops employed more than a dozen. Gristmills were the most widespread form of power industry.[3] They were usually set up by a waterfall, where the miller ground his neighbor's grain for about a sixteenth part. One able engineer, Oliver Evans of Philadelphia, applied scientific management, along with labor-saving improvements such as an elevator and a conveyer, to the milling business. Reducing his labor force by half, he took the grain "from wagon to wagon" with the continuing help of machinery. Here was a spirit of efficiency which was to be one element in the success of American industry.[4]

The father of the American cotton manufacture, and perhaps of the American factory system, was Samuel Slater. Having completed his apprenticeship with Sir Richard Arkwright's partner, he went to the United States in disguise to evade the British laws against the

[1] H. S. Nourse, *History of the Town of Harvard, Massachusetts* (Harvard, 1894), 78.

[2] Johnson and others, *Commerce*, II, 5.

[3] Coxe, *View*, 39. There were but five steam engines in the country in 1803; see Henry Adams, *History of the United States* (N. Y., 1889-1901), I, 70.

[4] C. A. Pillsbury, "American Flour," C. M. Depew, ed., *One Hundred Years of American Commerce* (N. Y., 1895), I, 267.

emigration of artisans. He soon engaged with Moses Brown, a philanthropic Rhode Island Quaker who had been experimenting with textile manufacture.[1] Although the spinning jenny had been known in America, it had not been much employed. In 1790, a year after his arrival, Slater by a marvelous feat of memory reproduced the complicated Arkwright power-driven frame and other machines at Pawtucket Falls, which neighborhood thus became a center of cotton manufacturing. Two Yorkshiremen, John and Arthur Scholfield, similarly introduced the woolen-factory system, which they set up in Massachusetts in 1793.[2] Soon New England was rivaling Pennsylvania.

The manufacturer in the eighteenth century had had the social status merely of a prosperous artisan, but the faint beginnings of prestige were now appearing, especially where men, already distinguished in another activity, took up industrial experiment — professedly, at least, from patriotic motives. Such a person was Colonel David Humphreys, a Yale graduate, a poet, member of Washington's official family in war and in peace, minister to Portugal and then to Spain, and Fellow of the Royal Society. That such a man should turn to manufacturing showed that it was becoming a respectable vocation. In 1803 he bought a mill site on the Naugatuck some ten miles northwest of New Haven and three years later set up factories to make woolen and cotton hosiery.[3] His introduction of labor-saving machines and his decision to employ women and children served the Hamiltonian ideal of harnessing every energy to build up the wealth and power of the nation. Farming,

[1] G. S. White, *Memoir of Samuel Slater* (Phila., 1836), chaps. ii-iii; Caroline F. Ware, *The Early New England Cotton Manufacture* (*Hart, Schaffner & Marx Prize Essays*, XLVIII), 19-22.

[2] A. H. Cole, *The American Wool Manufacture* (Cambridge, 1926), I, 88 ff.

[3] Humphreys, *David Humphreys*, II, 360-361.

it appeared, had not made sufficient use of women and children. President Washington inspecting a Boston duck manufactory some years before had seen fourteen girls spinning with both hands, while smaller girls turned the wheels for them. Tench Coxe praised an arrangement that took young folk out of idleness and early temptations to vice and placed them under proper care.[1] Colonel Humphreys certainly was no ruthless mill-lord grinding up his tender charges into profits. He maintained compulsory evening school in wintertime when the work stopped early, and persuaded the legislature to require such in all considerable manufactories. In large part he supported a minister. Model tenements and gardens were developed in his scheme. He was proud indeed of his establishment, and his tiny principality was proud of him as he clattered up the road from New Haven in an open carriage with four horses, with some distinguished visitor at his side.[2]

Another pioneer was Eli Whitney. A New England lad, who had shown a knack with tools in his father's shop, he had graduated from Yale, then had gone to Georgia and there found an opportunity to use his ingenuity in perfecting a machine to separate the seeds from cotton fiber. Returned to New Haven, he obtained a contract from the federal government to make 10,000 muskets. Previous manufacture of such firearms had been by gunsmiths working with crude appliances in little shops and building up each gun part by part. Fifty different pieces went into a musket; it was an intricate business. Whitney invented new power-machinery, machine tools, worked out a division of labor among his mechanics, each man constantly reproducing one part so nicely tooled that it could be counted on to

[1] Edith Abbott, *Women in Industry* (New York, 1910), 335-336; Coxe, *View*, 56.
[2] Humphreys, *David Humphreys*, II, chaps. xvii-xviii.

fit with others. Thus, at the beginning of the nineteenth century, he had devised and demonstrated manufacture by interchangeable parts, a method making possible standardized production, in the course of time to be welcomed or deplored by the rest of the world as the American method.[1]

By 1807 policies and institutions had been set up which stabilized business credit and conserved the country's capital. Moreover, this capital had in recent years been greatly increased by commerce and somewhat by manufacturing. Yet it would be well past 1830 before the manufacturer rivaled the merchant in importance, economically or socially. The manufacturer was obviously a potent influence toward cultural independence; the merchant-shipper might seem the contrary, but by his carriage profits, if nothing else, he increased American wealth and by his imports he constantly advanced the transit of civilization, brought in fine artifacts and ideas necessary in developing a culture that was respectable.

[1] Denison Olmsted, "Memoirs of the Life of Eli Whitney, Esq.," *Am. Journ. of Science and Arts*, XXI, no. 2, 201-254; W. P. Blake, "Sketch of Eli Whitney," New Haven Colony Hist. Soc., *Papers*, V (1894), 109-131.

CHAPTER IV

THE TURNPIKE ERA

THE young republic in 1790 desperately needed roads. Boundless possibilities were locked within the wilderness that still overlapped most of the original states and stretched toward the Mississippi; but natural resources would become goods only when men could get at them, use them, take them to other men. Distances, which in human terms meant time and effort, were the curse of the country and would continue so to be until dissolved in large part by engineering science. Till this could be accomplished the very integrity of the nation was in danger. The conquest of distance, quite as much as technical advance in production, was to revolutionize American life.

No striking improvement had occurred in travel, and therefore communication, since man learned the art of spreading cloth to catch the power of the wind. Nature's pathways, the ocean and the far-reaching streams and lakes, were used wherever possible. To go by water was far cheaper and more convenient than to go by land. But there were uncertainties that would irritate the modern traveler. The applicant must first find some skipper whose plans happened to match his own. Even then, the arrival date could be but roughly guessed. A traveler facing December winds spent eighteen days sailing from Eastport, Maine, to Portsmouth, New Hampshire, whereas the following June he did it in two days.[1] The hundred and fifty miles of navigation on the Hudson took three days when the weather favored, but a week

---

[1] Samuel Thomson, *Narrative* (Boston, 1822), 117-118.

was often needed and sometimes a fortnight.[1]   By 1820 large craft covering long distances made faster time, going from Boston to Charleston in good weather in less than two weeks and at a cost of fifteen dollars.[2]

Land traffic picked its tedious course as best it could. There was not a soundly paved road in the country when the federal government was set up.   Moreover, travel still wound its way, in large part, in shadow. The steady chopping of a hundred years had pushed the frontier line well up the Atlantic slope, but even near the sea immense unbroken areas remained.   Count Volney declared that in his journeys of 1796, including that from Boston to Richmond, he traveled scarce three miles together on cleared land.   "Everywhere I found the roads, or rather paths, bordered and overshadowed with coppices or tall trees . . . ," and he spoke feelingly of "the tormenting swarm of breeze-flies, moschettoes and gnats."[3]   Young Francis Baily, fresh from London, found it similarly gloomy: "To travel day after day, among trees a hundred feet high, is oppressive to a degree which those cannot conceive who have not experienced it."[4]   But, despite this general picture, much of the way ran through cultivated farm land, marked by zigzag rail fences, a quick expedient where wood and land were cheap.   In New England and New York the road was often flanked by dry stone walls, the slow laborious combing of the glaciated fields having thus turned a nuisance into a utility.

[1] John Maude, *A Visit to the Falls of Niagara* [1800] (London, 1826), 19.   Maude speaks also of a record passage in 16 hours, 6 minutes.

[2] William Faux, *Memorable Days in America, 1818-1820* (R. G. Thwaites, ed., *Early Western Travels, 1748-1846*, Cleveland, 1904-1907, XI-XII), I, 62.

[3] C. F. Volney, *A View of the Soil and Climate of the United States* (C. B. Brown, tr., London, 1804), 7-8.

[4] Francis Baily, *Journal of a Tour in the Unsettled Parts of North American in 1796-1797* (London, 1856), 417.

Along the highway passed the procession of life in its infinite variety.[1] Many trudged afoot, with burdens or without. Many went on horseback. On Sabbath mornings there might be placed behind the saddle a leather-covered cushion, or pillion, for the wife in best bonnet and kerchief bound for church. On remote wood paths pack trains of from two to twenty horses, generally of stunted breed, trucked their wares through the sparsely settled country, each pair of balanced panniers holding nearly two hundred pounds. Furs and hides were the usual staples on the townward journey; hardware and various small goods had their place as the train threaded its way back into the forest.[2] Hawkers were ubiquitous. There were drug and notion peddlers like the one Hawthorne pictured a little later in his *American Note-Books*.[3] Glib, insinuating and of easy honesty, he found wide markets for New England's manufactures, but too often left behind him a prejudice against the Yankee as a "slick one." Even Timothy Dwight, stout champion of New England virtues, deplored the tin peddler: "Many of the young men, employed in this business, part, at an early period with both modesty, and principle." [4]

In contrast to the peddlers were the loud-mouthed

[1] A good picture of road life may be gained from Fortescue Cuming, *Sketches of a Tour to the Western Country* (Thwaites, *Early Western Travels*, IV), chaps. vi-vii.

[2] Alice M. Earle, *Stage-coach and Tavern Days* (N. Y., 1900), 243-245. The packmen violently opposed widening and improving roads for wheeled traffic.

[3] Entry of July 27, 1838. Nathaniel Hawthorne, *Works* (Popular edn., Boston, n. d.), VI, 125.

[4] Timothy Dwight, *Travels in New-England and New-York* (New Haven, 1821-1822), II, 54-55. "The original load of a single horse, as I am told, is rarely worth more than three hundred dollars; or of a waggon, more than six hundred. Yet this business is said to yield the owner and his agents valuable returns, and their profit to be greater than that which is made by the sale of any other merchandise of equal value." See also Richardson Wright, *Hawkers and Walkers in Early America* (Phila., 1927), chaps. iv-vi.

wagoners, each guiding the four or six-horse team that hauled his great blue and red wagon. Boatlike in shape, with front and back wheels close together and its deep box rising fore and aft to keep the load from sliding whether the journey lay uphill or down, the vehicle was covered with a tunnel tent of white homespun hemp or linen stretched on hickory bows as a defense against the weather. A good driver so equipped could take fourteen barrels of flour over the five ridges of the Alleghanies and on easier grades could carry two tons.[1] Conestoga wagons and Conestoga draft horses, named from a creek in southeastern Pennsylvania, were probably unsurpassed in the world.[2]

Another stream of humanity consisted of the drovers. As the country increased in size their routes grew longer. By the beginning of the nineteenth century New York City was drawing meat supply from as far north as the Mohawk Valley, and Boston was laying New Hampshire and Vermont under tribute. As early as 1807 Fortescue Cuming passed a drove of a hundred and thirty cattle in Ohio being driven from near Lexington, Kentucky, to Baltimore.[3] Droves of horses and mules moved from the same state to the seaboard South. Mules were in special demand there because they could stand

[1] Anon., "Memorandums Made on a Journey through Part of Pennsylvania," *Literary Mag. and Am. Register*, I (1803-1804), 251. Christian Schultz, jr., *Travels on an Inland Voyage* (N. Y. 1810), has a table of freight rates in New York and Pennsylvania.

[2] John Omwake, *The Conestoga Six-Horse Bell Teams of Eastern Pennsylvania* (Cincinnati, 1930), chaps. vii-ix. The iron mountings of the wagon were oftentimes fine examples of folk art. To Omwake's book H. K. Landis contributes many drawings of details from specimens in his museum at Lancaster. Omwake says: "The wagoner was the first driver to drive from the left side . . . and inaugurated the American custom of passing approaching traffic to the right instead of following the English rule of driving to the left" (18).

[3] Cuming, *Tour*, 206. On the first drives from the Western states to New York, which took fully two months, see T. F. De Voe, *The Market Book* (N. Y., 1862), I, 411, and W. T. Bonner, *New York, the World's Metropolis* (N. Y., 1924), 541.

hot weather and the neglect and ill treatment incident
to the slavery régime and, being an infertile stock, they
had to be constantly replenished.[1]   They were also bred
in New York and New England for the Southern market.   Though hogs and sheep were driven in large numbers, beef was the main commodity transported on the
hoof.   Like peddlers, drovers had a name for sharpness.
Buyers sometimes lied outrageously about the price of
meat, worried the farmers into sales at twenty per cent
below the market and then cheated the city butcher at
the other end.[2]   Daniel Drew began his fortune, tradition says, through discovering new tricks even in that
trade.   The night before he reached the city he salted his
cattle well and then, just before entering, gave the
thirsty beasts all the water they could drink.   The water
cost him nothing, but a full-grown beef could drink
some fifty pounds of it, each of which on the butcher's
scales brought an added three cents.[3]

Steadily increasing traffic dramatized the need for better highways.   The science of road making, neglected
since the Romans, was now being redeveloped by Tré-
saguet in France and by Telford, Metcalf and Macadam
in Great Britain.[4]   Naturally, imitative enterprise was
stirred in America where such improvements were so
vitally needed.   New York in 1784 was the first state
to aid in the maintenance of local roads, but the small

[1] Edward Hooker, "Diary," Am. Hist. Assoc., Ann. Rep. for 1896,
I, 903; U. B. Phillips, A History of Transportation in the Eastern Cotton Belt to 1860 (N. Y., 1908), 68.

[2] N.-Y. Journal, Jan. 24, 1791; March 10, 1794.

[3] Bouck White, The Book of Daniel Drew (N. Y., 1910), 32-35,
42-54, 76-86.

[4] On the English revolution in road building, see E. A. Pratt, History
of Inland Transport and Communication in England (London, 1912),
98-107; Samuel Smiles, Lives of the Engineers (London, 1861), II,
chap. ii; Sidney and Beatrice Webb, English Local Government: the
Story of the King's Highway (London, 1913), chaps. vii-viii; and, on
the technical side, Reginald Ryves, The King's Highway (London, 1908).

sum voted had little importance save as indicating a new policy. Pennsylvania the following year appropriated two thousand pounds toward building the road from Cumberland County into Pittsburgh. In this and similar undertakings soon thereafter the legislature made state officials responsible for construction and maintenance, though in other instances it placed funds with county commissions to forward local enterprises.[1] New York in 1796 undertook a state-wide policy on similar principles, and the next year it organized a public lottery in order to provide additional funds.[2] Virginia and Maryland, after 1785, inaugurated the expedient of collecting maintenance costs from the users themselves by means of fees paid at pole gates, hinged or pivoted at the roadside and hence known as turnpikes.[3]

English precedent, reënforced by the prevalent zest for speculation, suggested that public good could be joined with private gain by forming road corporations which, as their profits were to come from tolls, were called turnpike companies. When the first such charter was granted in 1792 to a company engaging to build a sixty-two mile highway from Philadelphia to Lancaster, its stock was immediately oversubscribed. Within two years it constructed, at seventy-five hundred dollars a mile, a road declared to be a "masterpiece of its kind . . . paved with stone the whole way and overlaid with gravel, so that it is never obstructed during the most severe season."[4] This success inspired the formation of

[1] W. C. Plummer, *The Road Policy of Pennsylvania* (Phila., 1925), chap. iii.

[2] C. R. Webster and George Skinner, comps., *Laws of New York* [1802-1807] (Albany, 1807), V, 301-302, 354-356.

[3] J. A. Durrenberger, *Turnpikes, a Study of the Toll Road Movement in the Middle Atlantic States and Maryland* (Valdosta, Ga., 1931), chap. ii. Some early gates were raised by pulleys.

[4] Baily, *Journal*, 107; F. R. Diffenderfer, "The Philadelphia and Lancaster Turnpike," Lancaster Co. Hist. Soc., *Papers*, VI, 116 ff.

many other companies, notably in New England.[1] Because of financial difficulties no other turnpike was built in the Middle states during the eighteenth century. Nevertheless, by 1821 Pennsylvania had authorized a hundred and forty-six turnpike concerns and New York companies had built four thousand miles.[2] A glance at the road map of Massachusetts reveals why Boston was coming to be called "the Hub"; [3] but Baltimore was surpassing it and had become the third city of the Union by 1825 largely by reason of the seven trunk turnpikes which fed its trade.[4] Farther to the south only one important turnpike was built, a state enterprise from Charleston to Columbia, on which South Carolina expended a hundred thousand dollars between 1823 and 1828 besides the proceeds of the tollgates set up as fast as portions were completed.[5]

The earliest companies were usually granted their privileges in perpetuity, but later charters specified definite terms.   New York provided that a road should revert to the state as soon as the company recovered its investment and was realizing an annual profit of fourteen per cent, but apparently no turnpike ever earned so splendid a return. To induce subscriptions chartered companies were protected against direct competition. The toll rates, sometimes fixed by statute but generally left to the discretion of the directors, ran from three cents a dozen for driven sheep or swine up to twenty-

[1] F. J. Wood, *The Turnpikes of New England* (Boston, 1919), 10, 35, 63 and *passim*.

[2] Durrenberger, *Turnpikes*, chap. iii.   For the earlier phase in New York, see Benjamin De Witt, "A Sketch of the Turnpike Roads in the State of New York," Society for the Promotion of Useful Arts in the State of New York, *Transactions* (Albany, 1807), II, 190. By 1836 there are said to have been more than 500 such companies in New York.

[3] Wood, *Turnpikes*, opposite p. 57.   Massachusetts by 1814 had chartered about a hundred companies.

[4] F. J. Wood, "The Turnpikes of Maryland," *D. A. R. Mag.*, LIV, 565-574.

[5] Phillips, *Transportation*, 92.

five cents for a four-wheeled carriage. In most instances a company took over the improvement and maintenance of an existing highway. In laying out a new one it was given the right of eminent domain in buying land and even necessary materials.[1]

The provision in the Ohio enabling act requiring that a twentieth of the proceeds from its federal land sales be appropriated toward constructing roads had immediate effect and served for a time as a precedent with other new Western states. In 1808 Secretary Albert Gallatin, taking a national view of the problem, submitted to Congress a report contemplating a vast federal expenditure of sixteen million dollars, but circumstances, including the War of 1812 and the constitutional scruples of two presidents, prevented the achievement of this grandiose design.[2] The most notable federal enterprise was the Cumberland Road, starting westward in 1810 from the town of that name in Maryland. With a turnpike road to Baltimore, built by private capital, it was known as the National Road or, familiarly, the Old Pike.[3]

The construction of this artery worked miracles in the fortunate towns included on its route. For example, Wheeling, Virginia, had been a straggling, discouraged little settlement isolated on a cliff, but a decade after the Old Pike reached the Ohio it became an important market, with brick buildings and paved streets.[4] The running time to Baltimore was cut from eight to four days, and before long six-horse teams, their harness proudly

[1] The legal aspects are discussed in Durrenberger, *Turnpikes*, chap. iv; Wood, *Turnpikes*, 58; and Phillips, *Transportation*, chap. ii.

[2] A. B. Hulbert, *The Paths of Inland Commerce* (Allen Johnson, ed., *The Chronicles of America Series*, New Haven, 1918-1921, XXI), 120; Albert Gallatin, *Writings* (Henry Adams, ed., Phila., 1879), I, 334-335.

[3] T. B. Searight, *The Old Pike* (Uniontown, Pa., 1894), 14.

[4] Adlard Welby, "A Visit to North America, May 5, 1819-May 10, 1820," Thwaites, *Early Western Travels*, XII, 204, and *Sheppard's Wheeling Directory* (Wheeling, 1826), 89, both cited by Beulah Boyd in The National Road Comes to Wheeling (Master's essay, Columbia University Library), 33, 34, 36.

decked with rings, balls, rosettes and plumes, were hauling five-ton loads into its warehouses. It was natural
that less favored towns should be envious, Pittsburgh
fearing that it would lose its Eastern trade.[1] But the
Pittsburgh "pike" was constantly improved to meet this
competition, and gloomy prophecies were not realized.

Lengthening turnpikes accentuated the need for
strongly built bridges. While there had been bridges
since the seventeenth-century settlements, they were few,
short and none too sound.[2] A tree skillfully felled
across a narrow stream might afford the traveler a precarious passage while he swam his horse at the side.
Cart bridges, like those the English poet Thomas Moore
described in Virginia,

> Made of a few uneasy planks
> In open ranks
> Over rivers of mud,

added excitement to a journey.[3] In the older regions
stone arches could occasionally be found, but despite
their greater safety they required more capital than most
rural communities had to spare. There were no immense American structures like those which John Rennie
and "Pontifex Maximus" Telford were building in Great
Britain until the construction of the Rochester aqueduct
on the Erie Canal in the eighteen-twenties.

Wood, being cheap and plentiful, was used for extensive bridges, especially after the success of the one
from Boston to Charlestown, which replaced the ancient
ferry in 1785. Seven years later the West Boston bridge

[1] *Pittsburgh Mercury*, Feb. 14, 1821. It was estimated in 1818 that
over $18,000,000 worth of goods were carried annually from Phila-
delphia to Pittsburgh. See Caroline E. MacGill and others, *History of
Transportation in the United States before 1860* (Carnegie Inst., Publs.,
no. 215 C), 89.

[2] T. J. Wertenbaker, *The First Americans, 1607-1690* (*A History of
American Life*, II), 297-298.

[3] Quoted in Earle, *Stage-coach and Tavern Days*, 366.

was likewise built with pile piers, and others followed, the most famous being that across Lake Cayuga, measuring a mile in length and completed in the first years of the nineteenth century.[1] But the pile bridge, like the conventional row of masonry arches, did not always meet American conditions; those who guided lumber rafts or broad-beamed barges wanted as few piers as possible to impede the way, and wooden piers, when numerous, dammed up the spring ice floes.[2]

To meet these needs the wooden truss bridge was invented, the first important one being that finished in 1792 by Colonel Ewel Hale at Bellows Falls, Vermont, with two spans of a hundred and seventy-five feet each, resting on an island. During the years 1801-1805 Timothy Palmer placed the "permanent bridge" over the Schuylkill at Philadelphia at a cost of three hundred thousand dollars, and a little above it Lewis Wernwag, a young German-American, built the "colossus of Fairmount," whose single arch of three hundred and forty feet was never surpassed in a wooden road bridge.[3] This type carried the weight to the ends of a truss of arches and angles, a principle which, though once known to Leonardo da Vinci and Palladio, was independently discovered by these self-taught American engineers. In 1821 Ithiel Town, a Connecticut architect, published a description of a new kind of bridge, held up along each side by a lattice of planks.[4] Since timbers left exposed

[1] H. G. Tyrrell, *History of Bridge Engineering* (Chicago, 1911), 85-86, 126.

[2] Anon., *A Treatise on the Improvement of Canal Navigation* (London, 1796), 117.

[3] Owen Biddle, *Young Carpenter's Assistant* (Phila., 1815), 49-53; *Appletons' Cyclopædia of American Biography* (N. Y., 1887-1901), VI, 437.

[4] *A Description of Ithiel Town's Improvement in the Construction of Wood and Iron Bridges* (New Haven, 1821). Scientific bridge design in America, including close calculation of stresses and strains, dates from Squire Whipple, *A Work on Bridge Building* (Utica, N. Y., 1847), and Herman Haupt, *General Theory of Bridge Construction* (N. Y., 1851).

would quickly weather and decay, builders obviated this by roofing them like a long barn. Soon the covered bridge became a familiar sight in most Northern valleys. Frequently bridges, like turnpikes, were financed by companies. Seventy such corporations had already been organized by 1800.[1]

One great enterprise furthered by better roads and bridges was stagecoaching. During the first quarter of the nineteenth century it rose to its climax, thanks largely to the leadership of Levi Pease, a blacksmith of Shrewsbury, Massachusetts. Profiting by the knowledge of roads and horses gained as a military messenger during the Revolutionary War, Captain Pease began a passenger service which he was determined would surpass current standards. With courageous borrowing, ingenuity and zeal, he and a young partner accumulated sufficient rolling stock, four-horse teams and harness, and in 1783 undertook a through passage from Boston to Hartford, lasting from Monday to Thursday, with a branch line, served by a hired driver, leading to New Haven and the New York boat within another day.[2] During the first months many a trip was made without a passenger, but Pease's persistence was rewarded, and with another partner the route was put through to New York, forming thus the longest and most reliable link in a chain of stages reaching to Richmond in Virginia. Two years later he obtained the first mail contract of this kind granted by the Confederation government, a trust which was to give stagecoaching more prestige and an income upon which it could rely.

As with railroads in a later generation, rivalries

---

[1] J. S. Davis, *Essays in the Earlier History of American Corporations* (*Harvard Econ. Studies*, XVI), II, app. B.
[2] O. W. Holmes, "The Father of New England Stage-Coaching," *Journ. of Econ. and Business History*, III, 241-263.

brought reckless cutting of fares and eventual combination of lines, especially in eastern New England. The
Eastern Stage Coach Company, for example, was chartered in 1818 to operate north from Boston. Within
twenty years it was interlocked with turnpike, bridge
and bank companies and was paying dividends of ten
or eleven per cent. In such incorporations maximum
fares were generally set at five cents a mile and the public
interest was otherwise protected.

Service was extended rapidly to care for increasing
traffic.[1] Stages also penetrated the South, where the
dearth of towns and the prevalence of water travel had
earlier deterred them. One main route connected at
Petersburg, Virginia, with the northern lines, and continued down the piedmont till it branched to Charleston,
Savannah and finally to Montgomery, where river passage could be taken for Mobile. Another went up the
Shenandoah Valley and into Tennessee.[2] An Indiana
newspaper rejoiced to announce in September, 1820,
that a line of stages had been established to run from
Louisville through Vincennes to St. Louis.[3] In 1825
appeared the first guidebook of national scope for the
benefit of stagecoach travelers, and also the first paper
devoted chiefly to stagecoach news.[4]

The growth of communication is most strikingly illustrated by the development of the post office. When
the new federal government took charge, the main post

[1] R. P. H. Vail, "Along the Hudson in Stage-Coach Days," *Outlook*,
LXXX (1905), 489-496; O. W. Holmes, "The Stage-Coach Business
in the Hudson Valley," N. Y. State Hist. Assoc., *Quar. Journ.*, XII, 239-
240, 246-247; M. M. Bagg, *Pioneers of Utica* (Utica, N. Y., 1877),
501-502.

[2] Faux, *Memorable Days*, 72; Phillips, *Transportation*, 129; J. L.
Ringwalt, *Development of Transportation Systems in the United States*
(Phila., 1888), 62.

[3] *Indiana Centinel*, Sept. 2, 1820, quoted in Seymour Dunbar, *A History of Travel in America* (Indianapolis, 1915), III, 759.

[4] Daniel Hewett, *The American Traveller* (Wash.), and Badger &
Porter's Boston *American Traveller*.

route extended from Maine to Georgia, serving fifty offices, with lateral branches reaching half as many more. Vermont, Kentucky and Tennessee were still untouched, and the line to Pittsburgh, just inaugurated, was the farthest venture into the West. Since the government wanted to make considerable profit from the service, postage was high — it cost thirty-four cents to send a letter from New York to Savannah. At such rates, and especially as most letters were sent postage collect, correspondents made their messages as substantial and readable as possible. It was cheaper, and in many places necessary, to confide a letter to a friendly traveler or a wagoner, but this suffered from the disadvantage that the bearer might feel at liberty to unfold the paper and examine its contents and, if interesting, read it aloud at tavern firesides.[1]

In the 1790's the government, worried by uncertainties as to the loyalty of the trans-Alleghany folk and realizing the political significance of better communication, forsook the policy of profits, reduced the rates and pushed the service as fast as possible into the remoter regions. By 1792 an ordinary letter cost from six to twenty-five cents, according to the distance, though slightly upward readjustments later had to be made. In 1796 the post reached the garrison at Fort Niagara; a decade later Postmaster-General Gideon Granger announced that he had engaged "two faithful, enterprising, hardy young woodsmen" to carry the mails from Cleveland to Detroit, an arduous commission as it meant traversing the Great Black Swamp that stretched from Sandusky Bay to the Maumee River. There was an office at Memphis in 1800 and one at Natchez in 1801. As late as 1825 it was reported that half the mails were

[1] W. E. Rich, *History of the United States Post Office to the Year 1828* (*Harvard Econ. Studies*, XXVII), 67-75.

transported by horse and rider.[1] The office in the wilderness might be a settler's cabin, but even in the East the postmaster was seldom fully differentiated, usually giving out the mail from a corner in his general store or tavern or printing office. By 1830 the first postmaster-general to sit in the President's cabinet could report eight thousand offices and a hundred and fifteen thousand miles of routes, the longest reaching the Rockies.[2]

The stagecoach business was closely related not only to the post office but also in many places to the tavern. While stage men often found it expedient to acquire inns, landlords occasionally branched into staging, even in its early days.[3] The tavern, of course, was more than an adjunct to the stagecoach lines. It had existed long before the advent of wheeled traffic and was to persist after coaches had been laid away in the museums. Yet it was never more lively or more interesting than in the great days of the turnpike.[4] Lodging under its roof the traveler had an opportunity to survey its full activity. In the spacious taproom, especially on court day or during militia muster or a season of land sales, a thirsty multitude would crowd around the bar in the corner. From behind a grating would be served the strong staples — whisky, brandy, gin and rum — or an outrageous New England drink called "black strap." A party might call for a bowl of American flip, made up of strong beer with a dark rum into which a white-hot iron had been thrust to give it the desired burnt-bitter taste and then poured into mammoth glasses. Toddy and punch could likewise be concocted on demand, while

[1] *Ibid.,* 95.
[2] A. F. Harlow, *The Old Post Bags* (N. Y., 1928), 301-302.
[3] Holmes, "Stage-Coach Business," 231-235.
[4] For pictures of taverns, see Elsie Lathrop, *Early American Inns and Taverns* (N. Y., 1926), and for those of signs, Earle, *Stage-coach and Tavern Days, passim.*

simpler tastes were satisfied with hard cider.[1] But the taproom also sheltered other interests. If the traveler wished to write a letter, he had to use the same rough desk on which the host would calculate his morning's bill. If he sought diversion, and did not care for the juggler or the dancing bear performing in the stable yard, there were draughts, cards, the newspaper or, best of all, conversation around the mighty fire, where many a yarn was spun, though not always in the stately phrase of Longfellow's *Tales of a Wayside Inn*. On a favored night an attraction might be found in the upstairs long room, perhaps a group of strolling players, a lecture on the elements of science, a party caucus or a dance, when the spring floor, resting on shallow-arch trusses, throbbed with gayety.

Over all this animated scene presided the landlord, a man of consequence — a "topping man," as the Yankee phrase went—for no one in those days, when the temperance movement was just beginning, thought of bracketing publicans with sinners. The military officer, returning from the Revolution to readjust himself to civil life and noting the increase of traffic, oftentimes decided to capitalize his prestige by taverning. Europeans were astonished to be told that they could breakfast at Major Todd's and dine at Colonel Brown's, but they soon became familiar with this phenomenon of civil and political equality.[2] Owning a good-sized farm and possibly a mill or a distillery in addition to his inn, the landlord was the economic peer of most of his patrons. His daughter waited table without sacrifice of caste and would have been no less surprised than offended had a

[1] Alice M. Earle, *Customs and Fashions in Old New England* (N. Y., 1893), 163-183.
[2] Adam Hodgson, *Letters from North America* (London, 1824), I, 21-22; John Harriott, *Struggles through Life* (London, 1807), II, 110, 114, 117; Cuming, *Tour*, 42, 63; Thomas Cooper, *Some Information Respecting America* (London, 1794), 119.

Stage-coach in 1819

Covered Bridge in 1821

Eagle Tavern, Buffalo, in 1825

tip been offered.   He himself sat down with his guests.
Fenimore Cooper declared that,

> The inn-keeper of Old England, and the inn-keeper
> of New-England, form the very extremes of their class.
> The one is obsequious to the rich, the other unmoved,
> and often apparently cold.   The first seems to calcu-
> late, at a glance, the amount of profit you are likely
> to leave behind you; while his opposite appears only
> to calculate in what manner he can most contribute
> to your comfort, without materially impairing his own.
> . . . He is often a magistrate, the chief of a battalion
> of militia, or even a member of a state legislature.[1]

In taverns, however, as in most other respects, standards varied with the distance from the port towns.
There were special sectional differences, too, as among
the Pennsylvania Germans, where the stranger found
an unfamiliar cuisine.   Some, like the Moravians who
kept the Sun at Bethlehem, were famous bonifaces.   The
rougher country inns of that region impressed the traveler with their cleanliness, but the absence of sheets
between the feather ticks was deplored.[2]   South of the
Potomac inns were rare.   Where they were good, as the
Eagle Tavern at Richmond, the prices were accounted
high, though, here as everywhere, lodging was cheaper
than food, and could be had in the 1790's for less than
thirty cents.   But generally they were not good, often
a solitary cabin beside a ferry.   A traveler of good address, however, could usually find ample entertainment
at a planter's house.   "Hospitality," wrote Dr. Thomas
Cooper in 1794, "is relative: from Massachusetts to
Maryland, inns are plenty, and strangers frequent them
when they travel: from the south boundary of Penn-

[1] J. F. Cooper, *Notions of the Americans* (Phila., 1828), I, 64-65.
See also Dwight, *Travels*, I, 427-429, on New England innkeepers.
[2] W. C. Reichal, *The Old Sun Inn* (Phila., 1876); J. F. Sachse,
Wayside Inns on the Lancaster Road (Lancaster, 1912), *passim*.

sylvania to South Carolina, taverns are more scarce and dear, and hospitality is on the most liberal scale." [1] The same observation could have been made through the next forty years. If one found entry to a house, he might leave with a letter to a friend or relative of his host living a day's journey further on, where he would find a welcome from the servants even if the family itself chanced to be away. [2] A traveler with his store of news relieved the loneliness of plantation life.

It is a far cry from the frontier tavern-hut to the urban caravansaries just beginning to develop in 1790. The word "hotel," with its suggestion of French luxury, was apparently first used in America that year. [3] Certainly the City Hotel, opened four years later in New York, far outdid any existing hostelry. It had seventy-three rooms, whereas few others had more than thirty; it was financed by a stock company; and on both accounts had somewhat less the atmosphere of personal hospitality. In 1804 the Exchange Coffee House was begun in Boston, seven stories in height, and in 1807 a similar large-scale establishment with the same name opened in Philadelphia. Others soon followed in Baltimore and later in Washington. [4] At the earlier taverns it had been the habit of bachelors who lived near by to take their board, a practice which surprised Europeans. Now, with these enlarged facilities, whole families took up hotel life, engaging rooms by the month, if not the year.

But these places were hardly more than oversized inns.

[1] Cooper, *Some Information*, 52.

[2] Mrs. Basil [Margaret H.] Hall, *The Aristocratic Journey* (Una Pope-Hennessy, ed., N. Y., 1931), 224.

[3] Jefferson Williamson, *The American Hotel* (N. Y., 1930), 300, speaking of Corre's Hotel in New York.

[4] In Washington Captain Hall, who always desired the best, found in 1827 very satisfactory entertainment for himself, his wife, nurse and child for $6.50 per day, including bedroom fires and candles. Hall, *Aristocratic Journey*, 167-168.

At the very end of the period, in 1829, came something as new in spirit as it was in aspect—the first-class American hotel, the Tremont House in Boston. Not only was it the largest in the world, with a hundred and seventy bedrooms, a granite façade with Doric portico, and ten large public rooms with marble floors, but the whole physical arrangement was different. Gone was the swinging sign; the horse yard had changed into a flower garden; the public rooms were lighted with gas; and there was running water in the kitchen. Instead of the dinner being put on all at once, it was served *à la France* in courses. The barroom was set off by itself, and the "office" with the room-clerk's desk and stately stairway, the forerunner of the lobby, made its initial appearance. Every door had a patent lock with a special key; washbowl and pitcher stood by every bedside and soap was furnished free though not yet renewed for each arriving guest; "rotunda men" answered calls from the annunciator connected with each room. Service was the watchword, but still without loss of dignity.[1] It was obviously a place for the rich and the successful; at last democracy had its palace, where the poor might look if not linger. It was, moreover, in almost every feature a characteristically and peculiarly American institution.

[1] Williamson, *American Hotel*, 13-18, 22-38, 141, 195-199.

CHAPTER V

COUNTRY LIFE

IN the early days of the republic at least nine Americans out of ten, even in "commercial" New England, dug their living from the land. Self-esteem, if nothing else, led them to glorify country life as the noblest state of man. "Those who labor in the earth," said Jefferson, "are the chosen people of God. . . . They are the most vigorous, the most independent, the most valuable citizens." [1]   Rural simplicity and manly self-respect were contrasted with the cunning found in towns, where traders filled their pockets by overreaching other people —sentiments reminiscent of a passage from Plato or Vergil. [2]   One may smile who has noted among farmers no deep disgust for an unearned dollar when it chanced to come their way, but there was a core of truth in this praise of American husbandry. When land was parceled out to a great number of independent proprietors enjoying low taxes without ecclesiastical encumbrance or feudal imposition, the average farmer had a sense of liberty and opportunity which most European tillers of the soil might well have envied. [3]

The typical Northern farm comprised from a hundred to two hundred acres, seemingly a great deal for one family's care in a day of hand tools; but only a small part was planted at one time. On a hundred-acre farm

---

[1] This quotation was widely used by editors of farm journals.   A. L. Demaree, *The American Agricultural Press, 1819-1860* (Columbia Univ., *Studies in the History of American Agriculture*, no. 8), 185, 332.

[2] P. H. Johnstone, "Turnips and Romanticism," *Agricultural History,* XII, 224.

[3] J. B. Bordley, *Essays and Notes on Husbandry and Rural Affairs* (Phila., 1799), 3, 451.

in eastern Massachusetts but half-a-dozen acres would be in crops, a little more in meadows, plowed at infrequent intervals, and about the same amount in permanent pasture. The rest, if cleared, usually lay fallow until such time as sheer exhaustion of the tilled soil forced the transfer of crops to these fields, which were supposed to have regained their fertility during the period of idleness or, rather, their devotion to weeds and brush. But generally this remainder was only partly cleared and served as woodland range for swine and cattle. The price of fair farm land, except near cities, averaged between ten and fifteen dollars an acre, figures which seem surprisingly high. Many an Eastern farm must have sold in 1800 at a higher price than it did, with better buildings, in 1900.[1]

On good land as well as bad the farmer's methods were primitive and, by English standards, scandalously wasteful. To the modern scientific age it seems that he practised agricide, not agriculture. He knew little of the rotation of crops and would have been astonished to learn that certain plants would return to the soil values that others had extracted.[2] Maize was the mainstay of New England—"nearly as valuable to this country," said Timothy Dwight, "as all other kinds of corn united."[3] Wheat was failing in that region, partly because of the blight of parasites harbored in barberry bushes. At the end of the eighteenth century wheat lingered only in the western hills and in Vermont; and white bread largely

[1] James Warren, "Observations on Agriculture," *Am. Museum*, II (1787), 347; P. W. Bidwell, "Rural Economy in New England," Conn. Acad. of Arts and Sci., *Trans.*, XX, 392 ff.

[2] Only a few gentlemen-farmers were experimenting with crop rotation. See *Medical Repository*, V (N. Y., 1802), 311, for a review of Thomas Moore, *The Great Error of American Agriculture Exposed* (Balt., 1801). See also George Logan, *Fourteen Agricultural Experiments to Ascertain the Best Rotation of Crops* (Phila., 1797).

[3] Timothy Dwight, *Travels in New-England and New-York* (New Haven, 1821-1822), II, 73.

disappeared from the Yankee's table, giving place to "rye and Injun," a bread made from rye flour and maize meal.

Wheat had been a profitable staple from New York to Virginia until shortly before 1790, when it was attacked by the Hessian fly, so called because it was erroneously supposed to have been imported in the fodder bags of the German mercenaries during the Revolutionary War. Spreading rapidly, the pest entered Virginia by 1790 and crossed the Appalachians in 1797. Jefferson, fearing complete extinction of the ancient staff of life, induced the American Philosophical Society to make an elaborate study, and other agencies also attacked the problem. As a result, new varieties were found, especially the yellow-headed wheat, that would resist the insect, and since the latter perished with the first frost, the planting date was put forward a month in some places.[1]

Rye, for distillation among the Scotch-Irish and for bread among the Germans, was highly esteemed in the backcountry.[2] Oats, of poor quality, were grown for horse feed and, among the Scots, for oatmeal. Barley for brewing flourished here and there in the Middle states, and buckwheat had some vogue in New York and New Jersey for fodder and occasionally for griddlecakes. The Irish potato was becoming a staple food in the North and by 1800 was grown extensively in Maine and on Long Island.[3] New York seems to have been least unprogressive in agriculture, but there too the yield was low. Dr. Thomas Cooper observed that ten bushels of wheat an acre was a good average, though in France they raised eighteen and in England twenty-four.[4]

[1] P. W. Bidwell and J. I. Falconer, *History of Agriculture in the Northern United States* (Carnegie Inst., *Publs.*, no. 358), 95-96.

[2] William Strickland, *Observations on the Agriculture of the United States of America* (London, 1801), 47; *Pennsylvania Archives*, V, 229.

[3] Bidwell and Falconer, *Agriculture*, 97-98.

[4] Thomas Cooper, *Political Essays* (Phila., 1800), 40.

Tillage was chiefly by the strain and sweat of human limbs. The disgusted Richard Parkinson warned any English farmer who might plan to migrate to America that he would have to learn a new trade: "He will have to chop up trees, and cultivate the land by the hoe and pick-axe, instead of the plough and harrows." [1] But plows and harrows were available, such as they were. The common Carey plow was made entirely of wood save for an iron colter to cut the sod and oftentimes a sheathing of odd fragments of saw-plate, tin or iron sheets. With such an implement an acre was a good day's work. Strong arms were needed to hold it in the ground and twice the modern pulling power was required. [2] Oxen were the favored work animals, for over rough slopes, among the stumps and stones or in the half-drained swales, the ox alone could hold his footing, and his steady, patient pull was worth infinitely more than the fitful spurts of the less stolid horse. Besides, he could live on grass without grain and stand almost any exposure; and when he closed his service at about the age of ten he furnished beef and boot leather. As the land was smoothed during the early decades of the nineteenth century and harder roads, as we have seen, lamed the cattle, horses superseded them in many sections. [3]

The other tools were few. It is said that at the beginning of the nineteenth century a strong farmer could have carried them all on his shoulder except for his spike-tooth harrow, sledge and two-wheeled oxcart. Generally he dug with an iron-plated shovel though, if the metal were more plentiful, he pounded out his

[1] Quoted in *Literary Magazine and American Register*, V (1806), 222.
[2] C. L. Flint, "One Hundred Years of Progress," in *Report* of the Commissioner of Agriculture for the year 1872 (Wash., 1874), 278-279. Washington sometimes used what was called a duck-billed plow. P. L. Haworth, *George Washington, Farmer* (Indianapolis, 1915), 94.
[3] T. N. Carver, "Historical Sketch of American Agriculture," L. H. Bailey, ed., *Cyclopedia of American Agriculture* (N. Y., 1911), IV, 65, 100.

spades and two-tined forks upon his own anvil, or had them made at a blacksmith shop.[1]   The farmer sowing his seed in the spring gauged his area by what he could cut in the late summer days by the back-breaking labor of the sickle; but a new contrivance was making its appearance, the cradle, with its long scythe blade paralleled by a rack of wooden fingers.   Swinging this with strength and skill, the harvester might reap three quarters of an acre in a day.   About Thanksgiving time he beat the grain from the straw with his flail upon the barn floor and then held it in a half-moon basket for the wind to drive away the chaff.   Ground at the neighborhood mill beside the waterfall, it filled his larder or, binned in his stilted granary, awaited the needs of the cattle—or the rats.[2]

The farmer's livestock in 1800 were lean and rangy, partly by degeneration that followed neglect and partly as a result of adaptation to environment.   The old "black cattle," compounded by chance out of all sorts of importations, now showed so many colors as to make the old name inappropriate.   "The scimitar-ribbed, flat-sided lubberly big-legged cattle," cried one disgusted farmer, "what are they other than expensive masses of unimportant bone!"[3]   The average farm in eastern Massachusetts could show one or two horses, one or two yoke of oxen, fifteen head of cattle including five dairy cows, and about as many swine, while half the farms had flocks of from ten to twenty sheep.[4]   When butch-

---

[1] Few farm implements were made in quantity before 1810.   Shovel factories were established at Pittsburgh shortly after 1800, and by 1822 one at Easton, Mass., was turning out thirty thousand annually.   Flint, "One Hundred Years of Progress," 279-286.

[2] A. D. Mellick, *The Story of an Old Farm* (Somerville, N. J., 1889), *passim;* S. G. Goodrich, *Recollections of a Lifetime* (N. Y., 1856), I, 61-62.

[3] Bordley, *Essays and Notes,* 204.   See also Lyman Carrier, *Beginnings of Agriculture in America* (N. Y., 1923), 256.

[4] Bidwell and Falconer, *Agriculture,* 105, 110-111.

ering season came in early winter, there was fresh meat
for a few weeks, but most of it had to be cured for
future use, smoked, dried or pickled in the brine barrels
which lined every cellar. Sheep were raised for wool,
though the longest staple was scarce seven inches,
as compared with English records of three times that
length. As the farms in the Northern states matured,
better barns brought better stock. The natural grasses,
which grew lush on the bottom lands, were now less
valued, and the "artificial" timothy and clover began to
cram the mows for winter feeding.

In the milder climates to the southward intelligent
men deplored the custom of letting cattle run and feeding them from stacks in the fields. Wide-ranging cattle
were often at the mercy of the forest beasts, and farmers
even in the older regions had to keep alert to drive off
wolf, lynx, wildcat and bear.[1] Swine became as fleet
as the woodland enemies they eluded; often the owner
needed his gun to capture them.

Englishmen traveling in the United States missed the
hedgerows that so pleasantly striped their native countryside. Americans often marked the bounds of their
fields with stumps, laboriously pulled by ox chain and
forming a grotesque *chevaux-de-frise* no animal would
care to hazard. In New England and New York stones
for walls were all too plentiful, and wood was at hand
everywhere in the East. Chestnut or cedar rails were
split for fences that were "horse-high, bull-proof and
pig-tight," whether zigzagged or more thriftily set into
posts.[2]

The systematic application of manure to the soil was
rare. Where the cattle roamed wood pastures through

[1] Anon., "Memorandums Made on a Journey through Part of Pennsylvania," *Literary Mag. and Am. Register*, I (1803-1804), 251.
[2] H. S. Nourse, *History of the Town of Harvard, Massachusetts* (Harvard, 1894), 77.

the year it was impossible, but even in the North, where they were stabled, the accumulations of the barnyard were oftentimes considered as a nuisance, not an asset. Even after the Civil War a Kentuckian could write that in his youth he never knew of dung being put on land. Along the shores of New England and Long Island menhaden, or whitefish, were spread on the fields, to the olfactory distress of passers-by.[1]

The farm was a family unit. Extra hands at from fifteen to eighteen guineas a year, as Dr. Benjamin Rush estimated wages, or at from six to twelve dollars a month, as others testified, were beyond the reach of the average husbandman, though he might finance a man or two in harvest at fifty cents a day or an expert cradler at twice that sum.[2] The hired man, where he could be obtained, was generally a youngster waiting his chance to conquer Nature for himself, or a deficient man whom Nature had conquered at the start. With labor difficult to hire, the farmer and his sons tilled and reaped for the most part unaided and, except among the Germans and the Scotch-Irish, called upon the womenfolk for hard field work only in a desperate emergency.[3] In these circumstances it was unfair to compare the agriculture of the New World with that of the Old, where a Yorkshire yeoman, for example, would employ eight or ten laborers on his hundred and fifty acres and spread eight or nine hundred loads of manure.[4] "Though in America less grain is produced per acre than in England," wrote Dr. Cooper for English readers, "they get more per man.   There, land is plentiful and labour scarce.

[1] R. H. Gabriel, *The Evolution of Long Island* (New Haven, 1921), 39. It took 8000 to fertilize one acre.
[2] Benjamin Rush, "Information to Europeans," same author, *Essays, Literary, Moral & Philosophical* (Phila., 1798), 199; Thomas Cooper, *Some Information Respecting America* (London, 1795), 95, 125-126.
[3] Dwight, *Travels*, III, 205.
[4] Warren, "Observations on Agriculture," 347.

With you, it is the reverse. Hence the accuracy of British, and the carelessness of American cultivation." [1] In farming "carelessly" perhaps the American was farming wisely.

Though the work of the fields and barns absorbed the farmer's energies for much of the year, it was not his sole concern. His happiness often depended upon how he solved the problem of housing. Many of the rural folk along the coastal plain, it is true, had inherited colonial homes, but even for these the early years of the republic were a time of reconstruction. With the passing of the older frontier, primitive log cabins were being abandoned to the pigs and substantial frame houses were rising in front of them. Generally the farmer got out his own lumber from the wood lots, hewed the beams with a bent-handled broadax and even sawed the boards, though this was less necessary now that makeshift sawmills had been set up on every Eastern river. With the help of neighbors, summoned to his meat and drink, he joined and raised the frame. Then, when the boarding was finished, the simple hardware was attached, all made to order at the blacksmith's shop, and the glass was set in that he had secured for produce at the village store. Homemade shingles had been shaved at the rate of almost a thousand a day. Thanks to Jacob Perkins's invention of his nail-making machine, nails were no longer rare and costly as they had been when hammered out on small anvils. In 1790 an establishment to make nails was set up at Taunton, Massachusetts.[2]

The concern of architecture was, as always, how to

---

[1] Cooper, *Some Information*, 114. Washington had written in the same strain to Arthur Young. George Washington, *Letters on Agriculture to Arthur Young and Sir John Sinclair* (Franklin Knight, ed., Wash., 1847), 84.

[2] Tench Coxe, *A View of the United States of America* (Phila., 1794), 144-145, 266-268; R. M. Tryon, *Household Manufactures in the United States* (Chicago, 1917), 237-239.

serve the human need of shelter by adaptation to environment. In the South the main problem was to keep cool in summer on broad verandas and in well-ventilated halls; in the North it was to keep warm in winter. In New England wood was used for construction not only because it was cheap and easily handled, but because it was more quickly dried. Narrow eaves conserved the sunlight, and small doors and windows gave better defense against the searching January wind. Steep roofs delivered the snow, the sweeping lean-to at the rear making possible the narrow angle at the rooftree. With better commerce white paint grew cheaper and the new homes, no longer bare or coated in red, now gleamed in unwonted splendor.[1] In southern New York, Dutch lines persisted with the overhung roof sometimes supported upon posts, forming with the flagstone floor a rudimentary veranda. Here and in New Jersey and Pennsylvania houses were often constructed of plastered masonry.[2]

As an example of a better-class Connecticut home, we may glance at the parsonage at Ridgefield. An old house, it was still unpainted; at the rear the roof sloped spaciously down to a height of ten feet, slightly dipping at the jointure with the lean-to, thus making it a "breakback." Inside, the parlor at the right of the small square entry had whitewashed walls ornamented chiefly with a mahogany-framed mirror, and was brightened with calico curtains and a large homemade carpet. "To these," says the minister's son, "must be added eight chairs and a cherry table, of the manufacture of Deacon Hawley." The keeping room at the left of the chimney was also carpeted, and furnished with a table and a dozen rush-bottom chairs of various sizes. But the kitchen, twenty feet square, with its fireplace six feet

[1] Goodrich, *Recollections*, I, 78.
[2] Anon., "Journey through Part of Pennsylvania," 170.

A Pennsylvania Farm, about 1790

across and four feet deep, and its open door giving out on the garden and well sweep, was the "most comfortable room in the house; cool in summer, and perfumed with the breath of the garden and the orchard: in winter, with its roaring blaze of hickory, it was a cosy resort, defying the bitterest blasts of the season. Here the whole family assembled at meals, save only when the presence of company made it proper to serve tea [supper] in the parlor."[1] The carpetless chambers upstairs were doubtless strewn with mats of braided rags and of woolly sheepskins. The high-posted rope bedstead supported a straw tick, surmounted by a bed filled with goose feathers and luxurious with homemade linen sheets, quilts and blue-patterned wool coverlet. Overhead was the garret, hung with dried vegetables and fruits and savory, as well as boneset and tansy, which, compounded in the mortar with other herbs, would make spring tonic. Here, too, were flax and wool and the assorted implements for their processing. Deep below in the cellar stood the barrels of briny pork, corned beef and cider, and the heaps of tuberous vegetables awaiting the winter kettles.

Nearness to the soil and to domestic stock gave that generation the abundant food which unlimited families and hard outdoor work demanded.[2] "Settin' a good table" meant loading it with plenty, if not variety. Breakfast included boiled fish, beefsteak, ham and sausages. Count Volney, a dyspeptic Frenchman, writhed under the effects of "hot bread, half baked, soaked in melted butter, with the grossest cheese, and salt or hung beef, pickled pork or fish." Many European visitors rebelled at the prevalence of pork and grease. Physicians added their warning that Americans ate too much

---

[1] Goodrich, *Recollections*, I, 79.
[2] Anon., *The New American Cookery, or Female Companion* (N. Y., 1805), 61, 64; Fortescue Cuming, *Sketches of a Tour to the Western Country* (R. G. Thwaites, ed., *Early Western Travels, 1748-1846*, Cleveland, 1904-1907, IV), 236.

meat and too little of vegetables.[1] Dinner and supper
were merely elaborations of breakfast. Even the farmer's
fare was coarse and dull, especially "out of season," and
generally ill cooked and ill served.[2] All foreigners observed that Americans ate too rapidly and swallowed
almost without attempt at mastication.

For persons who liked vegetables the "sarse patches"
furnished most of those we know today except the
tomato.[3] Cauliflower, head lettuce, eggplant or "vegetable eggs," salsify and rhubarb were, however, rare.[4]
Cookbook references to such European delicacies as
borage, broccoli and sweet basil merely evidence too slavish copying from foreign sources.[5] Though oranges and
lemons had long been known, they were scarcely cheap
enough for common folk till after 1832, when Sicilian
cargoes were first shipped direct. Pineapples had come
in with the expanding commerce since the Revolution
and by 1804 bananas were known to a few. These
were regarded as dainties to grace a banquet table or to
serve as presents of affection, as when friends brought

[1] Jane L. Mesick, The English Traveller in America (Columbia Univ.,
Studies in English and Comparative Literature, 1922), 103-104; C. F.
Volney, A View of the Soil and Climate of the United States of Amer-
ica (C. B. Brown, tr., Phila., 1804), 257 ff.; Samuel Brown, M. D.,
"An Account of the Pestilential Disease . . . in the Summer and Au-
tumn of 1798," Medical Repository, II (N. Y., 1800), 364; Charles
Caldwell, M. D., Medical and Physical Memoirs (Phila., 1801), first
memoir, pt. iv.

[2] Mesick, English Traveller, 103-105; C. F. Adams, Three Episodes
of Massachusetts History (Boston, 1872), II, 808.

[3] The latter, picturesquely named the love apple, had been introduced
not as a food but as a curious decoration for the garden. The name was
a translation of the French pomme d'amour, which was a corruption of
the Italian pomo dei Moro, reflecting the introduction of the vegetable
from South America through "Moorish" Spain and Morocco into Italy.

[4] Bernard M'Mahon, The American Gardener's Calendar (Phila., 1806),
passim; J. T. Scharf, Chronicles of Baltimore (Balt., 1874), 229; J. B.
McMaster, A History of the People of the United States (N. Y., 1883-
1913), I, 18.

[5] See references in anon., New American Cookery, 155, 181, 186, and
anon., The Experienced American Housekeeper (N. Y., 1823), 48, 113,
159 and passim.

such viands to Aaron Burr awaiting his trial for treason at Richmond.[1] Country people contented themselves with peaches, pears, plums and berries, usually dried or preserved with sugar, and apples which kept most successfully and furnished the ubiquitous cider. Raisins, prunes and dried currants had been known at least since 1762. Spices were enumerated in the cookbooks, but most farm women relied, perforce, on garden thyme, summer savory and sweet marjoram.

If modern cattle would have astonished the farmer of 1800, so too would modern fruits which bear the old names. Now and then better varieties were come upon by chance and perpetuated, as when Loammi Baldwin near the end of the eighteenth century discovered the apple that bears his name. Grafting, such as produced the Concord grape, was practised in an elementary and empirical way, but nothing was known of cross-pollenation and other laboratory methods by which modern pomology has worked its miracles.[2]

Ice was cut by some enterprising farmers and ice houses were cleverly contrived. Rudimentary refrigeration, however, was practically confined to the larger towns where certain taverns installed the newly invented ice boxes. As early as 1799 the executive mansion at Washington was equipped with an ice house.[3] But few

[1] J. W. Harshberger, *The Botanists of Philadelphia and Their Work* (Phila., 1899), 118; J. W. Nix, "The Fruit Trade," C. M. Depew, ed., *One Hundred Years of American Commerce* (N. Y., 1895), II, 602-603; S. H. Wandell and Meade Minnigerode, *Aaron Burr* (N. Y., 1925), II, 199.

[2] M. A. De Wolfe Howe, *Boston, the Place and the People* (N. Y., 1903), 152; L. H. Bailey, ed., *The Standard Cyclopedia of Horticulture* (N. Y., 1914-1917), under names of the various fruits; U. P. Hedrick, *A History of Agriculture in the State of New York* (Albany, 1933), chap. xviii.

[3] Thomas Moore, *An Essay on the Most Eligible Construction of Ice-Houses* (Balt., 1803), 1-28; Cooper, *Some Information*, 131; Cuming, *Tour*, 163; A. Fothergill, "Observations on the Influence of Habit in Accommodating Animal and Vegetable Life to Diversity of Climate and Temperature," *Am. Medical and Philos. Register*, III (1812-1813), 19;

would have dared to drink ice water, to which Americans later became so addicted. In praising the water furnished to New York by the Manhattan Company the *Medical Repository* remarked, "In passing from the reservoir to its places of consumption, it loses that extreme coldness which renders water fresh drawn from deep wells dangerous to be drunk in hot weather, and frequently destructive of life." [1] Ice cream or, more properly, "iced" cream was known to epicures in the towns, but it is safe to say that few ordinary farmers had ever heard of it. [2]

Not only in shelter and food, but also in family clothing, the old farmstead had to be largely self-sufficing. In 1791 Hamilton complacently surveyed a "vast scene of household manufacturing" and computed that through it "two-thirds, three-fourths, and even four-fifths of all the clothing of the inhabitants are made by themselves." Twenty years later his great successor in the treasury, Albert Gallatin, made nearly as generous an estimate. [3] According to his figures, every person in the Union, countrymen as well as townsfolk, averaged six dollars' worth of cloth or other household goods, Rhode Island leading with $11.70 and New Hampshire, Georgia and Connecticut showing more than $8.50 each.

Woolens and linens were the chief concern. "The sheep being washed and sheared, the wool must first be picked by hand, and this was generally done by the family in the evening; then it must be . . . broke, as they

R. O. Cummings, *The American and His Food* (Chicago, 1940), 36-37. J. B. Bordley has a section on ice houses in his *Sketches on Rotations of Crops* (Phila., 1797) and in his *Essays and Notes*, 462-463.

[1] *Medical Repository*, IV (N. Y., 1801), 69. See also J. E. White, "Cursory Observations on the Soil, Climate, and Diseases of the State of Georgia," *ibid.*, IX (1805-1806), 357.

[2] Cummings, *American and His Food*, 40. See also anon., *Experienced American Housekeeper*, 166.

[3] *American State Papers* (Wash., 1832-1861), Finance, I, 132; II, 435. In households within the town of Providence alone 24,000 yards of linen were manufactured during the first nine months of 1791.

called it, and afterwards carded into rolls by hand, when it was fit for spinning." [1] The preparation of flax, more laborious than that of wool, was a responsibility of the men and older boys, who with flax brake and swingling knife separated the fibers from the woody portions. The matted fibers were then combed by the women with a spiked instrument called the hatchel, just as bunches of wool were drawn over a wire-studded block in carding. Spinning either flax or wool, being a relatively simple process, often fell to the older girls in the family, some of whom became so proficient as to secure employment as "spinning girls" in the neighborhood.

In Northern farmhouses at the beginning of the nineteenth century the hand loom was less in evidence than the spinning wheel. It was a time of transition even in communities somewhat distant from the centers of trade. If the fabrication of hats had already become a shop industry, the weaving of cloth and the making of shoes were entering the domestic stage, with the craftsmen either working in their own homes or more frequently going from house to house. [2] Whether she wore her own cloth or hired an itinerant artisan, the farmer's wife was generally ingenious in securing variety. Besides the better grades of woolens and linens and the coarser tow cloth, she contrived mixtures of wool and flax, known as linsey-woolsey, then popular on Northern farms and in frontier communities. Fustian was a mixture of cotton and flax, used chiefly in the South, while jeans, containing wool and cotton, figured prominently in men's clothing. [3]

The finishing of the cloth must have taxed the patience and skill of the womenfolk. In order to give their

[1] Levi Beardsley, *Reminiscences* (N. Y., 1852), 31.
[2] Goodrich, *Recollections*, I, 74; Bidwell, "Rural Economy," 262-268; Blanche E. Hazard, *The Organization of the Boot and Shoe Industry in Massachusetts before 1875* (*Harvard Econ. Studies*, XXIII), 24 ff.
[3] Tryon, *Household Manufactures*, 203.

linen a satisfactory whiteness, they soaked the yarn in warm water for three or four days, changing it frequently and rinsing in cold water; then they treated it with ashes or slaked lime and hot water. They next spread the woven fabric on the grass and sprinkled it hour after hour for several days. Thirty or forty bleachings were not uncommon. With woolens the process was less tedious, but strength was required to pound out the product of the hand loom after it had been shrunk in warm water containing strong soap or fuller's earth. Native barks—hickory, walnut and oak—berries and nuts usually supplied the dyes.[1] No housewife, however, turned away the indigo peddler, for his commodity more than any other colored the dye pot in its customary place by the kitchen fire. Mixed with native stains, it produced attractive shadings of blue when handled by those expert in its use.

The long and laborious manufacture of textiles was for the farmer's wife and daughters but an additional task in the perennial round of cooking, washing, sewing and cleaning. These other duties required similar skills. Light, for example, meant more than the cheerful glow from the fireplace. If one wished to read after dark, there must be blazing hemlock knots, or tow-wicked candles molded of bayberry, tallow or beeswax. Soap was made by combining lye from leached ashes with grease carefully saved for that purpose. Autumn brought the drying of fruits and vegetables against the long weeks of winter, and the butchering season was another busy time in the kitchen. So it was also in the spring, when the sap first began to run in the maples and preparations were made for the sugaring. In 1791 forty families in Oneida County, New York, made 13,000 pounds of sugar, while a few years later eighty families in the town of Cavendish, Vermont, produced 80,000

[1] Green vitriol, copperas, cochineal and madder were also used.

pounds. It was estimated that the average Vermont household at the end of the century turned out 250 pounds. Tench Coxe reported that in the better sections of the maple country, particularly northern New England and northern New York, it was possible for husband, wife and a ten-year old child to make 1000 pounds on a hundred-acre farm.[1]

The Northern farmer at the beginning of the nineteenth century was less self-sufficient than he had been fifty years earlier. He might still be a Jack-of-all-trades, but there was less reason for his being so. Perhaps his experienced eye still picked out the straightest hickory, ash and white oak to be saved from the capacious maw of the kitchen chimney so that he might deftly fashion cart tongues, oxbows, plow handles, ax helves and hoes. The heavy work with wood, however, was generally done at a near-by sawmill, and the services of an itinerant carpenter, with some pretension to the name of cabinetmaker, were often available. Hides from the family's cattle supplied numerous needs, but there were experts to do the tanning and to fabricate shoes and boots from the leather. Visits of traveling artisans, now becoming more frequent, brought the skill of the tailor, the weaver, the butcher and the chandler to lighten household burdens. The extent to which the farmer could rely upon such itinerant craftsmen was measured by the quantity of desirable commodities he could offer in exchange, or by his ability to secure cash in some market center for his small surpluses of grain, meat and wood.[2]

To the plain folk of the soil the passing seasons

[1] Tryon, *Household Manufactures*, 135; Samuel Williams, *Natural and Civil History of Vermont* (Walpole, N. H., 1794), 318 ff.; Coxe, *View*, 81.

[2] Few of these artisans earned a living from their craft. Like the mill owner and the country storekeeper, they depended upon farming for part of their income.

brought occasional opportunities to break the laborious cycle of the farm. Rural life in New England and certain sections of New York and New Jersey centered in the village, with its meetinghouse, tavern and town hall, each of which offered facilities for recreation. In such communities there was no isolation comparable to that of the frontiersmen on the slopes of the Alleghanies and in the Mississippi Valley. One could attend Sunday church services, midweek lectures, or the protracted meetings when some visiting preacher strove to breathe new zeal into a dispirited congregation. There was also the local tavern with its convivial cheer. "Dancing," wrote Jedidiah Morse in an early edition of his famous *Geography*, "is the principal and favourite amusement in New England; and of this the young people of both sexes are extremely fond." [1] But the older generation looked reprovingly upon youth who were drawn too often to public balls.

The farmer still found much of his recreation in close association with his work. "Bees" were organized on the slightest provocation—to get out a supply of logs for future building, to clear a field of stumps, to raise a barn in record time—and the toil was enlivened by gayety, sometimes spontaneous, more often induced through generous quantities of rum or whisky. Such gatherings usually culminated in a square dance under the enthusiastic direction of the local fiddler. Many a house "sprung up at the wagging of the fiddle-sticks, as the walls of Thebes sprang up of yore to the sound of the lyre." [2] For the womenfolk there were spinning and quilting bees, the social value of which fluctuated with the conversation, liberally spiced with unpremedi-

---

[1] Jedidiah Morse, *The American Geography* (Boston, 1789), 148; Goodrich, *Recollections*, I, 86.
[2] Washington Irving, *Knickerbocker's History of New York* (N. Y., 1916), bk. vii, chap. ii, p. 214.

tated gossip. But the most popular festivity came when
the maize was ready for husking. The young people
speeded up the work, well aware of the custom so pleasantly noted by Joel Barlow, the "Hartford Wit":

> The laws of husking every wight can tell
> And sure no laws he ever keeps so well
> For each red ear a general kiss he gains.[1]

After the ears had been stripped, time always remained
for foot races, leaping contests, shooting at the mark
and wrestling. These "athletic and healthy diversions"
received the approval of the generally censorious Jedidiah
Morse who was pleased to record that "the odious and
inhuman practices of duelling, gouging, cock-fighting
and horse-racing are scarcely known" in New England.[2]
Spectators' sports had little importance in the rural
communities of the Northeastern states. Professional
horse racing suffered from a legal ban, while few amateur
matches occurred in regions where men were not at ease
in the saddle and needed the animals for heavy work.
The genteel Narragansett pacer was slowly being replaced by the once despised trotter, but light harness racing had not yet been introduced. The few meets at
Albany, Poughkeepsie and elsewhere in New York
aroused little interest.[3] But the farmer and his sons
enjoyed the sports in which they could participate.
Hunting, fishing, swimming, skating, coasting and pitch-
ing quoits filled in the few leisure hours which they
allowed themselves. In the newer settlements along the
frontier from Vermont to Virginia game was so plentiful that circular hunts were necessary to drive out squir-
rels, foxes, wolves and other "vermin" of field and

[1] Joel Barlow, *The Hasty Pudding* (Brooklyn, 1833), 18.
[2] Morse, *American Geography*, 148; Goodrich, *Recollections*, I, 75-76;
M. N. Rawson, *When Antiques Were Young* (N. Y., 1931), 69-70.
[3] H. W. Herbert, *Frank Forester's Horse and Horsemanship of the
United States* (N. Y., 1857), I, 152; II, 67-70.

forest. At the same time sportsmen in Eastern villages were demanding some restraint on the indiscriminate slaughter of wild life. As early as 1788 the New York legislature in order "to prevent the destruction of deer" established the second six months of the year as the period in which they might be hunted. Three years later an act was passed to protect game birds, but it came too late to save the heath hen, which had long enticed hunters to Long Island.[1] The concern which lay behind such legislation was not shared by the farmer. He and his sons hunted and fished as inclination dictated or the demands of their work allowed.

During the winter months, particularly after January's snows had put a stop to work in field and wood lot, sleighing parties were organized, with rides to the village over the hard-packed surface to attend singing school or a dance at the tavern. The one-horse pung with its jingling bells was not well known in rural districts. The large sledge drawn by two strong horses was more popular, for sleighing was a social adventure. In the North it became, as that observant traveler Timothy Dwight remarked, a diversion to be enjoyed with passionate enthusiasm.[2]

However numerous the opportunities for recreation, the farm family indulged in few of them. If religious conviction did not enforce abstinence, accumulating tasks imposed restraints which only the shiftless could ignore. There were, of course, a few red-letter days in the almanac — training day, with its shooting at the mark in competition with one's fellows and then the descent on the tavern to quench one's thirst; election day, with its boisterous crowd and free-for-all fights, generally staged

[1] Jennie Holliman, *Early American Sports, 1785-1835* (Durham, 1931), 53-54; S. L. Mitchill, *The Picture of New-York* (N. Y., 1807), 173.
[2] Dwight, *Travels*, IV, 354; Sylvester Judd, *History of the Town of Hadley* (Northampton, 1863), 382.

by those ineligible to vote; county-court day, with its
interesting and amusing proceedings and perhaps some
wrestling after the judge had announced adjournment.
Infrequently a troupe of clowns and a traveling menagerie, with possibly a camel or an elephant—rudiments
of the American circus—came to a neighboring town,
arousing the curiosity of young and old. But, whatever
the diversion, there was no complete escape from the
perennial routine of chores.

The farmer could live in modest comfort, or at least
security, by a sort of skimming agriculture, and there he
stopped. He had little money income since no market
demand spurred him to produce a surplus. Without
good highways he could not economically haul his commodities to the few cities where he might have found
purchasers. The average countryman seemed invincibly
conservative. If he did not yoke the same number of
oxen to his plow, plant the same number of acres and
that too "in the old of the moon," and get the crops
in on the same day as did his father and grandfather,
he was shunned by the neighborhood as a visionary.[1]
With little incentive to increase his output, he saw no
reason to disturb the old round that insured his comfort.
For him, then, husbandry was a way of life and of getting a living. It was subsistence, not enterprise.

To this generalization there were, of course, striking
exceptions. Consider, for example, the farmer in New
York, Pennsylvania or Maryland, whose fertile acres
were convenient to water transportation. His position
was neither isolated nor independent. The call of warring Europe sounded in his grainfields. In 1800 seventy-
eight thousand quarters of wheat were shipped to Eng-

[1] On the conservatism of farmers, see C. L. Flint, "Agriculture in the
United States," Flint and others, *Eighty Years' Progress of the United
States* (N. Y., 1861), I, 23; A. L. Demaree, *The American Agricultural
Press, 1819-1860* (Columbia Univ., *Studies in the History of American
Agriculture*, no. 8), 48-51.

land alone, and the following year, because of scarcity
in the British Isles induced by failure of crops, America
supplied three and a half times as much. But in the
autumn word came of peace between England and
France. "It instantly operated almost like the hand
of death upon all business," wrote a land agent in western New York. "Wheat, corn and flour have been constantly on the fall!" [1] The American farmer, the merchant and the shipper joined in a common prayer that
"France and England get at loggerheads" again. When
war broke out once more in May, 1803, farmers' wagons
began to move in procession to the wharves. Next year
good harvests in England and a temporary opening of
trade with Prussia hurt the market for Americans, but
in 1806, after Napoleon had throttled Prussia, the fields
were levied on again and prices briefly maintained a
level never known before. Then in 1807 France and
England began to blockade each other and by the embargo the United States blockaded itself. In consequence, grain shipments to England fell to less than four
per cent of what they had been. Among those who had
a high stake in world politics during the Napoleonic
wars was the well-placed American farmer.[2]

Husbandmen with access to international markets
became interested in the agricultural experiments sponsored by a few who had found spacious living on large
estates. Many of these "gentlemen farmers" possessed
family fortunes made in commerce; some, like Robert
R. Livingston and Stephen Van Rensselaer, had long
rent rolls; still others had garnered money in land speculation, or, like John Jay, had piled up property in professional practice. The most influential was George

[1] Robert Troup to Rufus King, Dec. 5, 1801, Rufus King, *Life and Correspondence* (C. R. King, ed., N. Y., 1894-1900), IV, 27-28.
[2] W. F. Galpin, *The Grain Supply of England during the Napoleonic Period* (Univ. of Mich., *Publs.*, VI), chap. viii.

Washington, who so methodized the administration of
Mount Vernon that it almost paid its way. He was in
regular correspondence with the leading agriculturists in
England and was constantly experimenting with new
seeds and processes, keeping scientific records of results.
It was he, for example, who popularized the mule in
America, contributing good stock through his importa-
tion of asses from Spain and France.[1]

"Book farmers" such as these relied on English works
for guidance. But by reason of differences in climate and
soil, to say nothing of land tenure, labor and social tradition, the reader had to follow this guidance with caution.
In 1790 the Reverend Samuel Deane published a book
called *The New-England Farmer: or, Georgical Dictionary,* the first treatise on American agriculture to be
issued for a generation.[2] But the most important works
on general agriculture came from Maryland and Virginia.   John Beale Bordley, a lawyer who conducted
what was virtually an agricultural experiment station
on his sixteen-hundred-acre island farm, near where the
Wye flows into Chesapeake Bay, printed his *Essays and
Notes on Husbandry and Rural Affairs* in 1799.   He
condemned the three-field system that he had observed
in Maryland—maize, wheat or rye, spontaneous rubbish
pasture—and even more heartily the two-field system.
Instead, he worked out charts for eight fields, including
three of clover in the rotation.   Without the chemistry
to know the actual contribution of legumes he and his
followers had hit upon a saving principle.   John Taylor
of Caroline County, Virginia, insisted likewise on a
widely diversified crop system, but favored Indian corn,

[1] Washington, *Letters on Agriculture, passim;* P. L. Haworth, *George
Washington, Country Gentleman* (Indianapolis, 1925), 77, 92-96, 105-
124; Stephen Decatur, *Private Affairs of George Washington, from the
Records and Accounts of Tobias Lear* (Boston, 1933), 315, 318.

[2] There was a second edition in 1797 and a third in 1822.   In 1793
John Spurrier published *The Practical Farmer* (Wilmington), then the
best book on the subject.

whose waste could be mixed with cattle dung to enrich the soil.[1] To Thomas Moore of Montgomery County, Maryland, the great error of American agriculture was shallow plowing, which allowed the rains to wash away the topsoil and gave no room for roots to seek sustenance below.[2] Thomas Mann Randolph, Jefferson's son-in-law, is credited with leading the movement for cross-plowing slopes so as to stay erosion.[3] But Moore admitted that, since most farmers were "men of habit," improvement in plowing would be slow.

The plow itself must first be improved, and this proceeded along two lines. That the curvature enabling the moldboard to turn the soil most easily could be scientifically determined was Thomas Jefferson's discovery. Plowwrights could now build by a common pattern. The year before, in 1797, Charles Newbold of Burlington, New Jersey, patented an implement which save for beam and handles was cast in a solid piece of iron. The double basis of the modern plow was laid. But most farmers stubbornly clung to the familiar wooden variety, claiming that the iron poisoned the soil and pointing out that when such a plow was fractured the whole must be replaced. Not until the twenties, under various modifications, particularly that of the New York Quaker Jethro Wood in 1819, did the plow of standard iron parts bolted together come into common use.[4] It was the gentlemen farmers who prompted it.

They, too, experimented with gypsum, or plaster of Paris, as a soil amendment, bringing in boatloads from Nova Scotia as well as tapping beds in Maryland, New Jersey and New York. Robert R. Livingston, when

---

[1] *Arator* (Petersburg, 1818), 72-86.
[2] Moore, *Great Error of American Agriculture*, passim.
[3] A. O. Craven, *Soil Exhaustion as a Factor in the Agricultural History of Virginia and Maryland* (Univ. of Ill., *Studies*, XIII, no. 1), 90-91.
[4] F. W. Hirst, *Life and Letters of Thomas Jefferson* (N. Y., 1926), 333, 425; Robert Russell in *American Farmer*, II, (1820), 5.

minister to France in 1803, sent samples even across the Atlantic. John A. Binns acted as its prophet in Virginia, and Dr. George Logan and Judge Richard Peters in Pennsylvania, while Dr. S. L. Mitchill in New York and others wrote learned treatises upon it.[1] DeWitt Clinton in an oratorical flourish declared, "It has created a new era in agriculture."[2] But it had little merit in sandy regions and eventually was relegated to sour lands, where it really had beneficial effect. Marl, another new fertilizer, was early used in Maryland and New York, where calcareous deposits of marine shells were abundant. Its aid to acid soils was gradually recognized, and beginning in 1818 Edmund Ruffin spread its use throughout the upper South.[3]

In no way did the gentlemen farmers better serve their country than in the improvement of livestock, not so much by selective breeding of native cattle as by importations from abroad. The results of Robert Bakewell's experiments in England had marked a revolution: the average beef had increased from about three hundred pounds to more than eight. Three Marylanders sent an agent, Matthew Patton, to England to acquire specimens of robust Durham livestock; in 1794 Patton convoyed some of their progeny to Kentucky, and in 1800 his son took others to Ohio. In another five years descendants of these cattle were being driven back across the mountains.[4] In 1817 Henry Clay introduced Herefords into Kentucky, and during the twenties the familiar British dairy breeds—Alderneys and Guernseys—were imported in increasing numbers, Jerseys and Ayrshires coming

[1] J. A. Binns, *A Treatise on Farming* (Fredericktown, Md., 1803), passim; George Logan, *Agricultural Experiments in Gypsum* (Phila., 1797); Richard Peters, *Agricultural Inquiries on Plaster of Paris* (Phila., 1797).

[2] *Introductory Discourse before the Literary and Philosophical Society* (N. Y., 1815), 24.

[3] A. O. Craven, *Edmund Ruffin, Southerner* (N. Y., 1932), 53 ff.

[4] Carver, "Sketch of American Agriculture," 57, 59.

later.[1] Beef-fattening was an important industry in Connecticut and southern Pennsylvania, but dairy stock was more esteemed in most sections of the East. In 1790 eighty-five pounds of butter was thought in Massachusetts to be a good annual yield for a cow; by 1830 the average had been doubled, thanks to better breeding and more intelligent care.

At the opening of the century it would have taken a bold prophet to foretell that the United States would eventually become the chief pork-producing area of the world. American farmers had made gains, some with native animals but more with importations. During the last years of the eighteenth century came a notable consignment from the Duke of Bedford to George Washington—the Woburn stock. Quakers in Chester County, Pennsylvania, starting in 1820 with swine from Bedfordshire, developed a famous breed which bore their county's name throughout the Union.[2] Other stock of Chinese strain added weight and succulence to pork in many sections of the country, and by 1830 the Berkshires had arrived, arousing an unprecedented interest and causing a flurry of speculation.[3]

One of the most sensational episodes in the agricultural history of America resulted from the importation of Spanish sheep. The average flock of 1800, despite the efforts of a few leaders like Washington, was no better than that of 1700. Early in the nineteenth century two Frenchmen living in America, M. Du Pont de Nemours and M. Delessert, and two United States diplomats, Robert R. Livingston and David Humphreys, introduced specimens of merinos, the finest sheep in the

[1] Flint, "Hundred Years of Progress," 297; C. T. Leavitt, "Attempts to Improve Cattle Breeds in the United States, 1790-1860," *Agricultural History*, VII, 55-59.

[2] F. D. Coburn, *Swine in America* (N. Y., 1910), 35, 40, 55.

[3] Naval officers and consular agents were active in facilitating importations. *American Farmer*, IV (1822), 152, 176.

world. They attracted little attention until 1808 when American farmers began to see the possibilities of a market for raw wool in the attempts to manufacture textiles that would replace English imports cut down by war and embargo. Humphreys, Livingston and Du Pont, among others, established woolen mills, and by 1810 at least two dozen existed.[1] Merino rams were now quoted at a thousand, fifteen hundred, two thousand dollars, but such prices could not long be maintained, especially after the royal *cabañas* of Spain, hitherto inaccessible save through trickery or special royal favor, were broken up and scattered by the invading British army. Consul William Jarvis at Lisbon, for example, succeeded in shipping nearly five thousand to his own Vermont farm. Twenty thousand arrived in 1810 and 1811. Though this was a small infusion into flocks of seven million, the example had a stirring potency. Better stock and better markets—for after a temporary slump tariffs were to continue the protection the War of 1812 and its preliminaries had begun—established commercial woolgrowing in this country. [2] Pastoral profits meant much to the Northeast until Western competition toward the middle of the century brought the industry into decline; part, too, went literally to the dogs.

It was natural that the country gentlemen whose efforts we have traced should seek each other's company for discussion. As early as 1784 the South Carolina Agricultural Society had been established, but its interest

---

[1] In 1809 the New York legislature circulated Robert R. Livingston's *Essay on Sheep* as a public document.

[2] Samuel Bard, *Guide to Young Shepherds* (N. Y., 1811); F. L. Humphreys, *Life and Times of David Humphreys* (N. Y., 1917), II, 338; Mary P. S. Cutts, *Sketch of Mrs. William Jarvis of Weathersfield, Vermont* (Salem, 1887), 13. General accounts are available in L. G. Connor, "A Brief History of the Sheep Industry in the United States," Am. Hist. Assoc., *Ann. Rep. for 1918*, 93-109, and C. W. Wright, *Wool Growing and the Tariff* (*Harvard Econ. Studies*, V), chaps. ii-iii.

was somewhat specialized in rice culture.[1] Far more influential was the Philadelphia Society for Promoting Agriculture, formed the following year by Bordley. Its voluminous *Transactions* presented the results of the restless experimentation of its members. Judge Richard Peters, for example, regaled his colleagues with a hundred papers. New York and Massachusetts were soon in friendly rivalry, and county societies were organized and developed. One of the most progressive was that of Albemarle County, Virginia, over which Madison presided and for which Jefferson wrote the platform of objectives.[2] In 1803, as a sort of capstone, there was formed in Washington the American Board of Agriculture, a society whose list of leading members might serve as a roll of the chief statesmen of the country.[3]

The papers read by prominent landholders to their societies were entirely empirical; the good results reported had come from trial and error. To improve this situation Columbia College set up a professorship including agriculture among its responsibilities as early as 1792, but apparently Dr. Mitchill used it largely to illustrate favorite theories in chemistry and geology. At the end of the century Simeon DeWitt pleaded for "a state experimental garden" and later urged the establishment of an agricultural college. But little resulted. In 1823 Robert Hallowell Gardiner, a large proprietor in Maine, built the Gardiner Lyceum to educate youth in farming; the same year a course was offered in Washington (now Trinity) College, Hartford, and the next at the institute

<hr>

[1] Jefferson sent this society varieties of rice originally from the Philippine Islands. *Medical Repository*, I (N. Y., 1798), 120.

[2] R. H. True, "Early Days of the Albemarle Agricultural Society" and "Minute Book" of the Society in Am. Hist. Assoc., *Ann. Rep. for 1918*, 243-349.

[3] Bidwell and Falconer, *Agriculture*, 184 ff. See also *Medical Repository*, VI (N. Y., 1803), 342-343.

in Troy, newly founded by Stephen Van Rensselaer.[1] But a few years later agriculture's only contact with schools was as a support for students in certain institutions. The gentlemen farmers failed as patrons of agricultural education in formal institutions.

It was not their only failure. Though they had accomplished a great deal—importing livestock, testing new crops, experimenting with tillage methods and new implements—they had not reached the plowmen in the fields. The "dirt farmer" knew little about the agricultural societies, nor was he eager to learn more. He was especially impatient of attempts to instruct him from the printed page. This was theory, which in his mind meant dreamy speculation.

The gentleman who hit upon a novel expedient, especially appealing to farmers and their families, was Elkanah Watson of Massachusetts. Having introduced the first merino sheep into Berkshire County in 1807, he exhibited them on Pittsfield green in order to instruct his neighbors on their value. So spontaneous was the response that he organized a neighborhood cattle show and then a society to perpetuate it. "We take the liberty," said the announcement, "to recommend to farmers to select and prepare prime animals for exhibition, also for manufacturers to exhibit their best cloth, etc., for inspection and sale. . . . Innocent recreation will be permitted, but everything tending to immorality will be discountenanced." [2] Other cattle shows had been held, but none so successful. There were premiums for all kinds of produce and women's work, also community singing, an oration, and an "agricultural ball." The

[1] A. C. True, *A History of Agricultural Education, 1785-1925* (U. S. Dept. of Agr., *Misc. Publ.*, no. 36).

[2] Elkanah Watson, *History of the Berkshire Agricultural Society* (Albany, 1819), 14.

American county fair was born—a social institution for instruction and entertainment and not primarily for buying and selling. State aid was granted in 1817. The idea also operated elsewhere—the three-day exhibition held at Lexington, Kentucky, in 1814, for example, may have been of independent origin—but mostly it stemmed from Berkshire.

The state society of Massachusetts took up the plan in 1817 and it spread to New York in the same year. Watson, who soon moved to Albany, went about formally administering a sort of baptismal rite to new fairs held far and near. *Niles' Register* credited him with the parentage of fifty fairs, and by the end of the twenties they were to be found from Maine to South Carolina. True, when state aid was removed, they languished, but the impulse was never lost and, reviving about 1840 with more generous government patronage—and the added excitement of horse racing—they flourished into the twentieth century.[1]

Of greater practical benefit, however, was agricultural journalism. In 1819 John P. Skinner, the postmaster at Baltimore, established the *American Farmer,* the pioneer of the movement, though rivaled before 1830 by the *Ploughboy* (1819) at Albany, the *New England Farmer* (1822) at Boston, the *New York Farmer* (1828) at that city and the *Southern Agriculturist* (1828) at Charleston.[2] The editors all deprecated theoretical discussion and technical language, desiring to reach the "real, unsophisticated American." Their original essays were generally by men of the country-gentleman type, the *New England Farmer,* for instance, frequently attracting the pens of Timothy Pickering and Daniel Webster, but the style was as nearly as possible

[1] W. C. Neely, *The Agricultural Fair* (N. Y., 1935), 71-72. See also *American Farmer,* VI (1824), 287 ff.

[2] Demaree, *American Agricultural Press,* 13-14.

kept on the specified level. These journals constantly played fresh breezes of suggestion upon the stifling conservatism of the American farmer. The *Cultivator,* founded at Albany by Jesse Buel in 1834, was the first to attain a truly national circulation.[1]

American agriculture in 1830 was not sharply different from what it had been in 1790. Farm machinery, which was to effect a revolution in production, had scarcely taken form; the railroad, which was to bring large areas into market contacts, was merely a curiosity. State and federal experiment stations and scientific services and the great university schools of agriculture were in the distant future. Yet new forces were at work, set in motion almost entirely by the precept and example of gentlemen amateurs, who had time to read and discuss and capital to test new methods and materials.

[1] H. J. Carman, "Jesse Buel, Albany County Agriculturist," *N. Y. History,* XIV, 241-249.

CHAPTER VI

AGRARIAN EXPANSION

SLIGHTLY more than half the people who undertook the task of building a new nation lived south of the Mason and Dixon line in 1790. Numbering approximately two million, of whom three out of every eight were Negroes, the Southerners occupied a rural domain half again as large as the area of the seven Northern states. Their market centers were few and small, only Baltimore and Charleston having more than four thousand inhabitants. The latter, with sixteen thousand, still ranked first, but it was soon to be outstripped by the busy Maryland port. In Virginia, Richmond and Petersburg, despite inadequate facilities, were entering a period of unusual commercial activity, while Norfolk, tragic victim of the Revolution, was rising but slowly from its ashes. In all North Carolina no town contained more than two thousand inhabitants, and Georgia's metropolis, on a bluff above the Savannah River, was only a lively village, where the streets on hot, dry days reminded the traveler of the sands of the Sahara.[1]

Observant foreigners in the South were apt to comment on its "regionalism," even if they did not use the term. They noticed that political boundaries cut across areas which possessed similar, if not identical, interests and that within every state climate and soil combined to create natural differences which were reflected both in

[1] John Davis, *Travels of Four Years and a Half in the United States of America* (London, 1803), 102-103. See also anon., "The American Character," *Literary Mag. and Am. Register*, II (1804), 254, and George Sibbald, *Notes and Observations on the Pine Lands of Georgia* (Augusta, 1801), *passim*.

politics and in social customs. Such regional contrasts existed in Northern states as well—for example, between the Connecticut Valley and the New England hill country—but they seemed more conspicuous in the South.

One needed no peculiar gift to discern the superficial differences among the various physiographic divisions.[1] Southwestward from Chesapeake Bay stretched the great coastal plain, or tidewater as Virginians called it, reaching its greatest width of two hundred miles in the lowlands of the Carolinas and Georgia.[2] West of it was light, sandy soil, so infertile in some districts that only pine and scrub oak could grow. The pine barrens in North Carolina impressed President Washington in 1791 as the most desolate country he had ever seen, but he was pleased by the alluvial strips along the borders of all the larger streams that cut the coastal plain from the Potomac to the Savannah.[3] These were the areas in which the plantation system would within a generation reach a development surpassed only in the lower Mississippi Valley.

Between the coastal plain and the Appalachian foothills lay the great eastern plateau or piedmont, nowhere rising more than a thousand feet above sea level. Though its clay soils, drained by innumerable small streams, showed signs of long-continued erosion in the eastern districts, it was still excellent farm land. As one moved across it toward the Blue Ridge in Virginia or southwestward into North Carolina, the forests became more dense and the farmsteads smaller.[4] Closer to the

[1] R. H. Brown, *Mirror for Americans: Likeness of the Eastern Seaboard, 1810* (Am. Geog. Soc., *Special Publ.*, no. 27), chap. i.

[2] David Ramsay, *A Sketch of the Soil, Climate, Weather and Diseases of South Carolina* (Charleston, 1796), 2.

[3] Archibald Henderson, *Washington's Southern Tour, 1791* (Boston, 1923), 326-328.

[4] C. H. Ambler, *Sectionalism in Virginia* (Chicago, 1910), 1-3. See also J. W. Powell, ed., *The Physiography of the United States* (N. Y., 1897), 78-80, 308-309.

Appalachian range all evidence of farming and grazing disappeared, and hunters and fur traders were breaking new trails in search of pelts, quite unaware of the treasure of iron, coal, lead, manganese and oil that lay beneath their feet. But everyone knew the fertility of the long limestone valley extending from the Georgia border into Pennsylvania, which in its northern reaches was called the Shenandoah.[1]

The decline in American agriculture, which William Strickland thought he observed at the close of the eighteenth century, was in many districts merely a sign of temporary readjustment rather than of long-term collapse.[2] This was well exemplified in the South with reference to the older staples of indigo, rice and tobacco. Having thrown off the restrictive, but protective, mantle of British mercantilism, the South Carolina planters had lost their bounty on indigo and, as Great Britain found new supplies in the East Indies, its production almost disappeared from the sandy soils of the southern river valleys.[3] Though rice was still in considerable demand, especially for the Russian market, its cultivation after the Revolution was marked by a period of confused transition, for at the same time that indigo planters were trying to save themselves by concentrating on this more profitable staple, the rice fields were being shifted from inland swamps to any river bottom where tidal flooding could be advantageously used.[4]

In tidewater Maryland and Virginia, where tobacco had long held undisputed sway, acute distress also prevailed. Many a field, surrendering to the forest, bore silent witness to poor tillage and soil exhaustion, while

[1] L. C. Gray, *History of Agriculture in the Southern United States to 1860* (Carnegie Inst., *Publs.*, no. 430), II, 608-609.

[2] See earlier, chap. v.

[3] Gray, *Agriculture*, II, 610-611.

[4] John Drayton, *A View of South Carolina* (Charleston, 1802), 125 ff.

newly cleared acres produced crops for which there was no market.[1]   Maryland tobacco had lost its French customers during the Revolution and it was difficult to regain them.   European markets generally were so upset by the wars of the French Revolution, and the trade routes to America were so uncertain in the years of nonintercourse and embargo, that Europeans either imported tobacco from Cuba, Colombia and Sumatra or tried to produce their own.   As a result the American production for a long generation after 1790 declined in the tidewater regions and showed little increase in the piedmont.   Chesapeake Bay planters were turning over in their minds the possibility of migrating westward or of sowing their fields with grass and small grain.[2]

Wheat culture, far from being peculiar to Pennsylvania and New York, was, in fact, late in the eighteenth century pushing steadily southward under the impetus of high prices and a broadly speculative market.[3]   The Valley of Virginia, despite difficulties of transportation, was hauling its surplus grain into Philadelphia, while planters along the James River were growing corn for local consumption and wheat for export.   In the northern piedmont grain and livestock were replacing tobacco. Travelers reported new gristmills in the North Carolina backcountry, symbols of the expanding domain of wheat and corn.[4]

[1] Brown, *Mirror*, 221-222, citing William Tatham, *An Historical and Practical Essay on the Culture and Commerce of Tobacco* (London, 1800).

[2] *American State Papers* (Wash., 1832-1861), *Commerce and Navigation*, I, 241-242; *American Farmer*, IV (1822), 347; A. O. Craven, *Soil Exhaustion as a Factor in the Agricultural History of Virginia and Maryland, 1606-1860* (Univ. of Ill., *Studies*, XIII, no. 1), 77-78.

[3] Duke de La Rochefoucauld-Liancourt, *Travels through the United States of North America . . . in the Years 1795, 1796, and 1797* (London, 1799), III, 52, 113-114.   J. B. Bordley, *Essays and Notes on Husbandry* (Phila., 1801), 17-74, emphasizes Maryland's interest in small grain.

[4] Gray, *Agriculture*, II, 607; David Ramsay, *The History of South-Carolina* (Charleston, 1809), II, 216-217.

Though Virginia, largest and wealthiest state in the young republic, ranked for a time among the leading wheat producers, neither its tobacco nor its grain became the economic basis for Southern expansion. In 1790 the planters' great asset, as yet unrealized, lay in the ripening cotton boll. Great Britain's cotton industry, successfully imitating the cloths once imported from the Orient, had been revolutionized during the eighteenth century through the use of power-driven machines. By 1790 its mills and factories were slowed down, waiting for cotton fiber. The supply to meet that need was soon available, from American fields.

A few years after the War of Independence long-staple cotton began to appear on the export lists for England. The large amount of fiber in proportion to seeds made profitable their extraction by hand, pound by pound; but few pounds could be grown since climatic requirements confined it to a very narrow strip along the Carolina and Georgia shores and to the "sea-islands" near by. While still colonials, a few planters had tried to make some use of the short-staple boll, which grew so easily farther inland, but the tightly wrapped green seeds took too much labor in the separation to make a crop worth while.[1] Extensive cultivation was assured, however, in 1793 when Eli Whitney, the young Yale graduate then serving as tutor on a Georgia plantation, demonstrated both his Yankee ingenuity and his thorough training in his father's machine shop by making a contrivance which separated the seed from the lint cheaply and easily. The speed with which rivals appropriated the basic features of his invention left Whitney with little income beyond the sums necessary to fight infringements on his patents. But his device quickly converted the South to a new staple.[2]

[1] Drayton, *South Carolina*, 168.
[2] Eli Whitney, "Correspondence," *Am. Hist. Rev.*, III, 99-101.

That the cotton gin opened the uplands as well as the tidewater to short-staple cotton is strikingly revealed in the statistics of production. The crop of 1804 proved eight times as large as that of 1794, and almost three quarters of it was picked in the eastern districts of central Georgia and the northern counties of South Carolina.[1] The attractive prices presently whetted the appetite of the Georgia planters for fertile acres still in the hands of the Creek Indians.[2] North Carolina's piedmont, though producing chiefly for domestic consumption, also began to add to the bales which were handled either at Petersburg, Virginia, or at Charleston. In southeastern Virginia planters readily abandoned tobacco for cotton, just as some of their neighbors had turned to wheat and corn. The new staple was also becoming important across the mountains in central Tennessee and along the Mississippi, where merchants from Vicksburg to Natchez accepted it as a medium of exchange.[3] But it was not yet clear at the turn of the nineteenth century how greatly the cotton gin would give a new direction to economic and social trends in the South.

The organization of agriculture in many Southern regions at this period was not unlike that of the North. Except in the rice districts of Georgia and South Carolina and the tidewater of Virginia and Maryland, the typical unit could be more appropriately called a farm than a plantation. Its two or three hundred acres, only partially under cultivation, were usually divided into small fields by worm fences made of split rails from the adjacent woodland. Farmers generally followed a three-

---

[1] J. D. B. De Bow, *The Industrial Resources of the Southern and Western States* (New Orleans, 1852), I, 122.

[2] See C. R. Fish, *The Rise of the Common Man, 1830-1850* (*A History of American Life*, VI), 128.

[3] James Hall, *A Brief History of the Mississippi Territory* (Salisbury, N. C., 1801), *passim*; Gray, *Agriculture*, II, 683 ff.; U. B. Phillips, *American Negro Slavery* (N. Y., 1918), 159-160.

year rotation, hallowed by English precedent, which permitted each field one year in three to revert to "spontaneous rubbish pasture."[1]

At the close of the eighteenth century most of Maryland and the piedmont and Valley of Virginia, as well as the uplands of the Carolinas and Georgia, were in the hands of farmers and small-scale planters. The more prosperous among them tried to imitate the social amenities of the great plantations and hoped to ally themselves, by marriage or otherwise, with the aristocratic families of the seaboard. But the majority, descendants perhaps of indentured servants or of others who had found life difficult even in the New World, lived simply and independently, tilling their few acres alone or with their sons' help. They possessed few slaves and some had moral scruples against investing in such servants. Without education or leisure for self-improvement they tended to be narrowly provincial and intensely sectarian. Among travelers their hospitality was proverbial, but the accommodations which they had to offer seldom matched their warm generosity.[2] From southeastern Pennsylvania to the Georgia uplands, the low German speech of the "Pennsylvania Dutch" was increasingly heard in communities where many still spoke the English variants peculiar to Ulstermen or Highland Scots.[3] But whatever their national origins, they were inclined to give political allegiance to the agrarian republicanism of Thomas Jefferson and to respond quickly to the preaching of Methodist circuit riders and Baptist or Presbyterian itinerants.

[1] Bordley, Essays, 1, 17-33.
[2] Ramsay, South-Carolina, II, 448-449; Isaac Weld, jr., Travels in North America in 1795, 1796 and 1797 (London, 1807), I, 146-147; Jedidiah Morse, The American Universal Geography (Boston, 1802), 655-656; Phillips, Negro Slavery, 161-162.
[3] F. A. Michaux, Travels to the Westward of the Allegany Mountains . . . in the Year 1802 (London, 1805), 322-325, 339-340.

Out of their ranks came many young men who found their first economic opportunity as overseers on plantations. Aspiring to secure land in their own right, they occasionally realized their ambitions and rose above the social limitations of mere servants of the landed aristocracy. But most failed to maintain even its modest standards; they could not hold their own in face of the spreading large-plantation system based on considerable capital. Some, without prospect of inheritance and ill-adjusted to their social environment, found a life more to their liking in the mountains of western Virginia and North Carolina, where farming need not infringe too deeply on time more enjoyably spent in hunting and fishing. Isolated and illiterate, proud of their self-sufficiency, they perpetuated in their highland clearings seventeenth-century superstitions and folkways and preserved a consistent hostility to the nineteenth-century concept of progress.[1]

Poor and lazy though the mountain folk might be, they escaped the curse of that sluggish inexertion which caused the "poor whites" to be regarded with contempt in the older regions, even by the enslaved African. Physicians who visited the Carolinas and Georgia shortly after 1800 attributed to disease and bad diet the spiritual degradation of those whites known as "sand hillers" or "clayeaters." Dr. J. E. White sent an excellent clinical description to the *Medical Repository*:

> The countenance is pale and bloated; . . . the breathing is difficult, and is easily hurried by brisk exercise; the pulse is small and weak, but sometimes tense, and the carotid arteries in the neck beat with unusual force. . . . The person . . . is fond of a life of listless inactivity. The appetite is sometimes voracious, and

[1] Edward Hooker, "Diary," Am. Hist. Assoc., *Ann. Rep. for 1896*, I, 893-895, 903; U. B. Phillips, *Life and Labor in the Old South* (Boston, 1929), 342-343.

is often insatiable for eating dirt, which forms the characteristic symptom of the disease.[1]

But the malignant activity of the parasitic hookworm was not yet suspected.[2] "Malacia, or dirt-eating," said the observers, resulted from faulty diet — too much salt meat and greens — which had a more "debilitating" effect in the South than in the North. The prevalence of this habit explained, in Dr. White's opinion, the inertia which held men on unproductive pine barrens, indolently scratching the earth for a bare subsistence, when better lands beckoned in trans-Appalachia.[3]

If Southern agriculture, responsive to the demands of world markets, had not achieved a high general standard of physical comfort and social well-being, it had created, at least in Virginia and South Carolina, an aristocracy at once powerful and intelligent. These landed gentry honored English tradition long after political independence had been won, and some could claim noble lords or country gentlemen among their English forebears. At the close of the eighteenth century London was still the metropolis for the Virginia tidewater, for young Richmond as well as old Williamsburg transacted business in terms of bills of exchange originating in mercantile offices on the Thames. Though the planters found it increasingly difficult to finance elaborate country houses such as Nomini Hall, Mount Airy, Shirley and Westover, these colonial mansions and many others like them continued to serve as symbols of a standard of living which their owners were striving to maintain. Within the great houses there still was insistence on that courtly

[1] J. E. White, "Cursory Observations on the Soil, Climate, and Diseases of Georgia," *Medical Repository*, X (1806-1807), 121.

[2] See H. U. Faulkner, *The Quest for Social Justice, 1898-1914* (*A History of American Life*, XI), 233-234.

[3] White, "Observations," 122; Joseph Pitt, "Observations on the Country and Diseases near Roanoke River, in the State of North-Carolina," *Medical Repository*, XI (1807-1808), 337-342.

hospitality and social grace which superficially marked
the landed aristocracy.[1] Far more vital in the Virginia
tradition was the ancient custom of combining with
plantation management some training in law and a
career, however casual, in politics. Though Virginia
was the most populous of the thirteen states in 1790,
that fact alone does not explain the preëminence of her
sons in public service during the early years of the republic. They were now playing on a larger stage the
rôles to which generations of provincial leadership had
accustomed them.

In South Carolina the tidewater gentry wore their
social prestige with an urbanity scarcely equaled by the
Virginians. Charleston provided a focus for their interests and activities. Here the aristocracy of the rice and
indigo fields had joined with that of the wharf and
countinghouse to create, in a semitropical setting, a
graceful reminder of the variant groups whose customs
and traditions were determining the pattern of American
life. If London was still the mirror of fashion for
South Carolinians, their own little metropolis possessed
a distinctive flavor, a rare blending of influences emanating from the West Indies, France and Holland as well
as Great Britain. No other city in English America
was quite so "Continental." [2]

According to the 1790 census, Charleston was almost
as large as Boston and ranked fourth in the nation, containing more than sixteen thousand inhabitants of whom
six thousand were Negroes.[3] Its rapid recovery after
the Revolution was attested by the brigs, scows and

[1] John Bernard, *Retrospections of America, 1797-1811* (Mrs. Bayle
Bernard, ed., N. Y., 1887), 146-150; Davis, *Travels,* 355-356; Hooker,
"Diary," 850, 919-920. See also Dixon Wecter, *The Saga of American
Society* (N. Y., 1937), 25-26.

[2] Felix de Beaujour, *Sketch of the United States . . . from 1800 to
1810* (William Walton, tr., London, 1814), 77.

[3] Bureau of the Census, *A Century of Population Growth* (Wash.,
1909), 13, 78.

schooners in the harbor and by the new houses of brick and stone replacing the wooden ones which had been burned during the conflict. In adopting fire-resistant materials Charlestonians managed to escape the monotonous uniformity, so oppressive in the residential sections of Baltimore and Philadelphia, by covering the brick with stucco in delicate shades of blue, green, yellow and pink. Shingles likewise gave place to colored tiles rather than to drab slate, an additional symbol of the city's individuality. In most dwellings the Georgian style, with its balanced façade and ornate classical doorway, had supplanted the French and West Indian influences. Householders, reluctant to give up the two or three-tiered piazzas which helped ward off the heat, sometimes compromised by placing a pediment above the piazza and then constructing a partition with a false door on the street end. Such a façade, however skillfully designed, illustrated the willingness of Americans to sanction minor violations of European canons of taste in order to secure greater utility. If the effect was not always pleasing, it was at least distinctive; and it represented no revolt from Georgian dominance.[1]

The city was run by a planter oligarchy whose leaders, unlike their colonial predecessors, generally shunned trade just as the wealthy merchants ignored politics. The planters thought of themselves as agrarian republicans and their principles were often expressed in the vibrant phrases of the rights of man, but the manner and tone of their society would have shocked the Republicans who were joining Jefferson's party in Kentucky, western Pennsylvania, northern New York and the towns of Vermont. An observant Yankee called

[1] La Rochefoucauld-Liancourt, *Travels*, II, 376-377; Davis, *Travels*, 107; John Lambert, *Travels through Canada, and the United States* (London, 1814), II, 125-126; Mrs. St. Julien Ravenel, *Charleston, the Place and the People* (N. Y., 1906), 350.

Charleston, despite its ostensible Jacobinism, "the most aristocratic city in the Union." [1] The ruling class may have admired certain philosophers of the Enlightenment and have sympathized for a time with French revolutionaries, but such sentiments, even when reënforced by resentment against British creditors, furnished no solid foundation for democratic institutions. The framers of the state constitution had made sure that no one with less than a fifty-acre freehold could vote and that only the well-to-do could hold office.

Charleston society suited its plans to the convenience of the wealthy planter. He liked to visit his estate — sometimes fifty or sixty miles from the city — as soon as the November frosts had removed the danger of malaria or "country fever." [2] After the festivities of Christmas week in the plantation mansion, he brought his family back to town for the "season" from January to March. During the early spring, when the routine of rice culture was most demanding, he returned to the country, where he usually stayed until the ponds began to "green over." The enervating summer months might find him in the seclusion of his darkened town house, or in his summer cottage on Sullivan's Island or at such favored resorts as Virginia Hot Springs, Newport and, a little later, Saratoga. [3]

The "season" in Charleston was filled with concerts and balls of the St. Cecilia Society, supplemented by private dinner parties at which the raconteur was even more honored than the epicure. So general was the spirit of gayety that the Duke de La Rochefoucauld-Liancourt, probably in exaggeration, remarked that from four in the afternoon the people rarely thought of any-

[1] E. S. Thomas, *Reminiscences of the Last Sixty-Five Years* (Hartford, 1840), I, 33; Ravenel, *Charleston*, 378.

[2] Quinine was not yet in general use. Ravenel, *Charleston*, 385-386.

[3] Thomas Hunt, *Life of William H. Hunt* (Brattleboro, Vt., 1922), 3-4; Ravenel, *Charleston*, 384-385.

thing but pleasure and amusement.[1] Race week in February, followed by the Jockey Club ball, marked the climax. Upcountry planters joined heartily with those of the tidewater in supporting the Jockey Club; and numerous coaches, richly ornamented and bearing family crests, brought hundreds of spectators to the grandstand.

Because of their frequent dueling, reckless gambling and excessive drinking the Southerners whose social activities focused in Charleston were often judged to be indolent and self-indulgent, if not dissolute.[2] Yet the Duke de La Rochefoucauld-Liancourt, who knew the capitals of Europe, found in Charleston better company and livelier entertainment than he had expected, while that devout Calvinist, Jedidiah Morse, declared that in no part of America were "the social blessings enjoyed more rationally and liberally."[3] Life in plantation mansions and spacious town houses would have been less pleasant, had the aristocracy not possessed an army of servants unable to "give notice" at will, who kept the routine of the household functioning smoothly. While Northern communities were making the adjustments necessitated by the rapid decline of indentured servitude and the gradual emancipation of slaves, Southern families, especially in the tidewater, were enjoying the tradition of personal service which had slowly been created among the slaves and was now exemplified by Negroes several generations removed from their African origins.[4]

Throughout the South, slaves were growing more important as a base for the whole social structure. This was notably so in South Carolina where the lowland counties in 1790 reported almost three times as many

[1] La Rochefoucauld-Liancourt, *Travels*, II, 380.

[2] Ramsay, *South-Carolina*, II, 389-395.

[3] La Rochefoucauld-Liancourt, *Travels*, II, 379, 381; Morse, *American Universal Geography*, 683.

[4] Lambert, *Travels*, II, 163-164.

blacks as whites.[1] The Negro resisted the malaria of the moist rice fields and swamps much better than the white man, and he could be sacrificed, if need be, when yellow fever struck with epidemic force. As cotton spread into the uplands, the market for servile labor became wider and stronger. In 1790 only a fifth of the population of the South Carolina piedmont was colored; twenty years later the ratio had risen to a third. The retreat of the farmer who used only free white labor had already begun.[2] It was the Carolina rice planters who had blocked prohibition of the African slave trade in the Federal Constitution; and in 1803 the Carolina cotton planters took the lead in securing state legislation reopening the traffic.[3]

From the day the first Negroes were brought into Virginia there was persistent doubt, despite the hardening of custom into law, concerning the moral justification of hereditary bondage; and probably at no time were the slave owners themselves more deeply troubled than in the half-century after the Revolution. The system seemed peculiarly offensive in communities where liberty poles had but recently been raised and the "rights of man" were still much discussed at tavern and courthouse.[4] North of Maryland, as we have seen, this anomaly was slowly disappearing as gradual emancipation was written into state laws.[5] Though the Southern states, as well as the Northern, had eloquent opponents of slavery, the institution could not easily be modified in regions where climate, the routine production of staples

[1] Approximately thirteen hundred out of sixteen hundred heads of families in the rural counties of the Charleston district owned 42,949 slaves in 1790. Phillips, *Negro Slavery*, 95-96.

[2] Hooker, "Diary," 878, contains comments on the process by which large planters acquired and amalgamated small farms.

[3] Phillips, *Negro Slavery*, 136-138.

[4] Clement Eaton, *Freedom of Thought in the Old South* (Durham, 1940), 19-20.

[5] See earlier, chap. ii.

and large numbers of Negroes provided utilitarian arguments for its perpetuation.

Southern liberals at the close of the eighteenth century
were deeply impressed by the European philosophers of
the Enlightenment and desired to make their rationalistic
philosophy a force for social reform.[1] Yet their humanitarian program concerning slavery far outran their
actual achievements. Most of Virginia's great political
leaders agreed with George Mason, aristocratic owner of
Gunston Hall and three hundred blacks, who had written the state's bill of rights, that slavery was a slow
poison infecting the body politic. Jefferson rejoiced
that Chancellor George Wythe and St. George Tucker
were indoctrinating youthful abolitionists in the College
of William and Mary; he could not foresee that some
thirty years later Thomas R. Dew, from a professorial
chair in that same faculty, would formulate the historical
and theological justification of slavery.[2] The influential
liberals found strong supporters among the patrician
planters — many in Maryland and Virginia and a few
in South Carolina and Georgia — and for the generation
before 1800 they gave the stamp of social approval to
manumission; but in no Southern state were they able
to repeal those statutes without which slavery could not
long have survived.

The relation between master and man was not, in
the long run, to be determined by the libertarian doctrines of patrician planters or by the high ideals of humanitarian Quakers and other religious folk. More
influential was the achievement of those pioneers who

[1] St. George Tucker, *A Dissertation on Slavery with a Proposal for
the Gradual Emancipation of It in the State of Virginia* (Phila., 1796),
passim; George Buchanan, *An Oration upon the Moral and Political Evil
of Slavery* (Balt., 1793), 17-18; W. F. Poole, *Anti-slavery Opinions
before the Year 1800* (Cincinnati, 1873), 32-42.

[2] One of Wythe's most distinguished pupils was Henry Clay. Bernard
Mayo, *Henry Clay: Spokesman of the New West* (Boston, 1937), 78 ff.

went out and possessed the fertile river valleys between the Alleghanies and the Mississippi. This agricultural conquest of the West meant not the decline but the expansion of slavery — expansion into the pennyroyal districts of Kentucky, into the limestone basins of Tennessee and along the streams that watered the broad coastal plain as they flowed toward the Gulf of Mexico. Men of property were not numerous among these pioneers who first defied the menace of hostile Indians in order to seek new homes in the wilderness, and such property as they owned seldom included slaves. Yet the census of 1790 revealed that a sixth of the Kentuckians were Negroes. Already the tobacco planter had pushed his way through the mountain passes to escape the declining production of worn-out acres; and within a decade the cotton grower would start that steady advance into the fertile alluvial strips south of Tennessee, where the plantation system with slave labor was to dwarf all other forms of agriculture.[1]

Some Americans, observing the rapidity with which new states were admitted into the Union of the original thirteen, tried to analyze and describe this westward migration. Timothy Flint thought he could distinguish successive waves of settlers: first, the man with the gun, beating down old trails and blazing new ones in search of food and furs; second, the man with the ax, a descendant of those forest-farmers who had learned to cultivate their crops wherever the sun shone through the bare branches of girdled trees; then the man with the plow, eager to acquire tracts partly cleared, so that he might get forward more quickly with the routine of farming. To him, much more appropriately than to his predecessors, the term "settler" could be applied.

[1] Michaux, *Travels*, 75, 93-94; T. P. Abernethy, *From Frontier to Plantation in Tennessee* (Chapel Hill, 1932), 144-163; Phillips, *Negro Slavery*, 169 ff.

Finally came the man with the dollar. In a society where all were speculating on the rise in values which increased population would bring, he was peculiarly sensitive to opportunities for investing his capital, however small. Merchandising was usually the entering wedge, but it merely pried open the door to an undifferentiated activity in transportation, banking and manufacturing. Occasionally these variant types seemed to represent chronological stages in the process of settlement. More often migration was so rapid that their commingling became a distinctive aspect of frontier communities.[1]

During the 1790's Americans pushed up the Connecticut Valley into northern New Hampshire and Vermont, followed the Mohawk westward into central New York, floated down the Ohio from Pittsburgh, stopping more often on its southern than northern bank. Others deepened the ruts that gave uncertain accommodation to carts and wagons on the trails leading from Virginia and North Carolina into the valleys of eastern and middle Tennessee and north-central Kentucky. It is difficult, even with the aid of shaded population maps, to visualize the nature and extent of these frontier settlements. Crude huts strung along the river bank did not always become the nuclei of busy ports. Some areas were dotted with scattered clearings so few in number that isolation was a reality. Elsewhere there might be islands of detached but concentrated population, such as in the Blue Grass region of Kentucky. In the opinion of many travelers the most impressive feature of all the newly ten-

[1] Timothy Flint apparently encountered all these types in his travels. See his *Recollections of the Last Ten Years* (Boston, 1826). For excellent descriptions of these various types, see C. A. and Mary R. Beard, *The Rise of American Civilization* (rev. edn., N. Y., 1935), chap. viii. Many travelers commented on the homogeneity of the frontier population. Actually there was a considerable class of purposeless folk, carried along by the movement of the real pioneers.

anted districts was the speed with which the wilderness was compelled to yield to the requirements of a simple agrarian economy.

The process of becoming a landowner depended upon the locality which had caught the migrant's fancy. Before 1800 only a small minority settled directly on the public domain.[1] In that year Congress, accepting William Henry Harrison's proposals, liberalized the land law so that a prospective farmer could secure three hundred and twenty acres at two dollars an acre by paying one hundred and sixty dollars down and liquidating the balance over a period of four or more years.[2] Most frontiersmen, however, obtained their lands from the states or private speculators rather than from the federal government. In Tennessee, for example, nearly four million choice acres were entered by speculators under North Carolina's act of 1783. Pennsylvania's general land law of 1792 offered bona-fide settlers a chance to stake out claims at prices ranging from seven to twenty cents an acre, but the largest tracts were engrossed under warrants issued to land companies or other speculative operators.[3] The New England emigrant who liked the Genesee Valley in New York might strike a bargain with Theophile Cazenove, optimistic agent of that international syndicate, the Holland Land Company; or, if he preferred the river bottoms north of the Ohio, he found abundant opportunity to test his shrewdness by negotiating with the Ohio Associates at Marietta or the representatives of John Cleve Symmes in the

[1] Only fifty thousand acres, for example, were sold by the government under the land act of 1796. R. M. Robbins, *Our Landed Heritage* (Princeton, 1942), 17.

[2] Harrison was assisted by Albert Gallatin of western Pennsylvania. *Annals of Congress* (Wash., 1834-1856), 6 Cong., 1 sess., 209 ff.; *U. S. Statutes at Large*, II, 73.

[3] Abernethy, *From Frontier to Plantation*, 54; S. J. and Elizabeth H. Buck, *The Planting of Civilization in Western Pennsylvania* (*Western Pennsylvania Series;* Pittsburgh, 1939), 207.

vicinity of Cincinnati. A large part of Connecticut's Western Reserve had been granted to a company which pushed its sales by founding "Cleaveland" on Lake Erie in 1796.[1]

There was always the chance that eighty or a hundred dollars in cash would give one the right to clear a farmstead where water, timber and soil satisfied the most exacting demands. But for every such fortunate person there were scores of others — disillusioned victims, who had not properly discounted the land-company prospectuses; energetic speculator-farmers, seldom harvesting more than two crops in succession before they sold out and moved on; perennial squatters who managed to keep out of the way of surveyors; shiftless scratchers of the soil, who were content with open-faced cabins on inferior tracts, where inadequate drainage induced "the fevers" that sapped both strength and ambition. In general, the migrant farmer profited little from the competition among the large private companies, the states and the federal government to dispose of vacant lands. The net effect seems to have been confusion: uncertainty concerning titles, tardiness in making surveys, financial failure of prominent speculators and delay in providing transportation for remote settlements.

The universal symbol of the pioneer's first victory in his struggle against the encompassing forest was the erection of his cabin. West of the coastal towns the great majority of houses in 1790 were built of logs crudely notched and laid horizontally. Such a dwelling could easily be finished by half-a-dozen men in three or four days; and the cost was negligible, for the "raising" became a neighborhood enterprise enlivened by

[1] P. D. Evans, *The Holland Land Company* (Buffalo Hist. Soc., *Publs.*, XXVIII), 25-62; Ohio Company, *Records* (A. B. Hulbert, ed., Marietta, 1917), I, cxx-cxxv; B. A. Hinsdale, *The Old Northwest* (N. Y., 1888), 373-376.

Fig. 1. A Birch Canoe poled by an Indian.
2. A Birch Canoe paddled by Squaws.
3. A Baboose, or Indian Child.
4. A Log Fence.
5. Worm Fences.
6. Post and Rail Fence.
7. Virginia Rail Fence.
8. Dwelling House and Wings.

Plan OF AN AMERICA

M.ᶜ Intyre

NEW CLEARED *FARM*.

9. Barracks or Dutch Barn.
10. Barns rooffed with Singles.
11. Shade for Cattle to ly in Winter.
12. Shade for winning Indian Corn.
13. Fold for confining Cattle at night, &
in which they are milked.
14. A dwelling Log House covered with Bark.
15. An Indian Dog.

music, dancing and a tub of whisky. The cabins which Thomas Cooper saw in interior Pennsylvania in 1790 would accommodate a family, he thought, quite as well as the better cottages of England. He admired those that were sheathed with pine slabs and finished off inside with plain wainscoting, panel doors and glazed windows. They could be duplicated for one hundred and fifty pounds sterling, if one could get one's timber to a sawmill.[1]

But it was an exceptional frontiersman who spent much time on details within his cabin. If space permitted, there were two low-ceilinged rooms, one always dominated by the large fireplace, a sort of dictator of household routine. Chairs and tables revealed what could be done by inexpert hands with simple tools. A rough-hewn ladder gave access to the sleeping quarters, where there was sometimes space under the sloping roof for bed frames with rawhide or rope bottoms. Highly prized in every such household was that piece of furniture, perhaps a desk or a chest of drawers or a bedstead, which had been carried at great effort into the new country. It might be the only tangible link with that older community which had but lately been called "home." The simple furnishings of the frontier cabins indicate that in the westward migration the skilled artisans invariably sought the more populous towns.

A river, the first highway in every new area of settlement, was usually the dominant factor in the growth of towns. Along its banks appeared the initial commercial activities, housed at first in wood, but moving soon into buildings of brick and stone. Pittsburgh, where the colorful Conestoga wagon trains reached the headwaters of the Ohio, had fewer than four hundred

[1] Thomas Cooper, *Some Information Respecting America* (London, 1794), 51-52, 105-106; Isaac Finch, *Travels in the United States and Canada* (London, 1833), 318-319.

inhabitants in 1790, but a decade later its population
had increased fourfold. One visitor from the East was
so impressed that he described the town as "a reflex of
New York, the same earnest bustle in its business, and
that same national variety in its thickly thronging
strangers." [1] Among them were skilled artisans — cabi-
netmakers, cobblers, tailors, hatters, watchmakers and
silversmiths — as well as purposeful business men looking for investment opportunities. There was nothing
fortuitous about their coming. They had calculated the
potential profits in manufacturing enterprises which
could utilize Western materials to supply Western settlements at prices considerably below those charged for
Eastern imports. During the first decade of the nineteenth century they established glassworks, iron foundries, ropewalks and textile mills. Pittsburgh in 1810
bought seven hundred tons of spun yarn and hemp, a
hundred and twenty tons of cotton and ten tons of
tobacco from down river; and Zadok Cramer estimated
the town's annual trade at approximately a million dollars. Shipwrights were busy at the shipyards, and
carpenters along the principal streets. [2]

At the opening of the century the traveler who wished
to see the most active sector of the frontier would have
made arrangements at Pittsburgh for passage down the
Ohio and then down the Mississippi at least as far as
Natchez. Though he could not have looked forward
to a comfortable trip, there would have been compensa-
tions. "The *Ohio*," wrote Jefferson in his *Notes on
Virginia*, "is the most beautiful river on earth;" [3] and

[1] Quoted in Bucks, *Civilization in Western Pennsylvania*, 287.
[2] Fortescue Cuming, *Sketches of a Tour to the Western Country* (Pittsburgh, 1810), chap. xxxvii; Zadok Cramer, *The Navigator* (Pittsburgh,
1814), 17-20; L. D. Baldwin, *The Keelboat Age on Western Waters*
(Pittsburgh, 1941), 176-178.
[3] Thomas Jefferson, *Notes on the State of Virginia* (Phila., 1801), 15.

the settlers on its banks had scarcely marred the valley's natural beauty. So it appeared to John James and Lucy Audubon in the spring of 1808 as they floated downstream for the twelve days of their wedding journey to Louisville, Kentucky. On both shores the forest came down to the water's edge, its shadow broken here and there by the furrows of a newly plowed field. Overhead flocks of wild geese and ducks hurried northward to some lonely lake, their cries seeming to answer the shouts and songs of the boatmen. The ever changing face of Nature made the young voyagers forget the discomfort of a flatboat—crowded with farm implements, livestock and human beings—and the hazards of a river treacherous with shifting sand bars.[1]

But on many such journeys dangers other than those of navigation threatened the traveler and shipper. River pirates operated from small islands or secluded coves, while unscrupulous thieves, often in collusion with marauding Indians, lured boats into shore on the pretext that transportation was desired for passengers or goods. Sometimes the bargemen were in league with such plunderers.[2] Most of the transportation downstream was in flatboats, varying in length between twenty and one hundred feet, with the average vessel capable of carrying forty or fifty tons of produce.[3] They were usually classified according to their intended destinations or the type of goods they were designed to carry. On many an Ohio Valley creek "Kentucky" boats or "flour" boats

[1] For Audubon's description of the Ohio in 1810, see Maria R. Audubon, *Audubon and His Journals* (N. Y., 1897), II, 203-208.

[2] Cuming, *Sketches*, chap. xl; *Western Monthly Review*, III (1830), 354 ff.; O. A. Rothert, *The Outlaws of Cave-in-Rock* (Cleveland, 1924), 49-53, 157 ff.

[3] Primitive bull boats and pirogues continued to be used on the lower Ohio and Missouri, long after the keel boat and barge had become common on those streams, as well as on the Mississippi. Baldwin, *Keelboat Age*, 40-41, 44-47.

or "horse" boats were built and launched as soon as the rains had made the stream navigable.

A trend toward regional specialization in boat building early became apparent. The most important center was in the vicinity of Pittsburgh, along the Monongahela, the Allegheny and their major tributaries. Downstream, production was concentrated in Wheeling, Marietta, Cincinnati and Louisville, all destined to build ships of heavier tonnage as the commerce of the interior waterways increased.[1] As early as 1797 ships launched on the upper Ohio had reached the Atlantic and were engaged in the carrying trade out of Philadelphia.[2] In 1803 the brig *Dean*, which had been constructed on the Allegheny and had carried a cargo of cotton from a Cumberland River port to Liverpool, was described as "the first vessel which ever came to Europe from the western waters of the U. S."[3] No Western town had more extensive shipyards than those at Marietta. Some of the Ohio Company's first settlers were seamen and shipwrights from maritime New England, competent craftsmen who had learned much about the routes of world trade before they ever saw the banks of the Ohio. For a time it seemed as if they had hit upon the golden formula — abundant timber, cheap farm produce and high prices for ship and cargo in European markets — which would enable the Western river ports to surpass Philadelphia or Boston.[4]

Optimism was strong in the early years of the nineteenth century, but it represented the enthusiasm of

[1] A. B. Hulbert, "Western Ship-Building," *Am. Hist. Rev.*, XXI, 720 ff.; S. P. Hildreth, *Biographical and Historical Memoirs of the Early Pioneer Settlers of Ohio* (Cincinnati, 1852), 160, 161, 254, 309, 457.

[2] Francis Baily, *Journal of a Tour . . . in 1796 and 1797* (London, 1856), 330.

[3] Quoted in Baldwin, *Keelboat Age*, 164.

[4] By 1802 river shipments from Kentucky's settlements were estimated at $1,200,000 annually. 50 Cong., 1 sess., *House Exec. Docs.*, XX, no. 6, 182-183.

prospectors in a new country rather than sound financial calculation. As the shifting sand bars and turbulent rapids took a heavy toll of Western-built ships, so profitable markets were lost to the unpredictable ambition of Napoleon Bonaparte and to Great Britain's determination to maintain a balance of power in Europe. Many an Ohio River capitalist, long before the steamboat gained supremacy, came to the conclusion that building ocean-going vessels was of minor economic importance in comparison with handling cargoes which kept barge, keel and flatboat busy on the Mississippi and its navigable tributaries.[1]

It was this traffic, linking the frontier from western Pennsylvania to Louisiana and, in turn, binding it to the older part of the nation, which enabled the river towns to build steadily upon the production of the expanding agricultural districts. In 1800 no port between Pittsburgh and Natchez had as many as a thousand inhabitants, but the next decade brought rapid growth.[2] Over all these communities was the lingering mood of the backwoodsman, confident of the future and keen for any speculative enterprise. There was much that was coarse in the towns as well as throughout the countryside. Travelers commented on the incivility, boorishness, fighting and heavy drinking which they encountered, but the more discerning realized that in the settlement of any new country the rough would become rougher and that standards generally would decline.

The initial result of physical hardships wherever civilization met the wilderness was manifest in widespread

[1] C. H. Ambler, *A History of Transportation in the Ohio Valley* (Glendale, Calif., 1932), 73 ff.
[2] The largest settlement in this region, Lexington, Kentucky, was not a river town. In 1805 Espy thought that the "Main Street of Lexington has all the appearance of Market Street in Philadelphia on a busy day." Josiah Espy, *A Tour in Ohio, Kentucky and Indiana Territory* (Cincinnati, 1871), 8.

social leveling. Professional competence and craft skills were less highly esteemed when men were literally engaged in struggling for a living. For a brief period frontier society, as compared with the older communities from which its members had come, seemed to be singularly homogeneous. Men were equal, or nearly so, in challenging the natural forces which encompassed them. A sense of equality permeated their thinking about social relationships and was translated, somewhat imperfectly, into legal codes and political forms.[1]

On successive frontiers this phase of the transit of civilization seldom endured long. Social maturity, or at least the semblance of it, came quickly in crude settlements where pioneers were determined to conserve the best that they had known.[2] They had lost much but not all in the process of moving. Fortescue Cuming, commenting on life along the Ohio in 1807, found evidence on every side that the homogeneous frontier society was beginning to break up. Economic and political leadership was being assumed by men who had risen above their fellows, thanks largely to advantages which they had enjoyed in the communities whence they migrated. There were sons of Eastern land speculators, realizing profits from the unearned increment of town lots; Revolutionary officers whose recompense for former services had been commuted into Western acres; planters

[1] That this equalitarian influence did not break through all legal restraints on the propertyless appears in the constitutions of Kentucky (1792), Tennessee (1796) and Ohio (1802). See I. F. Patterson, *The Constitutions of Ohio* (Cleveland, 1912), 73-97, and B. H. Young, *History and Texts of the Three Constitutions of Kentucky* (Louisville, 1890), 9-48.

[2] There is much evidence in the histories of frontier towns, too numerous to list here, that the natural resources of the wilderness in the hands of acquisitive pioneers helped to create an economic aristocracy and that that aristocracy was essentially conservative in trying to reproduce the characteristics of the older communities whence its members had migrated. For a discussion of the acquisitive spirit of the West, see Abernethy, *From Frontier to Plantation*, 358-359.

who had exchanged farms in the tidewater for a chance
to work new and fertile soil with their slaves; merchants
sent out by Eastern houses, now able to establish independent stores; lawyers, well read in some preceptor's
office, advancing more rapidly than would have been
possible in any Eastern county.

The gap between the most prosperous and the least
fortunate seemed to be steadily widening. Alexander
Wilson, the ornithologist, noticed this during his travels
in 1810. The privations, which initially had been "the
offspring of necessity," became familiar habit with many
a squatter. While boasting loudly of the fertility of his
land, he was content to throw his seed into the ground,
neglect its cultivation, turn his hogs loose in the woods
and live on "pork, cabbages and hoe-cakes." His cabin
was often worse than a pigsty and his person ill-clothed,
dirty and diseased. "What a contrast," remarked Wilson, "to the neat farm and snug cleanly habitation of the
industrious settler[s] that opens their green fields, their
stately barns, gardens and orchards to the gladdened eye
of the delighted stranger!" [1]

Evidence of a rapidly maturing society was more impressive in the towns than in the rural districts. Lexington, though far from typical, stood as a symbol of
what could be accomplished within a single generation.
Situated in the heart of the Kentucky Blue Grass country,
Lexington in 1782 was little more than a military stock-
ade. A quarter-century later it had become the "Athens
of the West," with broad streets and substantial brick
houses, the seat of Transylvania University. Its three
thousand inhabitants supported a circulating library,
two newspapers and publishing houses, three boarding
schools for girls and five churches. The foreign merchandise handled annually by its twenty-two retail stores

[1] Alexander Wilson, "Letter from Lexington," *Port Folio*, n. s., III
(1810), 506.

was valued at over $300,000. More than a hundred small factories and artisans' shops produced cordage, sailcloth, cotton thread, nails, shoes, hats and furniture. Since this was much more than the local market could use, the surplus, together with the agricultural products of the countryside, supplied the Lower South or flowed out by way of the Mississippi into the channels of transatlantic trade.[1]

As commercial and industrial statistics revealed the growth of river ports and inland towns throughout the West, the opportunities for professional competence grew apace. More districts were able to furnish the support necessary for the specialized knowledge of the doctor or the lawyer. In 1790 Pittsburgh had two physicians; nine years later the number had risen to seven, two of whom had been trained in the Western country. Yet the degree of risk was still high for those who had the courage to carry to the frontier the elements of civilization. Faith played a mighty part in the westward transit of newspapers. In 1786 a Conestoga-wagon team had brought to the forks of the Ohio the press, type, ink and paper that were to make up John Scull's *Pittsburgh Gazette*. Here Fielding Bradford, who planned to assist his brother John in establishing a paper in Kentucky, learned something of the art of printing. Within a year John Bradford's flatboat, laden with another rude printing press and some type cut from dogwood, floated down the Ohio to the road which connected the river with the Kentucky metropolis. On Lexington's *Kentucky Gazette* worked a printer named Elihu Stout, who in 1804 dared to strap a press and type on pack horses and follow the trails that led to

[1] Cuming, *Sketches*, chap. xxvi. See also Bernard Mayo, "Lexington: Frontier Metropolis," E. F. Goldman, ed., *Historiography and Urbanization* (Balt., 1941), 25-29.

the little town of Vincennes deep in the old North-west.[1]

Many other pioneers of ideas and special competence were quite as daring. They were convinced that behind the thin edge of settlement, slowly cutting into the wilderness, the social soil was already prepared to sustain their particular specialties, that even on the frontier there were communities — literate, prosperous and expanding — where men and women would cherish the instruments and records of the human mind.

[1] J. C. Andrews, *Pittsburgh's Post-Gazette* (Boston, 1936), chap. i; R. G. Thwaites, "The Ohio Valley Press before the War of 1812-15," Am. Antiquarian Soc., *Proceeds.*, XIX, 310-311, 320, 345; Bucks, *Civilization in Western Pennsylvania*, 375, 378.

CHAPTER VII

THE CHALLENGE OF LIBERAL THOUGHT

DURING the early decades of its existence the United States of America was a highly dubious experiment. Political independence seemed more shadow than substance, for the encircling territories of Great Britain and Spain emphasized the new nation's economic and cultural dependence upon the European system from which it was striving to escape. With a domain stretching from the Atlantic to the Mississippi, between the Great Lakes and Spanish Florida, Americans faced the task, which many foreign commentators insisted was hopeless, of transforming particularistic British provinces into an enduring federal republic. Never had the attempt been made on so grand a scale.

Though the government was republican in form, it was far from democratic in spirit. Its leaders, with few exceptions, were of the older school of English liberalism and they believed that the theories of "the great Mr. Locke" had made clear the intimate connection between liberty and property.[1] If they thought of themselves as interested in the individual man, they were also aware that democratic license could produce such results as Rhode Island's fiat money and the Massachusetts uprising led by Daniel Shays.[2] Though they were committed by the logic of the Revolution to a government based

[1] C. E. Vaughan, *Studies in the History of Political Philosophy before and after Rousseau* (Manchester, 1925), I, 168-170; Merle Curti, "The Great Mr. Locke: America's Philosopher, 1783-1861," Huntington Library, *Bull.*, no. 11, 149-151.

[2] E. B. Greene, *The Revolutionary Generation, 1763-1790* (*A History of American Life*, IV), 38, 338-340.

on the consent of the governed, many remained skeptical
concerning democracy. Their republicanism was negative rather than positive. It is true that it embraced not
only hostility to monarchy and its attendant institutions,
but also distrust of any aristocracy which sought to
exploit the many for the benefit of the few. Even John
Adams, who was confident of the wisdom of the natural
aristocrats, was no believer in unlimited government by
wealth.[1] Yet there was little approval of equalitarian
doctrines.

In fact, this generation found it difficult to define the
proper bounds of its republicanism. In the attempt
much ink was spilled, for as men had differed in 1787
over the structure of the new government, so after 1790
they argued angrily over the manner in which it should
exercise its powers. Where were the limits beyond
which government ought not go lest it invade the rights
of the individual? How could property rights best be
protected? Could benefit for the many arise from special privilege for the few? Who should determine the
extent of the area in which the federal government was
competent to act?

Out of such questions arose differences of opinion
not unlike those which had marked the struggle over
the ratification of the Constitution. The division was
accentuated by the financial program of Secretary Hamilton, who found the new climate of opinion in commercial circles responsive to the needs of the rising capitalist order. Though he may have failed to understand
the deeply rooted prejudices of rural America, he appre-
ciated the fact that the common man throughout the
country still respected the gentleman. The day of the
tiewig aristocracy was waning but it had not yet closed.

[1] John Adams, *Works* (C. F. Adams, ed., Boston, 1850-1856), VI,
65; M. J. Dauer, "The Political Economy of John Adams," *Polit. Sci.
Quar.*, LVI, 546.

It was possible, therefore, to plan in terms of a philosophy which held that the masses would prosper if the interests of the rich and well-born were properly protected. Hostility to such an assumption rose slowly in a day when men were weary of strife and disorder, of business depression and political uncertainty.[1]

Furthermore, support of the Hamiltonian system stemmed in part from traditional Tory attitudes, and was one manifestation of the counter-revolutionary temper of the commercial groups whose business prospects had been steadily improving since the late autumn of 1787. Some observers sensed this situation. Writing to Richard Henry Lee in April, 1789, James Sullivan, who had just returned to Maine from a trip through the Middle and Southern states, expressed grave concern at the number of "anti-revolutionists" who had become politically active. He was convinced that they hated democracy, and he suspected they might attempt a drive for monarchy.[2]

On the other side, Fisher Ames, viewing the scene with characteristic alarm, commented on the "republican" minority in the first session of Congress. Some were former antifederalists, few in number and for the moment well disposed toward the new administration; others, proud in their local prejudices, feared lest the Eastern influence establish financial monopolies and enforce commercial regulations disastrous to both farmer and planter. Ames noted also the "new lights" in politics, who cherished a sublime faith in the people and placed the rights of man before the rights of property.

[1] See earlier, chaps. ii and iii. For the patrician direction of thought in the new republic, see Merle Curti, *The Growth of American Thought* (N. Y., 1943), 213-232.

[2] Thomas Amory, *Life of James Sullivan* (Boston, 1859), II, 391, 394. The sentiment in favor of monarchy is discussed by Louise B. Dunbar, "Monarchical Tendencies in the United States," Univ. of Ill., *Studies*, X, no. 1.

For them weak government was the safeguard of liberty.[1]

As Hamilton's measures became law, the opposition slowly took form. The well-disciplined Federalists, committed to business enterprise, sound finance and a vigorous foreign policy, faced a loose union of groups, known variously as anti-Federalists or Republicans, who cherished ideas of an agrarian republic, suspected the methods by which Hamilton had reached his objectives and resented the broadening of governmental powers so easily covered by the mantle of liberal interpretation of the Constitution. Like their opponents, they rejoiced in the establishment of the national credit and the enhancement of American prestige, but they felt that Federalist policies, however admirable the ultimate goal, were designed to exploit planters, farmers and laborers so that merchants, manufacturers and bankers might profit.[2]

What many vaguely perceived was stated with particularity by Colonel John Taylor whose mansion in Caroline County, Virginia, became a rendezvous for congressmen and other politicians traveling the main post road between Richmond and Philadelphia. He bitterly arraigned the "stock-jobbing interest in Congress" which held government securities and had invested in the bank; and he accused the Federalists of creating a new privileged class which might speedily outdo any aristocracy of the past — a class waxing strong at the expense of the agrarians out of whose pockets came every dollar made by Northern shippers, commission merchants and Hamilton's "paper" junto.[3] Thus, the "republicanism

---

[1] Fisher Ames, *Works* (Seth Ames, ed., Boston, 1854), I, 62.
[2] Analyses of the economic and social alignment appear in S. E. Morison, *Harrison Gray Otis* (N. Y., 1913), I, 46 ff., and C. A. Beard, *Economic Origins of Jeffersonian Democracy* (N. Y., 1915), 464 ff.
[3] *An Examination of the Late Proceedings in Congress* (Richmond, 1793); *A Definition of Parties* (Phila., 1794); *An Enquiry into the*

of the aristocracy of the Southern nabobs," to use Fisher Ames's words, arose out of self-interest as surely as did the Federalism of merchant-capitalists.

Though Republican leaders talked much of the rights of man, the phrase had chameleon qualities. It might mean the rights of "honest" farmers against their city creditors, as William Manning thought; or it might mean the rights of Virginia gentlemen against a domination of Northern business men, as John Randolph of Roanoke suggested.[1] If there were many who believed it meant the right of all men equally to share in government, their influence at the close of the eighteenth century fell short of their numbers.

No such leveling principle belonged to the political theory of Thomas Jefferson. "The people," whom he cherished, were not European mobs recruited from downtrodden peasants and exploited city workers. He thought and spoke in terms of the America of his day. A sound majority should be composed of farmers and villagers busy on their small freeholds or laboring earnestly to obtain such a stake in society. Social distinctions between the gentry and the others, or property qualifications for suffrage and officeholding, did not greatly disturb him. He had confidence that the politically active citizens in the United States would move steadily toward a more democratic system, for their domestic economy was relatively simple, being free from the complexities of Europe's stratified social arrangements.[2]

Principles and Tendency of Certain Public Measures (Phila., 1794). See also E. T. Mudge, *The Social Philosophy of John Taylor of Caroline* (N. Y., 1939), 145-146, and H. H. Simms, *Life of John Taylor* (Richmond, 1932), chap. iv. Taylor suspected a plot against Southern landholders by a coalition of Federalist and British commercial interests.

[1] William Manning, *The Key of Libberty* (S. E. Morison, ed., Billerica, Mass., 1922), 17-18; G. W. Johnson, *Randolph of Roanoke* (N. Y., 1929), 98.

[2] Thomas Jefferson, *Writings* (P. L. Ford, ed., N. Y., 1892-1899), VII, 356, 451. See also his First Inaugural.

More surely than Hamilton, Jefferson caught the spirit of the generation at the turn of the century. The former made use of a temporary reaction against popular excesses and economic maladjustments, while the latter based his philosophy upon that "fierce love of liberty" which Burke had once remarked. This it was which made him the great leader of the Republican forces.[1] In Virginia, Pennsylvania and New York local organizations had felt the quickening influence of his spirit and realized that his idealistic faith in humanity was tempered by a realistic sense of what was politically possible.[2]

The French Revolution made a momentous impact upon the direction of thought and action in the United States. As slow-sailing vessels brought belated news of the events of 1792 — the proclamation of the French Republic, the victory at Valmy and the November decree of the "war of all peoples against all kings" — American rejoicing became almost hysterical. Dispatches from Paris, published in the gazettes from Maine to Kentucky, stirred men's thoughts and filled their conversation.[3] In Savannah, Newport and Philadelphia there were dinners and balls, and the bands played "Ça Ira" and "Yankee Doodle." [4] In Boston the words "Liberty" and "Equality" were stamped on children's cakes, while merchants ostentatiously addressed one an-

[1] For the sources of Jefferson's political theory, see Richard Hofstadter, "Parrington and the Jeffersonian Tradition," *Journ. of the History of Ideas*, II, 391-400; Joseph Dorfman, "The Economic Philosophy of Thomas Jefferson," *Polit. Sci. Quar.*, LV, 98-121.

[2] George Cabot to Theophilus Parsons, Oct. 3, 1792, Theophilus Parsons, *Memoir of Theophilus Parsons* (Boston, 1861), 468-470; Alexander Graydon, *Memoirs of a Life* (Harrisburgh, 1811), 331-334; R. J. Ferguson, *Early Western Pennsylvania Politics* (*Western Pennsylvania Series*; Pittsburgh, 1938), 122-131.

[3] *National Gazette* (Phila.), Dec. 26, 1792; *Columbian Centinel* (Boston), Dec. 29, 1792; *Kentucky Gazette* (Lexington), Aug. 31, Nov. 16, 1793; C. D. Hazen, *Contemporary American Opinion of the French Revolution* (Johns Hopkins Univ., *Studies*, extra vol., XVI), 164-169.

[4] *Gazette of the United States* (Phila.), Feb. 9, 1793.

other as "citizen." At a great civic celebration the school children appeared in national cockades to watch their elders consume a huge roast ox, two hogsheads of punch and a cartload of bread in the name of the French Republic. "Citoyen S. Adams" presided over a more select banquet in Faneuil Hall.[1] The intensity and persistence of this feeling revealed a discontent which had been slowly spreading under the surface. Few could doubt that, whatever the outcome in Europe, the French upheaval had laid bare social antagonisms and democratic longings in America. It had given impetus and direction to the friends of the rights of man.

In equal measure it had aroused the friends of law and order to a sense of their danger. By 1794 there were many, like Noah Webster and the Reverend William Linn, who repented of their early enthusiasm for revolutionaries and turned to the defense of conservative principles. The Federalists classified all who disagreed with their philosophy of government as promoters of Jacobinical excesses.[2] Alexander Graydon complained of the "torrent of fanaticism" raging through Harrisburg and eastern Pennsylvania, with complete disregard for the "dictates of justice, humanity and consistency."[3] "There can be but two parties in a country," observed the editor of the Massachusetts Mercury, "the friends of order and its foes. Under the banners of the first are ranged all men of property, all quiet, honest, peaceable, orderly, unambitious citizens. In the ranks of the

[1] William Bentley, Diary (Salem, Mass., 1905-1914), II, 3; Justin Winsor, ed., Memorial History of Boston (Boston, 1880-1881), IV, 10-11.

[2] The conservatives were further alarmed by the influx of Irish rebels who joined French radicals in the Republican ranks. Rufus King, Life and Correspondence (C. R. King, ed., N. Y., 1894-1900), II, 481, 641-642. For the bitterness of the partisan controversy, see C. W. Upham, The Life of Timothy Pickering (Boston, 1873), III, 177-179; R. G. Harper, Select Works (Balt., 1814), 263 ff.; G. M. Dallas, Life and Writings of Alexander James Dallas (Phila., 1871), 195-197.

[3] Graydon, Memoirs, 339-340.

last are enlisted all desperate, embarrassed, unprincipled, disorderly, ambitious, disaffected, morose men." [1] He neglected to add, what Fisher Ames had already stressed, that one's choice may be determined, in part, by the nature of one's property interest. That consideration separated the seaport business men dependent upon British markets and London finance from most of the landholders of the frontier and slaveholding communities, who disliked all creditors, whether they were British or American. [2]

Stephen Higginson somewhat extravagantly insisted that French developments "drew a red-hot ploughshare through the history of America as well as through that of France." [3] Federalists became "Anglomen" or "Monarchists" while Republicans were denounced as "Francophiles" or "Jacobins." [4] An English traveler in 1794 asserted that he never took up a Western newspaper without finding violent abuse of his government, as if the editors wished to blow up the "hardly extinguished embers of the late war." [5] When the Federalist administration accepted Jay's treaty in 1795 as a settlement of the outstanding disputes with Great Britain, angry demonstrators in New York burned the treaty and hung Jay in effigy. Dr. Nathaniel Ames thought it were better the President's "hand had been cut off when his glory was at its height, before he blasted all his laurels." [6]

Standards of journalistic propriety sank lower as the

[1] Quoted in W. A. Robinson, *Jeffersonian Democracy in New England* (*Yale Hist. Publs. Miscellany*, III), 53.

[2] This cleavage had been pointed out by Ames in 1791. *Works*, I, 103-104.

[3] Stephen Higginson, "Letters," Am. Hist. Assoc., *Ann. Rep. for 1896*, I, 788 ff.

[4] *Aurora* (Phila.), July 2, 1796; May 22, 1797.

[5] William Priest, *Travels in the United States of America* (London, 1802), 56-57.

[6] *Aurora*, Aug. 22, 1795; Charles Warren, ed., *Jacobin and Junto* (Cambridge, 1931), 63.

political disputation grew more intense.[1] Probably at no period in American history unless it be immediately after the Civil War has the language of public controversy so constantly hovered on the verge of scurrility. John Fenno's hope that his *Gazette of the United States* might become the dignified journal of the "court party" soon vanished before the necessity of meeting the brilliant sarcasm of Philip Freneau in the *National Gazette* and the virulent abuse of Benjamin Franklin Bache in the *Aurora*.[2] In a generation which remembered the polemics of the Revolutionary era it was easy for party service to degenerate into vituperative attacks. From Europe came journalists already trained in the excesses of partisan warfare and political leaders seldom restrained them.[3] Country printers, imitating their city brethren, found their readers more amused than shocked by the batteries of slander. Bache's *Aurora* described even Washington as a cheat and an embezzler and, when the President retired from office, exulted that his name would cease "to give currency to political iniquity, and to legalize corruption."[4]

[1] In Philadelphia politics destroyed long-standing friendships, induced the boycotting of radical tradesmen and caused some gentlemen to arm themselves against personal aggression. Marriage across party lines was not always easy. George Logan, *Memoir of Dr. George Logan of Stenton* (Frances A. Logan, ed., Phila., 1899), 54-58.

[2] The *Gazette of the United States* was established in April, 1789, with financial support from Hamilton and other Federalists. Freneau's *National Gazette* was first published in October, 1791, after Jefferson had appointed him to a minor post in the state department. Bache founded the *General Advertiser*, later the *Aurora*, in the autumn of 1790.

[3] James Callender's reputation as a scandalmonger had been established in Scotland before he convinced Meriwether Jones of the *Richmond Examiner* that his work merited recognition; William Duane had been expelled from India by the British for seditious writings several years before he began to improve upon Bache's invectives in the *Aurora;* the *Gazette of the United States* had been a model of propriety in comparison with the billingsgate which William Cobbett, late from England, brought to the defense of Federalism in *Porcupine's Gazette.* Mary E. Clark, *Peter Porcupine in America* (Phila., 1939), *passim.*

[4] M. W. Hamilton, *The Country Printer: New York State, 1785-1830* (*N. Y. State Hist. Assoc. Ser.*, no. iv), chap. vi; C. A. Duniway, *The*

Beneath the swirling winds of journalistic controversy the structure and methods of politics were changing. The Federalist conception of a party as a well-disciplined army, dominated by a select group of officers who determined nominations and policies in the secrecy of local committees or legislative caucuses, was being challenged by Republican enthusiasts who unblushingly solicited votes from all who were qualified. "Jacobin emissaries," wrote Fisher Ames, "are sent to every class of men, and even to every individual man, that can be gained. Every threshing floor, every husking, every party at work on a house frame or raising a building — the very funerals are infected with brawlers or whisperers against government." [1] Reviving the techniques of American Revolutionary committees and stressing the social philosophy of Locke and Rousseau, the Republicans spun a web of Democratic Societies over the country. [2] Most of these clubs were organized after the arrival of the French minister, Edmond Genêt, in April, 1793, and recognized the close parallel between the aims of the Jacobin clubs in France and their own interest in American domestic and foreign policies.

The societies at Philadelphia, Charleston, New York and Lexington, Kentucky, led in spreading the doctrine that government officials were merely agents of the people and, as such, had no right "to prevent their employers from inspecting into their conduct as it regards the management of public affairs." [3] Membership was not limited by nationality or creed; Germans, Irish and

Development of Freedom of the Press in Massachusetts (Harvard Hist. Studies, XII), 143-144; W. G. Bleyer, Main Currents in the History of American Journalism (Boston, 1927), chap. iv.

[1] Ames, Works, II, 115.

[2] For their fight against neutrality, see Hazen, Contemporary Opinion, 196-200, and for their campaign to open the Mississippi, E. M. Coulter, "The Efforts of the Democratic Societies of the West to Open the Navigation of the Mississippi," Miss. Valley Hist. Rev., XI, 376-389.

[3] Aurora, Jan. 3, 1795.

French were prominent, though they were outnumbered by persons of English and Scotch ancestry. Many had been zealous patriots during the struggle with Great Britain, while others were too young to have played a part in that conflict. In Philadelphia the club minutes showed that half the members were artisans or mechanics, with only one in four either a merchant or a professional man.[1] The Federalists, recalling how well the earlier committees of correspondence had done their work, persuaded Washington to denounce all "self-constituted," secret, inquisitorial bodies.[2] Under presidential displeasure, as well as the stigma of sympathy with the "Whisky Rebels" in Pennsylvania, the membership and influence of the societies declined, but they had given political form to the Republicans and they left an important legacy of concern for a truly popular basis of government. "The collision of opposite opinions," wrote the Patriotic Society of New Castle, Delaware, "produces the spark which lights the torch of truth."[3]

If one fixes attention on the political clubs and the partisan press, it is easy to picture American society as servilely copying the quarrels of Europe. But the great majority of the people were attached to no country but their own. Cutting through the verbiage, a French observer reported that Republicans as well as Federalists accepted the Constitution, but that each group was learn-

[1] The most comprehensive account is E. P. Link, *Democratic-Republican Societies, 1790-1800* (*Columbia Studies in American Culture*, IX), which contains an analysis of membership in chap. iv.

[2] Washington's charges that the Democratic Societies were responsible for the Whisky Insurrection is not substantiated by the careful analysis in William Miller, "The Democratic Societies and the Whiskey Insurrection," *Pa. Mag. of History and Biog.*, LXII, 324-349.

[3] Link, *Democratic-Republican Societies*, 156. On the democratic attitude of Tammany societies, see E. P. Kilroe, *St. Tammany and the Origin of the Society of Tammany* (N. Y., 1913), 136, 138-139, 145, 194; M. W. Jernegan, *The Tammany Societies of Rhode Island* (Providence, 1897), 10-11, 14, 38; and W. T. Utter, "St. Tammany in Ohio," *Miss. Valley Hist. Rev.*, XV, 321-340.

ing how to use the document for its own designs.[1]   Ideas
concerning constitutional interpretation were still in flux.
The line between "strict" and "loose" constructionists
was meaningless, for circumstances constantly dictated
shifts across it, as New Englanders were to learn in the
first decade of the new century.   Though all accepted
the work of the Convention of 1787, few held that the
document was sacred.   The cult of the Constitution was
yet to be developed.[2]

Despite the dismay of the extreme Federalists as
Thomas Jefferson took office in 1801, most Americans
felt less apprehensive concerning the nation's future than
they had when George Washington became President.
Out of the tumultuous decade had come confidence in
severely tested processes of government.   Free discussion
seemed to bring that change which is necessary if government is to remain sensitive to the popular will.   Experience with the alien and sedition laws tended to con-
firm belief in freedom of speech, of the press and of
association, rights which the amendments to the Constitution in 1791 had specifically guaranteed.   The Virginia and Kentucky resolutions of 1798-1799, whatever their implications for the political theorist, had suggested that minority interests could be safeguarded without resort to violent revolution.   The rude electioneer-
ing of the Republicans had stirred many voters from their
apathy.[3]   In New England, where the proportion of

[1] Duke de La Rochefoucauld-Liancourt, *Travels through the United
States . . . in the Years 1795, 1796, and 1797* (London, 1799), II,
526-527.

[2] R. H. Gabriel, "Constitutional Democracy: a Nineteenth Century
Faith," Conyers Read, ed., *The Constitution Reconsidered* (N. Y., 1938),
247-248.

[3] For details of the Republican rise to political power in various states,
see D. R. Fox, *The Decline of Aristocracy in the Politics of New York*
(Columbia Univ., Studies, LXXXVI), chap. iii; W. R. Fee, *The Transition from Aristocracy to Democracy* (Somerville, N. J., 1933), chaps.
iii-iv; D. H. Gilpatrick, *Jeffersonian Democracy in North Carolina, 1789-
1816* (Columbia Univ., Studies, no. 344), chaps. ii-iv.

actual voters to the entire population was the lowest in
the country, activity at the polls increased notably.[1]
Rotation in office, based upon a belief in the need of
change, had challenged the long tenures characteristic of
many communities. Of course, annual elections did not
necessarily mean new incumbents, but they clearly de-
noted that the party system was not an evil and that no
governmental arrangement, however wise its sponsors,
should be permanent. The Federalists in their alarm
and the Republicans in their elation probably exaggerated the immediate significance of what Jefferson was
wont to call "the great revolution of 1800." Yet the
party with a creed had succeeded the party with a program, and that creed looked toward the establishment
of a more democratic way in America.[2]

There were no stauncher defenders of the old order
in politics and in religion than the Congregational
clergy of New England. Closely allied with merchants,
lawyers and the whole hierarchy of officialdom, they had
become accustomed to wielding political influence in the
interests of orthodoxy, to which they added Federalism
in the decade before 1800.[3] The compact groups in
Connecticut and Massachusetts, believing that they gov-
erned by divine right, were menaced by the rising democratic spirit.[4] Hence clerical voices quickly denounced

[1] Between the periods 1792-1797 and 1799-1802 the percentage for
Massachusetts rose from 3.9 to 7.4, for Connecticut from 2.8 to 5.6, for
New Hampshire from 3.4 to 6.7. See J. F. Jameson, "Did the Fathers
Vote?" *New England Mag.*, n.s., I (1889-1890), 484-490, and J. D.
Leutscher, *Early Political Machinery in the United States* (Phila., 1903),
25.

[2] Radical though this change was, it had been accomplished without
the violence that elsewhere marked the world-wide struggle of which the
Federalist-Republican battle was but one phase. See Link, *Democratic-
Republican Societies*, 41-43.

[3] R. J. Purcell, *Connecticut in Transition* (Wash., 1918), 319-323.

[4] Of Connecticut, John Adams wrote in 1808, "Half a dozen, or, at
most a dozen families, have controlled that country when a colony, as
well as since it has been a state." *Works*, VI, 530. The "Family Compact of Connecticut" is ridiculed in *Aurora*, Sept. 12, 1800.

the "atheism" of French revolutionaries and their Republican friends in America. From Charlestown, Massachusetts, Jedidiah Morse wrote of the "malignant aspect" which brooded over the country; he trembled in fear of a reign of American Jacobinism.[1] Timothy Dwight at Yale angrily questioned what the end of French influence would be: "Is it that we may change our holy worship into a dance of Jacobin phrenzy, and that we may behold a strumpet personating a Goddess on the altars of Jehovah?"[2] Some carried political controversy into the pulpit, which became a sounding board for party propaganda.[3] That their influence was potent is apparent from the bitter resentment of the Republicans, whose counteroffensive was weakened by their reluctance to be branded as enemies of religion and good morals.

Yet the social position as well as the religious authority of the clergy, even in rural New England, was waning. Among laymen they were no longer accorded the respect which had been theirs before the American Revolution. This they blamed upon foreign importations — English Deism and French rationalism — indiscriminately described as infidelism. Samuel Hopkins thought that infinite damage had been done to faith in Newport by the presence of the Allied troops during the American Revolution. Yet it would have been difficult for American officers to understand French infidelity; and most French officers were not followers of Voltaire.[4] It

[1] Jedidiah Morse, *Sermon on the National Fast, May 9, 1798* (Boston, 1798).

[2] Quoted in A. E. Morse, *The Federalist Party in Massachusetts to the Year 1800* (Princeton, 1909), 171.

[3] For examples, see David Osgood, *A Discourse Delivered on the Day of Annual Thanksgiving, Nov. 19, 1795* (Boston, 1795); Hezekiah Packard, *Federal Republicanism, Displayed in Two Discourses* (Boston, 1799); and David Tappan, *Christian Thankfulness Explained and Enforced* (Boston, 1795).

[4] Timothy Dwight, *Travels in New-England and New-York* (New Haven, 1821-1822), IV, 366.

is probable that early American Deism, like the English, owed as much to the indirect influence of Locke's essays, especially his *Letters on Toleration* and *The Reasonableness of Christianity*,[1] as it did to the direct impact of the Enlightenment.

However that may be, Deistical inroads were apparent late in the eighteenth century. President Charles Nisbet of Dickinson College complained that there were few who read the Bible or continued the custom of family prayers.[2] The Reverend William Linn of Rutgers College looked out upon a nation endangered by the decline of the family altar, the profanation of the Sabbath, the ostentation of those enriched in neutral trade, and the growth of infidelity.[3] Ethan Allen's coarsely written attack on the clergy may not have influenced many, but it betokened the direction of Deistic thought.[4] With revolutionary doctrines from the Paris faubourgs came French rationalism to reënforce this trend. Deistical clubs such as the "Theophilanthropists" in New York and the Druidical Society at Newburgh were formed, with many recruits enrolling from the Democratic Societies.[5] Students at Yale and Princeton took the names of favorite European rationalists, using them in preference to their own.[6] It was thought, though erroneously, that many were imitating that aggressive anticlerical or-

[1] H. M. Morais, *Deism in Eighteenth Century America* (Columbia Univ., *Studies*, no. 397), 16-17, 29, 35.

[2] Nisbet Papers, N. Y. Public Library, *Bull.*, I, 118-119.

[3] William Linn, *Discourse on National Sins* (N. Y., 1798). "Defections from the Platonic Christianity," Jefferson remarked, "are to Deism in Protestant countries and to atheism in Catholic countries." Adrienne Koch, *The Philosophy of Thomas Jefferson (Columbia Studies in American Culture*, no. 14), 28.

[4] *Reason the Only Oracle of Man, or a Compendious System of Natural Religion* (Bennington, 1784).

[5] J. W. Francis, *Old New York* (N. Y., 1865), 130-133; Morais, *Deism*, 133.

[6] Lyman Beecher, *Autobiography* (Charles Beecher, ed., N. Y., 1864), I, 43.

ganization, the Bavarian Illuminati.[1] With "youth in revolt" the earnestness of the rebels occasionally bordered on the absurd.[2]

In their attack on revealed religion the Deists pretended to be scientific, but they could launch no scientific attack except along Copernican lines, for their data were inadequate. The Rosetta Stone had not yet crushed the old chronology of Archbishop James Ussher; Sir Charles Lyell had not yet raised the curtain on the immense *Antiquity of Man;* modern biology had not yet brought its challenge against the separate-creation theory as it did, for instance, in Charles Darwin's *Origin of Species;* the critical apparatus of the Germans had not yet been turned against certain Scripture texts; the possibilities of the comparative method in studying the world's great religions were unexplored.[3] Deists, therefore, relied upon a "common-sense" exposure of revelation, supplemented in the manner of Voltaire by denunciation of the church as a social institution.

Their most popular apologist was Thomas Paine, whose *Age of Reason,* completed in 1796, created a greater sensation than his *Rights of Man.* It was largely a popularization of the older Deistical writers from the days of Lord Herbert of Cherbury to his own. Paine affirmed his belief in a God whose only revelation was "in the immensity of the creation" and "the unchangeable order by which the incomprehensible whole is governed." [4] There were some, though not many in Amer-

---

[1] See Vernon Stauffer, *New England and the Bavarian Illuminati* (Columbia Univ., *Studies,* LXXXIII, no. 1), *passim,* and J. K. Morse, *Jedidiah Morse, a Champion of New England Orthodoxy* (Columbia Studies in American Culture, no. 2), 51-58.

[2] "Striplings, scarcely fledged, suddenly found that the . . . light of wisdom had but just begun to dawn upon the human race." Dwight, *Travels,* IV, 376.

[3] D. R. Fox, *Ideas in Motion* (N. Y., 1935), 122.

[4] W. M. Van der Weyde, *The Life and Works of Thomas Paine* (New Rochelle, 1925), VIII, 43. *The Age of Reason* went through many edi-

ica, who recognized in this God of Nature the deity whom Jefferson had invoked in the Declaration of Independence. New York, Philadelphia and Baltimore were centers of rationalism, with active societies, frequent public addresses and periodicals. In the dissemination of tracts and cheap editions the Deists rivaled the Christian tract societies, and their influence extended far beyond a few seaboard cities. Travelers found French infidelity openly professed in western New York and western Pennsylvania, while Virginia earned the reputation, especially in the North, of being in the hands of skeptics and avowed unbelievers.[1]

In the eyes of professing Christians conditions had become alarming. The pulpits of Calvinism from Massachusetts to Kentucky thundered defiance, and the reverberations were heard for years.[2] Yet such sermons as Timothy Dwight's *Discourse on the Genuineness and Authenticity of the Old Testament* (1796) would not have been necessary for the generation which preceded or that which followed.[3] The "deistical fever" ran its course quickly, leaving not weakened but invigorated Christian sects behind it. Much that was regarded as French skepticism was probably little more than enthusiasm for French political liberalism. As the excesses of revolutionaries in France terrified some and the victories of Republicans in America satisfied others, Deism

tions, in which Moncure D. Conway counted more than 500 variations in the text.

[1] Anon., "The American Character," *Literary Mag. and Am. Register*, II (1804), 255; J. H. Hotchkin, *History of Western New York* (N. Y., 1848), 26; William Meade, *Old Churches, Ministers and Families of Virginia* (Phila., 1861), I, 29; Charles Nisbet to Charles Wallace, Sept. 2, 1790, N. Y. Public Library, *Bull.*, I, 118.

[2] Isaac Lewis, *The Political Advantages of Godliness* (Hartford, 1797); Jonathan Edwards, jr., *The Necessity of the Belief of Christianity* (Hartford, 1794), 12-14; N. H. Sonne, *Liberal Kentucky, 1780-1828 (Columbia Studies in American Culture,* III), 31-32.

[3] For attacks on Paine, see also S. S. Smith, *The Divine Goodness to the United States of America* (Phila., 1797), and Michael Hoge, *Christian Panoply; an Answer to Payne's 'Age of Reason'* (Phila., 1799).

declined. Philosophic rationalism could scarcely compete, except among intellectuals, with the emotionalism of evangelical religion.

More subtly subversive of traditional Christianity than the frontal attacks of European rationalism were the heresies which came to be known as Universalism and Unitarianism. In the transit of ideas the accident of the carrier is often of primary importance. So John Murray from London, thinking to bury his ruined life in the American wilderness, discovered that some persons in New England were ready for the gospel of universal salvation which he was under compulsion to preach. At Gloucester in 1779 and at Boston in 1793 he formed Universalist societies which became centers of his itinerant ministry. Within the precincts of Calvinism there was no doctrinal unity: Old Lights flared against New Lights, and the moderates strove to reconcile the position of these two groups while joining both in deep suspicion of the liberals among whom Unitarian teachings seemed to be gaining ascendancy. In such an atmosphere the heresy of John Murray at first seemed slight.[1]

Murray clung to the essential tenets of trinitarianism, but insisted "that *every individual* shall in due time be separated from sin, and rendered fit to associate with the denizens of heaven." [2] In 1791 at the New England General Convention of Universalists he met for the first time Hosea Ballou, who argued that society could well dispense with such doctrines as the deity of Jesus and human depravity. It was this form of Universalism which reached New Hampshire, Vermont and western New York in the wake of Ballou's successful preaching.

[1] John and Judith S. Murray, *The Life of Rev. John Murray* (new edn., Boston, 1870), *passim;* Richard Eddy, *Universalism in Gloucester* (Gloucester, Mass., 1892), *passim.*

[2] John Murray, *Letters and Sketches of Sermons* (Boston, 1812), I, 144.

The confession of faith adopted at Winchester, New Hampshire, in 1803 was broad enough to include his ideas, which within a decade dominated the first Universalist periodical, the *Gospel Visitant*, and represented the position of the Association.[1]

If Universalists thought that God was too good to damn a man, the Unitarians felt that man was too good to be damned. Long before an open break occurred in the ranks of Congregationalism, the ancient Socinian heresy had appeared among New England Calvinists.[2] The Boston Association was particularly affected, for James Freeman, having led the Episcopalians of King's Chapel in repudiating the doctrine of the Trinity,[3] busied himself with distributing Unitarian tracts and encouraging liberalism among the Congregationalists. By 1797 he reported that a "number of ministers . . . in the southern part of this state" were preaching Unitarian sentiments, while others were cautiously leading their hearers to embrace them.[4] Orthodox Calvinism was finding liberalism far more dangerous than French rationalism.[5]

In 1803 controversy came into the open, for Dr. David Tappan, Hollis professor of divinity at Harvard,

[1] J. C. Adams, *Hosea Ballou and the Gospel Renaissance of the Nineteenth Century* (Boston, 1903), 8-11; Richard Eddy, *Universalism in America* (Boston, 1884-1886), I, 354; II, 42-62; D. M. Ludlum, *Social Ferment in Vermont, 1791-1850* (Columbia Studies in American Culture, V), 26-30.

[2] G. W. Cooke, *Unitarianism in America* (Boston, 1902), 75, 80.

[3] See Greene, *Revolutionary Generation*, 370.

[4] Morse, *Jedidiah Morse*, 82-83. The orthodox in New York City were disturbed by a series of Unitarian lectures in 1794. S. I. Pomerantz, *New York, an American City, 1783-1803* (Columbia Univ., *Studies*, no. 442), 391.

[5] The trend of liberal thought appears in William Bentley, *Sermon Preached at Stone Chapel* (Boston, 1790), 21. Boston merchants, concentrating on profitable commerce, were not inclined to quarrel with Bentley's contention that "virtue alone secures heaven." His *Diary* traces the development of an emphasis upon a benevolent system of morals as the road to salvation.

had died and the conservative clergy were determined that no unorthodox person should replace him. The liberals in Boston proposed the name of Henry Ware, pastor at Hingham, whose Unitarian leanings were pronounced, even if he did not accept the humanitarian view of Christ. After a protracted struggle, in which the opposition was belligerently led by the Reverend Jedidiah Morse of Charlestown, Ware was appointed in 1805. Within a few months Professor Samuel Webber succeeded the deceased Joseph Willard as president, and Harvard was lost to the Calvinists. Some thought that the loss had occurred when the works of Priestley, Toulmin, Price and other English Deists had first been received into the college library.[1]

Liberalism, though triumphing at Harvard, won few notable victories beyond the borders of eastern Massachusetts during the first decade of the nineteenth century.[2] However democratic in its implications, it failed to stir the popular imagination. Even the colleges were apathetic or resistant. In New Haven, Timothy Dwight rejoiced at the renewed interest in the Scriptures, while he marshaled the forces of Congregationalism and Presbyterianism in Connecticut to support the standing order. Throughout the Atlantic Seaboard, especially among the Presbyterians of the Middle and Southern states, there was a growing determination to combat heretical teachings.[3]

In Kentucky, where Republican political philosophy became manifest in a state constitution providing for

[1] Sidney Willard, *Memoir of Youth and Manhood* (Cambridge, 1855), II, 117. For the Harvard controversy, see Morse, *Jedidiah Morse*, 82-100.

[2] For religious liberalism in Vermont, see Ludlum, *Social Ferment*, 31-33.

[3] *Evangelical Intelligencer* (Phila.), II (1808), 417; G. P. Fisher, *Life of Benjamin Silliman* (N. Y., 1866), I, 83; Elizur Goodrich, "Revivals of Religion in Yale College," Am. Educ. Soc., *Journ.*, X (1838), 289 ff.; C. E. Cuningham, *Timothy Dwight* (N. Y., 1942), 328-334.

universal manhood suffrage, liberal theology had strong supporters. Though various shades of heterodoxy existed, none exerted more influence than that associated with Unitarianism. Its ablest exponents were Harry Toulmin, son of Joshua Toulmin, the English Unitarian leader, and Augustin Eastin, a former member of the Elkhorn Baptist Association. Supported by such politicians as Governor James Garrard, Senator John Breckinridge and John Bradford, publisher of the *Kentucky Gazette,* who had fought in Virginia for the act establishing religious freedom, they dominated Transylvania Seminary for a decade after 1794, and for a generation carried on a struggle with the champions of orthodoxy for control of education in the state.[1]

Here, as in many other sections, the Presbyterians with their high regard for an educated clergy, their strong dogmatic emphasis and their middle-class constituency assumed the lead in intellectual conflict. Baptists and Methodists, on the other hand, eager to meet the spiritual needs of unlettered folk, strove to overcome the easy morals of frontier communities rather than to combat heterodox speculations. The contrast was dramatically revealed in the Great Revival. Though it first became manifest in Presbyterian churches, the Methodists and Baptists nurtured it and secured its best fruit.[2]

The Western revivals, unlike the quiet return to religion in Eastern villages early in the nineteenth century, were marked by phenomena which seemed distinctively American. In fertile river valleys against the background of forest and hills, preachers and people grappled clumsily but earnestly with an ancient problem, man's rela-

[1] Sonne, *Liberal Kentucky,* 33-44.
[2] R. H. Bishop, *An Outline of the History of the Church in the State of Kentucky* (Lexington, 1824), 76 ff.; W. B. Posey, *The Development of Methodism in the Old Southwest* (Tuscaloosa, Ala., 1933), 13 ff.; W. W. Sweet, ed., *The Baptists, 1783-1830* (same ed., *Religion on the American Frontier,* N. Y. and Chicago, 1931-1939, I), 20-21, 44.

tion to the unseen world, and its corollary, man's fortunes in eternity. It was drama on a grand scale. The participants, many of them Scotch-Irish acutely conscious that they had fallen far short of the standards set by Calvin and Knox, were of energetic stock, intense and quick to respond. The content of their religious meditations has been captured in the words of an old hymn:

> My thoughts on awful subjects roll,
> Damnation and the dead;
> What horrors seize a guilty soul
> Upon a dying bed![1]

Cowards they were not, yet they lived in perennial fear of dangers — the caprices of Nature, Indian attacks, the scourge of starvation, illness without benefit of medical aid. The terrors of hell they found easy to imagine. Most of them were lonely, especially the women, starving for human contacts and exciting incidents. Some were exiles from civilization: weaklings and criminals, who lacked self-control and fell easy victims to cumulative suggestion. Out of such lives came the emotional extravagances of the frontier revivals, miraculous to some, fantastic to others.

Beyond the Blue Ridge itinerant preachers in the generation after the Revolution followed settlers from Virginia and the Carolinas who had not entirely forgotten the tradition of George Whitefield.[2] Few in number, they resorted to union meetings, regardless of denominational affiliation; and such coöperative activity was a precursor of the revivals.[3] In 1796 there came into the beautiful Cumberland country from North Carolina a

[1] F. M. Davenport, *Primitive Traits in Religious Revivals* (N. Y., 1905), 99.

[2] See J. T. Adams, *Provincial Society, 1690-1763* (*A History of American Life*, III), 284.

[3] W. H. Milburn, *The Pioneers, Preachers and People of the Mississippi Valley* (N. Y., 1860), 356.

Presbyterian minister, James McGready, who assumed charge of three small congregations in Logan County, Kentucky, on the Gaspar, Red and Muddy rivers. Known at the time as "Rogues' Harbor," Logan County had more than its share of horse thieves, counterfeiters, robbers and murderers. McGready's preaching, with its emphasis on the wrath of an angry God, converted many, but these, as he later wrote, were "like a few scattering drops before a mighty rain, when compared with the overflowing floods of salvation" in 1800.[1]

In June of that year the Red River churches became the scene of unusual excitement occasioned by the preaching of the brothers McGee — John, who was a Methodist, and William, a Presbyterian. Enthusiasm spread rapidly through Kentucky and Tennessee, into the scattered settlements across the Ohio, and along the river valleys from western Pennsylvania to western South Carolina. Deeply moved by what he had seen in Logan County, Barton W. Stone carried the word into Bourbon County. There in August, 1801, a sacramental meeting was attended by a crowd variously estimated at from ten to twenty-five thousand. Eighteen Presbyterian ministers, as well as Baptist and Methodist preachers, were present, all preaching or exhorting "the distressed with more harmony than could be expected." Many worshipers remained from Friday until the following Thursday. "When a person is struck down," wrote one eyewitness, "he is carried . . . out of the congregation, when some minister converses with, and prays for him; afterwards a few gather around and sing a hymn suitable to his case. The whole number brought to the ground, under convictions, were about 1,000, not less." [2]

[1] "A Short Narrative of the Revival of Religion in Logan County," N. Y. Missionary Mag., IV (1803), 154.
[2] Catherine C. Cleveland, The Great Revival in the West, 1797-1805 (Chicago, 1916), 79-80.

After 1800 the camp meeting became a regular feature among Western Methodists and Baptists. In a region where large towns were few and the roads leading to them poor, it was necessary to hold such a religious fair in order to accommodate the crowds. The gathering usually assembled near some church, which might afford lodging for visiting clergy. After a rude platform had been constructed at one end of a near-by clearing, planks were laid across the tree stumps to furnish seats for some of the multitude. Around the edges of the space the wagons and tents, arranged in somewhat irregular rows, gave the appearance of a village sprung up in the forest. At night, blazing bonfires, lamps suspended from the trees and hundreds of flickering candles in the tents illumined the scene. "The uncertain light upon the tremulous foliage . . . the solemn chanting of hymns swelling and falling on the night wind; the impassioned exhortations; the earnest prayers" kindled the highly emotional. Weeping and sobbing gave way to shouts and shrieks; some were seized by the "jerks," their bodies torn by convulsions; others fell to the ground as in a trance, to lie for hours while friends sang and prayed over them. Occasionally barks were heard from those caught up in the exercise popularly known as "treeing the devil," or the "holy laugh" rang out, high-pitched and mirthless.[1] If falling was the most prevalent of these outbursts, jerking was the most spectacular.[2] To some these manifestations were the miracles of Protestantism.

Contemporary observers differed as to the influence of the Great Revival and the lesser ones which immedi-

---

[1] Cleveland, *Great Revival*, 60 *n.*, 88; P. G. Mode, *Frontier Spirit in American Christianity* (N. Y., 1923), 54; review of Z. M. Pike's *Account of a Voyage up the Mississippi River*, Medical Repository, X (1806-1807), 379.

[2] Peter Cartwright, *Autobiography* (W. P. Strickland, ed., N. Y., 1857), 48-51.

ately followed it. Some insisted that piety had overcome profligacy, while blasphemers, liars and drunkards
had forsaken their irreverent ways. Tangible results
appeared in the records of the evangelical denominations.
While the revival was at its height the Methodist membership in the Western Conference more than tripled. In
Kentucky alone the Baptists reported that during the
three years after 1800 approximately ten thousand converts were received.[1] New leaders rose up to carry the
gospel wherever the thin edge of settlement was pushing
up the river valleys—such men as Finis Ewing, seeking
out the religiously destitute in Kentucky and Tennessee;
James B. Finley, versed in forest lore, forsaking his dogs
and guns to go in search of souls; Peter Cartwright,
turning from cards and horse racing to become a lusty
exhorter in communities which Francis Asbury had once
visited; and Lorenzo Dow, "eccentric cosmopolite,"
leaving trans-Appalachia to carry the camp-meeting idea
into the English conventicle movement.[2]

Evangelism had its critics as well as its heroes. The
Presbyterians particularly scorned the hysterical outbursts. Falling, jerking, rolling and barking, they insisted, indicated that a doctor, not a preacher, was
needed. Moreover, the wholesome intercourse of
friendly family groups at the camp meeting, which has
played so large a part in the American tradition of public
gatherings, was sometimes marred by obscene conduct
and sexual irregularities which raised ugly doubts concerning the spiritual gains. In crowds so highly charged
with emotion it was not difficult for vagrant men and
women of easy virtue to cloak their vices in the respectable garb of religious ardor.

[1] Cleveland, Great Revival, 131, 148. But the Presbyterians lost members. Ibid., 146-147.
[2] J. B. Finley, Autobiography (W. P. Strickland, ed., Cincinnati,
1854), chaps. vii-x; Lorenzo Dow, The Eccentric Preacher (Lowell,
1841), 91-97; C. C. Sellers, Lorenzo Dow (N. Y., 1928), 113-115.

Some feared the misguided zeal of the converts. They were apt to be intolerant of sectarian regulations and, unhappy under the compulsion of theological dogma, ready recruits in factional quarrels. When the Presbyterian general assembly of 1809 refused to permit "illiterate exhorters" to shepherd the pastorless congregations of the Midwest, the Cumberland presbytery established an independent Cumberland Presbyterian Church, highly evangelical in method. At the same time there was developing in north-central Kentucky a dispute over the universality of salvation, which led Barton W. Stone and his associates to proclaim their rejection of all creeds, their reliance upon the Scriptures alone as the basis of Christian fellowship and their determination to strive for interdenominational unity. Assuming the name "Christian Church," they found a gratifying response in Kentucky and Ohio among former Baptists and Methodists.[1] Local congregations occasionally united with the Campbellites, followers of Thomas and Alexander Campbell, who had revolted against the sectarian exclusiveness of the Scotch Presbyterian Synod in southwestern Pennsylvania. From 1813 to 1830 they were ostensibly affiliated with the Baptists, though their views more nearly conformed to those of the Christian Church. No union occurred, however, and the Campbellites gradually emerged as the Disciples of Christ.[2] Thus religious leaders who were sworn foes of sectarianism sponsored movements which resulted in the creation of two new sects.

Americans who feared that uneducated exhorters ministering to the multitude might breed popular scorn of sound learning mistook the temper of their generation. An education was the goal of an increasing number,

[1] C. C. Ware, *Barton Warren Stone* (St. Louis, 1932), chap. xi.
[2] Alexander Campbell, *Memoirs* (Robert Richardson, ed., 2 vols. in one, St. Louis, 1868), I, chaps. xx-xxi; II, chaps. i-ii.

though many a boy at the beginning of the nineteenth century found it more difficult to obtain than had his father or grandfather. This did not arise from indifference on the part of political and religious leaders. In some communities it resulted from the limitations of a frontier environment; in others, it reflected the decline of education through the new apprenticeship which accompanied the growth of factories. Except for sections of New England, education in America, as in Europe, had always been a function of the family and the church. The creation of a republican government emphasized public responsibility for the instruction of youth, but the transition from private and parochial control to state support was slow and awkward. There was no lack of enthusiasm. It was a time of unbounded confidence in the regenerative power of education, of enthusiastic belief in the perfectibility of man and the perennial progress of the human race. The "nature of man points him to improvement," wrote Nathaniel Chipman, echoing the philosophers of the Enlightenment.[1]

"A people who mean to be their own governors," James Madison argued, "must arm themselves with the power which knowledge gives."[2] Education, therefore, could not remain the privilege of the few; it must become the possession of the many. Little doubt existed concerning objectives. Most educational reformers wished to end cultural dependence upon Europe, create an American social consciousness and inculcate patriotic devotion to the new nation.[3] It was high time, thought Robert Coram, to check all blind adherence to transatlantic poli-

---

[1] Nathaniel Chipman, *Principles of Government* (Rutland, 1793), 99.

[2] E. P. Cubberley, *Public Education in the United States* (rev. edn., N. Y., 1934), 90.

[3] James Sullivan (*pseud.*), *Thoughts upon the Political Situation of the United States* (Worcester, 1788), 18-21; Benjamin Rush, *Essays, Literary, Moral & Philosophical* (Phila., 1798), 7, 10-12; Lafitte du Courteil, *A Proposal to Demonstrate the Necessity of a National Institu-*

Browere's Thomas Jefferson

School Discipline

cies and to reject every European idea that would hamper human thought.[1] Benjamin Rush, who held a degree from the University of Edinburgh, agreed with Thomas Jefferson, graduate of the College of William and Mary, that American boys should not be educated in Europe. Rush feared that their minds would be poisoned against political democracy, while Jefferson doubted that America would accept foreign-trained leaders.[2] There were even suggestions that a prohibition be erected against American youth enrolling in European universities. Had it been taken seriously, an insignificant number would have been affected during the quarter-century after 1790.

Probably no educator in this generation was so determined as Noah Webster that the thought and action of his countrymen should have a distinctively American cast.[3] "As soon as he opens his lips," so ran Webster's prescription for the education of an American, "he should rehearse the history of his own country; he should lisp the praise of liberty, and of those illustrious heroes and statesmen who have wrought a revolution in her favor." [4] Education was the mold in which the national character would be formed and Webster labored mightily to help determine the pattern. This inspired much of his arduous work on his spellers and dictionaries, for he believed that uniformity in the pronunciation and use of words would break down provincial distinctions and

tion in the United States of America for the Education of Children of Both Sexes (Phila., 1797), 6, 23.

[1] Robert Coram, Political Inquiries (Wilmington, 1791), 98-99. See also A. O. Hansen, Liberalism and American Education in the Eighteenth Century (N. Y., 1926), 48-63.

[2] Jefferson, Writings, I, 467-468. But many Republican leaders had been born and educated in Europe.

[3] For the schoolbooks he prepared with this purpose in mind, see Greene, Revolutionary Generation, 374-375, 386-387.

[4] Noah Webster, A Collection of Essays and Fugitive Writings (Boston, 1790), 23.

that a simplified and regularized orthography would promote nationalism. His grammar included many examples of American prose writings, especially those dealing with the Revolution.[1]

There was substantial agreement among the articulate theorists that an educational system adequate for the United States should be national in scope and nationalistic in emphasis.[2] Samuel Knox, principal of Frederick Academy in Maryland, received an award from the American Philosophical Society for an essay which stressed the necessity of teaching youth to submerge sectional prejudices. Samuel Harrison Smith, editor of the Jeffersonian *New World* and founder of the *National Intelligencer,* proposed an extensive system of public schools. Less insistent than Knox upon uniformity in textbooks and curricula, he urged his country to take the best from all lands and use it for the world's benefit.[3] At the top of the ideal educational system stood the national university, a subject of much wishful thinking. Washington and Madison warmly indorsed the idea, the latter maintaining that a national "seminary of learning" could be established out of funds available from land sales in the District of Columbia.[4] In response, Dr. Samuel Latham Mitchill of New York prepared an elaborate report on the way in which a central school at the seat of government could roll "the flood of useful information throughout the land"; but he found no constitu-

[1] E. C. Shoemaker, *Noah Webster, Pioneer of Learning* (N. Y., 1936), 187-188; H. R. Warfel, *Noah Webster, Schoolmaster to America* (N. Y., 1936), 59-60.

[2] Merle Curti, *The Social Ideas of American Educators* (Comn. on Social Studies, *Report,* X), 47-48. Sectional prejudices were far too strong for any broadly national system of schools.

[3] Samuel Knox, *An Essay on the Best System of Education* (Balt., 1799); S. H. Smith, *Remarks on Education* (Phila., 1798).

[4] G. B. Goode, *The Origin of the National Scientific and Educational Institutions of the United States* (N. Y., 1890), 15-19.

tional warrant for such an appropriation of national funds.[1] Similar constitutional scruples may explain why Jefferson worked out the plans for his university in the state of Virginia.

Educational performance during the quarter-century after 1790 lagged far behind theory. John Adams might insist that the instruction of children of every rank and class, down to the lowest, was a public responsibility, but few taxpayers were eager to underwrite either a national or a state system of schools open to all without tuition. That legislators were aware of new forces demanding the democratization and secularization of education is apparent from the statutes which they enacted. But legal phrases did not describe actual conditions. The Massachusetts legislature, for example, in 1789 recognized the discrepancy between expectation and performance by providing that towns, which had long been obliged to establish elementary schools wherever there were one hundred families, might in the future defer such provision until the number of families had increased to two hundred.[2] Of the sixteen commonwealths in 1800, seven had written into their constitutions general statements concerning the state's duty to educate the people, but the laws to particularize such generalities were of various sorts. In New England the district schools were largely supported either by local taxes or, as in the case of Connecticut, by proceeds from the sale of Western lands. In the Middle Atlantic states public funds generally went to private or parochial schools to supplement their slender resources, or to charity societies which sponsored educational work for the poor. In the South some states diverted revenues from

[1] S. L. Mitchill, "Proceedings Relative to a National University," *Medical Repository*, XV (1811-1812), 122-126, esp. 124.
[2] *Laws of Massachusetts* (1807), I, 469-473.

lotteries and license fees into "literary funds" to be used for school purposes.

Despite the volume of legislation between 1790 and 1815 no part of the country had a comprehensive school system except on paper. Most of the laws were temporary expedients or were not enforced. Virginia, for instance, in 1796 authorized three "aldermen" in each county to set up districts, employ teachers and construct schoolhouses where all free children, male and female, might receive instruction without cost for three years; five years later not a single county had acted.[1] Delaware's legislature of 1796 directed that for ten years the money received from tavern and marriage licenses should be used for the erection of local schools, but within a year the legislators repented and devoted most of the revenue to other purposes.[2] The general common school law of 1795, whereby New York appropriated twenty thousand pounds annually to be allotted to counties which voluntarily raised amounts equal to one half of the state grant, remained in effect only five years. Not until 1812 did a law inaugurate a permanent state subsidy for elementary instruction.[3]

The district schools which received public support were "free" only in the sense that no white child was excluded because of the family's social position or financial status. The local taxes, even when supplemented by state subsidy, seldom sufficed to pay the teacher's salary, purchase fuel and other supplies and maintain the schoolhouse in serviceable condition. Whatever additional sum was needed to balance the annual budget

[1] General Assembly of Virginia, *Collection of Acts* (1803), 354-355; James Monroe, *Writings* (S. M. Hamilton, ed., N. Y., 1898-1903), III, 309.

[2] *Laws of Delaware* (1797), II, 1296-1298, 1352-1354.

[3] *N. Y. State Laws*, 18 sess., Apr. 9, 1795, ch. 75; also 35 sess., June 19, 1812, ch. 242. In 1812 Gideon Hawley became first state superintendent of common schools in the country. Cubberley, *Public Education*, 215.

was assessed against the families of the district according to the number of youths of school age. Parents unable to meet the rate bill were usually permitted to enroll their children with the understanding that they were "charity pupils." In Pennsylvania this stigma was made official by the preparation of a special list of those who requested exemption from payment. Throughout the rural districts, and to some extent in the cities, this regulation resulted in keeping many poor children away from school.[1]

In the cities the educational facilities for the poor were still largely provided by private and sectarian charitable associations, which occasionally received assistance from state or municipal treasuries. In 1801, for example, the free charity schools of eleven Protestant religious societies in New York City benefited from moneys which had become available under the law of 1795, and an equal amount was granted several years later to the school maintained by the Catholic Church. But it was chiefly children without church connections who were in need of free schooling. Their plight prompted the organization of nonsectarian groups which proceeded to mobilize benevolence for this purpose. Schools for both boys and girls were established in Philadelphia, Baltimore, New York and other cities.[2]

Among New York's benefactors were Thomas Eddy and John Murray, jr., members of the Society of Friends, who successfully sponsored the incorporation in 1805 of the Free School Society. Convinced that education was the best barrier against social unrest among the laboring poor, the leaders, under the presidency of De-Witt Clinton, announced that they would not only in-

---

[1] As late as 1835 there were more than 200,000 children, from five to fifteen years of age, who attended no school. F. T. Carlton, *Economic Influences upon Educational Progress in the United States, 1820-1850* (Univ. of Wis., *Econs. and Polit. Sci. Ser.*, IV, no. 1), 103.

[2] Pomerantz, *New York*, 422-423, 426.

culcate moral and religious truth without sectarian bias, but would also teach what was "essentially requisite for the due management of the ordinary business of life." In this venture private philanthropy soon received the aid of state and municipal appropriations, and the society became an important factor in the transition from private to public support of elementary schooling as well as in the secularization of instruction.[1]

Education beyond the elementary subjects depended chiefly upon private enterprise — upon clerical tutors, preparatory schools or tuition academies. In New England the Latin grammar school of colonial days, with its emphasis on college preparation, was being challenged by the academy. At Andover, Massachusetts, and Exeter, New Hampshire, there were models which other institutions with small endowments and no comparable prestige strove to copy. By 1815 Massachusetts had thirty academies and New York thirty-seven. South of Pennsylvania the progress was even more rapid. As early as 1783 Georgia had undertaken to establish one in each county. The academies varied widely in organization and control, and their educational programs expanded rapidly. Many were founded upon endowments raised solely by popular subscription or by generous gifts of a few philanthropists; some drew their support from particular religious sects; still others obtained public subsidies in addition to private funds. In New York, for example, the act of 1787 authorized the board of regents to incorporate academies and those which met state requirements received periodic appropriations from the state.[2] In some communities academy students ranged

[1] W. O. Bourne, *History of the Public School Society of the City of New York* (N. Y., 1873), 4 ff. For the later developments, see C. R. Fish, *The Rise of the Common Man, 1830-1850* (*A History of American Life*, VI), 202, 219.

[2] G. F. Miller, *The Academy System of the State of New York* (Albany, 1922), 21-22.

from boys and girls who had just learned to read to young men ready to enter college.

As late as 1830 public support of education was still largely "a gift to the destitute." This was as true of the Western states as of the slaveholding South.[1] In view of the provision in the land ordinance of 1785 setting aside the sixteenth section of each township in the Northwest Territory for public schools, the rapid development of a common-school system might have been expected. But not until 1824 did a reluctant Ohio legislature face the problem of how such a system could be created out of mere land grants. So it was in the sister states. Indiana in 1816 and Illinois in 1825 permitted the electors in each county to tax themselves for the maintenance of schools free to all, but few counties actually took advantage of the opportunity. The sale or leasing of land to pay the tuition of poor children at private schools was not abandoned until after 1830.

The secularization of education likewise proceeded slowly.[2] Eighteenth-century skepticism, as we have seen, had been largely overcome by the emotionalism of the revivals. The upswing of religious sentiment influenced the schools and in turn gained new strength from them. Not only did the churches maintain considerable supervisory power over elementary education — in Connecticut, for example, the schoolmaster had to be certified by the nearest minister of the established Congregational Church — but the curriculum stressed religious and moral precepts. In Noah Webster's spellers, Jedidiah Morse's geographies and John Pierpont's read-

[1] In 1818 a Virginia law gave elementary education to those willing to accept the brand of pauperism. W. A. Maddox, *The Free School Idea in Virginia before the Civil War* (Teachers College, Columbia Univ., Contribs. to Educ., no. 93), 90.

[2] Curti, *Social Ideas of American Educators*, 13 ff.; Purcell, *Connecticut in Transition*, 95.

ers the Christian spirit permeated the pupil's lessons, constantly reminding him of the hand of God in human affairs. Mingled with instruction on American governmental forms were suggestions that existing republican institutions had been divinely inspired. So patriotism had its religious side. There was a moral order in the universe, the student learned, upon which sound government rested, and that moral order was based upon revealed religion. Nowhere was this philosophy more explicitly stated, as we shall see in a later chapter, than in the colleges.

CHAPTER VIII

THE QUICKENING OF NATIONALISM

AMERICANS who desired to foster a strong national sentiment had their uneasy moments during the first quarter-century under the Constitution. Provincial jealousies were paraded in the press; the elimination of interstate customs barriers had but quickened the commercial rivalry among Atlantic ports; sectional interests clamored not so much for recognition as for primacy. From the communities beyond the Alleghanies came an insistent demand that preference be given the needs of the West: unrestricted navigation of the Mississippi, more effective means of transportation, removal of the Indian menace, and relief from the irritants of British in Canada and of Spaniards in Florida. Complaints of Eastern indifference, though fluctuating in volume, were continuous. In reply, New England merchants and shipbuilders, not yet convinced of the value of Western markets, angrily denounced the narrow sectionalism of Westerners and of Southern agrarians, insensitive to the needs of ocean-borne commerce. Secession, a word which had once risen easily to the lips of men in crude settlements beyond the mountains, now was often heard in the conversation of Northern countinghouses.

Yet through the conflicting economic interests, through the antagonism of aristocrat and democrat, there ran a note of confidence in the future which augured well for the young republic. Symbolic of this attitude was the new capital rising from the "mosquito-infested morass" along the Potomac. Its broad avenues, radiating from the Capitol and the President's House, in Major

L'Enfant's elaborate plan, bore little relation in 1801 to the causeway across the alder swamp and Tiber Creek, which was later to be known as Pennsylvania Avenue. Near the Capitol building, only one wing of which was completed, stood seven or eight boarding houses and several small shops; while more than a mile away, on the high ground hard by the President's House, were a half-dozen public buildings and some four hundred dwellings, perhaps one hundred of them brick. The District of Columbia contained thirty-two hundred inhabitants, including more than six hundred Negro slaves.[1]

Such was the Washington in which Thomas Jefferson was inaugurated. Both the place and the man bespoke the shape of things to come. Roads deep in mud did not deter ardent Republicans from seeing their hero installed in office. Among the thousands craning their necks to catch a glimpse of the tall, rather awkward Virginian as he strode from Conrad's boarding house to the Senate Chamber, there must have been some who regretted the transfer of the capital from the convenience and elegance of Philadelphia to this village so suggestive of the primitive frontier. Others may have sensed what was far more significant: that the capital slowly rising would become a new center of national interest, drawing to itself representatives of all groups and of all sections. Here could be seen in miniature — what would have been impossible in New York, Philadelphia or Charleston — the common characteristics as well as the divergent trends of national life. Here, on virgin soil, Americans could build a physical symbol of the national ideal toward which they were groping.

It would be easier in Washington than in Philadel-

[1] Henry Adams, The Life of Albert Gallatin (Phila., 1879), 252-253. See also anon., "An Account of the City of Washington," Literary Mag. and Am. Register, IV (1805), 123 ff.

phia to dramatize republican simplicity and bucolic virtue. The Federalists had not been long enough in the new capital to establish any precedents.[1] No formidable social régime confronted Thomas Jefferson. The small number of women — so few that the dining rooms of the boarding houses were described as monks' refectories — and the President's lack of a hostess facilitated the change from the courtlike ceremonial of earlier administrations. Dignity was combined with an easy informality in social intercourse. A few self-appointed leaders of society undertook to persuade Jefferson to maintain the custom of the weekly presidential levee, but his utmost concession was the institution of two receptions, one at New Year's and the other on Independence Day. Though his infrequent state dinners reminded the guests that he was a Virginia gentleman, his reactions, both instinctive and studied, oftentimes offended those who remembered the elegance of Washington's administration, or were familiar with the usages of European courts.[2]

Even during the brilliant reign of "Queen" Dolly Madison the chief characteristic of the capital's exclusive circle was its lack of exclusiveness. Anyone with the slightest claim on official attention was welcomed at the White House. In Mrs. Madison's drawing-rooms there was greater insistence upon the forms of aristocratic society, but those who enjoyed her impromptu musicales and dances were not all aristocrats. Indeed, Washington society in her régime reacted to forces beyond her control. When backwoods congressmen, inappropriately garbed and resentful of social gradations, mingled with foreign diplomats and distinguished visitors from European cap-

[1] Anne H. Wharton, *Social Life in the Early Republic* (Phila., 1902), 102-109.
[2] Gaillard Hunt, ed., *First Forty Years of Washington Society* (N. Y., 1906), 29, 31, 404-405.

itals, attempts to enforce precise rules of etiquette became ludicrous.[1]

If the capital reflected the decline of aristocracy throughout the nation, it also caught the spirit of optimism which dominated the newer communities. Foreign observers might scoff at the village on the Potomac — its swampy location, its grotesquely extravagant plan, its badly decorated public buildings and its ramshackle frame stores and offices — but Washingtonians foresaw a great future for their city.[2] Its magnificent distances, so inconvenient in a day of wretched roads, were but fitting for the seat of government of a great American empire. Its situation in a fertile district, intersected by navigable rivers and equally distant from the northern and southern boundaries of the nation, would make it an outlet for the increasing commerce of the West, the nation's great emporium.[3] Such optimism was closely akin to the mood of that speculative expansion which had carried thousands of men and women beyond the Alleghanies and had flung an advance guard across the Mississippi into the territory of Spain. It is impossible to say what direction this expansive thrust might have taken, had America been insulated against European influences. But the young nation was not so insulated. During the first two decades of the nineteenth century the reaction of America's confident spirit to the impact of European ideas and events determined the trend of national thinking as well as national policy.

Rumors of the secret treaty of San Ildefonso and the retrocession of Louisiana to France began to filter into

[1] A. C. Clark, *Life and Letters of Dolly Madison* (Wash., 1914), 108, 143, 464.

[2] John Melish, *Travels in the United States of America* (Phila., 1812), II, 16-17; H. B. Fearon, *Sketches of America* (London, 1819), 283-284.

[3] David B. Warden, *A Chorographical and Statistical Description of the District of Columbia* (Paris, 1816), 32.

the United States late in 1801.[1] Their full import was revealed when the Spanish *Intendant* of Louisiana revoked the privilege, granted in the treaty of 1795, of depositing goods at New Orleans free from all governmental exactions, pending transshipment to ocean-going vessels.[2] The prosperity of Westerners depended upon unrestricted use of the Mississippi and this right of temporary deposit. That fact was written large in the New Orleans customhouse books. In 1794, for example, thirty-one vessels entered from New York, Philadelphia and other Atlantic ports, while twenty-three river craft came from the American communities in the Ohio Valley. Five years later, however, some seventy-eight vessels arrived from the Atlantic Seaboard and one hundred and eleven barges and flatboats from the upriver settlements. By 1802 the customhouse at Natchez reported that tobacco, flour, hemp, cider, whisky and other commodities, valued at more than a million dollars, descended the great river annually.[3] If the unpredictable ambition of Napoleon replaced the feeble control of the Spanish monarch in Louisiana, there might be even more serious consequences than the damming up of a stream of goods at New Orleans. The expansion of the American people might be permanently checked.

The demand for action was nation-wide, but a storm of controversy arose over the course which that action should take. Belligerently nationalistic, the Federalists clamored for war against the Corsican. Mindful of their brief popularity some five years earlier as opponents of French aggression, they promptly announced

[1] Rufus King, *Life and Correspondence* (C. R. King, ed., N. Y., 1894-1900), III, 414, 469.

[2] *American State Papers* (Wash., 1832-1861), *Foreign Relations*, II, 523-524, 531-532, 534 ff.

[3] Louis Pelzer, "Economic Factors in the Acquisition of Louisiana," Miss. Valley Hist. Assoc., *Proceeds.*, VI, 109 ff. See also *American State Papers, Finance*, II, 56-58.

that Napoleon had "calculated to a pound of gunpowder and to a drop of blood, the means of severing Kentucky and Tennessee." It could be prevented only if the Westerners seized New Orleans before the arrival of the "scalers of the Alps and the conquerors of Venice." [1] Eastern Republicans, aware that the West was eager to defy both Spain and France, minimized the danger and staked all on an amicable negotiation at Paris. They found Napoleon badly shaken by General Leclerc's disaster in rebellious Santo Domingo and willing to dispose of all Louisiana before it should fall into the hands of Great Britain, his most formidable foe. So it was that the American representatives, authorized to purchase New Orleans and West Florida for a small sum, signed documents for the transfer of an empire at a much larger figure. [2]

Expansionists were surprised but delighted. In the end they had their way, for Jefferson's literalism in construing fundamental law yielded to the needs of the nation. For his constitutional scruples was substituted a vaguely formulated theory that "the good sense of our country will correct the evil of construction when it shall produce ill effects." Straightway the Republican press, though little informed concerning the empire beyond the Mississippi, proceeded to tabulate the value of the property acquired. There were forests for the building of a superior merchant marine and navy; vast prairies which could support a population larger than that of the British Isles, France, Spain and Portugal; deposits of gold and silver as well as quantities of lead, iron, plaster of Paris and salt. A great agricultural domain would flourish, whose farmers would buy the

---

[1] *Boston Gazette*, March 3, 1803, quoting the Baltimore *Republican; Connecticut Courant*, April 16, 1803.
[2] E. S. Brown, *The Constitutional History of the Louisiana Purchase* (Univ. of Calif., *Publs.*, X), chap. i.

products of Eastern mills and shops and feed the sea-board cities. This interplay of agricultural, manufac-turing and commercial interests would carry the nation far along the road toward complete independence from Europe.[1]

Some Americans could not see this attractive prospect. Such folk were generally Federalists, living mostly in New England and the seaboard communities of the Mid-dle Atlantic states. They feared that the westward movement of population, steadily bringing new states into the Union, would upset the balance of power and finally give the finishing stroke to the rapidly declining political influence of the Northeast. Some looked with foreboding toward the day when the opportunities of the West would lure the artisan from his craft and the sailor from the sea. Then mill owner and merchant would feel the pinch of labor shortage and high wages.

If such apprehensions lay beneath the surface, fear was openly expressed that republican government would founder in an area as vast as that which Tiberius gov-erned "by the swords of forty legions." Louisiana was inaccessible, unsuitable for extensive cultivation, an un-trodden waste for wolves to howl in. Its settlers would be outlaws and renegades who would defy the nation's laws and, when sufficiently strong, would proclaim their independence.[2] When the Mississippi was our boun-dary, lamented Fisher Ames, "we were confined within some limits. Now, by adding an unmeasured world be-yond that river, we rush like a comet into infinite space." [3] The spirit of separatism, which New England professed to dread in the new territory, became manifest among extreme Federalists, who discussed the possibility

[1] For a summary of newspaper comment, see Cecil Dryden, Public Ex-pression on the Purchase of Louisiana (Master's essay, 1927, Columbia University Library).

[2] Connecticut Courant, Aug. 3, 1803.

[3] Fisher Ames, Works (Seth Ames, ed., Boston, 1854), I, 323-324.

of a Northern confederacy to include New England, New York and possibly Pennsylvania. Though the conspirators had to abandon their scheme, they made unmistakable their belief that the Union could not long endure if the acquisition of new territory meant an increase of Southern power under the "federal ratio" which gave a planter with fifty slaves as much voice in national politics as thirty-one Northern freemen.[1]

On the other hand, Abraham Bishop, port collector at New Haven, speaking for a minority in Connecticut but probably a majority in the country, argued that Louisiana would strengthen the unity of the nation.[2] Tensions would be relieved both West and East. The removal of Spanish and French influence along the Mississippi would bind that section to the Union with newly enforced bonds, while the enlarged opportunities in the great valley would draw off from the East those most discontented with their social or economic inferiority. Their restless energy would be expended in the creation of a new society rather than in revolt against an older one.[3]

While Americans debated the possibilities of Louisiana, they knew neither the nature of the territory nor its precise boundaries. Meager accounts by trappers and hunters aroused curiosity concerning the rumors of a mountain of salt, one hundred and eighty miles long and forty-five wide; a vast prairie too fertile for the growth of trees, perpetually darkened by herds of buffalo; a tribe of Indians gigantic in stature and phenomenal in strength. Many had heard also of the white

[1] H. C. Lodge, *Life and Letters of George Cabot* (Boston, 1877), 344-346; William Plumer, jr., *Life of William Plumer* (Boston, 1857), 265, 304.

[2] Abraham Bishop, *Oration in Honor of . . . the Peaceful Acquisition of Louisiana* (Hartford, 1804).

[3] David Ramsay, *Oration on the Cession of Louisiana to the United States* (Charleston, 1804).

Indians along the upper Missouri, who spoke Welsh and treasured a Welsh Bible which they could not read.[1]

Such rumors were put to the test soon after the French flag was hauled down at New Orleans. In 1802 Jefferson, thinking of commerce and the expanding fur trade, secured from Congress a small appropriation which made possible the explorations of Meriwether Lewis and William Clark.[2] Permission had been obtained to cross French Louisiana, but by the time the party left St. Louis in May, 1804, it needed no documents from Paris. When the members returned more than two years later, they reported that they had crossed the western half of the continent by means of its two great river valleys, that they had discovered new passes over the continental divide and had collected much scientific information. The journals of Lewis and Clark, published in several editions before 1815, were profusely illustrated with maps and with drawings of birds, fish and animals, executed with meticulous care.[3] Alongside descriptions of the physical features of the country stood fascinating vignettes of Indian life — the ceremonials of the tribes, their customs, habitat and means of subsistence — and discussions of the language they spoke and the traditions they cherished. Other members of the expedition published their own versions of the exploration.[4]

Meanwhile the southern districts of Louisiana were being explored and described. The *Medical Repository*

[1] *American Universal Magazine* (1797), 399-400; *Moral and Sentimental Magazine* (1797), 333; *Medical Repository*, IX (1805-1806), 113; X (1806-1807), 289-290; Am. Philos. Soc., *Trans.*, VI (1809), 70.

[2] R. B. Guinness, "The Purpose of the Lewis and Clark Expedition," *Miss. Valley Hist. Rev.*, XX, 90 ff.

[3] Elliott Coues, *History of the Expedition under the Command of Lewis and Clark* (N. Y., 1893), I, 1-5.

[4] Patrick Gass, *A Journal of the Voyages and Travels of a Corps of Discovery, under the Command of Captain Lewis and Captain Clark* (Pittsburgh, 1807); R. G. Thwaites, ed., *Original Journals of the Lewis and Clark Expedition, 1804-1806* (N. Y., 1904-1905), VI.

carried accounts of the journey of William Dunbar and George Hunter into the Ouachita River country, as a result of which Dunbar made a scientific analysis of the waters of the hot springs in the present state of Arkansas. A few years later Captain Zebulon M. Pike reported somewhat inadequately (for the Spaniards had seized most of his papers) the details of his expedition to the sources of the Mississippi in 1805, and his circumspect reconnoitering two years later along the Arkansas and Red rivers and near the Spanish settlements of New Mexico.[1]

Descriptions of Louisiana interested the trapper, the miner or the trader more than the farmer.[2] The treeless prairies, rank with grass which seemed to be ever encroaching upon the woodland, constituted an alien terrain for forest farmers.[3] Moreover, Indian tribes, whose strength was untested and unknown, still controlled the choicest areas. In view of these considerations it was not entirely irrational for the agrarians, who had but recently come into possession of a great undeveloped domain, to clamor for still more land.[4]

As speculator and settler took title to the best tracts in western New York and pushed northward along the tributaries of the Ohio, Indian resistance stiffened and the frontiersman placed the blame upon the British

[1] See *Medical Repository*, IX, 305-313; XI (1807-1808), 299; *Am. Medical and Philos. Register*, II (1812), 33-40.

[2] For mining and fur trading, see E. C. Barker, ed., *Austin Papers* (Am. Hist. Assoc., *Ann. Rep. for 1919*, II), pt. i, 1 ff.; H. M. Brackenridge, *Views of Louisiana . . . in 1811* (Pittsburgh, 1814) ; Amos Stoddard, *Sketches, Historical and Descriptive of Louisiana* (Phila., 1812), chap. xv; H. M. Chittenden, *American Fur Trade of the Far West* (N. Y., 1902), I, *passim*.

[3] Pamphlet literature of the period contained much unfavorable comment on the agricultural possibilities of the trans-Mississippi region, not all of it reflecting Eastern opinion. Examples may be found in *Medical Repository*, IX, 307; XI, 189.

[4] See the hypothesis in L. M. Hacker, "Western Land Hunger and the War of 1812," *Miss. Valley Hist. Rev.*, X, 365 ff.

in Canada. The pioneer's desire for the fertile peninsula of Upper Canada helps to explain his insistence that the safety of the entire West required the expulsion of British power from North America.[1] "The waters of the St. Lawrence and the Mississippi," a Westerner declared in Congress, "interlock in a number of places, and the great Disposer of Human Events intended those two rivers should belong to the same people" — and he left no doubt as to the identity of that people.[2]

Governmental policy, with its agrarian implications, was designed to keep the course of Indian empire moving ever westward. Humanitarian principles yielded to the practical consideration of securing a maximum area for white settlement. The savages could and did point to broken promises, wanton murders, fraudulent treaties secured from dissolute chiefs. During the fourteen years after the treaty of Greenville the tribes of the old Northwest Territory alienated more than forty-eight million acres. Then came Tecumseh and his brother, the Prophet, towering above their fellow Shawnee and preaching a gospel of moral reform and intertribal amity. The braves who joined the confederation were expected to abstain from intoxicants, shun all unnecessary contacts with the white man and consecrate themselves anew in their ancient tribal rites. A union of sober and zealous warriors could stop the steady encroachment upon the Indians' domain.[3]

Noble in principle Tecumseh's confederacy may have been, but the men of the agricultural frontier viewed it solely in terms of menace. They believed it was a conspiracy secretly engineered by the British to preserve

[1] J. W. Pratt, *Expansionists of 1812* (N. Y., 1925), chap. i.

[2] A. K. Weinberg, *Manifest Destiny: a Study of Nationalist Expansionism in American History* (Balt., 1935), 53.

[3] *American State Papers, Indian Affairs*, I, 761-762, 776-780, 798 ff.; Dorothy B. Goebel, *William Henry Harrison* (Indianapolis, 1926), 104-107, 109-110.

the old routes of the fur traders by terrorizing pioneer settlements. In the congressional elections of 1810-1811 the frontiersmen spoke unmistakably, choosing men of expansionist temper eager to secure Canada and thus remove the Indian peril even at the cost of war with Great Britain. Such views were being expressed on Capitol Hill when news came of William Henry Harrison's victory over Tecumseh's forces at Tippecanoe. The war spirit was in the ascendant.[1]

Hostility to Great Britain, which reached a climax in congressional debates early in 1812, involved more than an expression of expansionist sentiment. Three decades of freedom had not sufficed to erase the memory of old grievances. Some New England Federalists might regret the attempt to make the Fourth of July an occasion for anti-British demonstrations, but most Americans still thought of their independent status as a happy release from British tyranny.[2] This was particularly true after the renewal of European war in 1804 brought the United States once more within the orbit of English sea power. Impressment of British subjects from American merchant vessels increased, as did also cases of mistaken identity. Protracted controversies over neutral rights monopolized the attention of the state department. British orders in council and Napoleonic decrees made American trade a gambler's profession. Men who had never gone down to the sea in ships, whose interests were not directly affected by confiscation of cargoes and impressment of seamen, swelled a mighty chorus demanding

[1] Pratt, *Expansionists of 1812*, 48; D. R. Anderson, "The Insurgents of 1811," Am. Hist. Assoc., *Ann. Rep. for 1911*, I, 165 ff. A. L. Burt minimizes the Indian menace and other frontier problems in discussing the causes of the War of 1812. *The United States, Great Britain and British North America* (New Haven, 1940), 269-316.

[2] *Aurora*, Aug. 24, 1803; *Spectator* (N. Y.), July 3, 1805; Oct. 20, 1810. See also F. O. Darvall, American Opinion with Regard to Great Britain during the Quarter Century Preceding the War of 1812 (Master's essay, 1930, Columbia University Library).

that somehow national honor be avenged. Some hot-heads even suggested that it might be necessary to fight France as well as England to prove America's complete independence of Europe. This warlike mood stimulated the desire of frontiersmen to be rid of foreign influence along the borders.

The government's policy was based on the assumption that economic pressure, following the lines of the non-importation agreements of the Revolutionary era, would make Great Britain or France, perhaps both, seek a compromise. "Peaceful coercion" reached its culmination in the embargo act, which forbade all vessels in American harbors to clear for foreign ports, prohibited all exports from the United States either by land or sea, except under special license, and closed the American market to the most important British exports. But instead of demonstrating England's commercial dependence upon the United States, the act revealed the extent to which Americans still relied upon Europe for markets and finished products.[1]

It is true that the embargo of 1807–1809 was not well enforced. The commerce of Lake Champlain, Lake Ontario and Lake Erie rose rapidly, and it was not diffi-cult to evade officials while carrying beef and flour into Canada and returning with British goods.[2] Vessels os-tensibly in the coastwise trade were driven from their courses by "unseasonable storms," only to find safe an-chorage and profitable markets in the West Indies. Shipping certificates, issued by the treasury department upon recommendation of the governor of a state, were bought

[1] L. M. Sears, *Jefferson and the Embargo* (Durham, 1927), 29-31, 51-60.

[2] *Evening Post* (N. Y.), June 27, Aug. 10, Sept. 6, 1808; John Lambert, *Travels through Lower Canada, and the United States* (London, 1810), I, 251-252; R. C. Ellsworth, "The Settlement of the North Country," A. C. Flick, ed., *History of the State of New York* (N. Y., 1933-1937), V, 197-198.

and sold in New York to cover transactions clearly outside the purposes for which they had been issued. Furthermore, the British government connived at violations. Customs officials ignored American ship captains who managed to get into a British port, even though they had infringed the British acts of trade. In 1809 fifteen thousand British licenses were issued for American shipments, as compared with fewer than three thousand in 1807.[1] Despite the reports in Republican newspapers of widespread suffering in England, her mill owners were more inconvenienced than distressed.[2] Moreover, British exports to Canada and South America rose in volume as direct shipments to the United States declined. France, to be sure, found it increasingly difficult to feed her possessions in the West Indies and to secure their products, but Napoleon was not apt to yield to pressure so long as he could confiscate American vessels, when they put into ports under his control, on the pretext that they had violated their own country's embargo.[3]

Americans, not Europeans, complained most bitterly of this attempt to use commercial coercion as a substitute for war. Republicans could not ignore the reports of idle ships and hungry seamen, of empty counting-houses and crowded tobacco barns, of bankruptcies in Philadelphia and mortgage foreclosures in Virginia.[4] Had violent protests been confined to extreme Federalists, the administration forces might have continued the ex-

[1] W. W. Jennings, *The American Embargo, 1807-1809* (Univ. of Iowa, *Studies*, VIII, no. 1), chaps. v-vi.

[2] G. W. Daniels, "The American Cotton Trade with Liverpool under the Embargo," *Am. Hist. Rev.*, XXI, 276 ff. Among the cotton-mill operatives there was genuine distress, but it had slight influence on public policy.

[3] Henry Adams, *History of the United States of America* (N. Y., 1889-1901), IV, 303-304, 328-331, 344.

[4] J. B. McMaster, *A History of the People of the United States* (N. Y., 1883-1913), III, 289-291; Jennings, *American Embargo*, 198-201.

periment, but there was schism in the Republican ranks
in New York; and New England, where Republicans
had made gains, was rapidly returning to its former
political allegiance.[1] When the unanimity of Southern
support of the embargo was broken, the time had come
to chart a new course. Congressman David R. Williams
of South Carolina informed the House that smuggling,
evasion of the law and sectional jealousies had created
a situation which made it necessary either "to enforce
the law with the bayonet" or to abandon it.[2] Reluctantly the Republican strategists accepted repeal (March
3, 1809) and turned to nonintercourse as a substitute.
At least this was "short of surrender" to British orders
and French decrees.

The war spirit was steadily rising, fed by streams
of variant opinion. It moved men to action not in the
commercial communities of the New England and Middle Atlantic states, but along the frontier from the Green
Mountains to the Kentucky Blue Grass and thence eastward into the Georgia uplands. These were the regions
of "expansionist enthusiasm," the strongholds of the
"war hawks." Yet many who joined the war party
were merely seeking an escape from economic distress.
From 1807 to 1812 the years had not been easy for
pioneer farmers in the valleys of the Ohio, Cumberland
and Tennessee. Markets were so few and prices so low
that the grower of hemp or tobacco or corn could not
secure enough cash to import necessary commodities and
to meet payments on land which he had bought a few
years earlier.[3] A heavy toll was taken from the frontiersman by cumbersome transportation methods, unre-

[1] *Evening Post*, Jan. 13, 1809; D. R. Fox, *The Decline of Aristocracy in the Politics of New York* (Columbia Univ., *Studies*,
LXXXVI), 99-104; Adams, *History*, IV, 409 ff.

[2] *Annals of Congress* (Wash., 1834-1856), 10 Cong., 2 sess., 1236.

[3] G. R. Taylor, "Agrarian Discontent in the Mississippi Valley Preceding the War of 1812," *Journ. of Polit. Economy*, XXXIX, 471 ff.

liable rumors concerning markets, inadequate financial facilities and crude marketing techniques; and the toll was exaggerated after 1807 by the restrictions imposed upon American commerce.

In the circumstances many were inclined to single out the extraordinary impact of the European war as the reason for their difficulties. It was to this factor that the Ohio legislature referred in 1808: "The unprovoked aggression of both England and France . . . has so materially affected the whole commerce of the United States, that it has almost put a stop to our circulating medium, and rendered the payment of the installments of the purchase money for the . . . lands almost impracticable." [1] "The farmer will see clearly," said the Lexington (Kentucky) *Reporter*, "that the orders in council prohibiting and interrupting all commerce to the continent is the only cause of his embarrassments . . . ." [2] Felix Grundy of Tennessee insisted that commercial privileges were as important for the welfare of the West as for the prosperity of Eastern shippers. "It is not the carrying trade," he reminded his fellow congressmen, "about which this nation and Great Britain are at present contending. . . . The true question in controversy is . . . the right of exporting the productions of our own soil and industry to foreign markets"; [3] to which the *Georgetown Telegraph* (Kentucky) responded, "We have now but one course to pursue — a resort to arms." [4]

The drive for war was at once sectional and partisan. Westerners and their Southern allies worked through the organization of the Republican party, whose elder statesmen were being pushed aside by young leaders impatient of the delays of diplomacy and sure of America's destiny.

[1] *Acts of Ohio*, 7th Assembly, 1 sess., 222-223.
[2] *Reporter* (Lexington, Ky.), Oct. 24, 1809.
[3] *Annals of Congress*, 12 Cong., 1 sess., 424.
[4] Cited in Taylor, "Agrarian Discontent in the Mississippi Valley," 498.

Henry Clay and Richard M. Johnson of Kentucky, Peter B. Porter of New York, Felix Grundy of Tennessee, John C. Calhoun and Langdon Cheves of South Carolina, all under forty, belonged to a different generation from that of Jefferson and Gallatin, Macon and Giles. They were sensitive, so they said, to the changing political climate.

But opposition to their plans quickly became articulate through the Federalist party. Its strength, so the student of election returns discovers, lay in New England, New York, New Jersey, Delaware and Maryland. Even in such districts, however, a considerable minority was inclined to support "Mr. Madison's War," but its influence was slight, especially in New England, in view of the ability of the majority to control press, pulpit and public platform. The Washington Benevolent Society, begun in New York in 1808 as the Federalist rival to Democratic secret clubs, spread through the Northeastern states, with many thousands of members working against Madison's administration in peace and war.[1] In Federalist eyes Great Britain was not the "traditional enemy" but "the world's last hope" against the scourge of Napoleon.[2] The governor of Massachusetts appointed a day of fasting and prayer, at which time the Reverend Jedidiah Morse of Charlestown described the war as "punishment for our national sins."[3] From the lower house of the Massachusetts legislature came an "Address to the People" urging them to make their condemnation of the war both "loud and deep."[4]

There was much partisan criticism of the federal government's attempt to secure volunteers, and some de-

[1] J. T. Adams, *New England in the Republic* (Boston, 1926), 272; Fox, *Decline of Aristocracy*, 89-99.
[2] John Lowell, *Mr. Madison's War* (Boston, 1812), 5-7.
[3] Jedidiah Morse, *A Sermon Delivered at Charlestown, July 23, 1812* (Charlestown, 1812), 1.
[4] Adams, *History*, VI, 401-402.

nounced the recruiting rendezvous as "hells of drinking, deception and degradation." [1] When the states were requested to place the militia at the service of the national government, the governors of Massachusetts, Connecticut and Rhode Island refused on the ground that it would be unconstitutional. Though New England possessed most of the nation's fluid capital, its citizens took less than one million dollars of the war loan, while residents of Philadelphia and New York subscribed for three times that amount. [2] So strongly did the commercial and financial leaders of the Northeast oppose the war that the government dared not move to curtail freedom of speech or to suppress hostile journals. One could jeer at "poor Jim Madison" or "Old Granny Dearborn" with impunity.

In parts of New England disaffection went beyond mere obstruction. As early as January 13, 1813, the *Columbian Centinel* in Boston boldly announced: "We must no longer be deafened by senseless clamors about a Separation of the States. . . . *The States are separated in fact* when one section . . . perseveres in measures fatal to the interests and repugnant to the opinion of another section." [3] Extremists, urged on by the fiery speeches of Josiah Quincy and the caustic letters of Timothy Pickering, seriously calculated the value of the Union. Though they generally avoided the words "nullification" and "secession," their arguments were reminiscent of the Kentucky and Virginia resolutions and contained the essentials of the political theory later propounded by Calhoun. [4] Such desperate sentiments found few supporters west of the Hudson. Most New York Fed-

[1] S. G. Goodrich, *Recollections of a Lifetime* (N. Y., 1856), I, 452.
[2] Adams, *History*, VI, 207.
[3] Cited in Adams, *New England in the Republic*, 274.
[4] F. M. Anderson, "A Forgotten Phase of the New England Opposition to the War of 1812," Miss. Valley Hist. Assoc., *Proceeds.*, VI, 176 ff.

eralists, mindful of the possibility of invasion from Canada, confined their resentment to criticism of the conduct of the war and pronouncements in favor of an early peace.[1] In New Jersey, where sentiment seems to have been nicely balanced, the Republicans in despair cried out against the Federalist "traitors."[2]

In New England expostulation gave way to action in October, 1814, when the Massachusetts legislature summoned a convention to meet at Hartford. The delegates, chiefly from Massachusetts, Rhode Island and Connecticut and ably counseled by Harrison Gray Otis, turned their secret sessions into a sort of safety valve for secessionist sentiment, with the result that their report was surprisingly moderate.[3] Yet its implications suggested that the Hartford Federalists would have been content to keep the nation, however small and feeble, forever under New England's domination. After proposing several amendments to the Constitution they poured scorn on the way in which the war had been conducted and denounced the government for aiding Napoleon.[4] Fortunately for the administration leaders, news of Jackson's victory at New Orleans and of the treaty signed at Ghent came as apparent vindication of governmental policy and condemnation of the "treason" of New England Federalists.

No war in American history has been more unpopular than that which James Madison reluctantly waged, and none has been quite so badly managed. Had Britain not been preoccupied with European affairs, the result could easily have been a major disaster, for the nation's resources of foodstuffs, equipment and military supplies,

[1] *Spectator*, Dec. 9, 1813; *Evening Post*, Jan. 4, 1813.
[2] *Centinel* (Newark), Jan. 25, 1814.
[3] S. E. Morison, *Life and Letters of Harrison Gray Otis* (Boston, 1913), II, 111.
[4] Hartford Convention of Delegates, *Proceedings* (Boston, 1815), 9, 12, 16.

though considerable, were not mobilized for war. The regular army of ten regiments, ill-equipped and half filled, was commanded by senior officers whom young Winfield Scott described as "generally sunk in either sloth, ignorance, or habits of intemperate drinking." [1] Of the 694,000 men enrolled in the militia of the several states, fewer than five thousand responded to the President's call at the beginning of hostilities. [2] Congress voted to raise a volunteer army, but neglected to make adequate provision for supplying the additional troops. [3] Nor was there a rush of volunteers at the recruiting stations. Not until 1814 did the effective fighting strength reach 35,000, so heavy were the ravages of various bilious fevers and pneumonia among the troops in northern New York and the Great Lakes region. [4] Service of supply soon degenerated into a congeries of quartermasters, commissaries, contractors and wagoners who quarreled incessantly with commanders in the field. At the moment in 1814 that it seemed impossible to feed Andrew Jackson's men in the Southwest, Sir George Prevost, British commissioner, reported that two thirds of the army in Canada were eating beef "provided by the American contractors, drawn principally from the states of Vermont and New York." [5]

When Calhoun boasted that within one month of the declaration of war Upper Canada and a portion of

[1] Winfield Scott, *Memoirs of Lieut-Gen. Scott, LL.D. Written by Himself* (N. Y., 1864), 31.

[2] *American State Papers, Military Affairs*, I, 298 ff.

[3] In 1814 newspapers were appealing to citizens who had cannon, pistols and other military articles to turn them over to the commissaries that the militia might be equipped for federal service. *Evening Post*, Aug. 28, 31, 1814.

[4] *Am. Medical and Philos. Register*, III (1812-1813), 497-503, reports an "epidemic" of pneumonia among troops in northern New York. See also J. D. Edgar, "The American Medical Department in the War of 1812," *Military Surgeon*, LX (1927), 301-313.

[5] "State Papers, Lower Canada," *Report on Canadian Archives for 1896* (Ottawa, 1897), 37.

The Boston Troops, as reviewed on President Adams's birth day on the Common by the Hon'l Lieut' Governor Gill & Major Gen'l Elliot, under the command of Brigadier Gen'l Winslow; also a view of the New State House &c.

Military Muster, Boston Common, 1799

Macdonough's Victory on Lake Champlain

Lower Canada would be seized, he forgot the problem of transportation. Control of the Great Lakes was a prerequisite for success, but few roads connected the Atlantic Seaboard with the trans-Alleghany basin. It was a major engineering feat to get heavy ordnance from the Hudson Valley either to the little town of Pittsburgh or to any port on Lake Erie.[1] Detroit, from which it seemed logical to launch an attack upon Upper Canada, had no nearer points of supply than Cleveland and Urbana. Wagon trains from either of these Ohio settlements had to cross the Black Swamp near the Maumee River, where roads and bridges were not yet constructed.[2]

Strategy on the high seas had to be planned in terms of the individual man-of-war rather than fleet action, for the navy consisted of only sixteen frigates, brigs and sloops, unless one counted about a hundred and sixty gunboats which could not survive a heavy sea. The navy's officers, young and energetic, had seen some service in handling Mediterranean pirates and were not dependent upon vague recollections of the Revolutionary War for their "military experience."[3] Yet the exploits of Isaac Hull, William Bainbridge and Stephen Decatur, in the tradition of John Paul Jones, could not compensate for the blockade of the coast line which Great Britain imposed in 1814; and the victories of Oliver H. Perry on Lake Erie and Thomas MacDonough on Lake Champlain were but balm for the wounds suffered in raids on Atlantic ports and in the capture and burning

---

[1] For the construction of the first road to Presqu'isle on Lake Erie, see Catharine V. Mathews, *Andrew Ellicott, His Life and Letters* (N. Y., 1908), 105-126.

[2] C. E. Slocum, *History of the Maumee River Basin* (Defiance, Ohio, 1905), 303-304. For the condition of roads in the Lake Champlain region, see Mordecai Myers, *Reminiscences, 1780-1814* (Washington, 1900), 14, 27, 44-45.

[3] A. T. Mahan, *Sea Power in Its Relation to the War of 1812* (Boston, 1905), I, 290, 297-300.

of Washington.[1] Even the gallant stand of Jackson's troops at New Orleans merely offset the terms of the treaty of Ghent, already signed, which said little about the disputes responsible for the war.

Nevertheless, Americans emerged from the struggle not humbled but exultant. The nadir of federal authority — when much of the capital lay in ruins, the states were raising armies for their own defense and the Treasury begged for loans from local bankers — was quickly forgotten. "The war," wrote Albert Gallatin to a fellow Republican, "has renewed and reinstated the national feelings and character which the Revolution had given, and which were daily lessened. The people have now more general objects of attachment with which their pride and political opinions are connected. They are more Americans; they feel and act more as a nation." [2] Sectionalism, for the moment, was overshadowed by national pride. The partisan had become the patriot.

This first generation of independent Americans had to build patriotic sentiments without that devotion to a personal hero which had been so potent an element in the romantic nationalism of European countries.[3] Though Washington's birthday was frequently celebrated as a holiday even before his death, veneration of the first President came only after the remembrance of his partisan attitude had slowly faded from men's

---

[1] The naval victories aroused more popular interest than any other phase of the war. Republican editors were quick to capitalize on this feeling in their attempts to promote cultural nationalism. See J. C. McCloskey, "The Campaign of Periodicals after the War of 1812 for National American Literature," Modern Lang. Assoc., Publs., L, 262-273. Many American newspapers, however, devoted more space to the fortunes of Napoleon than to the military conflict at home.

[2] Albert Gallatin, Writings (Henry Adams, ed., Phila., 1879), I, 700.

[3] Gaillard Hunt, Life in America One Hundred Years Ago (N. Y., 1914), 273-275.

minds.[1] But there were less vital symbols which evoked patriotic response. During the war years "Yankee Doodle" had virtually become a national anthem, so numerous and varied were the verses sung to its strains. By 1815 "Brother Jonathan" had lost his place to "Uncle Sam," who was emerging as a folk figure capable of arousing affection and loyalty.[2] Whatever else the British may have hoped to accomplish in their Chesapeake campaign, they had inspired a Baltimore attorney, Francis Scott Key, to write the "Star Spangled Banner," which (set, strangely enough, to the tune of an English drinking song) gave Americans a more vibrant sense of the symbolism of the flag.[3]

Among the youth of the nation the influence of such symbols was reënforced by lessons learned at school. Noah Webster was not the only textbook writer interested in molding the national character along patriotic lines. Successive editions of Jedidiah Morse's geographies, however inaccurate the information, declared the superiority of American institutions to those of Europe, while Caleb Bingham in his series of readers set the fashion, perpetuated by later compilers, of selecting resounding political oratory to stir young minds.[4] Indeed, most of those who wrote for the schools would have made good members of the "Association of American Patriots for the purpose of forming a National Character."[5] Though patriotic sentiments were sedulously

---

[1] William Bentley, *Diary* (Salem, Mass., 1904-1914), III, 30, 79, 173, 500. See also anon., "Guerra d'America," *Am. Rev. of History and Politics*, I (1811), 185.

[2] Albert Matthews, "Uncle Sam," Am. Antiquarian Soc., *Proceeds.*, XIX, 21 ff.

[3] J. C. Carpenter, "The Star Spangled Banner," *Century*, XLVIII (1894), 358 ff.

[4] Clifton Johnson, *Old Time Schools and School Books* (N. Y., 1904), 276, 318-336.

[5] This was an idea in which Noah Webster was interested. A. O. Hansen, *Liberalism and American Education in Eighteenth Century America* (N. Y., 1926), 237.

preached in Fourth of July orations, political sermons and magazine articles, there was no attempt to formulate a systematic philosophy of nationalism.[1]   The recurrent theme made clear that Americans were a chosen people, established in a divinely selected habitat, for an experiment unique in the annals of human freedom.[2]

What passed for nationalism after the War of 1812 was partly a sense of relief that the country had escaped from the radiating influences of Europe's quarrels, and partly resentment that sectional antagonisms and partisan bickerings had almost thwarted that escape.   Conditioned by a renewed confidence in the nation's future, this feeling found expression in a legislative program which would have gladdened the heart of Alexander Hamilton.   His "Report on Manufactures" of 1791 became the handbook of supporters of a protective tariff.   In defending the relatively high schedules of the act of 1816, Calhoun maintained that his purpose was not to befriend the manufacturer but to strengthen means of national defense through promoting economic self-sufficiency.   Hamiltonian, likewise, were the arguments which favored the creation of a Second Bank of the United States on the model of the institution whose charter had expired in 1811.   When it was proposed that the bonus, payable to the government under the bank charter, should be used to finance a national system of internal improvements, there could be no doubt that many a Republican had put on the mantle of Federalism.   It was no Federalist, but Calhoun, from the

---

[1] *American Museum*, VII-XI (1790-1792), contains numerous Fourth of July orations.   See also Archibald Buchanan, *An Oration . . . on the Fourth of July, 1794* (Balt., 1795); Samuel Dickinson, *An Oration, in Celebration of American Independence* (Northampton, Mass., 1797); and George Clinton, jr., *An Oration on the Fourth of July, 1798* (N. Y., 1798).

[2] For example, Abiel Abbott, *Traits of Resemblance in the People of the United States of America to Ancient Israel* (Haverhill, Mass., 1799); and Timothy Dwight, *Greenfield Hill* (New Haven, 1794), 18-27.

uplands of South Carolina, who declared, "Let us then bind the Republic together with roads and canals." [1]

Yet there had been no genuine triumph of nationalism over sectionalism. Though the language of separatism was less frequently heard in frontier taverns or on the quarterdecks of Massachusetts ships, men's opinions were still divided over the nature of the Union. The insistent problem — which had plagued the British imperial administrators before the Revolution — of distributing power and authority between governments had not yet been resolved. The fact that the Republicans had "put on Federalism," that Monroe was reëlected without opposition in 1820, did not mean that champions of state rights were dead. Despite New England's "treasonable" conduct during the war, the theory had not fallen into disrepute. It was available to any group which, as a conscious minority, felt that its interests were being neglected or injured in the broader policies of the nation.

The stranger in America was painfully impressed by the boasting he heard. "The national vanity of the United States," wrote an English traveler, "surpasses that of any other country, not even excepting France. It blazes out everywhere, and on all occasions — in their conversation, newspapers, pamphlets, speeches, and books." [2] Some observers attributed such displays to the poorly educated masses, while others admitted that Americans had a right to boast, particularly of the promise of the future.

Few, however, seem to have realized how far-reaching in America had been the revulsion against all things

[1] Quoted in McMaster, *History*, IV, 412. This nationalistic program was strongly supported by such publicists as Mathew Carey and Hezekiah Niles. See K. W. Rowe, *Mathew Carey* (Johns Hopkins Univ., *Studies*, LI, no. 4), 72-78.

[2] John Bristed, *The Resources of the United States of America* (N. Y., 1818), 460.

European in the years following the War of 1812. Even before that conflict, resentment had flared up over the manner in which foreign commentators had affected "contempt for the very low and degraded state of intellect in America." [1] Instead of reporting their experiences accurately, European observers either through ignorance or malice had filled their accounts with "moral and physical" caricatures of the United States and its people.[2] Offended by such criticism, especially when appearing in English reviews, many Americans resorted to hyperbole to state their country's merits. Wounded sensibilities found solace in minimizing the New World's debt to the Old and in bragging about American achievements. In the opinion of one enthusiast the young republic was rapidly becoming a land of "self-taught geniuses" in which learning and art met with proportionately more encouragement than in Great Britain.[3] "We already rival Europe in portraits and engravings," B. H. Latrobe reminded the Society of Artists in an optimistic oration which closed with the prediction that the glorious days of ancient Greece would be revived in the forests of America.[4]

This sense of cultural independence from Europe, however unrelated to reality, was mightily stimulated by the second war with England. The year 1815, as Henry Adams has insisted, marked a clear divergence between Europe and the United States, but that divergence was largely political. If Vienna began a chapter of Old World history in which Americans felt little interest, so Ghent was the symbol of America's turning from problems which originated across the Atlantic.

[1] Anon., "The Wanderer. Remarks on the Principal British Reviews," *Monthly Register*, III (1807), 351.

[2] Anon., "Literary and Philosophical Intelligence," *Monthly Anthology*, IV (1807), 217.

[3] Anon., "An Essay on the Liberal Arts," *ibid.*, III (1806), 301.

[4] *Port Folio*, May, 1811, 24.

When Europe took the road of political reaction, imposing fresh restraints upon individual liberty, Americans were undismayed. Their government, through President Monroe, proclaimed a positive policy of self-defense which reflected their growing sense of nationality. They were obviously less interested in Metternich than they had been in Napoleon. Though their sympathy for England was not deep-rooted, they got on better with that government after Waterloo than they had at any time since 1763. Some publicists gladly hailed the new era of peace, ushered in by the Rush-Bagot pact of 1817, providing for disarmament along the Canadian-American frontier, and the convention of 1818 which seemed to settle all outstanding disputes with Great Britain. Believing, for the moment, that they had escaped from the encompassing menace of the Old World, Americans were eager to concentrate upon their own problems. Expansion — in territory, in settlement, in agriculture, in commerce, in industry — was to be the stuff of their political preoccupation. This, in the long run, would determine the nature of the Union and the character of American civilization.

CHAPTER IX

THE DAY OF THE MERCHANT

THE *volte-face* which seemed to follow the "second war for American independence" was more a state of mind than a reflection of economic realities. In their business activities, if somewhat less in their political concerns, Americans were constantly affected by forces emanating from the Old World. However much they wanted to concentrate upon the problems of their own expanding economy, they could not escape the fact that success for them often depended upon conditions across the Atlantic. The price of cotton at Liverpool, of tobacco at Le Havre, of flour at Lisbon or Cadiz, vitally concerned American producers. So, too, the movement of goods, whether in foreign or domestic commerce, responded in part to the London money market. After 1815 European balances in American banking houses began to accumulate, and within a decade such New York brokers as Romulus Riggs and Nathaniel Prime faced strong competition from the resident agents of British bankers.[1] Short-term commercial credit, granted by London merchants to stimulate their own exports, was subsidiary to the investment of capital funds in various American enterprises.[2] Between 1815 and 1827 more than forty-three million dollars' worth of securities — government bonds, bank stocks, canal bonds — were sold in England. Already complaints were heard

[1] Edward Clibborn, *American Prosperity* (London, 1837), 3.
[2] R. W. Hidy, "The Organization and Functions of Anglo-American Merchant Bankers, 1815-1860," *Journ. of Econ. History*, supplemental issue (Dec., 1941), 53-66.

that foreigners had gained control of American industry.[1]

While the townsfolk of the Atlantic ports were still drinking toasts in celebration of the treaty concluded at Ghent, shipwrights and riggers were busy reconditioning the merchantmen which had been lying idle during the blockade. Some of these ships had not cleared for a foreign port since the days before the embargo. Now their owners proposed to carry on in the tradition of the prewar years. Commercial circles talked of clearances for Canton and Bombay as well as for Havana and Belfast and Liverpool. The water fronts of Boston, New York and Philadelphia resounded with the shouts of longshoremen unloading goods which the British had decided to "dump" upon a relatively empty market at rock-bottom prices. As New York received the bulk of these commodities, its auction rooms were soon filled with cotton and woolen goods, linens, hardware, cutlery and other articles. There was jubilation in South Street countinghouses, for the influx of imports set one of the main currents of world commerce flowing in the direction of New York.[2]

From the lamentations of manufacturers ruined by this cutthroat competition and the complaints of merchants injured by the activities of European factors or agents one might conclude that peace had brought hard times to the American people. Except for the manufacturing group, however, there was moderate prosperity throughout the country for three years after 1815.[3] It was the European situation, rather than the tariff of 1816, that served as a protective cushion. Though the channels of world trade were no longer

---

[1] C. K. Hobson, *The Export of Capital* (London, 1914), 105, 110.
[2] R. G. Albion, *The Rise of New York Port* (N. Y., 1939), 11-13.
[3] W. B. Smith and A. H. Cole, *Fluctuations in American Business, 1790-1860 (Harvard Econ. Studies, L)*, 20.

subject to war-time restrictions, the demand for American corn, flour, beef and pork remained large because of serious crop failures across the Atlantic. Moreover, speculation abroad in cotton and tobacco temporarily bolstered up those prices to the great advantage of American shipowners and traders. The depression which appeared at the close of 1818, and assumed the proportions of social crisis a little later, was attributed by some to the spirit of speculation, stimulated by abnormal business conditions, the optimistic extension of long-term loans and the consequent pyramiding of indebtedness.[1] Others, charging improper banking practices, suggested that fraud had played an ugly part. A case in point, they said, was the Second Bank of the United States which had been corruptly managed since its establishment in 1816; and its example had lured other banks into dishonest methods.[2]

The protectionists, claiming that American business had been sacrificed for cheap European imports, found an opportunity to moralize over the need for a higher tariff.[3] Mathew Carey, emphasizing another angle, contended that the national economy was out of balance. Too many farmers were raising foodstuffs for the constantly diminishing demands of European markets. American wheat and flour could not penetrate the barrier of the British corn laws, while on the Continent grain from Odessa was an active competitor. Much the same thing was true of cotton which had to meet com-

[1] An illuminating discussion appears in Samuel Reznack, "The Depression of 1819-1822, a Social History," *Am. Hist. Rev.*, XXXIX, 28-47.

[2] R. C. H. Catterall, *The Second Bank of the United States* (Univ. of Chicago, *Decennial Publs.*, ser. 2, II), 73-74, 91-92.

[3] John Melish, *The Necessity of Protecting and Encouraging the Manufactures of the United States* (Phila., 1818), in Am. Philos. Soc., *Pamphlets*, XXXIII. See also *Niles' Wkly. Register*, XVI, 215-220 (May 22, 1819); XVII, 1-5, 163-164, 165-166 (Sept. 4, Nov. 13, 1819).

petition from Brazil and the East Indies. Europe at peace was less eager for American staples than at any time since 1793. A vigorous development of the home market seemed imperative.[1]

In years of business depression social maladjustments appear in sharp definition. Then men give thought to the individual's responsibilities to society and the obligations of society to the individual. So it was in the crisis of 1819–1822. Much writing occurred on the rôle of government in the promotion of human welfare. Though Americans had never before faced such insistent problems of unemployment and pauperism, many nevertheless agreed with John Quincy Adams that government could do nothing but wait for "the healers and destroyers, Time and Chance," to bring either "catastrophe or the cure." [2] Others rejected this do-nothing attitude. Legislatures attempted to protect debtors against forced sales and the rigorous application of insolvency laws. Few states, however, adopted any comprehensive program of relief. Kentucky, Tennessee, Indiana and Illinois enacted stay laws, while Ohio and Tennessee and the fledgling state of Missouri accepted the principle that all property offered for sale under an execution must bring the minimum price fixed by a board of appraisers. Missouri also created a loan office for debtor relief.[3]

In the East private philanthropy rather than legislation provided a safety valve for discontent. Urban poor were fed at soup houses supported by generous citizens and the charity organizations of the churches, while so-

[1] Mathew Carey, *Essays in Political Economy* (Phila., 1822), 323-324, 399, 470-471, 492-494; Samuel Rezneck, "Rise and Early Development of Industrial Consciousness in the United States," *Journ. of Econ. and Business History*, IV, 800, 802.

[2] John Quincy Adams, *Memoirs* (C. F. Adams, ed., Phila., 1875), IV, 498; V, 129.

[3] J. B. McMaster, *A History of the People of the United States* (N. Y., 1883-1913), IV, 493-495, 508-510.

cieties for the prevention of pauperism undertook to study the subject systematically.[1] Their proposals generally took the form of platitudes concerning industry, sobriety and frugality. Humanitarian motives, as well as considerations of thrift, led to the founding of additional savings banks. The Savings Fund Society, created at Philadelphia in December, 1816, was followed within the year by the Provident Institution at Boston. In July, 1819, the New York Society for the Prevention of Pauperism sponsored a nonprofit savings bank, paying five per cent on deposits and soliciting the business of laborers, mechanics and tradesmen. Its first annual report showed more than three hundred thousand dollars in about three thousand accounts.[2]

Thrift, with its attendant virtues of economy and retrenchment, strongly appealed to the nation's taxpayers as a sensible way out of the depression. The government, as well as the individual, was urged to keep expenditures within income. Congress responded moderately to this pressure, finally effecting a saving of approximately two million dollars in 1821.[3] No one devised plans against a recurrence of economic depression. The nearest approach to a long-range program was that of the protectionists, with their balance between industry and agriculture, dependent upon a home market ever expanding behind the tariff wall. Even the President's reluctance to act in the crisis was but mildly criticized. Instead, distressed debtors let their wrath fall upon the courts, which in several states had invalidated

---

[1] See first five *Reports* of Society for Prevention of Pauperism (N. Y., 1818-1822), *passim.*

[2] Superintendent of the Banking Department of New York, "Annual Report," *Bankers' Mag.,* XII (1858), 857-858; O. C. Lightner, *The History of Business Depressions* (N. Y., 1922), 112.

[3] The land act of 1820, repealing the credit arrangements established in 1800, was hailed by Eastern business men as a check on speculation in Western lands. B. H. Hibbard, *A History of the Public Land Policies* (N. Y., 1924), 97-99.

relief legislation. In their resentment they denounced John Marshall's decision in McCulloch *v.* Maryland as a peculiarly flagrant example of federal interference with the state's taxing power. Ohio now declared that the doctrines asserted in the Kentucky and Virginia resolutions of 1798 were sound and Kentucky reiterated its earlier stand.[1] Thus problems of production and distribution finally led to a political dispute over the nature of the federal union, particularly the rôle of the courts in interpreting the Constitution.[2]

During the twenties American business seemed in the doldrums. Except for sharp rises in 1821 and again in 1825, wholesale commodity prices drifted steadily, though not alarmingly, lower, a trend more noticeable in the products of the factory than of the farm. The fluctuation of industrial prices corresponded rather closely with trends in Great Britain.[3] Public land sales fell off greatly. Only Indiana in 1824, Michigan in 1825 and Illinois two years later showed remarkable activity in this respect after the 1819 collapse.

Though foreign commerce also reflected the general decline of business, these years were rich in incidents of shifting trade routes, rising commercial centers and new forces in transportation.[4] Despite the enemy's solicitude for New England during the War of 1812, the British blockade, following hard upon embargo and nonintercourse, had taken a heavy toll. Salem, proud of her one hundred and eighty-two merchantmen en-

[1] McMaster, *History,* IV, 496-503; V, 412-417; Charles Warren, *Congress, the Constitution and the Supreme Court* (Boston, 1925), 194, 268.

[2] Rezneck, "Depression of 1819-1822," 46-47.

[3] Smith and Cole, *Fluctuations in American Business,* 60 ff.

[4] Southern ports interested in the West Indies commerce waged an unsuccessful struggle with Great Britain to regain their former share in trading with the Caribbean islands. F. L. Benns, *The American Struggle for the British West India Carrying-Trade, 1815-1830* (Indiana Univ., Studies, X, no. 56); T. J. Wertenbaker, *Norfolk: Historic Southern Port* (Durham, 1931), 158 ff.

gaged in foreign trade in 1807, had only fifty-seven eight years later. But her maritime energy survived. Salem captains still sought the Far East, opening Cochinchina to American commerce in 1819, daring to stop in the Fiji Islands and maintaining regular schedules in the Sumatra pepper trade. From Para, Brazil, if we may credit local tradition, they brought in 1824 the first shipment of pure gum "rubbers," heavy and clumsy, but equal to the slush of a Massachusetts winter.[1]

A significant movement of merchant-mariners occurred, from the smaller Massachusetts towns and from New Hampshire, Connecticut and Rhode Island to the ports of Boston and New York.[2] Beverly, Marblehead, Plymouth and Newburyport never recovered from the war until the noise of machinery filled their streets; but Gloucester and New Bedford found opportunities in the fisheries and whaling, the latter becoming the greatest whaling port in the country.[3] In other sections of seaboard New England, especially in Connecticut and Rhode Island, the road back to prosperity was marked by the growth of mill towns.[4]

As the smaller seaports declined in importance, Boston's commerce increased. The clouds which had hung low over State Street in 1814 were dispelled by successive annual reports of foreign trade. In 1806, the largest year of neutral commerce, over a thousand ships had entered Boston harbor from foreign ports. By 1830 that number had been surpassed and the arrivals represented greater individual tonnage.[5] The North-

---

[1] S. E. Morison, *The Maritime History of Massachusetts* (Boston, 1921), 217-222.

[2] R. G. Albion, "Yankee Domination of New York Port, 1820-1865," *New England Quar.*, V, 665 ff.

[3] Morison, *Maritime History*, 216-217.

[4] Timothy Pitkin, *A Statistical View of the Commerce of the United States* (New Haven, 1835), 523.

[5] W. P. Sterns, "The Foreign Trade of the United States from 1820 to 1840," *Journ. of Polit. Economy*, VIII, 34 ff.

west fur traffic, briefly reviving after 1815, fell off rapidly in the twenties because of the competition of English and American companies and the extensive activities of the Russians. If sea otter was now too scarce and costly for the China trade, sandalwood from the Sandwich Islands proved much in demand at the hongs of Canton. Boston merchants provided the Hawaiians with New England rum and Yankee notions until the sandalwood supply was virtually exhausted. With the New Bedford and Nantucket whalers they transformed Honolulu into a bit of Massachusetts in the Pacific. "Could I have forgotten the circumstances of my visit," wrote an American in 1833, "I should have fancied myself in New England." [1]

The traders of old India Wharf and newer Central Wharf were well aware that Boston's success depended upon her ability to draw extensive revenues from cargoes gathered in every harbor of the seven seas. Hence her merchant-shipowners pieced together profits from various ventures—supplying ice to the West Indies, carrying sugar from Havana to Göteborg for Swedish iron, selling domestic shirtings in Montevideo and Buenos Aires, importing pepper, fruits, nuts and olive oil from Mediterranean ports. In 1830 business-minded Bostonians believed, and rightly, that they were heading into a period of great maritime activity. [2]

It was New York, however, which people were now calling "the great commercial emporium of America." Though the port at the tip of Manhattan had taken first place in volume of exports and imports as early as 1797, its lead was not then great. In the last year before the War of 1812 the customs receipts indicated that New York, Boston and Philadelphia were almost equal

[1] Morison, *Maritime History*, 260-264. See also H. W. Bradley, *The American Frontier in Hawaii* (Stanford University, 1942), chap. ii.
[2] Morison, *Maritime History*, 225, 228-229, 237.

in the value of their foreign imports. In 1815, when that parity was upset by British "dumping," New York took a commanding position which it never lost.[1] This remarkable rise, occurring before the Erie Canal had increased its business, resulted partly from British preference for New York's harbor at the war's close. It was further stimulated by the state's favorable auction-sales laws and by the inauguration of the first packet line. The decade after 1815 contributed more to the success of New York port than the whole two centuries which had gone before.[2]

During the first quarter of the nineteenth century most American merchantmen were either "transients," picking up cargoes from port to port, or "regular traders," normally sailing a particular route between two or three ports and, in the European trade, managing to make two round trips each year. Few vessels undertook to meet previously announced schedules, and few owners coördinated sailings for the benefit of shippers. But the Black Ball Line in 1818 inaugurated a uniform service to Liverpool and soon had four packets, each making three round trips a year. No longer need New York auctioneers, drygoods merchants and manufacturers' agents rely upon the grudging accommodation of merchant-shipowners. The success of this pioneer line in weathering the depression years encouraged the formation of others until by 1830 thirty-six packets went to English ports, insuring three regular transatlantic sailings a week.[3] "Square-riggers" also maintained schedules from New York to Le Havre, to Belfast and to sev-

[1] In 1825 Boston and Philadelphia ranked next to New York in imports, while New Orleans was its closest rival in exports. E. R. Johnson and others, *History of Domestic and Foreign Commerce of the United States* (Carnegie Inst., *Publs.*, no. 215 A), II, 37-41.

[2] Albion, *New York Port*, 12-15.

[3] There are interesting details (not always accurate) and excellent illustrations in G. W. Sheldon, "The Old Packet and Clipper Service," *Harper's Mag.*, LXVIII (1883-1884), 217-237.

eral American ports, notably Charleston, Savannah, Mobile and New Orleans. Philadelphia had a line to Liverpool after 1821, but Baltimore's attempt met with little success. The packets specialized in "fine freight" of small bulk and high valuation, which helps to explain their success.

Their services were prized by the community beyond commercial circles, for scheduled sailings and relative speed soon won the patronage of transatlantic passengers. In 1826, for example, the cabin passengers on Liverpool packets were more than three times as numerous as those who arrived on other vessels. European news also rode the packets. Against the prevailing westerly winds of the North Atlantic these early ocean liners cut the trip to New York from an average of seven weeks to slightly over five, thus freshening up appreciably the stale "intelligence from Europe" in American newspapers. Of more importance were regular reports of commercial and financial news, which frequently gave New York merchants an advantage over their competitors in other seaboard cities.[1]

Mercantile success in the East depended largely upon the ability to distribute foreign imports to a wide inland market and to collect from country storekeepers goods for export. New York City was the natural mart for the Hudson Valley and the up-state counties, as well as for western Long Island, but the southwestern part of the state found an outlet down the Susquehanna toward Philadelphia, while the regions north of Albany belonged geographically to the commercial empire of the St. Lawrence.[2] New York's pretensions in Connecticut

[1] R. G. Albion, *Square-Riggers on Schedule: the New York Sailing Packets* (Princeton, 1938), chap. vii.

[2] Chilton Williamson, "New York's Struggle for Champlain Valley Trade, 1760-1825," *N. Y. History*, XXII, 433-436; D. G. Creighton, *The Commercial Empire of the St. Lawrence, 1760-1850* (New Haven, 1937), 248-250.

and other parts of western New England were somewhat challenged by Boston and New Haven, and in New Jersey the Philadelphia merchants held on to the Delaware River towns. East Jersey, however, looked toward Manhattan Island.[1] By 1820 New York's immediate hinterland had almost 1,600,000 inhabitants, slightly over a sixth of the country's entire population, but the growing port was handling a third of the national imports. Its exports were chiefly growth of the soil—ashes for making soap and glass or bleaching textiles; salt beef and salt pork for Caribbean consumption or for the rations of American and British mariners; flaxseed for Irish growers so that they might harvest their immature plants for manufacture into linens; and, above all, wheat, either fresh from the threshing floor, or ground and bolted in country mills and barreled as superfine flour. For a decade after 1815 New York lagged behind Philadelphia and Baltimore in the quantity of flour handled, but the extension of the market following the completion of the Erie Canal gave New York a decisive lead.[2]

At the same time the cotton bale was replacing the flour barrel as the great symbol of American export. In January, 1785, Liverpool had reported the first "bag" of Southern cotton. Twenty years later, thanks to Eli Whitney's gin, the United States had passed the West Indies as the source of British supply. Charleston and Savannah, both advantageously situated to receive the upland cotton from the backcountry, were the early outlets for this trade. By 1822, however, the westward advance of the South's new staple enabled New Orleans to surpass Charleston, while Mobile a decade later had

[1] W. J. Lane, *From Indian Trail to Iron Horse; Travel and Transportation in New Jersey, 1620-1860* (*Princeton History of New Jersey*, I; Princeton, 1939), 146-148, 211-215.
[2] Albion, *New York Port*, 76-83.

gathered the commerce of the Alabama rivers into a greater export trade than that of Savannah.[1]

New York importers maintained agents in Southern ports, sent them European goods to be exchanged for cotton, brought the fiber back and used it to meet their obligations to British merchants. By the twenties the famous "cotton triangle" (Charleston or Savannah or New Orleans to New York to Liverpool or Le Havre) was well established. Even after the Erie Canal boats began their east-west shuttle, Southern products handled in New York probably exceeded in value the Western commodities which have generally been credited with assuring that port's primacy.[2] Before 1830 Southern merchants were more likely customers than Western storekeepers for the British and Continental goods that reached New York's water front.

Every port dreamed of improvements of river, road or canal, which would bring Western products more rapidly to it. The enthusiasm for turnpikes was slowly tempered by experience with the inadequate facilities afforded by even the best roads.[3] The turnpike era merged imperceptibly into the golden age of steamboats and canals. But Secretary Gallatin's famous report on roads and canals in April, 1808, was prophecy rather than history.[4] Few projects had been completed. The Dismal Swamp Canal connected the lower end of Chesapeake Bay with the North Carolina sounds; the Santee and Cooper Canal, more than twenty miles in length, joined these two rivers just above Charleston; Boston was able to tap the Merrimack near the present site of

[1] U. B. Phillips, *A History of Transportation in the Eastern Cotton Belt to 1860* (N. Y., 1908), chaps. i-ii.

[2] See the excellent chapter on "The Cotton Triangle" in Albion, *New York Port*, 95-121.

[3] See earlier, chap. iv.

[4] Secretary of the Treasury, *Report on the Subject of Public Roads and Canals* (Wash., 1808).

Lowell by means of the Middlesex Canal. Many of the waterways described by Gallatin, however, were short works around falls or rapids in navigable rivers. Though New Yorkers had hoped for federal aid to connect the Hudson with Lake Erie, it was not until the canal promoters succeeded in interesting DeWitt Clinton that paper plans took more substantial form.[1] After his successful race for governor in the spring of 1817, he had the satisfaction of hearing his political foe, Martin Van Buren, plead for legislation which would make possible the diversion of Great Lakes commerce to the valley of the Hudson. On July 4, 1817, a small group at the little village of Rome watched a contractor lift the first shovelful of earth on the greatest construction job that Americans had yet undertaken.[2]

If rare foresight and imagination had conceived the idea of the Erie Canal, great resourcefulness and courage were required to build it. Buffalo, finally designated as the western terminus, was an unpromising port. Between the Mohawk and Lake Erie stretched a wilderness of forest and swamp broken infrequently by small villages. An air of defiant audacity marked Benjamin Wright who became technical supervisor of construction. His title of engineer rested more upon courtesy than upon training. One of his ablest assistants, Canvass White, had undertaken a minute examination of the canals of Great Britain, tramping the towpaths for two thousand miles, making drawings and gathering suggestions for new and better implements. With his asso-

[1] In March, 1817, Madison had vetoed Calhoun's bonus bill which the votes of representatives from Middle Atlantic and Western states had carried through House and Senate. Constitutional scruple prevented his signing a measure to devote federal funds to the construction of a national system of internal improvements. McMaster, *History*, IV, 410-415.

[2] N. E. Whitford, *History of the Canal System of the State of New York* (Albany, 1906), I, 83, 88. The use of Lake Ontario was avoided for safety not only against storms but against Canadian interference in case of war. This entailed a long canal with many locks.

ciates he solved the problem of stonework by developing from Chittenango stone a variety of hydraulic cement equal to the best in Europe. Ingenious devices either improved upon or replaced the tools which had fashioned the canals of the Old World. A cable attached high on a tree, and operated by an endless screw, enabled a single laborer to bring down the largest ones. A stump puller worked by seven men and a team could account for thirty or forty stumps each day. The familiar shovel and wheelbarrow were almost completely supplanted by scrapers and plows equipped with special blades for cutting roots and swamp underbrush.[1] Yankee ingenuity was supplemented by Hibernian brawn. Of the Montezuma marshes in the Onondaga Valley a resident of Rome wrote, "Bog trotters from the West of Ireland, cutting out the trees the width of the canal track, were set to work knee deep in the wet muck; they could wear no clothing but a flannel shirt and a slouch cap." They were part of that great army of Irishmen, which from the close of the eighteenth century to the Civil War dug America's canals.[2]

On October 26, 1825, a little fleet moved eastward along the canal to the accompaniment of cheers, band music and salvos of musketry, being attended down the Hudson from Albany by many gayly decorated steamboats. If we may credit newspaper accounts, thirty thousand visitors crowded New York City to witness the "wedding of the waters," as Governor Clinton opened the kegs brought from Buffalo and poured their contents into the sea. The union of Lake Erie and the Atlantic had been consummated.[3] Philadelphians might regard the ceremony and attendant celebrations as some-

[1] Whitford, *Canal System*, I, 91, 96-97, 104.
[2] A. F. Harlow, *Old Towpaths* (N. Y., 1926), 54.
[3] Whitford, *Canal System*, I, 127; C. D. Colden, *Memoir Prepared . . . at the Celebration of the Completion of the New York Canals* (N. Y., 1825), 273-274.

what absurd, but New Yorkers had reasons for rejoicing, even before they could be sure how much commercial advantage they had gained. With a population of less than a million and a half, the state had constructed two canals, the Champlain and the Erie, representing an investment of almost eight million dollars of public funds. Their completion marked a notable victory over forest and swamp, over typhoid and malaria, won despite the handicap of crude tools and makeshift methods. Even if traffic on the new waterways should prove of little consequence, their construction had made great contributions to the advancement of engineering in America.[1]

Any doubt concerning the value of the New York canals was soon dispelled. By 1826 it was clear that the produce of the Champlain Valley would not find its outlet down the St. Lawrence, enriching the merchants of Montreal and Quebec, but would follow the Champlain canal route southward to Albany and the Hudson.[2] Annual tolls were in the neighborhood of seventy-five thousand dollars. This amount, however, was a mere bagatelle compared with the seven hundred thousand earned each year by the Erie. It was not uncommon for the Albany press to list fifty arrivals from the West in a single day.[3] Moreover, the influence of Clinton's "Big Ditch" was steadily lengthening. The cost of transporting goods between the Ohio Valley and New York City was cut in half and the time reduced by a third. Travelers between New York and New Orleans no longer relied solely on coastwise packets. Some took the route up the Hudson and across the Erie Canal, then transferred to stagecoaches for the overland

[1] See later, 330-331.
[2] Williamson, "New York's Struggle for Champlain Valley Trade," 435.
[3] Joel Munsell, ed., *The Annals of Albany* (Albany, 1850-1859), VIII, 125, 161; X, 385.

ride to Pittsburgh, where Ohio River steamers made regular trips to the metropolis of Louisiana.[1]

In 1827 an observant English traveler recorded the effect of the canal on Rochester, which fifteen years earlier had been a wilderness of forest and underbrush. "Everything in this bustling place," he wrote, "appears to be in motion. . . . Here and there we saw great warehouses, without window sashes, but half-filled with goods, and furnished with hoisting cranes, ready to fish up the huge pyramids of flour barrels, bales, and boxes lying in the streets." [2] Up and down the Hudson there were exciting stories, told in tavern and countinghouse, of the "boom" towns along the canal. Utica rose in ten years from an unkempt village to the dignity of a prosperous city.[3] Syracuse, in 1820 a desolate hamlet of two hundred and fifty inhabitants, increased its population tenfold in a decade and boasted machine shops, leather mills, gristmills and marble yards.[4] Shrewd residents of Cleaveland (as they preferred to spell it) gauged the town's future by the growing lake traffic and the declining canal rates. Distance was but an "obsolete nuisance." Its elimination was enabling producers in the basin of the Great Lakes to plan in terms of a market at the port of New York.[5]

The prosperity of central and western New York aroused mixed feelings in Boston, Philadelphia, Baltimore, Norfolk and other Atlantic ports. Apprehension over New York's success stirred a desire to emulate its methods,[6] as the best way to tap the markets of the

[1] McMaster, *History*, V, 133-136; Harlow, *Old Towpaths*, 342 ff.

[2] Basil Hall, *Travels in North America in the Years 1827 and 1828* (Phila., 1829), I, 87.

[3] W. L. Stone, "Journal of a Tour from New York to Niagara," Buffalo Hist. Soc., *Publs.*, XIV, 207-264.

[4] M. C. Hand, *From a Forest to a City* (Syracuse, 1889), 183-184.

[5] *Cleaveland Herald*, March 23, 1827.

[6] R. G. Albion, "New York Port and Its Disappointed Rivals, 1815-1860," *Journ. of Business and Econ. History*, III, 602 ff.

hinterland. Rapidly the "canal craze" developed, reaching its climax during the thirties and then receding before the challenge of the railway.[1] Bostonians, eager to cut through the Berkshires, had to be content with improvements in the old Middlesex Canal which tapped the Merrimack rather than the Hudson.[2] Other projects in New England were on a less pretentious scale. The first boat passed through the Blackstone Canal from Worcester, Massachusetts, to Providence in 1828. New Haven's desire to secure the traffic of the Connecticut Valley led to the digging of a canal which by 1835 connected Northampton, Massachusetts, with the Connecticut port. Important though these projects were for local trade, none brought New England its contact with the transportation lines to the West.[3]

Philadelphia's commerce in the twenties was menaced not only by the Erie Canal but also by the probability that the traffic of the Susquehanna might find its permanent outlet at Baltimore.[4] To meet the latter threat work was revived on two canal projects of long standing—the Schuylkill and the Union—and in 1828 a waterway was opened to Middletown, New York. There remained the problem of how best to answer New York's bid for the trans-Alleghany commerce. Advocates of a railway were strident, but decision was taken in favor of a grand canal uniting Pittsburgh and Philadelphia. Though profiting from New York's experience, the builders of Pennsylvania's waterway failed to

[1] See C. R. Fish, *The Rise of the Common Man, 1830-1850* (*A History of American Life*, VI), 75-77, 84-85.

[2] Caleb Eddy, *Historical Sketch of the Middlesex Canal* (Boston, 1843), *passim;* Christopher Roberts, *The Middlesex Canal, 1793-1860* (*Harvard Econ. Studies,* LXI), 19-45.

[3] H. S. Tanner, *A Description of the Canals and Rail Roads of the United States* (N. Y., 1840), 43, 48-49.

[4] For an early warning of Pennsylvania's dilemma, see W. J. Duane, *Letters Addressed to the People of Pennsylvania, Respecting the Internal Improvement of the Commonwealth* (Phila., 1811), 88-90.

match Clinton's "Big Ditch." Neither tunnel nor lock could conquer the Alleghany barrier. Consequently, from Hollidaysburg to Johnstown the crest of the mountain ridge was surmounted by means of horse cars and inclined planes operated by stationary engines. As a carrier to the West the main line handled neither freight nor passenger boats as rapidly and cheaply as did the Erie.[1]

South of Philadelphia merchants were equally confident that canals would spell prosperity. Washington, Georgetown and Alexandria expected to share the increased commerce which the Chesapeake and Ohio Canal would bring to the Bay region. Richmond looked forward to the day when the James River and the Kanawha would be joined.[2] Norfolk, caught in the net which British regulations cast over her trade with the West Indies, found some hope of commercial recovery in the improved Dismal Swamp Canal, ready in 1828.[3] There were many similar ventures, some grandiose, others trivial. In the ten years before 1830 more than eight hundred miles of canals were opened in Maryland, Delaware, Pennsylvania and New York, while at the close of that decade an additional thirteen hundred miles were nearing completion. In New Jersey, Ohio, Indiana and Illinois a score of projects were emerging from the "blueprint" stage.[4]

Meanwhile Americans were making greater use of steam navigation. Its possibilities had been demonstrated on August 17, 1807, as Robert Fulton's *Clermont* moved slowly up the Hudson, sparks flying from

[1] T. B. Klein, *The Canals of Pennsylvania and the System of Internal Improvements* (Harrisburg, 1901), 16; Harlow, *Old Towpaths*, 92-103.

[2] W. F. Dunaway, *History of the James River and Kanawha Company* (N. Y., 1922), 110.

[3] Benns, *Struggle for the British West India Carrying-Trade*, 153-154; Wertenbaker, *Norfolk*, 173-177.

[4] Harlow, *Old Towpaths*, 73; R. T. Thompson, *Colonel James Neilson* (New Brunswick, 1940), chap. vii.

her smokestack and the clanking of her steam-driven machinery drowning out the splashing of her paddle wheels. The speed was not impressive, for the trip from New York to Albany took slightly more than thirty hours. Yet even those inclined to scoff sensed that great changes in transportation were in the making.[1] There had been forerunners of Fulton—John Fitch and James Rumsey experimenting on the Delaware and Potomac rivers;[2] David Wilkinson dismantling his steamboat in 1794 after a successful "frolic" in Providence Harbor; Oliver Evans trying out his surprising *Oruktor Amphibolos* on the Schuylkill in 1804; and John Stevens making trial runs from Hoboken to test the principle of the steam-driven screw propeller.[3] Toward the close of the eighteenth century "a sort of mania began to prevail . . . for impelling boats by steam-engines."[4]

In the *Clermont* venture Fulton's debt to others was heavy. Not only was he familiar with several of the American experiments, but he had also examined the equipment of an English steam tugboat. The engine and boiler, which made the *Clermont's* run possible, were manufactured by the British firm of Watt and Boulton and purchased by Fulton with the financial assistance of Chancellor Robert R. Livingston, an enthusiastic student of steam navigation, who had taken time from his diplomatic duties in Paris to explore suggestions which he found in French works. Livingston's

[1] H. W. Dickinson, *Robert Fulton* (N. Y., 1913), 217-218; D. L. Buckman, *Old Steamboat Days on the Hudson River* (N. Y., 1907), 11.

[2] E. B. Greene, *The Revolutionary Generation, 1763-1790* (*A History of American Life*, IV), 65-66, 345-346.

[3] Thompson Westcott, *The Life of John Fitch* (Phila., 1857), chap. xiii; J. W. Roe, *English and American Tool Builders* (2nd edn., N. Y., 1926), 119. See also Oliver Evans, "Steam Engines," *Medical Repository*, VIII (1804-1805), 317-321.

[4] B. H. Latrobe, "First Report to the American Philosophical Society," *Am. Philos. Soc., Trans.*, VI, 90.

Scene on the Erie Canal

The "Paragon," on the Hudson, about 1812

contribution was threefold. He brought direction to
Fulton's energy; his political influence secured from the
New York legislature an exclusive grant to navigate the
state's waters with steam; and his connections with the
merchants of New York City insured the attention of
men who could use the steamboat.[1]

It was the inland waterways, however, rather than
the safe reaches of New York Harbor and Long Island
Sound, that witnessed the most notable triumphs of this
new form of navigation. The first steamboat west of the
Alleghanies was built in 1798 at Bardstown, Kentucky,
by that same John Fitch who had given up his enterprise on the Delaware; his Western venture, however,
proved even less fruitful than his Eastern one. For another fifteen years most of the hardy woodsmen, who
annually floated downstream to New Orleans to dispose of their agricultural surpluses, were compelled to
make the long journey back on foot or, at best, on horseback. It was cheaper and easier to haul merchandise
from Philadelphia to Pittsburgh in wagons at one hundred and twenty-five dollars a ton than to force it against
the current of the Mississippi.[2] But in 1811 Nicholas
Roosevelt, in association with Livingston and Fulton,
persuaded the Louisiana legislature to grant an exclusive
use of the lower Mississippi for steamboats. Their first
vessel, the *New Orleans*, built at Pittsburgh, steamed
down the river to reach New Orleans early in January,
1812. Four years later the *Washington*, equipped with
stern paddle wheels and cleverly piloted by Captain
Henry M. Shreve, made two round trips between New
Orleans and Louisville, cutting the time upstream to a
quarter that required by the barges and keel boats. It

[1] See John Stevens, "Letter Relative to Steam Boats," *Am. Medical
and Philos. Register*, II (1812), 416-426.
[2] Josiah Lawton, *Oration on the Importance of Scientific Knowledge*
(Providence, 1826), 7-8; F. E. Dayton, *Steamboat Days* (N. Y., 1925),
332-333.

was an event, wrote Salmon P. Chase many years later, "of more momentous consequences to the West than the issues of a thousand battles." [1]

The Livingston-Fulton monopoly, however, made competition difficult, if not impossible. A suit in the Louisiana courts to break the exclusive grant reached the Supreme Court shortly before Marshall's famous opinion in Gibbons v. Ogden settled the principle at issue. Thomas Gibbons little knew how great a boon he was conferring on the producers and shippers of the Mississippi Valley when he opened a ferry line between Elizabethtown, New Jersey, and New York City, deliberately challenging Aaron Ogden, who was operating under a Livingston-Fulton license. The New York courts granted Ogden an injunction, but on appeal, which in 1824 finally reached the Supreme Court, Daniel Webster and William Wirt had the satisfaction of winning judicial approval for the doctrine of freedom of navigation subject only to congressional regulations.[2] "The navigable waters of this state, and of the United States, are again free," declared the New Jersey Journal, March 16, 1824. This was particularly pleasing to a young skipper in Thomas Gibbons's employ. His name was Cornelius Vanderbilt and already he had many plans for the steamboat.

The breaking of the monopoly was the signal for renewed activity in the shipyards, notably on the Ohio and the Mississippi.[3] By 1830 about two hundred boats were in operation in these waters, though the estimated losses ran as high as a hundred for the preced-

[1] Ohio Statutes, I, 11, cited in E. L. Bogart, Economic History of the American People (N. Y., 1936), 329, 353; Dayton, Steamboat Days, 334-336.

[2] 9 Wheaton, 1 ff.; Lane, From Indian Trail to Iron Horse, 185-194.

[3] C. H. Ambler, History of Transportation in the Ohio Valley (Glendale, 1932), 151-152.

ing twenty years. Even the most skillful pilot was lucky to avoid the shifting sand bars and submerged rocks; and no engineer, however competent, could protect passengers against the hazards of boiler explosions and devastating fires. When Charles Dickens a few years later somewhat reluctantly used this mode of transportation, he remarked, "It always conveyed that kind of feeling to me which I should be likely to experience, if I had lodgings on the first floor of a powder mill." [1]

Since the life of the average steamboat was short, profits had to be quick and large.[2] The *New Orleans*, for instance, earned half its cost of forty thousand dollars in its first year. Such profits, however, could not be maintained under the terrific pressure for greater speed and lower rates. The trip from New Orleans to Natchez, which took five and a half days in 1814, required only one day and twenty-one hours twenty years later. As fares declined and accommodations improved, the number of passengers increased. A trend toward gaudy designs indicated an effort to attract patronage.[3] In the year of Dickens's visit (1842) the tonnage of Mississippi steamboats exceeded that of the entire British Empire.[4]

But the steamboat did not solve the country's transportation problems. Its usefulness was greatest upon rivers, lakes and the protected bays and inlets of the Atlantic Seaboard. Even after the *Clermont's* successful trial run, sloops continued for several decades to transport the major portion of the products of the Hudson

[1] Cited in Dayton, *Steamboat Days*, 340.

[2] F. H. Dixon, *A Traffic History of the Mississippi River System* (Natl. Waterways Comn., Doc., no. 11), 13, 26-27.

[3] For an account of a trip down the Ohio and Mississippi rivers, see Mr. Hooper's "Journal," *Missionary Herald*, XVII (1821), 311-312, 345-346.

[4] A. B. Hulbert, *The Paths of Inland Commerce* (Allen Johnson, ed., *The Chronicles of America Series*, New Haven, 1918-1921, XXI), 182.

Valley to market.[1] Similarly on the Ohio and Mississippi and the lower reaches of the Missouri keel boats and flatboats kept on carrying bulky commodities downstream long after the wood-burning steamers had instituted regular schedules for freight and passengers. The first steamer on the Great Lakes, the *Walk-in-the-Water*, making its initial voyage from Buffalo to Detroit in August, 1818, proved so unprofitable as to discourage rival operators. Eighteen years later there were on the lakes only forty-five American steamboats, all primarily designed to carry passengers.[2] In like fashion the sailing packet maintained its supremacy in the coastwise trade, though some bay steamers ran from New York to Baltimore, Charleston or New Orleans during the twenties. After the experimental voyage of the *Savannah* to Ireland in 1819, more than a quarter-century elapsed before another American steamship attempted an Atlantic crossing.[3]

The transport lines, quickened by the steamboat, generally followed a north-south direction and therefore failed to connect Eastern ports with trans-Appalachia. Those links, begun by the turnpikes and the towpaths of canals, were later completed by the tracks of railroads. Just as the pack-horse men had resisted the first efforts to construct toll roads, so the turnpike companies and canal promoters did their utmost to discourage the railroad builders.[4] Equally hostile were the tavern keepers, freight handlers and draymen; and they found ready allies among persons who disliked change. Steam locomotion was impractical, said some mechanics; it was too

---

[1] J. S. Curtiss, "The Sloops of the Hudson, 1800-1850," *N. Y. History*, XIV, 61 ff.

[2] *Cleaveland Herald*, April 8, 1830; Dayton, *Steamboat Days*, 404.

[3] D. B. Tyler, *Steam Conquers the Atlantic* (N. Y., 1939), chaps. i-ii.

[4] For the struggle over canals and railroads in New Jersey, see Thompson, *Colonel James Neilson*, chap. vii.

costly to benefit the average producer, said others. Farmers believed that, if the advent of the railroad meant a lower cost of distribution for certain industries, this advantage would be gained at the expense of agriculture.[1] Furthermore, the dangers of steam navigation were insignificant in comparison with the hazards of railroads. A few even based their opposition on moral grounds: it was obviously sinful, in view of the Lord's plans for mankind, to travel at a speed of fifteen or twenty miles an hour.[2] Determined though this opposition seemed to be, it quickly disappeared when disputation gave way to demonstration.

America produced no Robert Fulton of the railroad, no counterpart of George Stephenson's achievement in England with the *Rocket*. Yet the basic ideas of the steam railway had an original development in this country almost to the point of practicality, even if the final importation was from Europe. Oliver Evans in later years remembered that his first speculations concerning steam carriages had been stirred in 1772 while apprenticed to a wagon maker and that he had turned seriously to work on steam wagons after reading descriptions of Thomas Newcomen's engine.[3] The Maryland legislature in 1787 gave him the exclusive right for fourteen years to make and use such wagons within the state, but even this grant did not induce private capitalists to provide the small sum necessary for experimentation. Scientists as well as laymen were skeptical. Thus Benjamin H. Latrobe reported to the American Philosophical Society in 1803 that Evans's ideas were

[1] Some farm journals, however, stressed the advantages of railroads over canals. Anon., "Comparative Advantage of Canals and Rail Roads," *New England Farmer*, III, 355 (June 3, 1825).

[2] T. W. Van Metre, *Early Opposition to the Steam Railroad* (N. Y., 1924).

[3] Oliver Evans, "On the Origin of Steam Boats and Steam Waggons," *Niles' Wkly. Register*, III (1812), "Addenda," 2-6.

absurd.¹ Satisfied by the profits from his flour-milling machinery and stationary engines, Evans never built his steam carriage.

Evans's resignation was not shared by Colonel John Stevens of Hoboken, New Jersey. Convinced by experiments with steamboats after 1796 that the railway was more practical than the canal, he presented his views to the New York commissioners for the improvement of inland navigation.² This, the first important railroad document published in the United States, failed to persuade the commissioners; but what New York rejected, New Jersey approved. In February, 1815, the legislators at Trenton granted Stevens a charter authorizing the construction of a railroad between the Delaware and the Raritan.³ Had the project materialized, New Jersey might have moved quickly out of the turnpike era into the railway age, but the charter lapsed, for in view of the rising canal agitation capitalists were hesitant to take risks when the experts disagreed. Yet Stevens and his talented sons, Robert Livingston and Edward Augustus, completed in 1826 a small circular track upon which they ran a locomotive of their own construction.⁴ Though it was the first steam locomotive built in America to operate on rails, it attracted little attention.

The discussion inspired by these experiments ac-

¹ American Philosophical Society, *Transactions*, VI, 92; *American State Papers* (Wash., 1832-1861), *Miscellaneous*, 916. When his offer to build for a $3000 bet a wagon "propelled by steam," able "to run upon a level road against the swiftest horse," aroused no response, Evans philosophically wrote: "When we reflect upon the obstinate opposition that has been made by a great majority to every step towards improvement . . . it is too much to expect the monstrous leap from bad roads to rail-ways for steam carriages, at once." Evans, "Origin of Steam Boats," 4-5.

² [John Stevens], *Documents Tending to Prove the Superior Advantages of Rail-Ways and Steam-Carriages over Canal Navigation* (N. Y., 1812).

³ *Laws of New Jersey*, 39th Session, 2nd Sitting, Statute 68.

⁴ A. D. Turnbull, *John Stevens, an American Record* (N. Y., 1928), 477-483.

quainted Americans with the work that was being done in England. In 1824 the Pennsylvania Society for the Promotion of Internal Improvements sent William Strickland across the Atlantic to investigate particularly the application of steam locomotives to tramways. Strickland's fifty-page report, published with numerous plates in 1826, was freely copied by Eastern newspapers.[1] A few American engineers were prompted to see the developments for themselves.[2] Strickland's opinions were sensationally confirmed by the success of Stephenson's *Rocket* when tried on the Liverpool and Manchester Railway in the fall of 1829. Thus the mingled contributions of Europe and America were laying the basis for the world's greatest railway system.[3]

Merchants, watching the expansion of their markets, seemed slow to realize what steam locomotion on land might mean to them, yet they were generally men of large vision. Among them a certain hierarchy had developed during the first quarter of the nineteenth century, though the lines were not rigid and a fusion of functions was much more common than specialization. Foreign textiles, for instance, might flow along such a channel as importer-jobber-retailer-consumer. The sequence was similar for American-made drygoods, if one substituted "domestic wholesaler" for "importer." But only in the larger cities were these gradations clearly defined. In such centers there might be two types of wholesalers — merchant middlemen and agent middlemen. The former took title to the various commodities which they handled, while the agent middlemen — com-

[1] William Strickland, *Reports on Canals, Railways, Roads, and Other Subjects, Made to "The Pennsylvania Society for the Promotion of Internal Improvements"* (Phila., 1826).

[2] Horatio Allen, then engineer for the Delaware and Hudson Canal Company, had an English locomotive, the *Stourbridge Lion*, tested on the tramway of the Carbondale and Honesdale Coal Company in 1829. Philip Hone, *Diary* (Allan Nevins, ed., N. Y., 1927), I, xiv.

[3] For later developments, see Fish, *Rise of the Common Man*, 78-84.

mission merchants or factors, brokers and auctioneers — avoided the risks normally involved in ownership.[1] Some wholesalers did a job-lot business, buying from importers who specialized in a single line of goods. Thus Joseph Hertzog of Philadelphia bought up varied assortments from importers in order to supply retailers along the Ohio and in St. Louis.[2]

Both foreign and domestic producers relied chiefly upon commission merchants, brokers and auctioneers to establish contacts with retailers.　The decade following the War of 1812 marked the heyday of the auction system.　It cut into the business of importers and wholesale jobbers, who were quick to protest.　Beginning in 1817, they vainly petitioned Congress for heavy duties on auction sales, but the delegates at a convention of the United Dry Goods Mercantile Association in New York in 1821 admitted that there was small chance of success without the coöperation of "those from populous towns, and sister cities, more or less remote," who frequented sales in New York and other seaports.[3]　The popularity of auctions waned only when improvements in transportation made it possible for many inland towns to become wholesale centers and when manufacturers began to send aggressive agents into all parts of the nation to solicit business from country merchants who had once flocked to the Eastern sales.[4]

[1] F. J. Jones, *Middlemen in the Domestic Trade of the United States, 1800-1860* (Ill. Studies in the Social Sciences, XXI, no. 3), 9-10.

[2] Sister Marietta Jennings, *A Pioneer Merchant of St. Louis, 1810-1820* (Columbia Univ., Studies, no. 462), 11-19.

[3] *Niles' Wkly. Register*, XXI, 103 (Oct. 13, 1821).　In 1828-1829 the New York Workingmen's party condemned the auction system as a form of monopoly "hostile to the equal rights of the American merchant, manufacturer, mechanic and laboring man."　Horace Secrist, *The Anti-Auction Movement and the New York Workingmen's Party of 1829* (Wis. Acad. of Sciences, Arts and Letters, Trans., XVII), pt. i. 154.

[4] For a summary of state laws controlling auctioneers, see Jones, *Middlemen*, 40-43.

The American commission merchant was a great boon to the European manufacturer or merchant who did not wish to sell outright to an American importer and who lacked the capital to establish a branch house. Into the commission merchant's hands, through his contacts with general storekeepers in small villages, came also the rising volume of marketable produce from Northern farms.[1] He was prepared to sell these commodities advantageously in the wholesale markets of the Atlantic Seaboard or to start them on their way to foreign buyers. Similarly, tobacco and cotton planters found their net returns higher by relying upon some commission merchant to gauge the trend of prices and to determine the most opportune moment to sell. Manufacturers, as they exhausted the possibilities of the local market, also turned to a middleman who knew how to utilize distant opportunities.

We may trace the various activities of a commission merchant in the letter books of Oliver Wolcott and Company. In 1803, a few years after retiring from the secretaryship of the treasury, Wolcott joined four leading merchants of New York City—James Watson, Moses Rogers, William W. Woolsey and Archibald Gracie — in a general wholesale and commission business. He obtained from Francis Baring and Company an advance of £10,000 sterling in order to finance transactions in which London exchange was essential. Through a voluminous correspondence his firm secured the latest price quotations from London, Liverpool, Lisbon and other markets and in return sent reports on crop prospects and prices current in New York. Commissions ranged from the purchase of a few lottery tickets for a principal in Maryland to the handling of

[1] On mercantile organization, see Margaret Martin, *Merchants and Trade of the Connecticut River Valley* (Smith College, *Studies*, XXIV), 102-130.

thousands of barrels of flour for Asa and Daniel Hopkins of Hartford, who were active in the West Indies trade. Both as agent and principal, Wolcott and Company were involved in speculative ventures in the Orient, Canton and Calcutta appearing in their ledgers almost as frequently as London and Amsterdam. But they did not neglect opportunities nearer home. There were many profitable transactions in Louisiana sugar, New York flour and Rhode Island textiles. There were also offsetting losses, for the risks of such far-flung operations proved great.[1]

The general commission merchant frequently performed the services also of shipper, warehouse proprietor, insurance company and banker, utilizing his own facilities rather than bringing his principals into contact with specialists in these several functions. The Neilson brothers of New Brunswick, New Jersey, for example, found that their shipping between the Raritan and New York City was more profitable during the twenties than their wholesale and commission business.[2] Christian Wilt, trading out of St. Louis on his own account and as a commission merchant, owned a fleet of river boats at the close of the War of 1812.[3]

As an embryonic banker, the commission merchant stood in his most intimate relation to retailers, urban and rural. Usually he sold on credit of from four to six months. When prompter payment was required he often made a financial advance in order to facilitate exchange. By the late 1820's it was becoming customary to grant Western retailers six months' credit without interest and then to extend the period for another six months at a charge of from six to ten per cent.[4] South-

[1] Letter Books, 1803-1808, Oliver Wolcott and Company, New York City, in the New York Historical Society Library.
[2] Thompson, *Colonel James Neilson*, 36.
[3] Jennings, *Pioneer Merchant*, 127-141.
[4] Luke Shortfield, *The Western Merchant* (Phila., 1849), 119-120.

ern planters expected advances as high as three fourths
of the market value of their cotton, tobacco or sugar.
In addition to financing the transfer of goods, the agent
middlemen performed other banking functions. They
might occasionally be called upon to buy or sell securities or specie, and they were frequently authorized to
draw, indorse, accept or sell bills of exchange, for which
they received two and one half per cent. While it is
impossible to determine the precise influence of these
merchants upon commercial activities, by 1830 they were
probably handling the major portion of the goods exchanged in this country on the basis of money payments.

Along the lines established by the commission houses
capital flowed into all sections of the nation. Retail
merchants were the transformers making it available
for commercial transactions, individually unimportant
but in the aggregate significant.

At the opening of the nineteenth century few retailers
could afford to confine their stocks to a particular kind
of goods. Typical of the limited market with slow
means of transportation and communication was the
general store, exchanging goods for goods and providing
an outlet, however small, for the community's surplus
produce. Its stock was always varied, sometimes inferior and seldom large. Observing the small country
stores in western Pennsylvania in 1806, Thomas Ashe
was reminded of a well-stocked magazine where one
could find "both a needle and an anchor, a tin pot and a
large copper boiler, a child's whistle and a pianoforte
. . . a glass of whiskey and a barrel of brandy." [1]
When Jedediah Barber opened the "Great Western
Store" at Homer, New York, in 1813, he managed to
crowd his merchandise into a room twenty-two feet by
thirty. Fifteen years later his establishment, consisting

[1] Thomas Ashe, *Travels in America, Performed in 1806* (London,
1808), I, 108-109.

of three stories besides an attic and a cellar, contained
an assortment of drygoods, staple and fancy, "equal to
any in the western country." Though the opening of
the Erie Canal had cut down the long haul for Albany
goods from a hundred and fifty miles to thirty, from
seven days to one, the Great Western continued to carry
the same wide variety of articles.[1] Indeed, the general
store in America changed little in a half-century. The
descriptions of it at the time Abraham Lincoln was born
are not inappropriate for the Offut establishment in
Salem, Illinois, where he later worked, or for the country
store flourishing in the year that he became President.

Though the rural retailer based his business largely
on barter, certain articles could not be purchased without
cash. Among them were tea, coffee and powder and
frequently leather, iron and lead. On the other hand,
some products were so much in demand and so easy to
transport that they passed currently as specie. Pennsylvania, Ohio and Missouri merchants were inclined to
place deerskins, furs, feathers, linen cloth and beeswax
in this category.[2] The system of barter held some advantages for the storekeeper. Whatever country produce he accepted was valued lower than the price at
which he expected to dispose of it, and he often had complete control of the marketable surplus in his immediate
neighborhood. At times, however, this scarcely compensated for the risks of transportation he was compelled to assume.

Whether sales were made for money or goods, the
country storekeeper rendered important services to the
community. His contacts with distant market centers,

[1] H. B. Howe, "Jedediah Barber, 1787-1876, Merchant of Homer,"
N. Y. History, XVII, 296-297.
[2] F. A. Michaux, Travels to the Westward of the Allegany Mountains
(London, 1805), 157; W. C. Howells, Recollections of Life in Ohio,
from 1813 to 1840 (Cincinnati, 1895), 137-138; Jennings, Pioneer
Merchant, 29-31.

domestic and foreign, enabled the people to concentrate upon those forms of production for which they were particularly qualified. For many of them these were the first tentative steps away from a self-sufficient economy toward economic specialization. Not least of the merchant's services was the extension of long-term credits. Probably a majority of his customers settled accounts only twice a year, in January and June, while some expected to be carried from one year's crop to the next.[1] That such concessions did not always prove sufficient is apparent from the yellowed pages of account books of the period.

In our admiration for the frontiersman blazing new trails, or the farmer clearing new land, we are apt to forget the pioneer merchant. He too was daring and determined. Many a Western community owed its origin to his decision to start a store at a particular crossroads or on the banks of a certain stream. As often as not, he preceded settlement, spying out opportunities for farm families who later contributed to his own prosperity. Shrewd and aggressive, he rendered signal public service, even when his acquisitive spirit was but slightly curbed by a sense of social responsibility. As his general store grew in size and his goods improved in quality, the range of his interests steadily widened. To farming — usually the initial accompaniment of shopkeeping — he proceeded to add milling and other forms of manufacturing. The grain which he accepted in exchange for wares was not all shipped to New Orleans or Eastern seaports; much of it was ground into flour at his own gristmill. An abundance of timber

---

[1] Samuel Stoddard, for example, settled his account of $33.78 covering eight months, January to August, 1831, by paying the storekeeper at Pinckney Corners, Lewis County, New York, 49 pounds of butter at 14 cents; three thousand shingles at $1.50; two skins, $1.25; two cords of wood, $1.25; and the balance of one dollar in cash. *Potsdam* (N. Y.) *Herald-Recorder*, May 6, 1932.

might lead him to erect a simple sawmill, or the opportunity to process other raw materials might result in his becoming a manufacturer of rope, bagging, paper or tobacco products.[1]

To a large extent the general storekeepers controlled the growth of their respective communities. The capital available for new investments was either in their hands, or was responsive to their suggestions. They became promoters of real-estate "booms," some of which collapsed in the depression of 1818-1819 only to be revived during the following decade. Many aspired to the rôle of merchant-bankers. Since banks were few outside the larger cities, the village merchant, with his commercial contacts in distant market centers, not only performed elementary functions of deposit, loan and discount, but also served as financial adviser to all comers. Thus to his own accumulations was added other people's money for investments or highly speculative ventures, as the case might be. Few knew so well as he the financial status of his neighbors; few therefore were so able to realize upon business opportunities.

If the typical merchant was not always stirred by philanthropic impulses, he vaguely believed that social progress automatically flowed from adherence to a stern code of morals. In his thinking that code was not sharply defined, but it included a strong sense of the right of private property, the necessity of hard work and thrift and the sinfulness of idleness and dissipation. Through it ran an abiding confidence in the future progress of one's village as well as one's country. For the unfortunate there was sympathy, but it was tempered by condemnation of the personal faults which caused an individual to fall far behind his fellows. Inner reform was more effective than charity. One should be frugal

---

[1] L. E. Atherton, "The Services of the Frontier Merchant," *Miss. Valley Hist. Rev.*, XXIV, 153-171.

in philanthropy as in all else. The country merchant was not unlike his neighbors in accepting these principles, but his imprimatur was more significant than their approval, for he wielded great economic power in local affairs. He became the embodiment of the common-sense philosophy of "Poor Richard" and the prototype of the American village magnate so revealingly delineated later in *David Harum*.

Much that has been said concerning the general store-keeper applies also to the business of the urban retailer. Yet there were differences. By the opening of the nineteenth century a tendency toward specialization was apparent in the larger towns. City directories in Philadelphia, New York, Boston and Providence classified most of the retail stores as dealers in groceries, drygoods, hardware and queen's ware, the favorite combination being groceries and drygoods. The gradual separation of these two branches was a development of the first three decades of the century. Such specialization did not prevent the proprietor from adding to his stock any commodities which he could conveniently handle for his customers. In other words, the urban retailer was a general storekeeper who concentrated upon one or two profitable lines. Specialty stores, which steadily increased in number, were usually closely associated with the work of skilled craftsmen. The cabinetmaker, venturing beyond the limits of customers' advance orders, sold furniture at retail; the cobbler's shop was listed as a shoe store; the clock maker became a jeweler. Similarly, the apothecary shop expanded into the drugstore with a lengthening array of patent medicines upon its shelves. As late as 1830, however, all these stores were artisans' shops rather than specialized retail establishments.[1]

[1] C. H. Haswell, *Reminiscences of New York by an Octogenarian* (N. Y., 1897), 77, 262-263.

Although the volume of domestic manufactures rose rapidly after 1815, many American consumers continued to show a partiality for imported goods. Shipments of broadcloths, flannels and kersey were quickly snapped up at the auction rooms; and retailers vied with one another to obtain Sheffield ware and the motley assortment of articles which ingenious Birmingham manufacturers turned out "for the American trade." That the world of fashion should demand laces, ribbons, silks and bonnets direct from Le Havre was natural, but the preference seemed to extend also to cheap muslins and calicoes. Price was not the determinant, for Fall River or Waltham could often undersell Manchester across New York and Charleston counters. Tench Coxe, pleading that Americans should manufacture and wear their entire cotton crop, discovered that in this respect at least his countrymen in the third decade of the century had not yet escaped from their colonial-mindedness.

CHAPTER X

THE CONSERVATIVE TRADITION

DURING the sixteenth century reformers in province after province of northern Europe undermined the prestige of the Catholic Church and set up sturdy rivals. For a generation this challenge strained the organization of the vast Christian establishment, then strengthened it. Zealous defenders of the ancient faith arose to combat heresy by clarifying old tenets; missionaries, especially those under Jesuit inspiration, encircled the world; new and far more effective institutions and methods of teaching Catholic doctrine were introduced. Thus counter-reformation finally limited the extent of the initial reform. So in Calvinistic New England at the opening of the nineteenth century, a reformation was taking place and its challenge was likewise met by an effective counter-reformation.[1]

Imperfect though this analogy may be, none can doubt the vigilant devotion of orthodoxy's champions in New England. They stubbornly resisted frontal assaults from Deists or flank attacks from liberals of Universalist or Unitarian persuasion; and they were resourceful in extending the areas of their own influence. Foremost in their ranks was the Reverend Jedidiah Morse of Charlestown, who gave and asked no quarter in the columns of his religious journal, the *Panoplist,* constantly striving to lay bare the lines of doctrinal cleavage and to convict the liberals of their Unitarian heresy.[2]

[1] See D. R. Fox, "The Protestant Counter-Reformation," *N. Y. History,* XVI, 19 ff; E. B. Greene, "A Puritan Counter-Reformation," Am. Antiquarian Soc., *Proceeds.,* n. s., XLII, 17-46; C. R. Keller, *The Second Great Awakening in Connecticut* (New Haven, 1942), chap. iii.

[2] See earlier, 168-169.

Finally in 1815, when a recent publication of the English Unitarians which referred to American clerical brethren by name fell into his hands, he reprinted the entire passage and declared that the fight was now to be in the open. And so it was.[1]

On many New Englanders the grip of John Calvin was still unrelaxed. Though the trinitarians had lost every Boston pulpit but one, and Harvard's defection was not merely temporary, they yet had the satisfaction of establishing in 1808 a training school for ministers of the old faith at Andover, Massachusetts.[2] The Andover seminary was probably the most important institution of Calvinist orthodoxy in America during the first half of the nineteenth century. Among others, Moses Stuart brought national distinction to its faculty. At a time when Hebrew scholarship had virtually disappeared from American colleges, he learned German that he might read Gesenius's *Hebrew Lexicon of the Old Testament*.[3] In 1813 he published his grammar, the first Hebrew work printed in America, whose type he had set up with his own hand. It was but the first of thirty volumes revealing the scope of his knowledge and the depth of his zeal.

Though the majority of Christians in the United States relied upon a learned clergy, theological instruction was rarely formal and systematic.[4] In a few colleges ministerial candidates attended lectures by professors of theology, but most received their special training

[1] The *Panoplist* was established in June, 1805. Thomas Belsham's *Memoirs of the Life of Theophilus Lindsey* was reviewed by Morse and Jeremiah Evarts in the issue for June, 1815, pp. 241-272.

[2] William Bentley, *Diary* (Salem, 1905-1914), III, 317, 403, 412. See also Leonard Woods, *History of the Andover Theological Seminary* (Boston, 1885), *passim*, and W. B. Sprague, *Life of Jedidiah Morse* (N. Y., 1874), 107 ff.

[3] Harvard did offer a little instruction in Hebrew.

[4] Prior to 1791 American Catholic clergy received their seminary training in Europe.

as apprentice-students in the homes of divines for six months or a year, perusing such doctrinal works as were suggested and preparing a few essays in sermon form. Standards of training, of course, varied with the tutor and the requirements of the denomination. Congregationalists and Presbyterians insisted that each applicant submit evidence of a college degree or its equivalent and satisfy a board of examiners as to his proficiency in Greek, Latin, English grammar, mathematics, logic, rhetoric, geography and natural philosophy.[1] In New England the Baptists strove to maintain similar standards, though their associations in the West and South did not. Few candidates who applied to the appropriate examining board for a license were rejected.

Superficial this sort of training might be, but it kept alive the tradition of a learned clergy at a time when some denominations tended to ignore formal tests of scholarship. In many Baptist associations, especially in the backcountry, a candidate's fitness to preach was decided by his neighbors in the congregation and depended upon personal attributes quite unrelated to sound learning. Frequently the Methodists likewise found among farmers and artisans men, like Paul of old, powerful in preaching the Word. Such self-trained exhorters became the circuit riders of trans-Appalachia at the beginning of the nineteenth century.[2] They prided themselves on being alumni of "Brush College," that is, the school of practical experience. Most of them possessed no more of a library than their saddlebags could hold, yet a few, reading as they rode, gained a knowledge of the great works in English literature.[3]

[1] J. H. Hotchkin, *History of the Purchase and Settlement of Western New York* (N. Y., 1848), 110.

[2] See E. S. Tipple, *Francis Asbury, the Prophet of the Long Road* (N. Y., 1916), 158-182.

[3] W. H. Milburn, *The Pioneers, Preachers and People of the Mississippi Valley* (N. Y., 1860), 355; W. W. Sweet, *Circuit Rider Days*

The coming of the theological seminary foreshadowed the secularization of the college throughout America, for a steadily increasing number of ministerial candidates sought their formal training in this type of professional school. As early as 1784 a group of Dutch Reformed ministers on Manhattan Island had given doctrinal instruction, precursors of the institution established in 1810 beside Queen's College (later Rutgers) at New Brunswick.[1] After 1804 John M. Mason, leader of the Associated Presbyterians in New York, collected five thousand dollars in Great Britain to support himself and a few colleagues in a similar enterprise.[2] But these were part-time activities of busy clergymen and scarcely merit the name of seminaries, the first example of which really was Andover in 1808. Though that institution resulted from dogmatic tensions in New England Congregationalism, it was quickly copied in other sections and denominations, notably by the Presbyterians, who founded divinity schools at Princeton (1812) and at Hampden-Sydney College in Virginia.[3] Within twenty years of the inaugural ceremonies at Andover seventeen seminaries were founded—the initial group of those institutions which during the ensuing century would impose a distinctive stamp upon American Protestantism.[4]

To most Protestants an understanding of doctrinal mysteries seemed less important than an extensive preach-

in Indiana (Indianapolis, 1916), 34, 41. For an eloquent tribute to "Brush College," see John Strange, quoted in J. C. Smith, Early Methodism in Indiana (Indianapolis, 1879), 38-39.

[1] Jedidiah Morse, The Signs of the Times (Charlestown, 1810), 45-46.

[2] Jacob Van Vechten, Memoirs of John M. Mason, D.D. (N. Y., 1856), 171-180, 224-238.

[3] Samuel Miller, jr., Life of Samuel Miller (Phila., 1869), I, 239, 313-315; J. W. Alexander, Life of Archibald Alexander (N. Y., 1854), 399.

[4] G. L. Prentiss, The Union Theological Seminary (N. Y., 1889), 3 ff. The Quarterly Register and Journal of the American Education Society, II (1829-1830), 35 ff., contains news of the workers seeking endowments for seminaries and scholarships for divinity students.

ing of the simple gospel message. Christianity, in America as elsewhere, had ever been marked by a spirit of proselytism. During the eighteenth century a goodly company of devout men, notably the Moravians, had gone into the wilderness to preach to the Indians.[1] These outposts had suffered severely during the Revolutionary War, but with the cessation of hostilities the work was extended as new contacts developed with the tribes of the trans-Alleghany region. At the beginning of the nineteenth century the Presbyterians were already making substantial progress in teaching Cherokee children to read the English Bible, to solve simple problems in arithmetic and to write, while the Quakers were carrying Christian friendliness along with better agricultural methods to the Cornplanter, the Shawnee and the Wyandotte.[2] By 1817 the Baptists were proud of their achievements among the Miami, Ottawa and Seneca. In the South, where they found themselves in friendly rivalry with the Methodists, they regarded the Creek as their special charge.[3]

In the Ohio and Mississippi valleys the Protestant missionary occasionally crossed the path of a black-robed priest following the forest trails which a long generation earlier had been marked by the Jesuits of New France.[4] With the expulsion of the Jesuits and the fall of Gallic power, Catholic missions among the Indians

[1] For the Moravian activities, see E. B. Greene, *The Revolutionary Generation, 1763-1790* (*A History of American Life*, IV), 104-105, 111-112.

[2] James Hall, *Brief History of the Mississippi Territory* (Salisbury, N. C., 1801); Abiel Abbott, *A Discourse Delivered before the Missionary Society of Salem and Vicinity* (Salem, 1816); Fortescue Cuming, *Sketches of a Tour to the Western Country* (R. G. Thwaites, ed., *Early Western Travels, 1748-1846*, Cleveland, 1904-1907, IV), 89 *n*.

[3] Isaac McCoy, *History of the Baptist Indian Missions* (Wash., 1840), chaps. xvi-xviii; Enoch Mudge, "History of the Missions of the Methodist Episcopal Church," Joseph Tracy and others, *History of American Missions to the Heathen* (Worcester, 1840), 621 ff.

[4] See H. I. Priestley, *The Coming of the White Man, 1492-1848* (*A History of American Life*, I), 278-279.

had practically disappeared. But when John Carroll received episcopal authority over the American churches in 1790, he sought to revive this phase of missionary activity. So slender were his resources, and so immense his newly created diocese, that his task seemed impossible. At that moment, however, the tragedy of the Catholic Church in Europe became a blessing for its isolated missions in America, since the French Revolution drove many priests from their own country.[1] Among them were members of the Society of Saint Sulpice, the greatest single influence in training the American priesthood and in restoring the Catholic missions of the Middle West. Between 1791 and 1800 twenty-seven French priests, including the Sulpicians, received assignments from Bishop Carroll.[2] They found the needs of the Indians less compelling than the appeals of the surviving French settlements in the Mississippi Valley. As they carried the sacraments into these long-neglected villages and the new communities being established by Catholic migrants from the Eastern states and Kentucky, their work among the savages became a secondary responsibility.

Similarly with Protestant missions, the need of the frontiersman supplanted that of the Indian. As the younger generation of Americans pushed into remote regions, parental concern and family sentiment followed them. Easterners, who could not bear a hand in the actual hanging of the crane, liked to feel that they were

[1] L. F. Ruskowski, *French Emigré Priests in the United States* (Catholic Univ., *Studies*, XXXII), 11-14.

[2] J. W. Ruane, *The Beginnings of the Society of St. Sulpice in the United States* (Wash., 1935), 3-4; T. T. McAvoy, *The Catholic Church in Indiana, 1789-1834* (Columbia Univ., *Studies*, no. 471), 63-66. In 1808 Bishop Carroll's great diocese was divided into five parts and within a few years bishops were appointed for the dioceses of Boston, New York, Philadelphia and Bardstown, Kentucky, in addition to Baltimore. Peter Guilday, *The Life and Times of John Carroll* (N. Y., 1922), 463-477, 578-579.

helping the pioneers to maintain proper standards of faith and morals.[1]   In 1793, for example, the General Association of Connecticut Congregationalists was supporting nine pastors, who had arranged itineraries of four months' duration through the Northern and Western settlements.   By the close of the century these missionaries had traversed a great arc from northern New Hampshire through Vermont, New York, Ohio and Kentucky into western Tennessee.[2]   After Anthony Wayne's victory and the treaty of Greenville in 1795, Bishop Francis Asbury reminded the Methodists that a mission field greater than New England existed in the communities along the rivers of trans-Appalachia.[3]

These were fruitful years in transforming enthusiasm into continuing support, and that along interdenominational lines.   Presbyterians and Baptists were active in forming the New York Missionary Society in 1796 and the Northern Missionary Society of New York the following year.   It was the need for concurrent action in 1801 that brought the famous Plan of Union of Congregationalists and Presbyterians, devised by the younger Jonathan Edwards while president of Union College. By this scheme, in operation for more than thirty years, the former took control of missions on the northern frontier of New England and the latter, because of better organization, those of the West.   As a result, Presbyterianism never became deeply rooted east of the Hudson, nor Congregationalism west of it.[4]

[1] It is difficult to determine how much home missionary enterprise was furthered by conservative Easterners who feared the irreligion of the West.   S. J. Mills and Daniel Smith, *Report of a Missionary Tour* (Andover, 1816), 16-17.

[2] J. B. Clark, *Leavening the Nation* (N. Y., 1903), chap. ii.

[3] O. W. Elsbree, *The Rise of the Missionary Spirit in America, 1790-1815* (Williamsport, Pa., 1928), 32.

[4] A. E. Dunning, *Congregationalists in America* (N. Y., 1894), 327; R. H. Nichols, "The Plan of Union in New York," *Church History*, V, 29-51; D. R. Fox, *Yankees and Yorkers* (N. Y., 1940), 208-210.

Though home missions had but a casual connection with the counter-reformation, it was quite otherwise with the movement to evangelize the heathen overseas. At Williams College stands a famous monument recalling five students who in 1806 pledged themselves to forward Christian enterprise among the millions living in "the moral darkness of Asia."[1] Out of their personal dedication developed a small society, the Brethren, whose memorial in 1810 to the General Association of Massachusetts caused a group of Congregational ministers to form the American Board of Commissioners for Foreign Missions. This was not only the first administrative base for world evangelization from America, but also the first general organization of Congregationalism.[2] At the Tabernacle Church in Salem on February 6, 1812, five members of the Brethren, all Andover seminarians — Gordon Hall and Luther Rice of Williams, Adoniram Judson of Brown, Samuel Newell of Harvard and Samuel Nott, jr., of Union — were ordained as missionaries to India.[3] En route to the Orient in different ships, two of them became convinced of the truth of Baptist dogma and abandoned orthodox Calvinism. These conversions were as a sign to the Baptists, quickening missionary zeal in the Eastern associations.[4]

The diversion of the pioneering spirit of American Protestantism into distant lands was no accident. Behind the resolution of a handful of college boys lay a

[1] Gardiner Spring, *Memoir of S. J. Mills* (2nd edn., Boston, 1829), 22-27; Calvin Durfee, *A History of Williams College* (Boston, 1860), 110-122.

[2] Rufus Anderson, ed., *Memorial Volume of the First Fifty Years of the American Board of Commissioners for Foreign Missions* (Boston, 1863), 15-16.

[3] Leonard Woods, *A Sermon Delivered at the Tabernacle in Salem, February 6, 1812* (Boston, 1812). The problems of these first missionaries were complicated by the fact that Great Britain and the United States were soon at war.

[4] H. S. Burrage, *A History of the Baptists in New England* (Phila., 1894), 151-154.

Ordination of the First American Foreign Missionaries

The First Planned Campus in America

quarter-century of growing interest in China, India and other parts of the Orient. Stories of travelers to the Far East had been widely read as monthly magazines increased their circulation and gave space to whatever the editors considered exotic. Moreover, Boston and Salem were forging ahead of all others in the China trade; and Salem's seamen by 1812 were quite at home in Whampoa or Calcutta or Bombay, though they probably did not think of those ports as outposts for Christian missions. Nor were Americans unaware of the beginnings of scholarly study of Oriental languages.[1]

Religious journals in America, as in Great Britain, managed to deflect some of this secular interest into spiritual channels. The *Theological Magazine*, started at New York in 1795, began publishing extensive accounts of the English missionaries, and similar reports appeared in the *Connecticut Evangelical Magazine*, founded in 1800 at New Haven, and in the *Boston Analytical Repository* in 1801-1802.[2] The *New York Missionary Magazine*, established in 1800, devoted itself primarily to forwarding the cause of missions, and this example led to the publishing of the *Massachusetts Missionary Magazine* in 1803, which fourteen years later became the *American Baptist Magazine*. In 1816 New Englanders were able to support the *Boston Recorder*, the first weekly paper devoting its pages exclusively to religious news.

[1] In 1785 Charles Wilkins, an Englishman, had completed the first extensive translation into English from the literature of the Brahmins. Shortly afterwards Englishmen organized at Calcutta the Asiatic Society to promote interest in Hindu antiquities, science and letters, and in 1801 Joseph Hagar, a German philologist, published *An Explanation of the Elementary Characters of the Chinese Language*. Samuel Miller, *A Brief Retrospect of the Eighteenth Century* (N. Y., 1803), II, 78-87; F. A. Cox, *History of the Baptist Missionary Society from 1792 to 1842* (London, 1842), I, 107-109; *Panoplist*, III (1807-1808), 530-533.

[2] For evidence of English inspiration in the American missionary enterprise, see J. O. Choules and Thomas Smith, *The Origin and History of Missions* (Boston, 1834), II, 234 ff.

If the religious periodicals constitute an accurate index, the prosecution of missions became Protestantism's most popular appeal. *"Eight hundred millions of human beings,"* declaimed an orator in 1814, ". . . are either lost in the darkness of pagan idolatry, or degraded by the bloody brutality of Moslem fanaticism, or hardened into incarnate fiends by the absolute rejection of all religious belief." [1] The Presbyterian General Assembly in 1811 agreed to support the American Board of Commissioners for Foreign Missions, maintaining that position until the schism of 1837 caused the Old School Presbyterians to establish their own board; and in 1826 the Dutch Reformed Church also decided to make its contributions through the American Board.[2] For a time it seemed that the Baptists might likewise coöperate, but in 1814 that individualistic sect formed the "General Convention of the Baptist Denomination in the United States of America for Foreign Missions and Other Important Objects Relating to the Redeemer's Kingdom," thus making its first venture into nation-wide organization.[3] And the American Board soon faced other friendly rivals in the foreign field.[4]

During the years from 1815 to 1830 American missionaries were riding into the outer darkness of heathendom — on camels out of Beirut, on elephants out of Serampore, in clumsy carts along the ancient roads from Hong Kong, in strange native boats threading the crowded traffic of the Mekong in Siam and along the shadowed shores of old Ceylon. Wherever they went, "from Greenland's icy mountains to India's coral

[1] John Bristed, *An Oration on the Utility of Literary Establishments* (N. Y., 1814), 11-12.

[2] W. E. Strong, *The Story of the American Board* (Boston, 1910), 150-151.

[3] Anderson, *Memorial Volume*, 19-20.

[4] Walter Chapin, *The Missionary Gazetteer* (Woodstock, Vt., 1825), vii.

strand," they carried "the simple story of Christ cruci-
fied." [1]   The language difficulties were appreciably lessened whenever a native convert learned English and
assumed his share of responsibility.   Soon steps were
taken to train such proselytes in the United States.   Congregational circles in Connecticut had been deeply stirred
by the fascinating story of Henry Obookiah, a Hawaiian
lad who after receiving a good education under the
tutelage of Connecticut Calvinists had announced his desire to preach Christian doctrine to his own people. [2]
For the proper instruction of such missionaries a school
was established beside the Cornwall green in the Litchfield hills, and a goodly company of earnest young men
— Polynesians, Melanesians, Chinese and American Indians — went forth from its classrooms to their several
ministries. [3]   Galagina, the Cherokee who had assumed
the name of New Jersey's famous philanthropist, Elias
Boudinot, returned to his people in the southern Appalachians to carry forward the educational work begun
by the talented Sequoyah. [4]   Typhus fever cut short
Obookiah's life during his first year at the Foreign Mission School, but three of his classmates helped to persuade King Kamehameha II to accept Christianity and
started a "Great Awakening" in the Sandwich Islands. [5]
The expansion of evangelical Protestantism overseas

[1] Francis Wayland, *The Moral Dignity of the Missionary Enterprise*
(Boston, 1824), 30.   Bishop Reginald Heber's famous missionary hymn
was published in the English *Christian Observer*, XXIII (1823), 97.

[2] E. W. Dwight, *Memoirs of Henry Obookiah* (Elizabeth-Town,
N. J., 1819), 88.

[3] The school closed in 1827 as a result of a tragic controversy over the
marriage of one of the students, a Cherokee Indian, with the daughter of
a prominent Cornwall family.   For the consequences of this marriage
across race lines, see R. H. Gabriel, *Elias Boudinot, Cherokee* (Norman,
1941), 66-80.

[4] Grant Foreman, *Sequoyah* (Norman, 1938), 10-14; Gabriel, *Elias
Boudinot*, 95-105.

[5] *A Narrative of Five Youth from the Sandwich Islands* (N. Y., 1816);
Tracy and others, *American Missions*, chaps. xi-xii.

had momentous consequences at home. The furtherance of missions provided the first organized religious work for Protestant women in America. Not only did they accompany their husbands to the far frontiers of Christendom, but they gathered for prayer and study in American village homes and organized societies to popularize the idea of giving one cent a week to missionary enterprises. Such "mite societies," spreading rapidly through New England, New York and other states, assured a steady revenue from many thousand members.[1] One can easily imagine the cultural influence of these hundreds of weekly meetings. Housewives dreamed of tinkling temple bells, of juggernauts and pagan sacrifice, of Moslem mosques and Buddhist shrines. It was dreamed in horror, for the candid study of comparative religion never intruded to challenge the assumed superiority of the white man's Christianity. But it brought a picture, however distorted, of other lives far away. In some inquiring minds it stirred a desire to read about the history and geography of the lands to which their benevolence bound them.

Among the ventures of orthodox Protestantism none was more thriving than the plan for wholesale distribution of the Bible.[2] Again following an English model, a society for this purpose was organized at Philadelphia in 1808. Within two years fifteen others had been formed in America.[3] As with missions, women became the effective workers, and the mite societies diverted a portion of their revenue into this affiliate of home missions. Young Samuel J. Mills, who had been the leading spirit of the little band at Williams College, made two extensive tours through the Western wilder-

[1] Clark, *Leavening the Nation*, chap. xix.
[2] Directing Committee of the Connecticut Bible Society, *Report* (Hartford, 1810) ; Emerson Davis, *The Half Century* (Boston, 1851), 321 ff.
[3] Morse, *Signs of the Times*, 45.

ness during the second war with Great Britain.   In New Orleans, where he could not buy a Bible, he made arrangements for distributing three thousand copies of a French translation of the New Testament.   More than seventy-six thousand families in the Southwest, he estimated, lacked access to the Scriptures.[1]   As his report became available in print, men began to ask how the Bible societies could supply such a demand without coöperative effort.   Having created a movement out of sentiment, they proceeded in typical American fashion to institutionalize it.   While nationalist feeling ran high at the close of the War of 1812, delegates from thirty-five societies meeting at New York in 1816 established the American Bible Society.   Within a decade there were glowing reports that through an intensive campaign virtually every family in the United States which lacked a Bible and desired one had received a copy of the King James version.

More effective in reaching uninstructed minds were short, simple stories of Christian triumph over evil.   In 1795 Mrs. Hannah More, the English essayist, had started a movement which fruited in the London Religious Tract Society, an organization which prompted emulation in America.[2]   The first tract society, formed in Connecticut in 1807, was quickly followed by others in Vermont, New York, Pennsylvania and Maryland.   Nationalization along interdenominational lines, though deterred by local prejudices, finally resulted in 1825 in the American Tract Society with headquarters in New York.   Judicious editing, though without sacrifice of fundamental orthodoxy, rendered the texts of pamphlets acceptable to all constituent sects.   While many were reprints of little essays which had been popular

[1] Mills and Smith, *Missionary Tour*, 35-36, 47.
[2] "Distribution of Religious Tracts," Am. Educ. Soc., *Quar. Register and Journ.*, II, 38-41.

in England, some were of American authorship, even by such eminent divines as Timothy Dwight and Gardiner Spring. There was a message for everyone: *An Affectionate Address to a Married Couple; Advice from a Master to His Apprentice; To Christian Females on Simplicity of Dress; Advice to the Keeper of a Turnpike Gate; The Well Conducted Farm*—and in large editions with woodcut illustrations. In 1827 the Society was printing more than fifty-three million pages annually and consigning them to local centers as far west as Illinois.[1]

Highly important in the new Christian propaganda was the Sunday School, which began as an educational philanthropy for poor children. In 1790 Philadelphia had a "First Day or Sunday School" sponsored by admirers of Robert Raikes's achievements with the neglected youths employed in the pin factories of Gloucester, England. It was copied the next year in Boston, and presently New England manufacturers such as Samuel Slater and David Humphreys set up such schools for their mill families, following the custom of using the Bible as a reading text and placing emphasis upon writing and simple arithmetic. By 1815 the Sunday School existed in a score of places from New Hampshire to Maryland.[2] This advance was not made without struggle, for some disliked the institution because of its origin in England, while others doubted the propriety of conducting schools on the Sabbath. To the latter it was pointed out that the exclusive use of the Bible as a textbook should be sufficient justification, and this educational feature began to stir the interest of

[1] American Tract Society, *Tenth Annual Report* (N. Y., 1835); W. A. Hallock, *A Sketch of the Life and Labors of Justin Edwards* (N. Y., 1855), 182-184.

[2] O. S. Michael, *The Sunday School in the Development of the American Church* (Milwaukee, 1918), 51-58; Francis Eddy, *The Sabbath School Century* (Hamilton, Ohio, 1882), 83-91.

churchmen.[1] Lyman Beecher, deploring the disappearance of the catechism from the schools, urged his parishioners at Litchfield, Connecticut, to enroll their children in regular attendance on Sabbath lessons.[2]

Whether from this example or from other factors, the Sunday School expanded into a vital part of Protestant Christianity. In several respects its development varied from its English prototype: it ministered to all young people; and it gradually substituted for instruction in reading and writing a program of religious education that avoided sectarian indoctrination. In 1824 the Philadelphia Union became the nucleus of the movement for nationalization, assuming the name American Sunday School Union and inviting affiliation from local groups.[3] The institution, having lost its secular form, was taking on its modern characteristics, with the pastor's class for adults, with book prizes for attendance and for proficiency in memorizing Scripture texts, and with many children's classes subscribing for the monthly *Sunday School Magazine*.[4]

While the Sunday School was bringing thousands within the orbit of revealed religion, other organizations sought to lay restraints upon the conduct of the unchurched. Moral societies, sounding a warning against Sabbath breaking, profanity, intemperance and other human frailties, gave expression to a neo-Puritanism, in some respects more rigorous than the Puritanism of the preceding generation. The Connecticut Society for the Reformation of Morals, formed in 1813, soon had local

[1] Ward Stafford, *New Missionary Field* (N. Y., 1817), 18-19.

[2] Lyman Beecher, *The Building of Waste Places* (Litchfield, 1814).

[3] Eddy, *Sabbath School Century*, 81-105.

[4] Asa Bullard, *Fifty Years with the Sabbath Schools* (Boston, 1876), 59-69. The influence of the Sunday School library was enhanced by the lack of other opportunities for reading. In Brooklyn, for example, the Sands Street Methodist Church circulated about 1000 volumes, long before there was a free public library. R. F. Weld, *Brooklyn Village, 1816-1834* (D. R. Fox, ed., *N. Y. State Hist. Assoc. Ser.*, VII), 116.

auxiliaries throughout the state.[1] The religious journals reported similar groups in other parts of the country.[2] As always, reform had its fanatics. Some communities now intensified their hostility to the theater and frowned upon even dancing and card playing, which had gone largely unrebuked earlier in the century. Horse racing, as it grew more popular in the North, encountered similar opposition. Pennsylvania in 1820 not only prohibited racing, but forbade any person to "print or cause to be printed, set up or cause to be set up, any advertisement mentioning the time and place for the running, trotting or pacing of any horse, mare or gelding."

The protest against intemperate drinking made the greatest headway. In 1810 it was estimated that fourteen thousand or more distilleries produced over twenty-five million gallons of ardent spirits annually. Ten years later the census enumerators reported that it was meaningless to classify distilling as a separate industry since it was carried on generally throughout the rural districts.[3] Inspired largely by the writings of Dr. Benjamin Rush, who had begun declaiming against distilled liquors while holding the post of physician general during the Revolutionary War, Dr. Billy J. Clark in Saratoga County, New York, brought together forty of his neighbors in a formal society early in 1808 and set a precedent of organization to diminish the use of strong drinks.[4]

Rush based his arguments mainly on grounds of hygiene. Others warned of the waste of money, time and labor efficiency. It was Lyman Beecher who in-

[1] *Panoplist*, X (1814), 198-203, 236.

[2] Besides the *Panoplist*, the following religious periodicals carried news of the moral societies: the *Religious Remembrancer* (Phila., 1813), the *Recorder* (Boston, 1816), the *Christian Herald* (N. Y., 1816), and the *Christian Disciple*, a Methodist weekly founded at Boston in 1819.

[3] Adam Seybert, *Statistical Annals* (Phila., 1818), 463-464; *U. S. Fourth Census* (1820), *Digest of Manufactures*, 3-4.

[4] J. A. Krout, *The Origins of Prohibition* (N. Y., 1925), 77-80.

fused the aggressive spirit of evangelical Protestantism into the movement. Of his first Consociation meeting in Connecticut in 1810 he reported, "the sideboard, with the spillings of water, and sugar, and liquor, looked and smelled like the bar of a very active grog-shop. None of the Consociation were drunk; but that there was not, at times, a considerable amount of exhilaration, I can not affirm." [1] Aroused to action, he helped organize the Connecticut moral society in order to set a higher standard of conduct among the clergy as well as to wage war generally on "Sabbath-breakers, rum-selling, tippling folk, infidels and ruff-scruff." [2]

From Maine to the Mississippi the movement spread, easily blending its crusading spirit with the rising missionary zeal of the Protestant churches. Wherever a religious revival deeply stirred village and countryside, there the friends of temperance found fertile soil in which to sow their seed; and it multiplied abundantly. In 1826 the Boston leaders nationalized the movement by forming the American Temperance Society, which had jurisdiction over state, county and village auxiliaries. [3] Its membership significantly overlapped those of the national tract and Bible societies and the missionary boards; and its most effective propagandist was the Protestant clergyman, who indicted intemperance as the great barrier to the church militant as it marched on to become the church triumphant. [4]

[1] Lyman Beecher, *Autobiography, Correspondence* (Charles Beecher, ed., N. Y., 1864-1865), I, 245.

[2] Cited in R. J. Purcell, *Connecticut in Transition, 1775-1818* (Washington, 1918), 329.

[3] American Society for the Promotion of Temperance, *First Annual Report* (Andover, 1828).

[4] *Permanent Temperance Documents,* I, 242; Krout, *Origins of Prohibition,* 113-114. This close association of pulpit and reform propaganda quickly led to the charge that the temperance movement was designed to effect the union of church and state. See J. H. Hopkins, *The Primitive Church* (Burlington, 1836), 129-153, and Calvin Colton, *Protestant Jesuitism* (N. Y., 1836), preface and chap. v. The link be-

The temperance leaders won their most notable victories either in New England or in sections settled by Yankee stock, for community control of individual conduct had been a folkway in New England from the start.[1] Now, social welfare was to be advanced by moderation in the use of ardent spirits. Some even wished to go further. In 1825 pledge signers were asked to place a letter T beside their names if they would promise to avoid all ardent spirits. Within a decade the attitude of the "teetotalers" had become the objective of most societies and had been indorsed by the national convention after several stormy sessions.[2] By that time the word "temperance" had acquired a peculiarly American meaning: abstinence from the use of all alcoholic beverages.[3]

The religious revival gave impetus to so many humanitarian reforms that enthusiasts thought they had Satan on the run. The millennium, which American students had repeatedly predicted from their meticulous exegesis of the Scriptures, seemed to be at hand.[4] Religious journals told of renewed interest in Bible study and the spread of the "concert of prayer" throughout the land and declared that the Great Revival of 1801 now was being enacted on a national stage.[5] Most inspiriting of all were the evidences of joint efforts in Christian work. "Various denominations," wrote Sereno Dwight, "already commune together at the sac-

tween church and state had been broken in New Hampshire in 1817, in Connecticut in 1818 and in Massachusetts in 1833. These were the last states to maintain religious establishments.

[1] See map in Krout, *Origins of Prohibition*, 130.

[2] *Permanent Temperance Documents*, I, 455, 474.

[3] C. R. Fish, *The Rise of the Common Man, 1830-1850* (*A History of American Life*, VI), 262-264.

[4] For a discussion of the millennial prophecies, see D. R. Fox, *Ideas in Motion* (N. Y., 1935), 110-119.

[5] For reports of revivals, consult files of *Connecticut Journal*, Feb.-May, 1819; *Boston Recorder*, March, 1820-Jan., 1822; *Religious Intelligencer*, Jan., 1817-July, 1818.

ramental table; and those who do not are relaxing in their rigidness.   While the great divisions of the Church are thus growing truly liberal toward each other, they unite more cordially than ever in opposing fundamental error." [1]

But those who thought that Christians would present a united front against error, or even that they agreed in defining error, greatly underestimated the divisive power of sectarian loyalty and doctrinal dispute. Though fear of the continuing rationalist temper and the growing liberalism of Eastern churches induced some interdenominational coöperation, it was short-lived.   A vigorous minority of Baptists soon opposed the entire foreign missionary enterprise, Methodists were in revolt against their own episcopal tradition, while High-Church Episcopalians like Bishop John H. Hobart of New York and Bishop John H. Hopkins of Vermont warned against too much easy-going fellowship with other Protestant groups.[2]   Presbyterians quarreled vehemently over the methods of such revivalists as Charles G. Finney, and Congregationalists could not reconcile Dr. Nathaniel Taylor's "new divinity" with the ages-old doctrine that

> In Adam's fall,
> We sinned all.

On every side schismatics fanned anew the flame of denominational rivalry.[3]

In the story of the religious and humanitarian enterprises of this period the figure of the evangelical clergyman looms large.   It was not otherwise in education. "The Christian College," said the Methodist Episcopal Conference in 1824, "is the bulwark of the Christian

[1] S. E. Dwight, *Thy Kingdom Come* (Boston, 1820), 22.
[2] J. H. Hobart, *The High Churchmen Vindicated* (N. Y., 1837).
[3] Davis, *Half Century*, 355-367.

Church." Few discerned any conflict between such a view and secular learning; indeed, the dominant note in most colleges was religious, if not sectarian. Though less attention than formerly was given to training for the ministry, faculty members tended to feel they were churchmen first and scholars afterward.

The American college president was, in the language of biology, a throw-off from the clergyman, and early in the nineteenth century he was very imperfectly detached. More than nine tenths of the college heads during the forty years after 1790 were ordained ministers, who saw life from the sacred desk quite as steadily after their induction as before.[1] Originally the president had been the entire staff or, at best, had had one or two tutors or instructors under him; but by the close of the eighteenth century differentiation of function had separated from him three or four "specialist" professors. Still he remained chief executive with all that that implied in keeping records, maintaining discipline, raising money and promoting cordial relations between the institution and its constituency. He also served as college pastor and taught theology or ethics or moral philosophy, sometimes all three.[2] Few carried their burdens with the easy dignity of Timothy Dwight of Yale, who became a great exemplar of the tradition which brought immense prestige to the college president in the United States.[3]

It would be difficult to describe the typical professor, whatever caricatures may have caught the fancy of alert undergraduates. The staff of the Western University of Pennsylvania (1822), to take an extreme example,

[1] Approximately forty per cent of them were natives of New England. G. P. Schmidt, *The Old Time College President* (Columbia Univ., Studies, no. 317), 146-147.

[2] *Ibid.*, 77-145.

[3] C. E. Cuningham, *Timothy Dwight, 1752-1817* (N. Y., 1942), chap. vii.

consisted of the local clergy in the town of Pittsburgh.[1] In nearly all instances churchmen were numerous. The professor, then, evolved from the clergyman, either directly, like the college president, or indirectly through the slow division of the president's teaching functions into specialized fields of instruction. Toward hastening this process and insuring that science would not undermine faith, Timothy Dwight made an influential contribution. He encouraged young men like Jeremiah Day, Benjamin Silliman and James L. Kingsley, who could accept the Westminster Catechism and the Saybrook Platform, to devote their lives to the advancement of learning in nontheological fields.[2]

Some colleges sought out foreign scholars of wide repute, while Harvard sent a number of superior students abroad for extensive study.[3] Thus the Reverend Edward Everett, named to the newly endowed professorship of Greek literature in 1815, and Joseph G. Cogswell, who had taught Latin at Cambridge, and George Bancroft, who was to write history, all traveled widely in Europe. Tarrying at Göttingen, they came to understand not only the meaning of scholarly achievement, but also how far short of the ideal American colleges had fallen. In their company belongs George Ticknor, for he managed to bring something of the spirit of the German university to Harvard Yard.[4] In his own department of foreign languages Ticknor steadily widened the scope of the courses, strengthening the staff with European-trained scholars and following the best Ger-

[1] S. J. and Elizabeth H. Buck, *The Planting of Civilization in Western Pennsylvania* (Western Pennsylvania Series; Pittsburgh, 1939), 375, 398.

[2] C. F. Thwing, *A History of Higher Education in America* (N. Y., 1906), 258-263; Cuningham, *Timothy Dwight*, 198 ff.

[3] S. E. Morison, *Three Centuries of Harvard* (Boston, 1936), 224-225.

[4] O. W. Long, *Literary Pioneers* (Cambridge, 1935), 41 ff.

man models of instruction. Other colleges might have profited by imitating this first American professorship in modern languages, but it is doubtful that many knew what was happening at Cambridge.[1]

Historians have portrayed the American college of this period as a vested institution, untouched by the life about it and belligerently resistant to change. Such a picture contains much distortion. "Experience has shown," wrote the Reverend John M. Mason, provost of Columbia College early in the nineteenth century, "that with the study or neglect of the Greek and Latin languages, sound learning flourishes or declines."[2] College leaders who approved this dictum—and they constituted a majority—were just as sincere in seeking to prepare the rising generation for effective public service as President Eliphalet Nott experimenting at Union or Thomas Jefferson planning his university in Virginia. Far from being complacent reactionaries, the conservatives were genuinely alarmed. They feared the decline of sound learning if they yielded too readily to the demand for more practical courses. In education, they had observed, "practical" could easily become a synonym for cheap or inferior.

The traditional college curriculum consisted of four divisions: the classics; mathematics and natural philosophy; rhetoric and *belles-lettres;* and metaphysics and moral philosophy.[3] The crowning glory of the last year was the course in which the "moral professor," usually the president, ranged widely over the whole field of knowledge, pausing wherever he was interested. It was from this side of the college president that there

[1] Morison, *Three Centuries of Harvard*, 226-228.
[2] Van Vechten, *Memoirs of John M. Mason*, 239.
[3] A view of the course of study at various colleges in Am. Educ. Soc., *Quar. Register and Journ.*, I (1827-1829), 228-232. See also L. F. Snow, *The College Curriculum in the United States* (N. Y., 1907), chap. iv.

developed in the course of time the political science, economics, sociology and philosophy departments of the modern university. At Pennsylvania the "moral professor" in 1826 taught logic, philosophy, metaphysics, theology, natural and political law and during his spare moments dabbled in composition and rhetoric.

The senior course in moral philosophy was based upon the assumption that it would enable the preceptor to present an ingeniously unified interpretation of life. That such a task lay beyond the ability of many college teachers, then and later, is obvious; yet Benjamin Silliman spoke of the eagerness with which students looked forward to President Dwight's lectures, while Jefferson Davis never forgot the inspiration he received as he listened to Horace Holley at Transylvania.[1] Whatever the differences in organization and emphasis, the content of such lectures was usually drawn from the writings of eighteenth-century Scottish philosophers and their contemporary, William Paley, the great Anglican theologian, and, of course, that perennial reliance, John Locke.[2]

Within the limits of such indebtedness some American teachers formulated their own textbooks. At Columbia in 1795 the Reverend John Daniel Gros issued his *Natural Principles of Rectitude*. He was far more inclined to modify the masters than was Samuel Stanhope Smith of Princeton, who published two volumes avowedly dependent upon the common-sense philosophy of the Scottish school. "*Reason,*" wrote Gros, "*is religion, because religion is the greatest perfection of reason, and gives it the happiest direction.*"[3]   Morality, he continued, is based upon God's will as it is revealed in

---

[1] G. P. Fisher, *Life of Benjamin Silliman* (N. Y., 1866), I, 32; Varina H. Davis, *Jefferson Davis, a Memoir* (N. Y., 1890), I, 26.

[2] Schmidt, *Old Time College President,* 112 ff.

[3] J. D. Gros, *Natural Principles of Rectitude* (N. Y., 1795), preface.

Nature, in everyday experience and in reason; and individual happiness may be achieved if the moral sense responds to these revelations. In stressing the happiness of the individual and man's development within the limits of his environment the common-sense philosophers looked toward the Greek ideal, but they saw it in distortion through the refracting medium of Calvinistic tradition.

On the periphery of such discussions there was an occasional treatment of topics which would be classified today as fragments of political and social science. In the early decades of the nineteenth century sporadic instances of specialization appeared, too few to establish an unmistakable trend. At Columbia the comprehensive course had embraced natural jurisprudence, civil government and the law of nations; but by 1811 a separate course on the law of nature and nations had been set up, and seven years later the Reverend John McVickar was offering political economy as a senior subject.[1] Likewise at William and Mary College the moral philosophy course, which as early as 1779 had included lectures on natural law, the law of nations and general principles of politics, had by 1815 been subdivided. Moral philosophy was offered in the first year, natural and national law in the second, government and political economy in the third, and municipal law as an elective for seniors.[2] When Levi Frisbie was appointed at Harvard in 1817, civil polity was on a parity with natural religion and moral philosophy in his tripartite professorship.[3]

The textbooks in political theory used for several

[1] Brander Matthews and others, eds., *A History of Columbia University, 1754-1904* (N. Y., 1904), 89-92; E. V. Wills, "John McVickar, Economist and Old-Time College Teacher," *Education*, LII, 112-113.

[2] College of William and Mary, *The Officers, Statutes and Charter* (Phila., 1817), 62.

[3] Anna Haddow, *Political Science in American Colleges and Universities, 1636-1900* (F. A. Ogg, ed., *The Century Political Science Series*; N. Y., 1939), 57-58.

decades after the Revolution were either such classic works as Grotius's *Of the Rights of War and Peace* and Locke's *Two Treatises Concerning Government,* or the eighteenth-century essays of Burlamaqui, Montesquieu, Vattel and Rousseau. Bishop James Madison at William and Mary recommended Thomas Paine's *Dissertation on First Principles of Government* and *The Rights of Man,* but the only application of theory specifically to the political conditions of the new nation came from the extensive use of the *Federalist* after 1790. Political economy, still closely associated with political philosophy, dealt with governmental activity in such fields as finance, commerce and industry, and public welfare.[1] Bishop Madison may have used Adam Smith's *The Wealth of Nations* even before it was first listed in 1798.[2] Professor McVickar at Columbia, finding no satisfactory treatise, prepared in 1825 his *Outlines of Political Economy,* little more than an article by J. R. M'Culloch, elaborately annotated to illustrate American problems. A year later Thomas Cooper, then president of South Carolina College, published a volume designed to distinguish political economy from politics.[3] The embryonic social sciences drew slight sustenance from history, as then taught, for that subject was merely a supplement to studies of classical civilization. Exceptional among the history textbooks was David Ramsay's *History of the United States,* which covered the period from the first settlements to 1806.

As political science and public law were evolving from the comprehensive courses in moral philosophy, so botany, chemistry, geology and zoology were slowly

[1] Haddow, *Political Science in American Colleges,* 74-82.
[2] E. R. A. Seligman, "The Early Teaching of Economics in the United States," *Economic Essays Contributed in Honor of John Bates Clark* (N. Y., 1927), 294-302.
[3] Thomas Cooper, *Lectures on the Elements of Political Economy* (Columbia, S. C., 1826).

emerging out of the data still classified as natural philosophy or natural history. Despite the pretensions of many college catalogues, little time was set aside for natural history and few undergraduates had an opportunity to attend the lectures.[1] Harvard permitted students to elect the subject, but Yale finally restricted enrollment to medical candidates. At Princeton and Williams the lectures by eminent naturalists were considered extracurricular. Meager apparatus and equipment for experimentation constantly improved, enabling Samuel L. Mitchill at Columbia, Benjamin S. Barton at Pennsylvania and Benjamin Waterhouse at Harvard to arouse widespread interest in their reports and other writings. But the long struggle for academic recognition was not easily won. For more than forty years Benjamin Silliman persistently worked at Yale to secure proper laboratory facilities and degree credit for scientific experiments.[2]

The preponderant emphasis upon classical studies caused vehement controversy. It was raging as early as 1790. Dr. Hugh Williamson thought that Columbia College should substitute natural history for some of the required Greek and Latin, pointing out that the ancient Greeks had had the good sense to study their own language and literature.[3] Dr. Benjamin Rush voiced the fears of those who saw pagan immorality undermining Christian virtue.[4] Others insisted that the ancient languages symbolized the dead hand of tradition—students needed more time for the component parts of natural

[1] *Medical Repository*, XII (1808-1809), 155.
[2] W. M. and Mabel S. C. Smallwood, *Natural History and the American Mind* (*Columbia Studies in American Culture*, no. 8), 285-287.
[3] T. E. V. Smith, *The City of New York in the Year of Washington's Inauguration* (N. Y., 1889), 193-195.
[4] *Literary Mag. and Am. Register*, III (1805), 426-428; IV (1805), 137, 185-191. President Joshua Bates of Middlebury College thought that this problem could safely be left in the hands of pious professors. *An Inaugural Oration* (Middlebury, Vt., 1818), 19 ff.

history; for modern languages, which were growing ever more important with the expansion of international trade; and for political philosophy and allied subjects, which were peculiarly useful to the citizens of a republic.[1] Of the numerous answers to such attacks none was more convincing than that of the eminent scholar, Moses Stuart, at Andover Seminary.[2] Though the ancient classics might seem remote from practical problems in the United States, the study of them, he argued, led to clear thinking, an appreciation of beauty and a sense of literary form. Latin, long the living language of scholarship throughout Christendom, was basic to an understanding of English and many other modern languages, while Greek was the great avenue of approach not only to the life of an ancient people of remarkable intellectual vigor, but also to the truths of the New Testament.

Preoccupied with classical studies the colleges may have been, but the instruction was surprisingly superficial. In 1825 George Ticknor asked,

Who in this country, by means here offered him, has been enabled to make himself a good Greek scholar? Who has been taught thoroughly to read, write, and speak Latin? Nay, who has been taught anything, at our colleges, with the thoroughness that will enable him to go safely and directly onward to distinction in the department he has thus entered . . . ?[3]

Even if allowance be made for Ticknor's foreign sojourn and his exceptionally high standards, it seems obvious that college boys were not being trained for scholarly work.

[1] Miller, *Retrospect of the Eighteenth Century*, II, 37-40.
[2] Moses Stuart, "Letter on the Study of the Classics," Am. Educ. Soc., *Quar. Register and Journ.*, I, 85-98.
[3] [G. S. Hillard and others], *Life, Letters, and Journals of George Ticknor* (Boston, 1876), I, 363.

Attempts to modify the traditional college curriculum accomplished little. Jefferson's plans for the University of Virginia, designed to admit scientific interests and provide superior professional schools, proved more alarming than inspiring. Conservatives even frowned upon Eliphalet Nott's modest proposals at Union College, where he established a parallel course in which modern languages might be substituted for Greek.[1] His example may have encouraged Amherst in 1827 to give credit for modern languages, English literature, history, political economy and experimental work in natural science in lieu of the classical courses.[2] It would be possible to list other innovations, yet as the third decade of the nineteenth century ended the classicists were still in control. A Yale report on the curriculum in 1828 eloquently defended the place of ancient languages and literatures in the whole scheme of a liberal education. Faculty and trustees alike indorsed it.

College authorities apparently spent more time discussing disciplinary than instructional problems. In some institutions the students lived in drab quarters under a "benevolent despotism" more efficacious in promoting rebellion than in maintaining order. Riots in commons over unsatisfactory fare suggest that income from inadequate endowments was sometimes eked out by economies at table. Furthermore, no intercollegiate athletics or compulsory physical training existed to take some of the mischief out of exuberant youth.[3] In most colleges extracurricular activities were neither numerous nor varied, but it was only the unsocial student at Harvard who could not find amusement or instruction in the

---

[1] Cornelius Van Santvoord, *Memoirs of Eliphalet Nott* (N. Y., 1876), 155-156.

[2] Snow, *College Curriculum*, 155.

[3] E. M. Coulter, *College Life in the Old South* (N. Y., 1928), chap. iv; K. P. Battle, *History of the University of North Carolina* (Raleigh, 1907), I, 199, 452; Schmidt, *Old Time College President*, 78 ff.

musical, literary and religious societies, or in the clubs dedicated exclusively to nonsense.[1]   On every campus rough-and-tumble games were played without violating college rules.   By 1830 some variation of "four-old-cat," or "bat and ball" as it was called in New England, had become popular.   Primitive football, a crude adaptation of the English sport, often provided the means for settling differences between classes.   Like their elders, American boys were eager to test individual prowess, but they lacked indoor facilities to measure and compare strength and skill.   The gymnasium was still a curiosity on the college campus.[2]

Colleges were rapidly increasing in number.   At the opening of the century there had been twenty-two degree-granting institutions; three decades later they totaled fifty-six, not counting those that had failed to survive.[3]   This increase came out of a complex in which religious zeal, educational aspiration, local pride, political rivalry and real-estate interests were closely commingled.   Sectarianism, reënforced by a desire to keep learning close to the people, was a major factor in scattering colleges widely over the country.   In the opinion of the American Education Society, this was indicative of a democratic spirit "which will not rest till it has brought within the reach of every enterprising youth, the means of a liberal education." [4]   Some, however, re-

[1] Morison, *Three Centuries of Harvard,* 201-205.

[2] The first gymnasium in the United States, established by Germans who had fled from Metternich's agents, was at the Round Hill School in Northampton, Massachusetts, in which George Bancroft was interested.   See Charles Beck's translation of Friedrich L. Jahn's *Treatise on Gymnastics* (Northampton, 1828).

[3] E. G. Dexter, *History of Education in the United States* (N. Y., 1904), 270; D. G. Tewksbury, *The Founding of American Colleges and Universities before the Civil War* (N. Y., 1932), chap. i.

[4] In 1830 New England had one college for every 1231 inhabitants; the Middle states one for every 3465; the Southern states one for every 7232; and the Western states one for every 6060.   "General Summary of Colleges," Am. Educ. Soc., *Quar. Register and Journ.,* II, 242.

gretted that Americans had not followed the example of the British and the French in creating a few great centers of learning. Others felt that no further additions should be made to the "multitude of colleges." [1]

According to Jedidiah Morse's *Geography Made Easy* (1802), the colleges were "generally well furnished with libraries, apparatus, instruments and students." The trustees of these institutions, however, would scarcely have recognized the description. The productive funds of the twenty-two colleges in 1800 were estimated at slightly more than $500,000. In 1804, when Nott became president, the expenditure of Union College was only $4000, but the income was even less — a situation which he promptly corrected by conducting several lotteries under state authorization. As late as 1830 Yale had only about $20,000 income from endowment, while Harvard secured half its total revenue of $45,000 from student fees and rents. These were the more substantial schools. From the West came incessant pleas for books, equipment and funds. [2]

Following the depression of 1819 there were numerous complaints that student enrollments were declining. A survey made by the American Education Society in 1829 listed Yale first with 359 undergraduates drawn from a geographic range wider than that of any other college. Harvard stood second with 247, followed by Union (227), Amherst (207) and Dartmouth (137). [3] Fifty colleges had fewer than 135 students each. The professors were peculiarly interested in fluctuating enrollments at a time when salaries were partially based upon

---

[1] *Analectic Magazine*, II (1813), 310-311; R. S. Baldwin, *Considerations Suggested by the Establishment of a Second College in Connecticut* (Hartford, 1824).

[2] Thwing, *Higher Education*, 271-280.

[3] Am. Educ. Soc., *Quar. Register and Journ.*, II, 238. Ten years later the figures were Yale 411; Union 286; Virginia 247; Princeton 237; Harvard 216.

fees in courses. Though Columbia abandoned the fee
system in 1810, offering its professors $2500 annually
and the use of a dwelling house, many colleges, especially in the West and South, continued to eke out fixed
salaries with fees, whenever income from endowments
and special gifts seemed uncertain.[1]

The library was the weakest point in any comparison
of American colleges with European universities. At
the beginning of the century Dartmouth reported 4000
volumes while Princeton had no more. Both institutions, like many others, also relied upon the collections
of the literary societies.[2] To its 2700 volumes in 1790
Yale added more than 4000 in thirty years, making its
entire collection no larger than the magnificent private
library built up by Thomas Jefferson. Like many other
institutions, Yale specialized in theological works, almost
a third of the titles falling into that category. From
Göttingen, George Ticknor wrote in 1816, "I cannot
better explain to you the difference between our University in Cambridge and the one here than by telling you
that here I hardly say too much when I say that it consists in the Library, and that in Cambridge the Library is
one of the last things thought and talked about." [3] Yet
Harvard had been singularly fortunate on this score. In
1812 its library contained some 15,000 volumes — a
number not reached by Columbia until after the Civil
War — and in 1830 more than 35,000 books, maps
and other items. No other college could match its
treasures.[4] In 1790 Thomas Cooper had remarked that
American libraries consisted "almost entirely of *modern*

[1] Matthews and others, *Columbia University*, 92.

[2] Thwing, *Higher Education*, 410.

[3] When he returned to Cambridge, Ticknor was shocked by the inadequate collection of books and manuscripts. [Hillard and others], *George
Ticknor*, I, 72.

[4] President of Harvard University, *Fifth Annual Report to the Overseers* (Cambridge, 1831).

books" and did not contain "the means of tracing the *history* of questions"; but he lived long enough in academic circles to see the changes as college librarians tardily became aware of the slowly expanding curricula.[1]

"I cast my eye, for a moment," wrote Moses Stuart in 1828, "on the catalogues of the New England Colleges, which contain *exposées* of the course of study. Here I see navigation, surveying, guaging, spherical trigonometry, fluxions, integral and differential calculus, conic sections, calculation of eclipses, chemistry, mineralogy, the law of nations, political economy, and many other studies of the like nature . . . ."[2] He could have added to this lengthy list. Yet the curriculum still revolved about the classics, moral philosophy and "evidences of Christianity." Alexis de Tocqueville might well have used the colleges to give point to his observation in the early thirties that, despite the lack of a national church, religion was the foremost institution of the country, more influential in America than in any other land.

[1] Thomas Cooper, *Some Information Respecting America* (London, 1794), 65.

[2] Am. Educ. Soc., *Quar. Register and Journ.*, I, 199.

CHAPTER XI

LAWYERS AND DOCTORS

AT the close of the Revolution the legal fraternity was notoriously unpopular — nowhere more so than in New England. "The most innocent and irreproachable life," remarked John Quincy Adams in 1787, "cannot guard a lawyer against the hatred of his fellow citizens." [1] The reasons were various. As the lawyers who remained loyal to the Crown either retired from active practice or fled the country, pettifoggers took the vacant places and soon found more than a living in collecting debts contracted during the war-time inflation. Both bar and bench declined further in popular esteem during the paper-money controversies, so strikingly dramatized by Shays's Rebellion. [2] Attorneys and counselors came to be regarded as hirelings of the creditor interests, English as well as American. There was muttering also against prominent lawyer-politicians who aided returning Loyalists in suits to regain possession of their property. [3] But while these prejudices lingered long among mechanics and small farmers, the early years of the nineteenth century brought a remarkable change of sentiment. European visitors now noted that the lawyer was "the first man in the state," occupying a social position alongside clergymen and physicians and wielding great political power. Some commentators shrewdly attributed this prestige to the rapidly growing

[1] John Quincy Adams, *Writings* (W. C. Ford, ed., N. Y., 1913-1917), I, 37.

[2] See E. B. Greene, *The Revolutionary Generation, 1763-1790* (*A History of American Life*, IV), 338.

[3] Charles Warren, *A History of the American Bar* (Boston, 1911), 213-214.

demand for legal services in business and land affairs.[1]

But the professional status of the lawyer was still precarious. No group in the United States corresponded to the upper bar in England, possessing special privileges and prerogatives by reason of affiliation with the Inns of Court. The Revolution had swept away the aristocracy of American barristers trained at the English Inns, who had been notably strong in the Southern provinces.[2] For several decades thereafter the term barrister was frequently used, but it became an honorary title accorded by common consent to outstanding lawyers.[3] The English distinction between the practitioner in law (attorney) and in equity (solicitor), faintly persisting in New Jersey and Delaware, generally disappeared; and the functions of the counselor or barrister were also assumed by the attorney. In New York, for example, the leaders of the bar apparently intended to follow the English system, but the provision that solicitors might easily become counselors and the subsequent requirement that counselors in chancery must also be attorneys gradually modified distinctions once more sharply defined.[4] Out of the modifications of English and colonial precedents there emerged the general practitioner, whose sign read "attorney and counselor at law."

Control over admissions to the bar varied. In 1800 Kentucky, Virginia and North Carolina were the only states where neither rule of court nor legislative act fixed

[1] John Bristed, *America and Her Resources* (London, 1818), 293-295; Achille Murat, *A Moral and Political Sketch of the United States of North America* (London, 1833), 146. Fortescue Cuming remarked in 1807 that the lawyers constituted "a very numerous class which assumes an air of superiority throughout the whole country." *Sketches of a Tour to the Western Country* (Pittsburgh, 1810), 71.

[2] E. A. Jones, *American Members of the Inns of Court* (London, 1924), xxviii-xxix; Greene, *Revolutionary Generation*, 381-382.

[3] Anon., "The American Character," *Literary Mag. and Am. Register,* II (1804), 255.

[4] P. M. Hamlin, *Legal Education in Colonial New York* (N. Y., 1939), 131, n. 16.

definite periods for legal training. While no uniformity existed, the court regulations usually called for a clerkship of from three to seven years with appropriate credit for courses completed in college. The preparatory work in several states was below the standard set during the colonial period, and from time to time the training term was shortened during the early decades of the nineteenth century.[1] Ohio's first constitution (1802) included every clause of the territorial code except that relating to the education of lawyers. Indiana in 1817 substituted a superficial system of examinations for the traditional clerkship. These were but straws in the wind. The general decline in standards came after 1830 as frontiersmen and urban workers demanded that the lawyer's special privileges be made more easily available to ambitious young men.[2]

The clerkship was usually an informal arrangement. In some parts of the East, particularly New England and New York, the bar associations, motivated by self-interest as well as concern for the profession, undertook to regulate the relation between clerk and counselor. Of the attorneys practising in Massachusetts between 1800 and 1830 more than ninety per cent were college graduates and began their legal education in law offices.[3] The value of such training depended upon the time which the attorney, busy with the details of his private practice, was willing to devote to instruction, however unsystematic. Few preceptors were so inspiring as George Wythe, who during his Richmond years taught young Henry Clay, or so methodical as Lemuel Shaw, who became chief justice of Massachusetts. Shaw prescribed a regular program based upon his clerks' previous read-

[1] *Ibid.*, 125-126.
[2] A. Z. Reed, *Training for the Public Profession of Law* (N. Y., 1921), 83-87.
[3] This is based on data compiled by Austin L. Moore, now professor of history at Akron University.

ing and designed to acquaint them with the routine of local practice as well as with the philosophy of the law.[1] Most young men "reading law," however, spent their time copying papers, looking up cases, preparing abstracts and briefs and learning legal procedure by haunting the county courts. Even Joseph Story, fortunately apprenticed in Samuel Sewall's office at Marblehead, complained he had little opportunity to ask for explanations "to light up the dark and intricate paths." [2]

If the student turned to his preceptor's library for help, he was apt to be disappointed. Few of the texts possessed sufficient literary merit to make subtle refinements easy for him. After a careful reading of Bacon's *Pleas and Pleading* John Quincy Adams found the subject "so knotty" that he would have to read the work "once or twice more." [3] Story, having finished Blackstone's *Commentaries,* was directed by Sewall to read Coke on Littleton. He "took it up, and after trying it day after day with very little success . . . sat down and wept bitterly." For a time he was completely confused by the "intricacies of the middle ages of the common law, and the repulsive and almost unintelligible forms of process and pleadings." [4] In most offices books were few, especially in the days before court reports were widely published, but the student-apprentices read earnestly, if not extensively. Webster went through Vattel's *Law of Nations* three times, while John Quincy Adams devoted the same attention to Blackstone's *Commentaries.*[5] Less widely read than Blackstone, but well known, were Ward's *Law of*

---

[1] F. H. Chase, *Life of Lemuel Shaw* (Boston, 1918), 120.
[2] W. W. Story, *Life and Letters of Joseph Story* (Boston, 1851), I, 73.
[3] J. Q. Adams, *Life in a New England Town* (Boston, 1903), 158.
[4] Story, *Life and Letters of Joseph Story,* I, 74.
[5] F. A. Ogg, *Life of Daniel Webster* (Phila., 1914), 56.

Nations, Lord Bacon's *Institutes,* Hawkins's *Pleas of the Crown,* Pufendorf's *Of the Law of Nature and Nations* and Rutherforth's *Institutes of Natural Law,* which was really a commentary on Grotius. No comprehensive commentary on American law was available until James Kent's four volumes appeared between 1826 and 1830.

From a well-conducted office with two or three students trying to master a few texts, it was but a short step to a small private law school. That step was taken late in the eighteenth century. Sometime between 1782 and 1784 Tapping Reeve at Litchfield, Connecticut, began a series of formal lectures to students in his office and announced that he would conduct a law school.[1] For a half-century he or his associates, James Gould and J. W. Huntington, trained young men from every part of the country, more than a thousand in all. Students who completed the course spent fourteen months — eight in the first year and six in the second — attending lectures, reading cases, writing weekly examination papers and participating in moot court or the programs of the forensic societies. Though Reeve was not a vigorous lecturer, judged by the oratorical standards of his generation, he possessed the qualities of an inspiring teacher. A goodly number went out from Litchfield to win recognition in private practice or in public office; and if they were not Federalists it was no fault of their preceptor. Fifteen became United States senators and ten governors, two were appointed to the Supreme Court and forty were named to the state judiciary. High on the list stand the names of John C.

[1] S. H. Fisher, ed., *Litchfield Law School, 1784-1833* (Litchfield, 1900), *passim.* More than one hundred students were trained in the law school established by Peter Van Schaack in 1786 in his home at Kinderhook, New York. H. C. Van Schaack, *Life of Peter Van Schaack* (N. Y., 1842), 443 ff.

Calhoun, Horace Mann, George Y. Mason and Levi Woodbury.[1] It was said that the student learned more at Litchfield in one year than could be gained in five by the "ordinary method of securing an acquaintance with legal principles."[2]

Tapping Reeve's school did not stand alone except in national renown. Occasionally his students followed his example, turning their own offices into legal academies. Samuel Howe at Northampton, Amasa Parker at Albany and Edward King at Cincinnati sponsored courses not unlike those offered in Litchfield. There were other undertakings of similar kind. At New Haven the school established in 1800 by Seth Staples, and continued by Samuel Hitchcock, set high standards of legal instruction for twenty-four years when Judge David Daggett brought additional distinction to its staff. In 1826 Daggett was appointed an instructor in law at Yale, and his proprietary interest in training lawyers slowly became the nucleus of the Yale Law School.[3]

There had been earlier experiments by American colleges in professional training for the law. Besides George Wythe, who in 1779 had been named at William and Mary to the first professorship of law, James Wilson tried a decade later to inaugurate a three-year course in the College of Philadelphia.[4] In 1794 James Kent delivered his introductory lecture as professor of law in Columbia College, announcing his intention to make

[1] D. C. Kilbourn, The Bench and Bar of Litchfield, Connecticut, 1709-1909 (Litchfield, 1909), 178-215.

[2] United States Law Journal (1822), 400-401.

[3] W. L. Kingsley, ed., Yale College, a Sketch of Its History (N. Y., 1879), II, 91.

[4] L. G. Tyler, "A Few Facts from the Records of William and Mary College," Am. Hist. Assoc., Papers, IV, 129 ff. Though John Vardill had been named to the chair of natural law in King's College in 1773, he probably taught political philosophy rather than anything designed to prepare young men for the bar. Anna Haddow, Political Science in American Colleges and Universities, 1636-1900 (F. A. Ogg, ed., The Century Political Science Series; N. Y., 1939), 85.

his instruction contribute to a liberal education. But
neither Wilson nor Kent succeeded in arousing interest.
Their lectures were apparently too technical for the average undergraduate and too theoretical for the young
apprentices-at-law who came to hear them.[1] There was
a similar lack of response to the rather half-hearted
efforts of Isaac Parker, chief justice of Massachusetts,
who was named first Royall professor of law at Harvard
in 1816. Though Parker persuaded the Corporation
to adopt his plan for "a school for the instruction of
resident graduates in jurisprudence," it was not until
Joseph Story accepted the Dane professorship in 1829
that a serious attempt was made to transform the course
into systematic professional training in law.[2]

Whatever his legal education, the neophyte became
familiar with judicial procedure by frequenting the
county courts rather than by reading treatises and reports. There was much to be learned — the functions
of the various court officials, the possibilities in challenging potential jurymen, the rules of evidence, the nuances
in handling witnesses and the legal erudition sometimes
paraded in the charge to the jury. Ceremonial precedents were few and simple, causing foreign observers
to deplore the failure to maintain the dignity of the
courts. Judges were abandoning the English custom of
wearing carefully curled wigs and scarlet robes.[3] Black
suits and black gowns were the only distinguishing costume of bench and bar in most parts of the country.
Sporadic attempts to preserve the judicial garb of colonial days were discountenanced as incongruous in a simple

[1] Brander Matthews and others, eds., *A History of Columbia University,
1754-1904* (N. Y., 1904), 340. Kent was reappointed in 1823.
[2] Roscoe Pound, "The Law School," S. E. Morison, ed., *The Development of Harvard University* (Cambridge, 1930), 472-473; S. E. Morison, *Three Centuries of Harvard* (Cambridge, 1936), 239-240.
[3] G. M. Towle, *American Society* (London, 1870), I, 89; Theophilus
Parsons, *Memoir of Theophilus Parsons* (Boston, 1859), 154.

republican government, or as unseemly survivals of English practice.

Court time was frolicking time. Taverns at the county seat were filled with litigants, attorneys and spectators who had come to enjoy the sparring of rival counsel and to participate in the wrestling, gambling, drinking and horse racing which filled the intervals between sessions. Even the judges spent the evenings in smoking, drinking and "cracking jokes indifferently with all." [1] James Kent, riding the western "eyres" of New York, was often distressed by the easy informality of lawyers, litigants and jurymen, especially in "democratic" counties, but he admitted that court procedure, however lacking in pageantry, was orderly and marked by a simple dignity. [2] On a small platform in the courtroom sat the judge behind a high desk with the clerk below him, quill behind his ear and armed with the papers of the case. On either side of the clerk's desk attorneys for plaintiff and defendant sat at tables, while the jury occupied hard wooden benches close to the witness box and the prisoner was seated on an inclosed bench guarded by the sheriff or his deputies. A conspicuous iron stove made court sessions during the winter months endurable, if not always pleasant. [3]

In most states the attorneys and judges of both appellate and county courts rode circuit. For the beginner this proved excellent schooling since he learned from the conversations of older practitioners, often in reminiscent mood, lessons which would help him handle difficult cases of his own. But circuit riding put lawyers,

[1] John Palmer, *Journal of Travels in the United States of North America . . . 1817* (London, 1818), 203-206; Chase, *Lemuel Shaw*, 44-45; Warren, *American Bar*, 206-207.

[2] J. T. Horton, *James Kent* (N. Y., 1939), 126-130.

[3] Towle, *American Society*, I, 103-105; James Stuart, *Three Years in North America* (London, 1833), I, 330; Rufus Choate, *Works* (S. G. Brown, ed., Boston, 1862), I, 280.

young and old, to the test. Its physical discomforts
were slight in comparison with its professional disad-
vantages. There was little opportunity to confer with
clients and witnesses; and reference to legal authorities
frequently was limited to whatever could be conveniently carried in one's saddlebags. So aggravating was
the situation in Berkshire County, Massachusetts, that
in 1815 the members of the bar formed a Law Library
Association to provide books for use during court
sessions.[1]

Lawyers and judges at the opening of the century
were better acquainted with European legal treatises
than with applications and modifications of English
precedents in the United States. Not only were there no
satisfactory commentaries on American law, but there
were few systematic compilations of the statutes of the
several states.[2] As for court reports, Ephraim Kirby's
first volume of *American Law Reports,* containing Connecticut decisions, appeared in 1789, and the following
year Alexander Dallas began to record Pennsylvania
decisions.[3] But at best these early compilations were
fragmentary in a day when judicial opinions were seldom written.[4] To Judge James Kent goes much of the
credit for establishing the written decision as normal
court procedure. His own opinions were so carefully

[1] Anon., *History of the County of Berkshire, Massachusetts* (Pittsfield, 1829), 109.

[2] In 1795 Zephaniah Swift published *A System of the Laws of the
State of Connecticut,* which seems to have exerted some influence upon
instruction in New England's private law schools. Nathan Dane's *General
Abridgment and Digest of American Law* in nine volumes appeared between 1823 and 1829.

[3] R. J. Purcell, *Connecticut in Transition* (Wash., 1918), 304 *n.*
Lord·Mansfield praised Dallas's *Reports of Cases Ruled and Adjudged in
the Courts of Pennsylvania before and since the Revolution,* but Dallas
had been forced to use the recollections of jurists and the rough notes of
attorneys in order to supplement the official record. Raymond Walters, jr.,
Alexander James Dallas (Phila., 1943), 23-24.

[4] Law reports were published in the Southern states earlier than in most
of the Northern states. Warren, *American Bar,* 330-331.

formulated and so cogent that colleagues in the New York supreme court had to follow his example in self-defense. As a result, New York's courts steadily grew in influence beyond the borders of the state. In view of the scarcity of contemporary reports and commentaries it is easy to understand why lawyers were confused concerning the validity of precedent and the direction of interpretation. But the situation was probably not so chaotic as Kent thought when he became New York's chief justice in 1804.[1]

American courts and legislatures seem to have departed farther from English precedents than was generally realized. The common law, which had been imperfectly understood but widely venerated in colonial times, was considerably modified by statute and judicial decision in the half-century following the Declaration of Independence. Hostility to British tradition in Pennsylvania and Kentucky led to legislation forbidding counsel to cite British decisions.[2] If the common law did not "escape the odium of its origin," it was also attacked on more specific counts: the brutality of its punishments; its bias against debtors and mortgagors; and its doctrines of criminal conspiracy, seditious libel and inalienable allegiance.[3]

Most American critics of "judge-made" law rested their case on the competence of their own legislatures to

[1] Horton, *James Kent*, 151. Lacking precedents, judges fell back upon their own conceptions of law, which may explain the popularity of the doctrine of the higher law early in the nineteenth century. H. S. Commager, "Constitutional History and the Higher Law," *Pa. Mag. of History and Biog.*, LXII, 38.

[2] Ingenious counsel, however, could cite English and American law texts which were based upon English decisions. Roscoe Pound, *The Formative Era of American Law* (Boston, 1938), 140. For a discussion of the popular prejudice against English court decisions, see Warren, *American Bar*, 228-239.

[3] Julius Goebel, jr., "The Courts and the Law in Colonial New York," A. C. Flick, ed., *History of the State of New York* (N. Y., 1933-1937), III, 42; Joseph Hawley to Ephraim Wright, April 16, 1782, *Am. Hist. Rev.*, XXXVI, 777; Warren, *American Bar*, 236-239.

create an autochthonous jurisprudence based on natural rights.[1] One of them, William Sampson, was so persistent that in 1828 he goaded New York's legislature into a general revision and codification of its statutes. The job was done with such thoroughness that James Kent, learned in the English tradition and champion of propertied interests, stood aghast at the "extent of demolition" effected by "an edict as sweeping as the torch of Omar." Yet an English commentary conceded that the new code rendered the law of descent of real property more simple, the rules of construction more conformable to common sense, modes of transfer cheaper and more direct, and title to property more clear.[2]

Despite the impact of popular prejudice, of critical legislatures and innovating judges, the spirit of the English common law continued to form the main current of American legal philosophy. In large measure this was the achievement of the bench and bar during the early decades of the nineteenth century. "John Marshall found a copy of Blackstone's *Commentaries,*" wrote the English legal historian, Frederick W. Maitland, "and the common law went straight to the Pacific."[3] But in this respect Joseph Story, Lemuel Shaw and Theophilus Parsons in Massachusetts, James Kent in New York, Benjamin Tilghman and John B. Gibson in Pennsylvania, Thomas Ruffin in North Carolina and Edward Livingston in Louisiana take rank with Marshall. Theirs was the substantial work of reconciling

[1] Edward Livingston's famous codifications in Louisiana contained abundant evidence of the utilitarianism of the Benthamite reformers. W. B. Hatcher, *Edward Livingston* (University, Louisiana, 1940), 255, 267.

[2] C. P. Daly, *The Common Law* (N. Y., 1894), 52-57.

[3] F. W. Maitland, *English Law and the Renaissance* (the Rede Lecture for 1901, Cambridge, Eng., 1901). Such common-law procedures as the student learned from Blackstone had been transformed, in American usage, by several generations of provincial experience. The English commentator had never been an inerrant guide to American practices.

social changes in the New World with the common-law tradition, modified to meet the necessities of a steadily expanding commercial and industrial society.[1] Complicated questions of partnership, bottomry, marine insurance, bills and notes were clarified in the light of the reports of cases decided in the Court of King's Bench during the time of Lord Mansfield, or perhaps the commercial codes of Continental Europe were explored and the writings of Emerigon and Valin placed under tribute.[2] So in New York the law merchant assumed new and substantial form. Furthermore, reports of Chancellor Kent's cases were cited in chancery proceedings from Maine to Florida.[3] An English publicist remarked that "all our doctrines" have met with approbation in the American courts of equity. "We confess," he concluded, "that we did not wish to find the homage to English authority carried to so great an extent." [4]

Whatever the source of the legal framework within which they labored, the lawyers were primarily concerned with the causes of litigation that brought them clients. Except in New England, where maritime questions frequently arose, they found their most lucrative practice in serving the interests of the landed gentry and land speculators. At the same time, however, the ramifications of expanding domestic and foreign commerce, the extraordinary problems imposed by nonintercourse, embargo and war, and the growing investment in ma-

---

[1] William Kent, *Memoirs and Letters of James Kent* (Boston, 1898), 112, 117; Pound, *Formative Era of American Law*, 20, 107. These years were marked also in America by the entrenchment of the doctrine of judicial review, feared by Jefferson and other opponents of "judge-made law." H. S. Commager, *Majority Rule and Minority Rights* (N. Y., 1943), 36-38.

[2] Horton, *James Kent*, 103-105.

[3] "No English books of chancery decisions are more respectfully cited in the courts of South Carolina than the seven volumes of Mr. Johnson's reports of Kent's decisions," wrote a commentator in 1822 in *London Law Mag.*, VI, 132.

[4] *American Jurist*, XXII, 234, cited in Horton, *James Kent*, 109.

chine industry steadily emphasized the importance of
the law merchant. Legal business was increasing so
rapidly, especially in the port cities, that conditions
seemed favorable for specialization within the profession.
It was retarded, however, by the fact that in most communities the personnel of the landowning and mercantile
groups was closely related and by the inclination of both
groups to make investments in industrial enterprises.[1]

Country lawyers, quite as much as their colleagues in
the cities, used the law as a gateway to business opportunities. The small town, often the frontier village,
beckoned to the beginner. If not already a qualified
attorney, a season of teaching school might precede the
day when he had satisfied all requirements and could
hang up his shingle. However that might be, his ultimate success depended upon his ability to withstand
months of anxious waiting for clients and other tedious
months of filling out writs and serving summonses or
of drudgery over deeds, conveyances and bad debts.
Once he had won the confidence of his neighbors, there
came a period of widening business activity as he learned
of mortgages to be foreclosed or of choice tracts of land
where a small speculative investment might return proportionately large profits. Political preferment, at first
a welcome supplement to insufficient income, came to be
valued as a badge of power and prestige. Many country
lawyers built their lives into the communities where
they first sought clients; others regarded the small town
as merely a way station to the city. Rufus Choate,
starting practice in the busy port of Salem, quickly
removed to Danvers, where he would not have to face

[1] Business interests and their legal advisers constantly sought judicial
recognition for the unincorporated association. Their efforts gave a certain
semblance of specialization to the work in some urban law offices prior to
1830. For a discussion of legal aspects of the problem of business organization in this period, see Shaw Livermore, *Early American Land Companies* (Columbia Univ. School of Law, *Publs.*, 1939), chaps. vii-viii,
and Julius Goebel's "Introduction."

the eminent lawyers of Essex County. When he ran for Congress, it was charged that he did not reside in the district since he was only stopping there "while he oated his horse" for Boston.[1]

The income of the legal profession in America varied greatly. George Ticknor, visiting Philip Barbour, an eminent Virginia lawyer, found that he was making less than seven thousand dollars in 1824.[2] A few years later William Wirt was told that six or eight thousand dollars was a good practice in New York City while ten thousand was the maximum.[3] Even such figures must have seemed astronomical to small-town lawyers, especially when farm prices sagged and speculative land values broke sharply.

Self-interest dictated many of the regulations of the bar associations — limitation of the number of students who might study in each lawyer's office, imposition of varying periods of training prior to admission to the bar, the fixing of minimum fees for legal services, provision for investigating unfair practices — yet fear of the possible overcrowding of the profession was mingled with a desire to raise the standard of professional ethics.[4] Most of these associations manifested a sense of social responsibility not always easily communicated to their individual members.[5] That the legal profession enjoyed greater popular esteem in 1830 than it had forty years earlier, there can be no doubt.

[1] Choate, Works, I, 18.

[2] [G. S. Hillard and others], Life, Letters, and Journals of George Ticknor (Boston, 1876), I, 347-348.

[3] S. E. Baldwin, The American Judiciary (N. Y., 1905), 355-356. By 1830 Lemuel Shaw, who was at the head of his profession in Boston, may have been earning as much as $15,000 a year. Chase, Lemuel Shaw, 131.

[4] Foreign commentators thought that lawyers' fees were moderate. One remarked that "going to law is a cheap amusement." Murat, United States, 248-249; Stuart, Three Years in North America, I, 348-349.

[5] See, for example, Rules of the Bar of Suffolk County, Massachusetts, Adopted in 1819 (Boston, 1827).

The faint line of social concern which ran through many regulations of the bar associations was more distinct in the proceedings of the medical societies. The problem of malpractice, ever weighted with the possibility of fatal consequences, was more serious for the physician than for the lawyer and received greater attention from state legislatures. Although medical societies had existed in colonial times, the desire of the states after the Revolution to enforce legislation against unlicensed practitioners stimulated a demand for greater professional competence. Organizations among the doctors fell into three categories: societies which were granted specific regulatory functions by state action; voluntary associations without such powers; and informal groups, usually in the larger towns, interested in special phases of medicine.[1] By 1830 all the states save Pennsylvania, Virginia and North Carolina had societies recognized by law.[2]

New York in 1806 placed regulation in the hands of a state medical society, a method first tested by Massachusetts in 1781. After four years' apprenticeship, one year of which might be spent in a classical college or medical school, a candidate could submit a dissertation and take an examination prepared by one of the thirty-five county medical societies. If successful, he was licensed. Doctors already practising were not subject to the new regulations. Unlicensed practitioners were outlawed, but a fatal amendment in 1813 exempted those whose prescriptions were confined to indigenous herbs.[3] The exemption was a concession to deluded folk

[1] H. B. Shafer, *The American Medical Profession from 1783 to 1850* (Columbia Univ., *Studies,* no. 417), 218.

[2] N. S. Davis, *Contributions to . . . Medical Education* (N. Y., 1877), 49 ff.

[3] *Laws of New York* (rev. edn., Albany, 1813), II, 219 ff. Dr. David Hosack lamented that "the hand of fellowship [was still] allowed to the illiterate and the vulgar, when it ought to have been reserved for the

who believed that medical standards were set up for the doctors' benefit and not in the public interest.

Regardless of the state's policy, medical societies strove to formulate codes of professional conduct and to insure compliance. Modeling their by-laws on the Englishman Thomas Percival's *Medical Jurisprudence or Code of Ethics* (1803), they suggested the precepts that should guide the physician in his relations with patients and colleagues. If he hit upon an efficacious formula, he was expected to share it with the profession. Few, however, resisted the temptation to keep their prescriptions secret. In 1797 the Connecticut Medical Society gave nation-wide publicity to Elisha Perkins by expelling him because he had patented "painted metallic instruments" which, he alleged, possessed inherent powers of curing many diseases. Expulsion apparently did not prevent the discoverer from reaping a small fortune from the sales of "Perkins Tractors."[1] After considerable deliberation the physicians of Albany dropped Dr. Elias Willard's name from their rolls because he refused to reveal the nature of his reputed cure for scrofula and cancer.[2] Likewise, Massachusetts expelled Dr. Lyman B. Sarbin of Wrentham who held the patents to Dr. Lee's Gravel Specific and Peges Vegetable Cyrup.[3]

Suspicion of motives hindered the work of the societies, for many felt that the primary purpose of such organizations was purely selfish — to increase patronage and maintain high charges for service. In New Haven and elsewhere it was said that the way to bring a full attendance at a meeting was to advertise a discussion of

educated and virtuous." "Present State of Medical Science." *Am. Medical and Philos. Register*, III (1812-1813), 87.

[1] *Medical Repository*, I (N. Y., 1798), 115; Connecticut Medical Society, *Transactions* (1796), 40; (1797), 50; B. D. Perkins, *The Efficacy of Perkins Patent Medicine Tractors* (n.p., n.d.), *passim*.

[2] S. D. Willard, *Annals of the Medical Society of the County of Albany, 1806-1851* (Albany, 1851), 24.

[3] Massachusetts Medical Society, *Medical Papers*, VII, 88-90.

The Pennsylvania Hospital, in 1802

fees. But there is no conclusive evidence to indicate how closely individual physicians followed the rate schedules so determined.[1]

Practitioners who failed to meet the standards of allopathic medicine proved a perennial source of trouble. It was not easy to draw the line between harmless herbalists and dangerous quacks.[2] Probably no irregular commanded more followers than Samuel Thomson, who in 1813 patented a system combining steam baths with the use of varying vegetable compounds in which the emetic properties of lobelia leaves were important. From "Thomsonism" stemmed a host of "botanics" and "steam doctors," whose regimen may have helped, if it could not cure, perennially hopeful patients. Dr. Benjamin Waterhouse of Boston, openly indorsing Thomson's ideas, was criticized by a profession which dared not discipline him for his temerity. Even Benjamin Rush and Benjamin Smith Barton of Philadelphia had a good word for the "botanics."

As the list of irregulars — botanic, regular botanic, Thomsonian, reformed Thomsonian, magnetical, electrical, rootist, herbist, florist — steadily lengthened, state legislatures began to retreat from their attempts to promote higher standards in medicine.[3] There was an impression abroad that some sort of conspiracy existed in medical circles to deprive the poor man of his cheap cures. As a Massachusetts farmer wrote in 1798,

[1] *Boston Medical Intelligencer*, II, 151-152.

[2] Regular practitioners were often more distressed by evidence of empirical folk science than by the vagaries of superstition. *Medical Repository*, IV (N. Y., 1801), 285 ff.; Joseph Johnson, *Oration before the Medical Society of South Carolina* (Charleston, 1808), 24-25.

[3] The herbalists, attacking regulatory legislation, helped to perpetuate belief in the efficacy of the rabbit's foot, the beaver's tail, the snake's skin and scores of weird concoctions in the cure of disease. Some paraded as "botanists," who should have been called sorcerers. See the prescriptions in *The New and Complete Medical Family Herbal* by Samuel Henry, botanist (N. Y., 1814), and Daniel Ballmer, *A Collection of New Receipts and Approved Cures for Man and Beast* (Shellsburg, Pa., 1827).

The Doctors have established their Meditial Societyes
. . . by which they have so nearly enielated Quacary
of all kinds, that a poor man cant git so grate cures of
them now for a ginna, as he could 50 years ago of an
old Squaw for halfe a pint of Rhum. The bisness of
a Midwife could be purformed 50 years ago for halfe
a doller & now it costs a poor man 5 hole ones.[1]

Here was the crude but forceful expression of the spirit
which from that day to this has resisted advances in
medical science.[2]

Self-interest spurred the licensed practitioner in his
running fight with the patent-medicine industry. In
America, as in England and the German provinces, there
was fear that the competition would undermine the
position of the medical profession.[3] The Medical Society of the City of New York in 1827 carefully investi-
gated Swain's Panacea, Potter's Catholicon, Columbian
Syrup and other popular "remedies" for rheumatism,
syphilis, scrofula and chronic eruptions. They reported
most of them to be ineffective, nothing more than compounds of sarsaparilla and varying amounts of harmless drugs.[4] Manufacturers of such concoctions found
golden rewards in indulging man's eternal craving for
cheap and painless cures. Others, equally reprehensible
in the eyes of the medical societies, published books of
prescriptions guaranteed to cure two types of diseases:

1 William Manning, *The Key of Libberty* (S. E. Morison, ed., Billerica,
Mass., 1922), 26.
2 For the decline of state regulation after 1830, see C. B. Cartwright,
"History of Medical Legislation in the State of New York." *N. Y. Journ.
of Medicine*, IV, 160. R. H. Shryock discusses its relation to the general
philosophy of *laissez faire* in his "Public Relations of the Medical Profession in Great Britain and the United States, 1600-1870," *Annals of
Medical History*, n.s., II, 322-323.
3 *Medical Repository*, XV (1811-1812), 113; *Literary Mag. and Am.
Register*, II (1804), 233 ff.; *Boston Medical Intelligencer*, Feb. 28, 1826.
4 Medical Society of the City of New York, *Report on Nostrums or
Secret Medicines* (N. Y., 1827), 29-35.

those which baffled the scientist and those which the
victim in shame wished to conceal.[1]

At the close of the eighteenth century the leaders in
American medicine were men with European training,
most of them having studied at Edinburgh or Leyden.
In 1803, however, the editor of the *Medical Repository*,
glancing over the latest list of Edinburgh graduates,
noted that of the twenty-four candidates "there was not
a single one from the United States. The schools of
Philadelphia, New York, Cambridge, Baltimore, Lexington [Kentucky], and Dartmouth are engaged in the
business of medical education to an extent that is pleasing
and surprising." [2] It was being loudly proclaimed, and
increasingly believed, that one could become a first-class
doctor without studying abroad. In fact, the American
medical schools were not only well established, but they
were sending their graduates into distant parts of the
country, there to found new schools and to raise professional standards. It was one of the achievements to
which Americans constantly pointed in their boasts of
cultural independence.

Though such training determined the nature of leadership in the profession, only indirectly did it affect the
rank and file of American physicians. The vast majority
in 1800 had gained their skill and knowledge not in a
medical school but by apprenticeship. In a physician's
office the apprentice, besides sweeping floors and keeping
fires, read his master's books, pounded out the powders
with his master's pestle and made up pills. From it he
followed his master to the sick room, handed him the
necessary tools and watched his practice, much as a
plumber's helper does today.[3] As his knowledge grew,

[1] Shafer, *Medical Profession*, 202-203.
[2] *Medical Repository*, VI (N. Y., 1803), 434.
[3] Asa Greene's *Life and Adventures of Dr. Dodimus Duckworth,
A. N. Q.* (N. Y., 1833), I, 239-240, contains a satirical description of
the medical apprentice who learns by just watching the doctor.

he took a hand himself, but the master was entitled to such fees as came from the apprentice's extracting of teeth, bleeding or other minor operations. In return the master taught the pupil everything he could. Occasionally a successful doctor might take several young men into his office and lecture to them as a class. Such opportunities, however, were exceptional. Instruction of apprentices in medicine, as in law, was usually casual and fragmentary.

The inadequacies of the American doctor's office as a training school strongly impressed all who had studied in Europe. Chemistry required an "elaboratory," Dr. Samuel Bard of New York observed, botany a garden, and, above all, diseases could not be systematically studied save in a hospital.[1] These considerations pointed to the desirability of well-equipped medical schools located in the larger cities. But not all schools sprang from such sound motivation. Some resulted from professorial jealousies and professional quarrels. In New York City, where these disputes were particularly intense, three schools were founded — in 1792, 1811 and 1826 — whose graduates received their degrees through Rutgers College in New Brunswick. So inharmonious was the medical faculty at Columbia that the College of Physicians and Surgeons was chartered in 1807. Well might DeWitt Clinton lament, "Look at New York . . . three contended where there should have been one grand temple dedicated to the healing art."[2] That grand temple was long in building, for after Physicians and Surgeons had absorbed the Columbia medical faculty in 1813 and had crushed the Rutgers school a few years later, it still had to face another rival in the twenties and the vigorous competition of New York University in

[1] *Am. Medical and Philos. Register*, II (1811-1812), 369-370.
[2] DeWitt Clinton, "Introductory Discourse," Literary and Philosophical Society, *Transactions* (1815), I, 19 ff.

the next decade. A similar schism produced a school to challenge that of the University of Pennsylvania, but Philadelphia's doctors, however vehement their disagreements, never equaled their New York colleagues in acrimonious dispute.

During the two decades after 1810 medical faculties were established with unprecedented rapidity, most of them granting their degrees under the charter of some liberal arts college.[1] Except for those in New England — at Brown (1811), Yale (1813) and Bowdoin (1820) — these newer schools generally ministered to the needs of frontier regions or rural communities. The one at Winchester, Virginia, served the valley of the Shenandoah, while as early as 1813 young men from the Mohawk Valley were attending courses instituted by Lyman Spalding, who had come from Dartmouth to Fairfield, New York. The medical department of Middlebury College opened at Castleton, Vermont, in 1818; about the same time Lexington, Kentucky, welcomed the medical department of Transylvania University; and the restless spirit of Daniel Drake, who held a degree from the University of Pennsylvania, found a temporary abode in the Ohio Medical College at Cincinnati before moving farther west.[2]

Prior to 1830 the South's medical dependence on Northern schools and hospitals was almost complete. During colonial days Southerners interested in medicine, as in law, had formed a disproportionately large contingent among the provincials studying in Europe. At the opening of the nineteenth century, however, Edinburgh was being supplanted by Philadelphia, New York

[1] For a summary of medical schools founded between 1800 and 1830, see Shafer, *Medical Profession*, 38-39.

[2] Drake's ability as a physician was marred by his contentiousness. He held eleven chairs in six different schools between 1817 and 1852. E. D. Mansfield, *Memoir of . . . Daniel Drake* (Cincinnati, 1855), *passim*.

and other American institutions.[1]   But neither foreign study nor Northern schooling was thought to fit young doctors to meet the challenge of diseases which were peculiarly Southern.   Furthermore, the Southerner, coming from a "Yankee" school, had to revise many of his notions in the light of native conditions.   It was Charleston, where scientific interest had long flourished, which finally established in 1823 the Lower South's first medical school — the Medical College of the State of South Carolina.[2]

The mushroom growth of training institutions pleased Americans like Daniel Drake, who felt that such activity would free the country from European influences, but the *Boston Medical Intelligencer* in 1826 viewed "the multiplication of medical schools" with alarm.   "In all England," the editor wrote, "there is but one medical school, one in Ireland, in Scotland two (for that at Aberdeen scarcely deserves the name) ; and in all France but three. In the United States there are already 17, and scarcely a month but we learn of the establishment of a new one." [3] What the *Intelligencer* failed to realize was that the settled parts of the United States in 1826 extended over an area nearly three times that of France and the British Isles combined, and that distance was an important factor in the availability of medical instruction.

As new schools reached out to serve a rapidly increasing and perennially migrant population, it became difficult to maintain earlier standards.   Gradually the degree of bachelor of medicine was abandoned, and the doctorate was cheapened by bestowal on those who met little more than the former bachelor's requirements.   At the very moment Edinburgh was lengthening its medical

[1] Edward Hooker, "Diary," Am. Hist. Assoc., *Ann. Rep. for 1896*, I, 916.
[2] R. H. Shryock, "Medical Practice in the Old South," *S. Atl. Quar.*, XXIX, 166-167.
[3] *Boston Medical Intelligencer*, III (1826), 40.

course from three years to four, American schools were accepting two terms, each of which had been shortened from four months to twelve or thirteen weeks to suit the convenience of students who had to travel long distances from their homes.   Standards suffered also from the failure to retain natural history and natural philosophy as a background for the young doctor's science and from the withering of the dissertation, that guild masterpiece long essential to the doctorate.   One melancholy critic said that a medical diploma was as "little respected as the license of many of our county medical societies." [1]

A perusal of medical-school circulars and catalogues reveals virtual uniformity at any given time in the arrangement and sequence of courses.   Despite some evidence of progressive differentiation in subject matter, most professors, as well as most physicians, took all medicine for their province.   At Dartmouth Nathan Smith was the entire faculty for almost a dozen years.[2] James S. Stringham taught chemistry in the Columbia medical faculty, but later in the College of Physicians and Surgeons he taught medical jurisprudence.   David Hosack was considered equally proficient in botany, midwifery, theory and practice of physic and clinical medicine.

Basic for the student was the work in anatomy, physiology and chemistry, followed by more advanced courses in therapeutics, botany and materia medica, midwifery, diseases of women and children and medical jurisprudence.   Slowly the schools followed the lead of the University of Pennsylvania after 1805 in separating the course in surgery from that in anatomy.   Not until 1813 was the lecturer on midwifery, whose subject was still regarded as folklore of women, given equal stand-

[1] *Medical Repository*, XIII (1809-1810), 176.
[2] Davis, *Contributions to Medical Education*, 26.

ing with other members of the medical faculties.[1] By
1820 the requirement was well established that each
student should attend lectures, sometimes five or six a
day, in all subjects during his first term and then go to
the same lectures again during his second year. This
regulation probably had originated at a time when textbooks were so scarce and lecturers so few that a return
engagement by each professor was necessary in order to
cover the subject matter properly.[2] Later, as repetitive
attendance on a professor's lectures became conventional,
there were few protests in faculties where aggregate fees
determined salaries.

Even a cursory survey of the textbooks shows the
continuing dependence upon Europe. French and German works usually reached this country by way of Edinburgh or London, but some, notably the *General Anatomy* of Xavier Bichat, famous French physiologist,
were translated by Americans. Native textbooks, at first
limited to translations or revisions of European authors,
grew steadily in volume. In 1811 Caspar Wistar of
the University of Pennsylvania published the first American study of anatomy. More popular was W. E.
Horner's *Treatise on Special and General Anatomy*
(1826), which went through seven editions in twenty
years. In 1817 Lyman Spalding persuaded the New
York Medical Society to summon a conference for the
purpose of framing a national pharmacopœia. Under
the leadership of Samuel L. Mitchill of New York the
committee in 1820 completed the *United States Pharmacopœia*, subject to revision every ten years.[3]

----

[1] Where the instructional staff was small, physiology, anatomy and
surgery remained one branch; botany, materia medica and pharmacy
another; and theory and practice of medicine a third. Shafer, *Medical
Profession*, 55-56.

[2] Committee of the American Medical Association, *Circular Addressed
to Medical Colleges of the United States* (Phila., 1856).

[3] J. A. Spalding, *Dr. Lyman Spalding* (Boston, 1916), 283.

Although the importance of dissection in the study of anatomy had been clearly recognized since the days of Vesalius, this phase of medical training, even in the larger American schools, was seriously handicapped by lack of adequate equipment and by popular prejudice against the use of cadavers in teaching the subject. In April, 1788, some boys, noticing a severed human limb hung out of a New York City hospital window to dry, straightway raised a riot which required the combined efforts of governor, chancellor, mayor and militia to quell.[1] An especially aggravating case of body-stealing at the Yale school in New Haven necessitated a two days' military guard for the professor of anatomy. At Berkshire, choleric Major Butler Goodrich threatened to burn the college down unless corpse-snatching ceased. While medical faculties sought to quiet the public by promising expulsion for "any attempt, proved on a student, to disinter the dead," such appeals as that of Dartmouth, offering fifty dollars for each corpse, not only spurred irrepressible youngsters to activity but also sent surreptitious merchants of cadavers to medical-college doors. The bodies of executed criminals had long been available, but not until 1830 did Massachusetts take the lead in devoting to science those of unclaimed paupers dying in state charge. Though the law was slowly liberalized in other states, the popular aversion to dissections long persisted, handicapping the "clinical professor" in his systematic research and often preventing the autopsy in private practice.[2]

Other barriers discouraged the search for the true nature of disease. Medical men were distracted, and their work was often disrupted, by the recurrent pes-

---

[1] *American Museum*, III (1788), 389-390.
[2] E. E. Atwater, ed., *History of the City of New Haven* (N. Y., 1887), 271; C. R. Bardeen, "Anatomy in America," Univ. of Wis., *Sci. Ser. Bull.*, III, 139.

tilence which ravaged American cities in the three decades after 1790. To the profession these visitations were a terrific challenge, not only exacting a heavy toll in human lives but subtly influencing medical theory and practice. When yellow fever or typhoid or malaria struck in epidemic form, the insistent demand was for immediate treatment to forestall death. The yellow-fever visitation of 1793 in Philadelphia was one of the worst the United States has ever experienced. The unadorned narrative of Mathew Carey describes it no less vividly than the fictionized account in Charles Brockden Brown's *Arthur Mervyn*.[1] There had been sporadic outbreaks of this disease, particularly in New York in 1702 and again in the early forties.[2] But in 1803 a Philadelphia journal could say: " 'Till the year 1793, we, in this part of America, at least, the present generation, had only heard and read of pestilence. Since that period it has visited us five years out of ten . . . . by which the city would be, for two or three months, almost entirely depopulated . . . ."[3]

There and elsewhere, especially in the Atlantic ports, its periodic returns continued until the 1820's. The horror of those times when cities lost thousands of their residents, when corpses were hurried through the night-black streets or abandoned where they lay, when rows of houses bore the tragic chalk mark, when impromptu hospitals were rigged up at the town's edge to be tended by heroic men who volunteered as nurses, when every desperate expedient at prevention and cure was tried on hearsay, when crime flourished amid the prevalent dis-

---

[1] Mathew Carey, *Short Account of the Malignant Fever* (Phila., 1793).

[2] *Medical Repository*, XIV (1810-1811), 182.

[3] *Literary Mag. and Am. Register*, I (1803-1804), 7. See also James Hardie, *An Account of the Malignant Fever, Lately Prevalent in the City of New-York* (N. Y., 1799).

traction — such horror could not be overstated. Nor was the dread destroyer confined to the seacoast. Between 1797 and 1803 the *Medical Repository* reported epidemics, diagnosed as yellow fever, in western New York, central Pennsylvania, southeastern Ohio and several settlements along the Mississippi. In neighborhoods where poverty prevented flight the list of victims was always long. "A poison," remarked a journalist in 1801, "which, in the city of New-York, has destroyed, within three months, the lives of more than twenty practitioners of medicine, well deserves to be traced and understood by the survivors." [1]

If understanding was not vouchsafed to this generation, speculation concerning probable causes and cures was voluminous.[2] These variant explanations seemed to support two contending schools of thought. The "importationists" insisted that yellow fever was brought by ships from the tropics, while the "domesticians" attributed it to poisonous acid gases arising from rotting refuse or foul ships. Samuel L. Mitchill, spreading fear of this lethal agent, which he called septon, recommended that it be counteracted by alkalis, especially lime.[3] But not all domesticians subscribed to the "septon theory." Some associated fevers with the cosmic maladjustments that produced droughts, meteors, earthquakes and volcanic eruptions. Noah Webster wrote a seven-hundred-page history showing the relation between disturbances in the physical world and the incidence of pestilence—a work which Benjamin Rush

[1] *Medical Repository*, V (N. Y., 1802), 182.
[2] In the first six volumes of the *Medical Repository* (1797-1803) more than ninety essays or papers discussed the history and phenomena of pestilence. American treatises, with learned commentaries appended, were translated in German, Spanish and Italian medical journals.
[3] *Medical Repository*, IV, 91-93; C. R. Hall, *A Scientist in the Early Republic; Samuel Latham Mitchill* (N. Y., 1934), 53.

warmly recommended to Joseph Priestley, for it confirmed the Philadelphian's own observations concerning
epidemics and earth tremors.[1]

Less fantastic was the suggestion that fever, or at least
malaria, was generated in stagnant water and some even
mentioned the mosquitoes which bred there. A writer
in Savannah held the surrounding marshes responsible
for the "autumnal insalubrity" while a North Carolin-
ian blamed the swampy land near Edenton.[2] But many
scoffed at such theories. The editor of the *Medical
Repository*, pointing out that "writers have been very
fond of considering a plentiful generation of insects to
be the forerunner or concomitant of epidemic diseases,"
concluded: "Common as this opinion is, and strenuously
as it has been urged, the careful observer of the seasons
in America has now acquired satisfactory proofs that
insects, even in great variety and number, are not the
necessary harbingers or companions of popular dis-
tempers."[3] The agency of the *stegomyia calopus* in
spreading yellow fever and that of the *anopheles* in
malaria were not to be known for many decades.[4]

Catastrophe is often the prelude to social change.
Just as the Chicago and San Francisco fires cleared the
way for more carefully planned cities and the tidal wave
at Galveston and the Dayton flood brought new forms
of municipal government, so the yellow fever induced
doctors and laymen to undertake new researches and investigations. Observation of climatic conditions in vari-

[1] Noah Webster, *Brief History of Epidemics and Pestilential Diseases,
with the Principal Phenomena of the Physical World, which Precede and
Accompany Them, and Observations Adduced from the Facts Stated*
(Hartford, 1799); *Medical Repository*, V, 32 ff.; J. L. E. W. Shecut,
Medical and Philosophical Essays (Charleston, 1819), chap. iii.

[2] *Medical Repository*, XIII, 154-157; *Am. Medical and Philos. Register*, I (1810-1811), 323.

[3] Vol. X (1806-1807), 198-199.

[4] See H. U. Faulkner, *The Quest for Social Justice, 1898-1914* (*A
History of American Life*, XI), 230-232.

ous sections of the country became more scientific. Vital statistics, not yet carefully recorded under government auspices, assumed a new social significance. The campaign for health through cleanliness received a prodigious impetus; [1] there were demands that streets be widened, paved and cleaned at municipal expense, that slaughter pens and boarding houses be placed under rigid inspection, that wells be dug deeper and more adequate water supplies be provided.[2] Philadelphia began to harness the Schuylkill into an effective public water system, the first in the country, while New York incorporated the Manhattan Company to serve its own metropolis.[3] Skeptics pointed out that an increase in public and private cleanliness was followed by even more violent epidemics; nevertheless, sanitation — the world was not yet in use — made steady headway, largely at the insistence of the doctors.

But it is less clear that the impact of pestilence advanced the theory and practice of medicine. On the contrary, preoccupation with the cause and cure of epidemic fevers probably contributed to the lag in pathological research. For thirty years after 1790 American medicine lingered under the spell of dogmatic theorists who looked to Edinburgh for continuous guidance. Controversy rose and fell between the Cullenians, who held that Nature provided much of its own healing by the use of spasms exciting a debilitated heart, and the Brunonians, who believed that cures depended on the physician's ability to balance natural action by means of agents which would irritate or tranquilize.

[1] The anonymous author of *The Town and Country Friend and Physician* (Phila., 1803) believed that more people ought to bathe: "I mean here to inculcate the indispensable necessity of *domestic baths*, so well known among the ancients."

[2] *Am. Medical and Philos. Register*, II, 14 ff.; *Medical Repository*, VI (N. Y., 1803), 37 ff.

[3] *Medical Repository*, III (N. Y., 1800), 65.

An original variant of Scotch and English theories was Benjamin Rush's monistic interpretation, which stressed "excessive action" in the arterial walls as the cause of all illness and proposed depleting procedures, notably bleeding and purging, as the effective remedy. Hundreds of admiring students introduced his system into every part of the nation, oftentimes in extreme form. In many communities bleeding and dosing with calomel became the weapons against every kind of fever.[1] Rush's critics, though numerous and bitter, generally met his "vascular system" with an equally conjectural nosology. In the 1820's, for example, David Hosack announced his theory of "acrimony" in the blood, which seemed to be a revival of the humoralism expounded at Leyden a century earlier by Hermann Boerhaave.[2] Neither Hosack nor his supporters had the evidence, which later generations amassed, to warrant some of their speculations concerning therapeutics.

While the humoralists failed to convince, Rush's disciples fell into disrepute. During the twenties American physicians were losing the complacent, indeed boastful, attitude which had marked the profession when the century began. A small minority lamented the wasted opportunities for clinical observation and post-mortem investigation. Medical journals, once filled with reprints of Scotch and English articles, now carried occasional items discussing new developments in French medicine—the reorganization of hospitals, larger funds for research and rigorous clinical examinations prior to diagnosis. Indeed, the needle of professional interest seemed to be swinging away from Edinburgh toward Paris. By 1826 a small group of American students were studying in French hospitals. They constituted

[1] Nathan Goodman, *Benjamin Rush, Physician and Citizen* (Phila., 1934), esp. chaps. vii and viii.

[2] *Phila. Journ. of Medical and Physical Sciences*, II, 297; IV, 344.

the vanguard of a larger migration. Returning to Philadelphia, Boston and New York, they endeavored to follow French procedures and to emulate the work of such pathologists as Laënnec and Louis.[1]

But many doctors scorned the careful study of cases as mere empiricism, while others tended to regard hospitals as charitable institutions subtly subversive of the principles of private professional gain. In any event, physical examinations could not be very thorough when clinical thermometers were unknown and stethoscopes just coming into use. Nor could study of the body proceed to much discovery until the introduction of the achromatic microscope in the 1830's. Nevertheless, Americans had made some contributions, even if the implications were not fully understood at the time.[2] Nathan Smith of New Haven was in the forefront of those who emphasized the need for exact descriptions, and his accounts in 1824 of typhoid, then called typhus, surpassed most clinical observations of his day.[3]

The empiricism of the French school gave added impetus to the process of professional specialization. Americans were not yet aware of the work in histology and embryology which was already in its incipient phases in Europe, notably in France and the German states.[4] Medicine, however, was steadily detaching itself from the great body of natural science of which it had long been a part. Furthermore, in communities where social support permitted, the family doctor no longer considered himself chemist, pharmacist, dentist and veterinarian as well as surgeon and physician. But

[1] For a discussion of the French influence, see R. H. Shryock, "The Advent of Modern Medicine in Philadelphia, 1800-1850," *Yale Journ. of Biology and Medicine*, XIII, 715-738.

[2] John C. Otto of Philadelphia was probably the first to give a complete account of hæmophilia. *Medical Repository*, VI, 3.

[3] E. H. Clarke and others, *A Century of American Medicine* (Phila., 1876), 23.

[4] Bardeen, "Anatomy in America," 148.

the lines of differentiation were seldom sharply drawn, the pharmacist still prescribing for numerous ailments just as the doctor derived much of his income from purveying drugs. Nevertheless, practitioners secured increasing recognition for their specialties from a rapidly growing society. Philadelphia was the pioneer in establishing in 1821 a college for the professional training of pharmacists,[1] while nineteen years later Horace H. Hayden of Baltimore organized the first college of dentistry in the world.[2]

The trends in medical theory and practice were recorded, sometimes tardily and inadequately, in the columns of the professional journals. First among them was the American *Medical Repository*, founded in 1797 and continuing for twenty-seven years with Samuel L. Mitchill as its versatile editor. At the close of its first decade it could say it was older than the most distinguished medical periodicals in Great Britain. Its early rivals were David Ramsay's *Charleston Medical Register* (1803) and the Philadelphia *Medical Museum* (1804), established by Dr. John Redman Coxe. Others rose and fell in New York, Philadelphia, Boston, Baltimore, Charleston and Cincinnati. In 1828 Nathaniel Chapman's *Philadelphia Journal of Medical and Physical Sciences*, then eight years old, became the *American Journal of the Medical Sciences*, which still flourishes.[3]

[1] In the 1760's Dr. John Morgan had urged the separation of pharmacy from medicine, but it was almost sixty years later that the University of Pennsylvania announced it would award the degree of Master of Pharmacy. Thereupon the pharmacists of the city organized their own college in 1821. H. M. Lippincott, *Early Philadelphia* (Phila., 1917), 192-194.

[2] The dentist was not entirely a throw-off from the physician, but rather an example of the union between the doctor and the artisan-manipulator. Hayden was a naturalist who became interested in dentistry late in his career. C. A. Harris, *A Dictionary of Dental Science* (Phila., 1849), 359-360.

[3] Shafer, *Medical Profession*, 181-183. New medical journals were established as follows: 1800-1810, six; 1810-1820, ten; 1820-1839, twenty-eight.

Much of the sound discussion in these periodicals was marred by exaggerated accounts of medical curiosities and by chauvinistic disputes with foreign journals. Physicians, like other Americans, were occasionally irritated by reminders of their debt to Europeans and too often replied in bombastic vein.[1]

No medical library in the United States compared with the great collections of the Old World, though the Pennsylvania Hospital had made an impressive start. Its catalogue listed not only foreign works, but also a steadily increasing number of books by American writers. Thirty-one were published in the first decade of the nineteenth century, not including pamphlets and graduates' dissertations; seventy-two in the second; and eighty-six in the third.[2] This literature reveals how much medical theory still depended upon trial-and-error methods and upon generalization from isolated incidents. If the leaders were concerned with local pathology, the army of general practitioners had not yet abandoned bleeding and purging in varying proportions for everything from rheumatism to "the fevers." The weight of professional opinion still favored copious doses of medicine, and prescriptions were occasionally as long and involved as those given by Thomas Sydenham in the seventeenth century. By 1830, however, some American doctors, who found post-mortem examinations unsystematic and therefore inconclusive, were demanding that a more scientific study of morbid anatomy be undertaken.

There was also much complaint by 1830 that the profession was overcrowded. A Cincinnati journal thought there were twice as many doctors as were needed

[1] Phila. Journ. of Medical and Physical Sciences, I, cover; Am. Journ. of Medical Sciences, V, 8; Boston Medical and Surgical Journ., III, 115-116.

[2] Clarke and others, American Medicine, 294; Shafer, Medical Profession, 177; Shryock, "Advent of Modern Medicine," 724.

and suggested that some return to farming.[1] It is impossible to determine whether the average income of physicians was lower than today, but it was estimated in 1833 that rural practitioners seldom received more than five hundred dollars yearly in money and in kind. Account books of city physicians tell a different story. The most successful doctors, who professed competence in minor surgery, probably earned more than eight thousand dollars a year in New York and Boston, where fees were largest.[2]

If professional prestige was not so high in 1830 as it had been in 1790, public esteem for the family physician had not declined. From Maine to Louisiana there were general practitioners who touched so intimately the lives of their fellows that they became the confessors of the families to which they ministered. Confidence in their advice was unlimited and that advice was often more valuable in healing the spirit than the body. Unable to summon skilled specialists to their aid, they took all medicine for their province and met each new problem as best they could. With meager instruments—knife, lancet, forceps and probe—they faced the multiform hazards of surgery and did not always lose. Their heroism reached out to the fringe of frontier settlements, where they rode through miles of almost pathless forest to stake energy and skill against death in a lonely cabin. Out of their ranks rose a William Beaumont, whose years of patient observation brought an epochal analysis of the digestive process; a Samuel Guthrie of Jefferson County, New York, discoverer of chloroform; and an Ephraim McDowell, practising in Kentucky and performing the first ovariotomy a decade before Europeans attempted it. It was men like these who finally made medicine a science.

[1] Western Journ. of the Medical and Physical Sciences, II (1829), 495.
[2] Shafer, Medical Profession, 167-169.

CHAPTER XII

THE SCIENTISTS,
AMATEUR AND PROFESSIONAL

WRITING to Dr. Benjamin Waterhouse in 1818, Thomas Jefferson enthusiastically remarked, "When I contemplate the immense advances in science and discoveries in the arts which have been made within the period of my life, I look forward with confidence to equal advances by the present generation . . . ." [1] More than fifty years later Simon Newcomb, looking back upon the same period which Jefferson had in contemplation, concluded it had been negligible in the rise of science in America. In fact, most histories of scientific progress find it unnecessary to mention the United States from the 1780's to the 1830's. Apart from some discoveries in medicine, that half-century was undistinguished in its contributions. Not only was there no considerable corps of productive scientists, but no genius appeared comparable to Benjamin Franklin or even David Rittenhouse in the preceding era. One contemporary found the explanation in the fact that his countrymen's energies had for some time been "swallowed up" in "the gulph of politics." [2]

Yet Americans were keenly interested in natural science. Most of their knowledge, to be sure, came from Europe. In geology they debated the rival theories of James Hutton of Edinburgh and Gustav Werner of Freiburg; in biology the rival classifications of Linnæus,

[1] Thomas Jefferson, *Writings* (P. L. Ford, ed., N. Y., 1892-1899), X, 103-104.
[2] Anon., "The American Character," *Literary Mag. and Am. Register,* II (1804), 255.

Buffon and Cuvier. But it was socially significant that these ideas found a general hospitality.[1] They were not imported for a small and artificial market, as they were into Russia by the exotic academy which Catherine the Great sponsored.

At the close of the eighteenth century the naturalist in the United States was but imperfectly detached from the physician. Most courses in natural science were taught in the medical schools and credited toward a medical degree; and the *Medical Repository* served as the best general scientific magazine for twenty years after its foundation in 1797.[2] Timothy Dwight, James Kent and DeWitt Clinton were among its readers eager to secure whatever scientific crumbs might fall from the doctors' table — and there were many. In 1810 a physician, Archibald Bruce, established the *American Mineralogical Journal,* the first in that field. When Dr. Richard Harlan's work *Fauna Americana* appeared in 1825, nearly half the subscribers were physicians.[3]

The scientific work of the doctors, so closely related to their professional interest, was supplemented by the widespread activities of amateurs, men who faithfully represented a people confident that any problem could be solved with a little information and common sense. For example, the Congregational clergyman, Jeremy Belknap, cultivated natural history as an avocation. A discriminating reader of Buffon's *Natural History,* he prepared for the third volume of his *History of New Hampshire* (1792) an extensive list of the plants and

---

[1] For a summary of the Huttonian and Wernerian systems, consult T. C. Gray, "Systems of Geology," *N. Am. Rev.,* VIII (1819), 396-414.

[2] Max Meisel, comp., *A Bibliography of American Natural History* (N. Y., 1924-1929), II, 67-76, contains a list of the papers on natural history in the *Medical Repository.*

[3] Harlan's volume was a translation and careful revision of A. G. Desmarest's *Mammalogie.* Henry Simpson, *The Lives of Eminent Philadelphians Now Deceased* (Phila., 1859), 247-266.

animals of that region, admirably arranged and classified. It was the more authoritative because he had taken
counsel with William Dandridge Peck, who later won
national recognition as professor of natural history at
Harvard, and the Reverend Manasseh Cutler, the first
native writer on botany in New England.[1] Thus was
a high standard set for other naturalists among the
clergy: L. D. von Schweinitz, the Moravian, seeking
fungi with scarcely less avidity than human souls; Henry
Muhlenberg, the Lutheran, writing treatises which
placed him in the front rank of American botanists; and
F. E. Melsheimer, so carefully studying insects that his
work constituted a beginning in American entomology.[2]

But the most prominent exemplar of amateur interest
was Thomas Jefferson, whose *Notes on the State of
Virginia* (1785) contains the earliest scientific survey
of a region in America. He eagerly encouraged fossil
hunting, which was already providing clues that would
change man's conception of the antiquity of the earth.
When he went to Philadelphia as Vice-President, he
took with him the bones of a prehistoric monster to
articulate. While the country was torn by controversy
over the embargo, he withdrew often to a great un-
furnished room of the executive mansion to sort out
three hundred bones that he had received from Big Bone
Lick, Kentucky.[3] Of equal importance were his botanical contributions, revealing a familiarity with European
writings which gave distinction to his descriptions of
American specimens.[4]

[1] Jeremy Belknap, *The History of New Hampshire* (Boston, 1792),
III, 96 *n.*

[2] W. M. and Mabel S. C. Smallwood, *Natural History and the American Mind* (*Columbia Studies in American Culture*, no. 8), 108, 265,
300.

[3] G. B. Goode, "The Beginnings of Natural History in America," U. S.
Natl. Museum, *Report* (Wash., 1901), pt. ii. 355 ff.

[4] R. H. True, "Thomas Jefferson in Relation to Botany," *Scientific
Mo.*, III, 345 ff.

Other country gentlemen, less prominent in politics, shared Jefferson's enthusiasm for studying plant life. Stephen Elliott, the South Carolina planter, began serial publication of his *Sketch of the Botany of South Carolina and Georgia* in 1817. At Philadelphia during the 1790's Humphrey Marshall continued to maintain the garden of exotic and native plants which he had established several decades earlier.[1] In Europe botanical gardens frequently were created as laboratories for university instruction in natural history; in America this was the exception. Though the University of Pennsylvania received a legislative grant in 1807 for such a garden, that was the fourth in the vicinity of Philadelphia. Charleston already had a garden in addition to the hundred and ten acres acquired by André Michaux for his extensive experiments.[2] In New York there was a tenuous connection between Dr. David Hosack's botanical garden and instruction in medicine, but students of materia medica probably derived less benefit than the citizens who came to regard the area as a public park.[3]

The museum was the companion piece of the botanical garden. To the naturalist its "curiosities," like the clues sought by the detective, offered intriguing possibilities for the solution of long-standing mysteries. Charleston claimed priority in developing the museum idea because its Library Society as early as 1773 had invited gentlemen to send in specimens — animal, vegetable and mineral — from every part of the state. This collection, permanently housed in 1785, was steadily enlarged through the efforts of such amateur naturalists as Charles Cotesworth Pinckney, Henry Middleton and

[1] J. W. Harshberger, *The Botanists of Philadelphia and Their Work* (Phila., 1899), 82-83.
[2] Smallwoods, *Natural History*, 150-155.
[3] David Hosack, *A Statement of Facts Relative to the Establishment and Progress of the Elgin Botanic Garden* (N. Y., 1811).

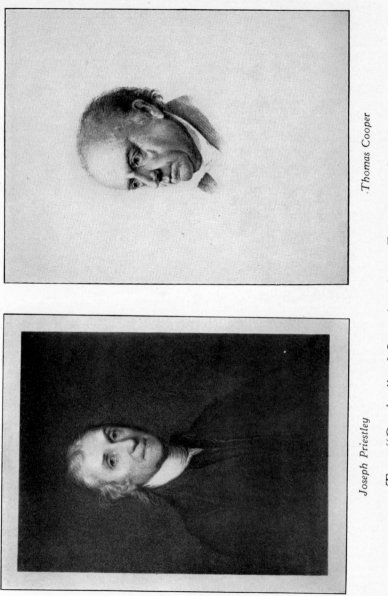

Joseph Priestley

Thomas Cooper

Two "Carriers" of Learning from Europe to America

Charles Willson Peale, in his Museum

Stephen Elliott.[1] Quite independently, and somewhat accidentally, Philadelphians became interested in a natural-history museum. Happily combining an artistic sense with superb showmanship, Charles Willson Peale stirred such popular interest in his collection of specimens that many others copied his methods. Though not a trained scientist, he developed the educational aspect of museum work until in 1821 his staff included such professional naturalists as Thomas Say in zoology, Dr. Richard Harlan in comparative anatomy and Dr. Gerard Troost in mineralogy.[2] Contact with European museums enabled Peale to introduce a semblance of natural habitat into his exhibits, an innovation which added greatly to their interest.[3] In New York, Boston, Albany and other cities the museum was still a private enterprise rather than a public institution, and it was apt to suggest an enlarged curio cabinet designed not so much to instruct as to amuse.

Those who took natural science as a side line did not content themselves with a mere fragment of human knowledge. They assumed that not enough was known about anything to dismay anyone who had a "talent for inquiry and observation." Dr. Samuel Latham Mitchill, for example, was "equally at home in studying the geology of Niagara or the anatomy of an egg, in offering suggestions as to the angle of a windmill or the shape of a gridiron, in deciphering a Babylonian brick or investi-

[1] Laura M. Bragg, "The Birth of the Museum Idea in America," *Charleston Museum Quar.*, I, 3 ff.

[2] Peale was remarkably successful in securing supporters. Through Jefferson's interest and the coöperation of the American Philosophical Society he excavated two mammoth skeletons, one of which is still in the Museum of Natural History in New York City. Thomas Jefferson, "Letters to C. W. Peale, 1796-1815" (H. W. Sellers, ed.), *Pa. Mag. of History and Biog.*, XXVIII, 138 ff.

[3] O. C. Farrington, "Rise of Natural History Museums," *Science*, n.s., XLII, 197-208; H. S. Colton, "Peale's Museum," *Popular Sci. Mo.*, LXXV, 221-238. For the geographic spread of museums, see *Medical Repository*, VI (N. Y., 1803), 237; XIV (1810-1811), 88-89.

gating bivalves and discoursing on conchology." [1] He also wrote on subconscious thinking, icebergs and mineralogy and, as we have seen, developed a theory of pestilential effluvia as the cause of fever epidemics.[2] Besides, he was a persuasive orator and a successful politician. Though the modern scientist may smile at him, his general scientific interest typified the learned men in his generation.[3]

The persistent desire for cultural independence had a fortunate influence upon American science. While we were colonials, wrote Dr. John Shecut of Charleston, deference to Europe seemed appropriate. Since our emancipation, however, there was no excuse for the shameful neglect of the arts, sciences and literature in America.[4] A further stimulus came from the national sentiment so widely diffused following the War of 1812. American investigators proudly announced their own discoveries "instead of blindly using the eyes of foreign naturalists, or bowing implicitly to the decisions of a foreign bar of criticism." [5] The North American Review rejoiced that botanical science was flourishing under "the legitimate auspices of Americans" and that a convincing answer had been given to the prevalent Euro-

[1] Martha J. Lamb, "An Illustrated Chapter on Beginnings," Magazine of American History, XVI, 217-218.

[2] Medical Repository, III (N. Y., 1800), 420-422; IV (N. Y., 1801), 196; V (N. Y., 1802), 205-218.

[3] C. R. Hall, A Scientist in the Early Republic; Samuel Latham Mitchell (N. Y., 1934), 3-5.

[4] J. L. E. W. Shecut, Medical and Philosophical Essays (Charleston, 1819), 54-55.

[5] James DeKay, Anniversary Address Delivered before the New York Lyceum (N. Y., 1826), 7. There was great satisfaction that Thomas Nuttall, though English-born, had developed his scientific interests in the United States. During the decade after 1817 he published two works that commanded attention in Europe—The Genera of North American Plants (Phila., 1818) and An Introduction to Systematic and Physiological Botany (Cambridge, 1827). Similarly Alexander Wilson, a Scot, had come to America to study bird life. His American Ornithology, a pioneer work on the subject, appeared between 1808 and 1814 and was published in Philadelphia.

pean belief in the inferiority of the soil and produce of North America.[1] From the observed natural phenomena of the New World would come other evidence modifying scientific theories of the Old.

Acceptable observation in this generation, however, depended upon proper assumptions on the observer's part. Jeffersonian science, for example, was widely suspected as Deistic. Doubtless Thomas Say, C. A. Lesueur, Gerard Troost, William Maclure and other students who joined in Robert Owen's New Harmony experiment also worried the orthodox.[2] Yet the majority of scientific men were convincingly sound on the Scriptures.[3] George Turner, working over his fossil specimens in 1797, summed up the purpose of Nature: "The Author of existence is wise and just in all His works. He never confers an appetite without the power of gratifying it." [4] Benjamin Silliman and Samuel L. Mitchill agreed in accepting a homocentric universe, and Amos Eaton pointed out with great satisfaction the coincidences between geology and the Bible.[5]

[1] "Botany of the United States," *N. Am. Rev.*, XIII (1821), 100-134. Muhlenberg thought that new species discovered in the United States should be named only by Americans. William Darlington, comp., *Reliquiae Baldwinianae* (Phila., 1843), 20-21.

[2] C. A. Browne, "Some Relations of the New Harmony Movement to the History of Science in America," *Scientific Mo.*, XLII, 483 ff.

[3] Amos Eaton's *An Index to the Geology of the Northern States* (Leicester, 1818) and Jeremiah Van Rensselaer's *Lectures on Geology* (N. Y., 1825) arranged their geologic chronology with reference to the Noachian deluge. When Benjamin Silliman published the first American edition of Robert Bakewell's *Introduction to Geology* (New Haven, 1829), he included a chapter on "The Deluge and Diluvial Action," to which Thomas Cooper, then at South Carolina College, replied in a pamphlet, *On the Connection between Geology and the Pentateuch*, chiding Silliman for accepting the Biblical account of the flood. Dumas Malone, *The Public Life of Thomas Cooper* (*Yale Hist. Publs. Miscellany*, XVI), 350-353.

[4] George Turner, "Memoir on the Extraneous Fossils," Am. Philos. Soc., *Trans.*, IV (1797), 578.

[5] S. L. Mitchill, "Discourse," N. Y. Hist. Soc., *Colls.*, II (1814), 155; H. H. Ballard, "Amos Eaton," Berkshire Hist. and Scientific Soc., *Colls.*, II, 212.

The science cultivated by such naturalists was descriptive and systematic. "One of the most remarkable improvements of the recent century," said the *Literary Magazine* in 1804, "is the practice of reducing the whole body of human knowledge into a comprehensive and systematic order." [1] Much of this, according to Dr. Waterhouse, had been merely the work of identification. Classification, at least in the case of such naturalists as C. S. Rafinesque, had sometimes depended more on ingenuity than on scholarship. [2] Laboratory study of natural structure could accomplish little without delicate and efficient instruments, and that indispensable aid, the achromatic microscope, was not yet invented. But the naturalist was not always disturbed by this lack, for man-made experiments were suspect in many quarters. "Nature is the best experimenter," complacently remarked the *Medical Repository* in 1800. "To *observe* and *interpret nature* is the way to be truly wise and scientific." [3]

Such observation required patience and the courage to overcome forbidding obstacles. "No one in Europe," wrote Stephen Elliott to a friend in London, "can, probably, appreciate correctly the difficulty of the task in which I have engaged. The want of books, the want of opportunities for examining living collections or good herbaria, the want of coadjutors, have all served to render my task arduous, and to multiply its imperfections." [4] America presented a magnificent challenge to the field worker, but he who accepted it joined a small company of the heroic. Michaux, penetrating the deep-shaded streams of Florida in cypress dugout and trudg-

---

[1] *Literary Mag. and Am. Register*, I (1803-1804), 420.
[2] Benjamin Waterhouse, *The Botanist* (Boston, 1811), ix-xiv; A. H. Barkley, "Constantine Samuel Rafinesque," *Annals of Medical History*, X, 66 ff.
[3] *Medical Repository*, III, 300.
[4] *Am. Journ. of Science and Arts*, IX (1825), 276.

ing nine hundred miles through the hostile Indian country of western Carolina and Georgia in search of plants and flowers; Maclure in heavy, thick-soled shoes crossing the Alleghanies fifty times, always with bag and hammer that he might secure new specimens of rock formation: Audubon drifting down the Mississippi and pushing into the solitary reaches of Louisiana bayous to preserve forever the images of yawning pelicans and snowy egrets — these men and their like still quicken the pulse and fill the imagination.[1] But there was compensation for their battles with the wilderness, not so much in the plaudits of the scientific world as in the opportunities of a vast continent where Nature offered unexpected treasures to be described and classified.

The naturalist's attainment of a professional status apart from the medical man was marked in 1818 by the launching of Benjamin Silliman's scientific periodical. That doubt existed whether the new profession could support a special journal is evident from the title, *American Journal of Science and Arts,* and from the occasional articles on painting, sculpture and literature. This conjunction of interests, which had been implicit in the activities of the American Philosophical Society in Philadelphia, the American Academy of Arts and Sciences in Boston and the Connecticut Academy of Arts and Sciences in New Haven, was rapidly disappearing as the naturalists defined with greater precision the area of their particular concern.[2] In 1812 a physician, an apothecary, a dentist and a mineralogist became the founders of the Academy of Natural Sciences in Phila-

[1] Many courageous explorers, though not interested primarily in scientific investigation, brought back invaluable data for the naturalist. Such contributions by Lewis, Clark, Dunbar, Pike, Long and Schoolcraft are admirably summarized in S. L. Mitchill, *Discourses . . . at Schenectady* (Albany, 1821), and DeKay, *Anniversary Address.*

[2] *Medical Repository,* XI (1807-1808), 273; DeWitt Clinton, *Introductory Discourse* (N. Y., 1815), 21-22; S. E. Baldwin, "Address," Conn. Acad. of Arts and Sci., *Trans.,* XI, xvii-xxii.

delphia. Five years later a similar group in New York City established the Lyceum of Natural History, which subsequently became the New York Academy of Sciences.[1]

These societies and their counterparts in other cities were primarily organizations of amateurs interested in promoting research and preserving data. Through the efforts of resident and corresponding members they financed expeditions to collect specimens, established libraries and museums, sponsored courses of popular lectures and published voluminous proceedings. The Philadelphia society, for example, maintained a *Journal* for several years after 1818 while the New York Lyceum inaugurated its *Annals* in 1824. Reports and essays in these pages reveal the trend toward a more professional attitude, especially as compared with the indiscriminate data in the early issues of the *Medical Repository*. Though this trend was not confined to any section of the country, it was less apparent in New England than in the seaboard communities of the Middle and Southern states.

Adequate training in science developed slowly. At the close of the eighteenth century, as we have seen, the college gave little time to any scientific interest. "How deeply it is to be regretted," lamented the *Medical Repository* in 1808, "that the knowledge of those things of which the Creator has formed the world we inhabit, should be . . . considered as of low value, in what is called a liberal education!"[2] College presidents of vision, however, like Bishop James Madison of William and Mary and Timothy Dwight of Yale, made a place for the subject in their curricula. In 1789 the College

---

[1] H. M. Lippincott, *Early Philadelphia* (Phila., 1917), 189-191; DeKay, *Anniversary Address*, 72-73; H. L. Fairchild, *A History of the New York Academy of Sciences* (N. Y., 1887), 25-27, 99 ff.
[2] *Medical Repository*, XII (1808-1809), 155.

of Philadelphia, soon to be merged in the University of Pennsylvania, named Benjamin Smith Barton to the first professorship of natural history in the Western Hemisphere.[1] A year earlier, however, Benjamin Waterhouse had been appointed lecturer in that subject at Harvard, and his work was less concerned with the medical curriculum than that of Barton. Soon there were others: the versatile Samuel L. Mitchill at Columbia; Benjamin Silliman emphasizing chemistry in his lectures at New Haven; Thomas Cooper developing his geological interests at Dickinson College; Parker Cleaveland discussing minerals with Bowdoin students. No naturalist had so many educational contacts, especially in the secondary schools, as Amos Eaton who in public lecture and school textbook stressed the necessity of instruction in natural history and allied subjects.[2] Though such courses had become commonplace in the college catalogues by 1830, scientific work seldom achieved full recognition, and it was slightly valued save where it touched, as in the case of botany and chemistry, the training of the physician.[3]

Medicine, as we have seen, threw the utility of the chemist into bold relief. His subject matter was but slowly differentiated in the curricula of the early medical schools. Dr. Benjamin Rush had begun giving lectures on chemistry at the Philadelphia Medical College as early as 1769; and at Harvard Aaron Dexter combined it with materia medica in his professorship from 1783 to 1816. Surveying the country at the opening of the

[1] W. S. Middleton, "Benjamin Smith Barton," *Annals of Medical History*, n.s., VIII, 477 ff. Daniel Treadwell was named professor of mathematics and natural history at King's College in 1757, but there is no evidence that he taught natural history. Brander Matthews and others, eds., *A History of Columbia University, 1754-1904* (N. Y., 1904), 21-22.

[2] Eaton believed in coeducation, and his classes included, among others, such future leaders in the education of women as Emma Willard and Mary Lyon. Ethel M. McAllister, *Amos Eaton, Scientist and Educator, 1776-1842* (Phila., 1941), 184-211, 354-355.

[3] Smallwoods, *Natural History*, 288-313.

nineteenth century, Dr. David Ramsay rejoiced that in
New York, New Jersey and Pennsylvania there were
three professors of chemistry — Samuel L. Mitchill,
John Maclean and James Woodhouse — equal to the
greatest European scientists.[1] The eccentric Woodhouse,
sweating amidst his laboratory forges, arranged experiments that fascinated his students.[2] He learned much
from the technique of his friend Joseph Priestley, who
in 1794 had established a scientist's laboratory as well as
a philosopher's study in the little frontier settlement of
Northumberland at the junction of the branches of the
Susquehanna. From this wilderness retreat the famous
English refugee vehemently defended that ancient error,
the doctrine of phlogiston, as the source of chemical
phenomena, against the newer theories advanced by
Lavoisier and his followers.[3] The controversy stirred
American scientists, but few of them did more in their
theoretical treatises than restate the ideas of the rising
French school.[4]

With the attempt to define chemistry as a separate
subject of instruction went increasing emphasis upon its
practical phases. In Philadelphia the Chemical Society
publicized Priestley's observations on the diffusion of
gases and the solution of glass by caustic alkalis.[5] His
discovery of carbon monoxide in 1799 by passing steam
over heated charcoal led to numerous communications
in the *Medical Repository* and the *Transactions* of the

[1] David Ramsay, *Review of the Improvements, Progress and State of
Medicine* (Charleston, 1800).

[2] James Woodhouse, *The Young Chemist's Pocket Companion* (Phila.,
1797) ; E. F. Smith, *James Woodhouse* (Phila., 1918), 68-70.

[3] Joseph Priestley, *The Doctrine of Phlogiston Established and That of
the Composition of Water Refuted* (Northumberland, Pa., 1800).

[4] *Medical Repository*, I (N. Y., 1798), 515-522; II (N. Y., 1800),
263-271; III, 423.

[5] Felix Pascalis, *Annual Oration . . . before the Chemical Society of
Philadelphia* (Phila., 1802), *passim;* E. F. Smith, *Priestley in America,
1794-1804* (Phila., 1920), 134, 142.

American Philosophical Society. There was also much speculation concerning potential uses of Robert Hare's device — the oxyhydrogen blowpipe — and of James Cutbush's successful experiments in pyrotechnics.[1] Lecturers like Dr. John Griscom in New York and Dr. Patrick Rogan in Philadelphia translated the findings of the scientist into terms which the public could understand. By 1813 courses in chemistry, for ladies as well as gentlemen, were popular in the larger cities, and the preceptor frequently enlivened his discourse by demonstrations of the exhilarating effects of nitrous oxide.[2] The *American Journal of Science and Arts,* surveying scientific achievements in 1827, rejoiced at the increased emphasis on "the chemical branch of physics" and the lengthening list of contributions made by that branch to the arts and manufactures of the country.

In the last year of his life Thomas Jefferson, sketching the course that the new professor of natural history was to give at the University of Virginia, listed twenty-four lectures each on botany, zoology, mineralogy, geology, chemistry and miscellaneous.[3] The very nomenclature indicated that the naturalist, who had broken off from the physician, was himself beginning to break up. When the state surveys were organized, starting with North Carolina in 1824, the personnel included, not several naturalists, but a geologist, a botanist, a zoologist and perhaps other specialists.[4]

The professionalizing of amateur scientific activities would have proceeded at a slower pace had Americans

[1] *Medical Repository,* VIII (1804-1805), 169; E. F. Smith, *James Cutbush* (Phila., 1919), 82-83.

[2] J. H. Griscom, *Memoir of John Griscom, LL.D.* (N. Y., 1859), 53-54; Smith, *James Cutbush,* 35, 40-42.

[3] P. A. Bruce, *History of the University of Virginia, 1819-1919* (N. Y., 1920), I, 323-328.

[4] G. P. Merrill, *The First One Hundred Years of American Geology* (New Haven, 1924), 127, 180.

not been convinced of their utility.[1] To encourage the federal government's patronage of science Dr. Edward Cutbush and Thomas Law organized the Columbian Institute in 1816. Two years later Congress passed an act of incorporation and subsequently granted land in Washington to be used as a botanical garden. As one of the Institute's active members John Quincy Adams heartily indorsed these attempts to put scientific knowledge to work in the nation's service.[2] The botanical garden would reveal the possibility of growing plants once regarded as exotic, while the mineral cabinet would direct attention to the country's unexploited resources. Though the Columbian Institute never actually effected its desired liaison between government and private enterprise, it stood for twenty years as a symbol of the terms on which society was willing to support the man of science.

The intense interest in the practical application of scientific principles was underscored by the need of a large and rapidly growing country for better transportation and communication, for labor-saving devices and improved methods of production. But indirectly abstract science was also benefited. Thus mathematics recruited its ablest students partly from the ranks of practical surveyors or engineers, such as Jared Mansfield, United States surveyor, 1803-1812, and Andrew Ellicott, who became professor of mathematics at West Point.[3] On the other hand the navigators, working constantly with figures and the stars, contributed little to mathematical theory, though Nathaniel Bowditch of

[1] For manifestations of the practical application of natural science, see *Am. Medical and Philos. Register*, I (1810-1811), 58; II (1811-1812), 33-40; *Medical Repository*, X (1806-1807), 340; XII, 194-195.

[2] J. W. Oliver, "America's First Attempt to Unite the Forces of Science and Government," *Scientific Mo.*, LIII, 253-257.

[3] Catherine V. Mathews, *Life of Andrew Ellicott* (N. Y., 1908), *passim*.

Salem was an impressive exception.[1] Robert Adrain, an Irish school-teacher who found refuge at Pennsylvania, Rutgers and Columbia after the revolt of 1798, published unique contributions to the law of probability of error.[2] Compared with the French mathematicians, however, "the contemporary American professors were mere Lilliputians."[3] The awakening came with the advent of Continentals like Ferdinand Hassler, who introduced analytic trigonometry at West Point after 1807, and Claude Crozet who brought to the same institution descriptive geometry, which had been used in France for a quarter-century.[4]

Closely related to mathematics was astronomy. Unfortunately, apparatus for observation had not been improved beyond the meager telescopes available to David Rittenhouse in the eighteenth century. Astronomical theories were rather pale imitations of those held in Europe. The Newtonian system was not quite universally accepted; meteorites were believed to be aggregations of mineral particles in the atmosphere; speculation concerning the composition of the sun caused some to maintain it was made of "electron," the substance which gave off electric energy.[5]

Whatever their theories, Americans devoted earnest thought to the age-old riddle of the skies, a curiosity

[1] Alexander Young, *Discourse on the Life and Character of Nathaniel Bowditch* (Boston, 1838), *passim;* Samuel Newcomb, *Sidelights on Astronomy* (N. Y., 1906), 282. Bowditch's *The New American Practical Navigator* was published in 1801.

[2] *Mathematical Correspondent* (N. Y., 1804) ; *The Analyst* (N. Y., 1814).

[3] Florian Cajori, *The Teaching and History of Mathematics in the United States* (Bur. of Educ., *Circular of Information*, no. 3), 98.

[4] Florian Cajori, *The Chequered Career of Ferdinand Rudolph Hassler* (Boston, 1929), 50-51; Claude Crozet, *Treatise on Descriptive Geometry* (N. Y., 1821).

[5] American Philosophical Society, *Transactions*, VI, pt. ii; *Medical Repository*, XIII (1809-1810), 263; XIV, 69; Joseph Young, *Principles of Astronomy* (N. Y., 1800), *passim.*

strengthened by constant need for astronomical knowledge in its practical application as, for example, in establishing boundary lines and running the meridians. The maps of this period show great variation in the basic line of reckoning. Local pride led Timothy Dwight to determine the longitude of the eastern United States with reference to New Haven. But neither such sectional prejudices nor a reliance on the meridian of Greenwich could satisfy the rising national spirit. At the instance of Congressman William Lambert of Virginia, an amateur naturalist, an act was passed in 1810 to fix the meridian of Washington as the American standard, but Congress withheld funds for a national observatory to make calculation accurate.[1] Though President John Quincy Adams later became interested, the project elicited more ridicule than support.[2] Busily engaged in wringing a living from this earth, most Americans did not see the utility of these "lighthouses of the skies." There was no organized observatory until President Joseph Caldwell set up complete equipment at the University of North Carolina in the early thirties, but during the next dozen years seven or eight observatories were erected. The way was cleared for the Maria Mitchells and Simon Newcombs of the future.[3]

Physics, though the name was not yet used in a definite sense in America, had begun a rapid advance in Europe late in the eighteenth century. One of the contributors was the Massachusetts-born Benjamin Thompson, who had left his native land in 1776 because of Loyalist sympathies and, under the title of Count Rumford bestowed by the Bavarian government, carried forward his experiments in friction as a source of heat,

[1] *Medical Repository*, X, 77-80.
[2] R. A. Proctor, "Astronomy in America," *Popular Sci. Mo.*, X, 76-77.
[3] See C. R. Fish, *The Rise of the Common Man, 1830-1850* (*A History of American Life*, VI), 240.

which later became basic in thermodynamic theory.[1] Europeans were advancing even more rapidly in electromagnetism and here, too, an American made his mark. Joseph Henry began his laboratory tests at Albany Academy just seventy-five years after Franklin had established the identity of lightning and electricity.[2] Henry, working independently, anticipated in some respects results obtained by Michael Faraday, but the Englishman's prior publication gave him credit for demonstrating the induction of electric currents and the relation between magnetism and electricity. By 1831 Henry was describing experiments with electromagnets that pointed toward the dynamo and the telegraph. Unlike Faraday he failed to draw from his findings their full theoretical implications.[3]

The practical application of scientific principles went forward not so much in the academic laboratory as at the blacksmith's forge and the artisan's bench. Jacob Perkins served as a goldsmith's apprentice before he perfected a process for silver-plating shoe buckles, invented a machine to cut and head nails and designed unique steel plates for engraving bank notes. Peter Cooper was a hat-maker's apprentice and a skilled craftsman long before he began turning out his numerous inventions.[4] Many American inventors, to be sure, were college-trained, but John Stevens found no work in mechanics at pre-Revolutionary King's College and Eli Whitney graduated at Yale a dozen years before Benjamin Silliman began the simple experiments which accompanied

[1] G. E. Ellis, *Memoir of Sir Benjamin Thompson, Count Rumford* (Boston, 1871), 168-169.
[2] See J. T. Adams, *Provincial Society, 1690-1763* (*A History of American Life*, III), 307-308.
[3] W. B. Taylor, "Henry and the Telegraph," Smithsonian Inst., *Ann. Rep. for 1878*, 262-360.
[4] H. P. and Margaret W. Vowles, "Jacob Perkins, 1766-1849," *Mechanical Engineering*, LIII, 785-790; Allan Nevins, *Abram S. Hewitt, with Some Account of Peter Cooper* (N. Y., 1935), 51.

his lectures in chemistry and natural history. As late as 1830 the best work in science was being done by the staff at the United States Military Academy at West Point, especially after the reforms effected in 1817 by Superintendent Sylvanus Thayer.[1] Seven years later Stephen Van Rensselaer's generosity and the energy of Amos Eaton made possible the founding at Troy, New York, of Rensselaer Polytechnic Institute, indirectly inspired by the Fellenberg Industrial School of Hofwyl, Switzerland.[2] At the same time Franklin Institute in Philadelphia opened its doors to young men desiring a technical training.

Though the creation of a corps of trained engineers had been one of the objectives in the establishment of West Point in 1802, there was no engineering profession in the early decades of the century. Builders of turnpikes, bridges, canals and engines were usually self-educated or, like Loammi Baldwin, who turned from law to construction work, had profited by travel and study in Europe.[3] Wherever they received their academic instruction, it seldom went beyond mathematics, surveying, and elementary principles of weights and tensions. Their great laboratory was the series of engineering projects undertaken to meet the needs of a rapidly growing country.[4] The Erie Canal became a training school for young men like John B. Jervis who rose from an axman in a surveying corps to one of the most famous railroad builders of the pre-Civil War era.

[1] E. C. Boynton, *History of West Point* (N. Y., 1863), 217-218.

[2] P. C. Ricketts, *History of the Rensselaer Polytechnic Institute, 1824-1934* (N. Y., 1934), 14-29.

[3] G. L. Vose, *Sketch of the Life and Works of Loammi Baldwin, Civil Engineer* (Boston, 1885), 8-15.

[4] Approximately 475 books dealing with various phases of engineering were known to Americans prior to 1830, but in many instances it would have been difficult to secure a copy of a particular book. R. R. Shaw lists 252 titles printed in England and 223 in America. See his study, "Engineering Books Available in America Prior to 1830," N. Y. Public Library, *Bull.*, XXXVII, 38, 157, 209, 301, 539.

His principal assistant was Horatio Allen, a Columbia graduate with honors in mathematics, who learned his engineering on the Chesapeake and Delaware Canal. It was a goodly company of apprentices in canal and road building who brought honor to the name of civil engineer in a later generation.

The most potent force in the rise of professional engineering was, in America as in Europe, the steady advance of industrial invention. A cursory glance at the patents awarded between 1790 and 1830 discloses the wide range of mechanical skill preparing the way for more spectacular developments later. Five years after perfecting the cotton gin in 1793, Eli Whitney demonstrated the principle of interchangeable parts. The first two decades of the nineteenth century brought the multitubular boiler, the screw-cutting machine, the circular saw, the power loom and Thomas Blanchard's profile lathe.[1] As the mechanization of industry progressed, as transportation moved along new routes under new forms of power, more complicated problems of applied science required a competence which gave a professional meaning to the term "engineer." In London the Institution of Civil Engineers was formed in 1818; two years later it elected Jacob Perkins, talented Yankee inventor, to membership. Though such organization lay far in the future for Americans, the third decade of the nineteenth century witnessed the development of advanced technical schools, the prelude to professional status and a symbol of the nation's growing industrialization.

[1] Olmsted, *Eli Whitney*, 47-50; A. H. Waters, *Biographical Sketch of Thomas Blanchard and His Inventions* (Worcester, Mass., 1878), 6-15.

CHAPTER XIII

CULTURAL ASPIRATIONS AND ACHIEVEMENTS

THE desire for cultural independence was strong. Though a lively sense of indebtedness to the Old World still persisted, it was overshadowed by the hope that American art and letters would soon break through the bonds of imitation and make original contributions commanding respect in foreign lands. That hope was briefly stimulated by John Trumbull's paintings, Samuel McIntire's houses and the public buildings inspired by Thomas Jefferson. Such artistic achievement required a standard of taste which the succeeding generation failed to maintain, but at the moment the promise for the future seemed bright.[1]

Adequate patronage of the arts came tardily in a country where there was neither royal court nor established church to assume responsibility. "A people must secure a provision of absolute necessaries," wrote one magazine editor, "before they think of convenience, and must enjoy conveniences before they indulge in the agreeable arts of life." Only when accumulated wealth provided patronage for painting and sculpture could native talent escape the need of quitting the country in order to be suitably trained and rewarded.[2] Some interpreted Gilbert Stuart's return in 1793 from study with the Pennsylvania-born Benjamin West in London

[1] C. R. Fish, *The Rise of the Common Man, 1830-1850* (*A History of American Life*, VI), 228.

[2] *Literary Mag. and Am. Register*, VI (1806), 76-77.

as evidence of an imminent change.[1] American youth might continue to seek instruction in the Old World, but an increasing number would find teachers as well as patrons at home.

The artistic achievement of Americans was not necessarily a measure of their cultural separation from Europe. Whatever the reasons for Gilbert Stuart's return to his native land, he repudiated little that he had learned in England. His portraits, invariably revealing manual brilliance and a distinctive style, nevertheless encouraged European mannerisms among his imitators and exalted Old World standards of taste among his numerous admirers.[2] Neither his great portraits nor his career contributed much to the growth of an indigenous artistic tradition. That growth really depended upon scores of nonprofessionals. Lay painters, concerned with the typical in their environment, carried on in the manner of colonial limners; master craftsmen in carpentry found time to plan and execute ornamental designs in building; hewers of wood, like William Rush, who fashioned figureheads for ships, and workers in stone, like John Frazee, who carved tombstones, became pioneers in arousing interest in the plastic arts.[3] The contribution of these laymen, whose work may be regarded as folk art, was generally ignored, but some of them finally earned the right to professional status and helped direct European influences into American channels.

In architecture two forces were important during the republic's early years. One flowed across the Atlantic,

[1] William Dunlap, The History of the Rise and Progress of the Arts of Design in the United States (Boston, 1918), I, 229; Oskar Hagen, The Birth of the American Tradition in Art (N. Y., 1940), 146-147.

[2] G. C. Mason, The Life and Works of Gilbert Stuart (N. Y., 1879), 89-91.

[3] Wilfred Jordan, "William Rush, the Earliest American-Born Sculptor," Art and Archaeology, XI, 145-146; Dunlap, History of the Arts of Design, III, 34-38.

either with those European architects who sought favor in the United States or with Americans returning from foreign study. The other originated with native carpenters and master builders, whose practical experience led them to study the function of design. The subtle fusing of these forces resulted in the modification of older models along utilitarian lines. Though that adaptation was far from unimaginative copying, there was genuine cultural continuity, well exemplified in the creation of the national capital on the Potomac. France, England and Ireland trained several of the men who laid out its general plan, designed and constructed its first public buildings, and later rebuilt the executive mansion after the raid on the city during the War of 1812.[1]

American architects and builders were inclined to turn from Tudor and Georgian models and to find their masters in the admirers of ancient Greece and Rome. There was an intensely personal quality about Jefferson's classical enthusiasm, but he was far from unique.[2] Ever since the Revolution popular conversation had been filled with allusions to republican Rome, and correspondents in the public prints had delighted in signing their communications with the names of legendary Roman heroes. The Society of the Cincinnati indicated that this interest was not confined to aggressive democrats. Roman influence in architecture was strengthened by the desire, not peculiar to Jefferson, to

[1] Major Pierre Charles L'Enfant's design for the city of Washington was thoroughly French. Stephen Hallet and Benjamin H. Latrobe, who worked on the Capitol, were trained in France and England, respectively. The winner of the competition for the executive mansion was James Hoban of Dublin. The unifying influence came from the continuing interest and counsel of Thomas Jefferson. I. T. Frary, *They Built the Capitol* (Richmond, 1940), 8-107. The most extensive work achieved by a foreign architect outside Washington was J. J. Ramee's balanced group of buildings at Union College in Schenectady.

[2] Fiske Kimball, *Thomas Jefferson, Architect* (Boston, 1916), 81-83.

be free from the domination of English art forms. The
spirit of independence was admirably expressed in the
Capitol at Washington, the great country house at Monticello and the new university at Charlottesville. It was
manifest also in state capitols and other public buildings
from New York to Savannah.[1] Foreign visitors during
the early decades of the nineteenth century were impressed by Philadelphia's banks and mercantile houses
and New York's churches, designed chiefly by amateurs
whose architectural apprenticeship had been served as
carpenters or builders' assistants.[2]

In New England, more than in any other section, the
colonial tradition was honored and English precedents
remained basic. On many a village green in Massachusetts and Connecticut, Congregational churches rose
with delicate towers and slender white spires. Some of
the most beautiful symbols which Calvinists and Episcopalians ever erected were made possible by profits from
neutral trade during the Napoleonic era. There was
usually a suggestion of ancient models in the English
manner of Robert Adam, but few were so patently in
the classical tradition as Ithiel Town's Center Church at
New Haven.[3] In New England also there was abundant
evidence of a somewhat independent American style.
Samuel McIntire, erstwhile wood carver, became architect extraordinary to the Salem merchants in the fabu-
lous years of the Old China trade. His contemporary,
Charles Bulfinch, one of the first Americans to deserve

[1] I. T. Frary, *Thomas Jefferson, Architect and Builder* (Richmond,
1931), 43-54 and plates.

[2] John Duncan, *Travels through Parts of the United States* (Glasgow,
1823), 189; Peter Neilson, *Recollections of a Six Years' Residence in
the United States* (Glasgow, 1830), 14; R. T. Coke, *A Subaltern's
Furlough* (N. Y., 1833), I, 30.

[3] Timothy Alden, jr., *An Account of the Several Religious Societies in
Portsmouth* (Boston, 1808); C. A. Wight, *Some Old Time Meeting
Houses of the Connecticut Valley* (Chicopee Falls, Mass., 1911), plates
opp. 94, 116; Aymar Embury II, *Early American Churches* (N. Y.,
1914), 5-6.

the title of professional architect, finally convinced Boston of his outstanding ability after he had remodeled Faneuil Hall, designed the state houses in Boston and Hartford and assumed charge in 1818 of the work on the national Capitol. Though Bulfinch and McIntire were deeply indebted to English masters, each contrived to adapt contemporary European forms to the conditions peculiar to the region in which he was working. Originality in detail enabled each to rival the classical enthusiasts in their contributions toward a distinctively American school.[1] Bulfinch, more than any other, transformed boxlike Puritan meetinghouses into austere but beautiful churches.[2]

Throughout the first quarter of the century there were numerous indications of an interest in Greek design, which was to dominate the architectural taste of the next generation. Before 1800 Benjamin H. Latrobe, lately arrived from England, had written, "Wherever, therefore, the Grecian style can be copied without impropriety, I love to be a mere, I would say, a slavish copyist . . . ."[3] This was the spirit in which the Greek revival in architecture came to America. Just as adaptation of English Georgian to wooden buildings in this country had emphasized the beauty of variations in the elaborate main doorway, so modifications of Greek models fixed attention on the majestic simplicity of the column. One did not need to build a complete temple in order to make use of the classic portico. In New

[1] See earlier, 11-12; also William Bentley, *Diary* (Salem, 1905-1914), III, 256-257; Fiske Kimball, "The Elias Hasket Derby Mansion in Salem," Essex Inst., *Colls.*, LX, 273-292; C. A. Place, *Charles Bulfinch, Architect and Citizen* (Boston, 1925), chap. iii.

[2] Bulfinch's influence was particularly noticeable in the work of Asher Benjamin, carpenter-builder, whose publications between 1797 and 1833 bulked large in the literature of the developing profession. A. J. Wall, *Books on Architecture Printed in America, 1775-1830* (Cambridge, 1925), *passim;* Aymar Embury II, *Asher Benjamin: a Reprint of the Country Builder's Assistant, 1805* (N. Y., 1917), 1-3.

[3] B. H. Latrobe, *Journal* (N. Y., 1905), 139.

England and New York as well as in Virginia and the Carolinas such a portico adorned many a Georgian dwelling. James Madison's Montpelier was thus remodeled and James Monroe set the same example in building Oak Hill. In 1826 a massive Doric portico was added to the mansion at Arlington across the Potomac from Washington. By the 1830's new state capitols and county courthouses were rising in templelike form, while the portico on the more pretentious country houses had become a symbol of dignity and prestige.[1]

Americans resembled Europeans in their enthusiasm for the exquisite beauty of the Greek orders and moldings. Throughout the western world romantic interest in ancient culture, breaking through mere academic concern with classical languages and literatures, was stirred anew by Lord Elgin's announcement of the removal to London of the Parthenon frieze and the sculptures from the Acropolis, and by the Greeks' heroic revolt against Turkey.[2] But the Greek revival in American architecture was more than an incidental part of a world-wide romantic movement. Laymen as well as professional architects came to think of Greek forms as the media through which distinctively American styles might be developed.[3] In 1830 Asher Benjamin remarked in *The Practical House Carpenter* that since the appearance of his last book some fifteen years earlier the Grecian School had almost completely superseded the Roman. Already Latrobe's able pupils, Robert Mills and William Strickland, were enthusiasts, while Ithiel Town and Alexander J. Davis in New York were convinced that the

[1] Howard Major, *The Domestic Architecture of the Early American Republic: the Greek Revival* (Phila., 1926), 17-50.

[2] Myrtle A. Cline, *American Attitude toward the Greek War of Independence* (Atlanta, 1930), 19-51; E. M. Earle, "American Interest in the Greek Cause," *Am. Hist. Rev.*, XXXIII, 44-63.

[3] Talbot Hamlin, "The Greek Revival in American Architecture," *Columbia Univ. Quar.*, XXXI, 171-175; Rexford Newcomb, "Ithiel Town of New Haven and New York," *Architect*, XI, 519-522.

inspiration of the Greek orders would provide an escape from servile copying of contemporary English and Continental designs.

Though some foreign-trained professional architects, like Latrobe in Philadelphia and Joseph Mangin in New York, had settled in Eastern cities after the Revolution, their colleagues were usually either skilled master craftsmen or talented amateurs who turned to architectural work as an avocation. As late as 1833 Asher Benjamin complained that many who would not think of "instructing a carpenter in the art of sawing boards" essayed the more difficult task of designing buildings.[1] They had learned whatever they knew about drawing plans and elevations either in the school of apprenticeship and experience or from the pages of pattern books. These convenient manuals, simplifying the styles popular in London as well as in Philadelphia and New York, long inspired the best architectural work in rural America.

The pervasiveness of Old World influences became apparent inside the homes of the wealthy. William Bingham's residence in Philadelphia was described in 1794 as furnished in the best English taste, a characterization that would have fit the town houses of the aristocracy anywhere from Boston to Charleston at the close of the eighteenth century. As in London, whitewashed walls were disappearing in a riot of color: either painted plasters or scenic wallpapers.[2] The latter, more common in Northern than in Southern houses, were available in series of tropical scenes, European landscapes, Chinese motifs or conventionalized designs from

[1] Asher Benjamin, *The Practice of Architecture* (Embury Reprint), 139-140. The first pattern book published by a native American was Benjamin's *Country Builder's Assistant* (Greenfield, Mass., 1797).

[2] By 1800 the product of domestic paper manufacturers was almost as highly esteemed as the imports from Paris. Nancy McClelland, *Historic Wall Papers* (Phila., 1924), 255, 266-267.

classical subjects.[1] At the windows rich damasks and
brocades were giving way to printed linen and chintz
hangings, while floors, once highly polished, were now
completely covered with carpets. Wedgwood ware with
its decorative Grecian designs enjoyed as high favor as
Lowestoft china; and tables heavy with European cut
glass were sometimes lighted by large candelabra moved
about on castors.

While many of the wealthy imported their chairs and
tables from Seddon's in London, there was no need for
them to do so. Native craftsmen, studying the style-
books of the great Georgians, Chippendale, Hepplewhite and Sheraton, modified these English forms with
French ornamentation or with American national symbols, and for a quarter-century fashioned furniture
which has not yet been surpassed.[2] Bookcases and secre-
taries usually had two doors, each with thirteen panes
of glass in honor of the original states. The gilded eagle
perched on the top of countless mirrors and wall clocks,
and a carved bust of Washington often surmounted the
backs of formal chairs. In New York the Georgian
styles were Americanized largely through the work of
Duncan Phyfe, a Scotch lad who had served an apprenticeship in Albany before becoming cabinetmaker to
Knickerbocker society. But his influence proved scarcely
greater than that of Henry Connolly in Philadelphia or
John Seymour and Michael Allison in Boston. In New
England the unusual success in reproducing the delicacy
of Hepplewhite's designs probably came from the fact
that artisans, who specialized on trim and cabin equip-

[1] *Salem Gazette*, Aug. 6, 1822. See also Essex Institute, *Historical
Collections*, LXII, 4-7.
[2] Thomas Hope, *House Furniture and Decoration* (London, 1807) ;
C. M. Stow, "The Influence of the Great Georgian Designers," J. M. Bell,
ed., *The Furniture Designs of Chippendale, Hepplewhite and Sheraton*
(N. Y., 1938).

ment in the shipyards, spent their slack time in fashioning fine furniture.[1]

Shortly after the treaty of Ghent, French influence, long held back by the Napoleonic wars, moved into American drawing-rooms, introducing Empire styles sharply divergent from those of the English Regency. To meet the change of fashion American craftsmen now turned from London to Paris for their models. Thus Duncan Phyfe's pieces in the decade of the twenties were more massive and ornate than anything he had done earlier. There was a suggestion, but only a slight one, of the decline in taste which was to come at mid-century when the aristocratic tradition, still imperfectly understood by the newly rich, no longer commanded the respect of the multitude.

Other artistic standards early in the century were largely borrowed from Europe. In painting, for example, the controlling influence emanated from the London studio of Benjamin West, where many a young artist received his inspiration.[2] Late in the eighteenth century this American expatriate had welcomed Gilbert Stuart, John Trumbull and Robert Fulton, while his last groups of students included Washington Allston, Samuel Waldo and Samuel F. B. Morse.[3] But these represented the fortunate minority. Not more than forty-five in all crossed the Atlantic for brief periods of European training during the forty years after 1790.

[1] C. O. Cornelius, *Early American Furniture* (N. Y., 1926), 100-179; Nancy McClelland, *Duncan Phyfe and English Regency, 1795-1830* (N. Y., 1939), 91 ff.; T. H. Ormsbee, *Early American Furniture Makers* (N. Y., 1930), 63-73.

[2] See E. B. Greene, *The Revolutionary Generation, 1763-1790* (*A History of American Life*, IV), 148, 299.

[3] Dunlap, *History of the Arts of Design*, I, 143-144; J. H. Morgan, *Early American Painters* (N. Y., 1921), 63 ff. Morse forsook England for France, where John Vanderlyn, protegé of Aaron Burr, also studied. Carleton Mabee, *The American Leonardo* (N. Y., 1943), chap. iii.

Yet it was difficult otherwise to secure proper guidance. The few professional artists in America were not always willing to take pupils, even if the ambitious youth had overcome parental prejudice and financial difficulties. Chester Harding recalled that, after he had met with some success in portraiture, his grandfather insisted, "I think it is very little better than swindling to charge forty dollars for one of those effigies. Now I want you to give up this course of living and settle down on a farm and become a respectable man." [1] Painting, like architecture, was closely allied to the practical arts. Many artists discovered their true interest and talent by serving an apprenticeship as sign painters, engravers, house painters or paper hangers.

Philadelphia still retained its primacy as a center for art students, a position which it had won in the days when members of the Continental Congress sat for their portraits. New York and Boston, however, were not far behind. In the latter city lived the great Stuart, but Washington Allston was even more popular with students. In New York two Scots, Alexander and Archibald Robertson, set up the Columbian Academy of Painting in 1792, and others were advertising drawing schools early in the nineteenth century. [2] Both the Pennsylvania Academy of Fine Arts (1805) and the Society of Artists of the United States, established at Philadelphia in 1810, undertook to provide instruction, but neither was able to maintain a school. A growing professional pride and protests against dependence on Europe gave support to Samuel F. B. Morse's efforts to organize in New York the National Academy of the

[1] Chester Harding, *My Egotistigraphy* (Cambridge, 1866), 41.
[2] Andrew Robertson, *Letters and Papers* (Emily Robertson, ed., London, 1895), 9-10; Dunlap, *History of the Arts of Design*, II, 157; III, 233.

Arts of Design. From the first exhibition in 1828 its primary objective was improvement of standards through careful training of young artists.[1]

Such financial support as the painter received grew out of interest in portraiture. Normal human vanity was reënforced, at least among the aristocrats, by rumors of the vogue of portrait painting across the Atlantic. Religious scruples against personal adornment and decorative embellishment, which had never been confined solely to the Quakers and other pietistic sects, yielded gradually to the desire to preserve the likenesses of the Revolutionary hero and the republican statesman. An improved market attracted foreign artists. Thus, John Vallence, a Scotch limner, opened a studio in Philadelphia in 1791; from Denmark came Joshua Carter, who settled in Charleston in 1792; two years later Févre de Saint-Mémin, the French refugee, arrived and perfected his profile portraits in crayon.[2] Even mediocre artists, carrying on in the tradition of colonial limners, began to discover that their talents had commercial value. A veritable army of them moved over the countryside, receiving in some districts a welcome not unlike that accorded to the peddler. Most were compelled to eke out a living by supplementary work. Ezra Ames in Albany maintained himself over slack periods by varnishing chairs, engraving silver spoons, painting sleighs and hanging wallpaper. Others re-

[1] Society of Artists of the United States, *Catalogue of the First Annual Exhibition* (Phila., 1811); Samuel Isham, *The History of American Painting* (N. Y., 1905), 186-189. An Academy of Fine Arts, organized in New York by Robert R. Livingston, John Trumbull, DeWitt Clinton and other prominent citizens, received its charter in 1808 and for several years conducted a drawing school. A. T. Goodrich, *Picture of New York and Strangers' Guide* (N. Y., 1828), 369-370.

[2] Dunlap, *History of the Arts of Design*, II, 112, 283; III, 332. Of two hundred portrait painters, selected at random, who worked between 1790 and 1830, forty-four were foreign-born. G. C. Groce, jr., ed., *American Poetry Inventory. 1440 Early American Portrait Artists, 1663-1860* (Newark, N. J., 1940), *passim*.

paired jewelry, conducted dancing schools or earned what money they could as hairdressers.[1]

These itinerants — and even the most talented traveled in search of patrons — were an important influence in elevating popular artistic taste. Though they usually sought such cultural centers as Philadelphia, New York and Boston, any decline in business activity, particularly that of 1818-1820, was apt to send them farther afield. John Wesley Jarvis's brilliant wit and Bohemian manners, so amusing to the New York of Washington Irving's Knickerbocker days, were known from Albany to New Orleans.[2] Rembrandt Peale and Samuel Waldo could not resist the charm of Charleston during the winter season when the wealthy planters were in town and sitters were numerous. William Dunlap never forgot the hospitality of Norfolk and Richmond and the gracious living in Virginia's great country houses.[3] Though the artists' frontier still ran close to the coast line, there were regions even in trans-Appalachia which offered generous patronage to portraitists. Pittsburgh's wholesalers and manufacturers made that river metropolis worth visiting, while the planters of the Kentucky Blue Grass enabled Chester Harding to earn enough for his European training.[4] By 1830 one venturesome miniaturist had reached Detroit.

Most portrait painters yielded to the "miniature craze," which was at its peak early in the nineteenth century. If Gilbert Stuart could boast he had painted few miniatures in more than eleven hundred and fifty

[1] Ezra Ames, Yearly Expense Books, covering years 1799-1826, in New York Historical Society; William Kelby, "Notes on American Artists," N. Y. Hist. Soc., Quar. Bull., III, 67, 112; IV, 114.

[2] H. E. Dickson, "John Wesley Jarvis, Knickerbocker Painter," ibid., XXXIV, 51-52.

[3] Dunlap, History of the Arts of Design, I, 319 ff.

[4] Harding, Egotistigraphy, 27-41. In six months at Paris, Kentucky, Harding painted nearly one hundred portraits at twenty-five dollars each.

portraits, at least a score of his contemporaries devoted themselves almost exclusively to this form of art. Edward Malbone of Boston and Charles Fraser of Charleston ranked with the best Europeans of their day. There was also a host of lesser artists in this medium.[1] These delicate small portraits on ivory, so charmingly intimate, were prized as highly by agrarian democrats as by the tie-wig aristocracy in seaport towns. Benjamin Trott toured the regions beyond the Alleghanies on horseback, carrying his materials in his saddlebags, in order to reach remote hamlets which itinerant painters never visited.[2] Not until the perfection of the daguerreotype did the popularity of the more lovely miniature decline.[3]

The portraitists of these years made an incalculable contribution to the historical record. As a result of their work posterity feels better acquainted with Washington and his younger colleagues than with any American leaders until the photographer's art recorded accurately the features of Lincoln and Lee. Gilbert Stuart's gallery alone included the first five presidents, as well as Samuel Adams, James Otis, Josiah Quincy, Fisher Ames and other public figures.

How much the painting of historical incidents contributed to the upsurge of national sentiment, which followed the War of 1812, is difficult to estimate, but it seems significant that in 1816 John Trumbull was commissioned to enlarge four of his historical pictures for the rotunda of the Capitol at Washington.[4] Except

[1] Theodore Bolton, *Early American Portrait Painters in Miniature* (N. Y., 1921), 54 ff., 99 ff.; H. B. Wehle, *American Miniatures, 1730-1850* (Garden City, 1927), 64-65.

[2] Dunlap, *History of the Arts of Design*, II, 204; Richardson Wright, *Hawkers and Walkers in Early America* (Phila., 1927), 134 ff.

[3] See Fish, *Rise of the Common Man*, 97-98.

[4] The subjects were "The Declaration of Independence," "The Surrender of Burgoyne," "The Surrender of Cornwallis" and "The Resignation of General Washington." John Trumbull, *Autobiography, Reminiscences and Letters* (N. Y., 1841), 275.

for American themes, however, such canvases in the grand style aroused little interest. Neither the Biblical scenes of Allston nor the classical subjects of Vanderlyn were at first commercially successful; but their exhibition in theaters and museums throughout the country may have brought to some Americans a new appreciation of the European masterpieces, which they occasionally saw in reproduction.

Unlike portraiture, sculpture had neither colonial tradition nor English precedents. Against that lack of background must be set a widespread prudery which derived only in part from the Puritans' mortal fear of sensuous beauty. When Robert E. Pine late in the eighteenth century brought over a plaster cast of the Venus de Medici, he was not permitted to keep the statue in a studio where it could be generally seen.[1] The copies of Louvre models, which Nicholas Biddle sent to the Pennsylvania Academy of Fine Arts, stood Philadelphia on end. One day each week the figures were swathed in muslin sheets for the benefit of feminine visitors to the gallery.[2] As late as 1820 John Trumbull stated that "nothing in sculpture would be wanted in this country for yet a hundred years."[3]

Those who agreed with Trumbull overlooked two facts: first, the growing demand for statues and memorials to commemorate the struggle for independence; and, second, the pioneer work already done by Americans who had learned to model in wax, wood or clay. From this group of early modelers, few in number, came the inspiration for our first native sculptors. The skill of Patience Lovell Wright, who worked in wax, won her recognition in London where she took up her residence after 1772. Mrs. Wright's European success

[1] B. A. Konkle, *Joseph Hopkinson* (Phila., 1931), 146.
[2] H. M. Lippincott, *Early Philadelphia* (Phila., 1917), **184-185**.
[3] *North American Quar. Mag.* (July, 1835), 17.

exerted an inspiriting influence on her son, Joseph Wright, in New York, and on Daniel Bowen in Boston, both of whom became proficient in wax portraiture. Standards of performance were constantly raised by the friendly emulation of German, Italian and English artists who settled in America during the first quarter of the nineteenth century.[1]

Craftsmen working in wood or stone were the immediate forerunners of the professional sculptor. William Rush, whose hand had acquired skill in shaping figureheads for ships, used wood as his medium in carving his full-length statue of George Washington for Independence Hall and his "Nymph of the Schuylkill," later in Fairmount Park, Philadelphia.[2] The first portrait in marble by a native American was executed in 1824 by John Frazee, who had become expert in carving mantelpieces and tombstones.[3] About the same time Hezekiah Augur, son of a New England carpenter, finished in Carrara marble his copy of the bust of Apollo.[4] Yet in 1830 Americans still depended largely upon Europeans for memorials of their national heroes, as they had a generation earlier when Houdon and Canova made statues of Washington for the states of Virginia and North Carolina. Native sculptors were acclaimed not so much for their talent as for their success in attracting the favorable attention of foreigners.

[1] A. J. Wall, "Wax Portraiture," N. Y. Hist. Soc., *Quar. Bull.*, IX, 3-26; Ethel S. Bolton, *American Wax Portraits* (Boston, 1929), 18-31.

[2] Jordan, "William Rush," 246-247.

[3] S. G. W. Benjamin, "Sculpture in America," *Harper's Mag.*, LVIII (1897), 658-659.

[4] *American Journal of Science and Arts*, IX (1825), 173. John H. I. Browere, contemporary of Augur and Frazee, perfected the process of taking casts of the human face, so that he might create a national gallery of the busts of famous men and women. Lack of popular interest and financial support thwarted his elaborate plans, but the busts for which his life masks were models remain as the best likenesses of the leaders of his generation. Many of them may be seen in the gallery of the New York State Historical Association at Cooperstown, New York. C. H. Hart, *Browere's Life Masks of Great Americans* (N. Y., 1899), 13-27.

If the people had little opportunity to see Europe's artistic masterpieces, they were becoming aware of their own achievements.   Public exhibitions were arranged from time to time by the Academy of Fine Arts in New York, the Pennsylvania Academy in Philadelphia, the South Carolina Academy in Charleston and the Athenaeum Gallery in Boston.   There were also small collections such as those at Harvard College, the Redwood Library at Newport, the Longworth Gallery in New York and Peale's Museum in Baltimore.   In addition, many artists displayed their paintings in their own studios or rented halls for exhibitions.   Thus, John Trumbull's historical pictures were shown in most of the larger Eastern cities before they were placed in the Capitol rotunda.[1]

At a more popular level, motives largely commercial established the vogue of the panorama.   One of the earliest of these canvases was the "City of London" which William Winstanley, an English artist, brought to New York in 1795.   The harbors of Charleston and New York, the siege of Tripoli and the various battles of Napoleon became favorite subjects.[2]   Probably the best panoramas were prepared under the supervision of John Vanderlyn, who for a dozen years after 1818 exhibited his work in a circular brick building in New York.   Such pictures did little to improve public taste. Generally they were mediocre, if not inferior, examples of American painting, and the best seldom won more plaudits than the worst.   Those who purported to be art critics afforded little help, for their commentaries in the magazines and newspapers were devoid of any standards of excellence.[3]   In artistic as in literary circles the

[1] Niles' Wkly. Register (XVI, 1819, 384) reported that "The Declaration of Independence" earned $1700 in Boston in three weeks.
[2] Dunlap, History of the Arts of Design, II, 77 ff.
[3] See Port Folio, VIII (1812), 538; North American Review, II, (1815-1816), 73; American Monthly Magazine, II (1834), 345-346.

critics easily identified questions of taste with those of morality.

Although the professional artist had no literary medium peculiarly his own, his work was discussed occasionally in the magazines, and of these there were many.[1] The typical periodical was general in content and highly imitative of English precedent. Between 1790 and 1800 more than fifty such literary journals were established, but only three lasted more than two years and none enjoyed a wide circulation. Financial difficulties, however, did not deter optimistic editors, for it is estimated that at least five hundred were able to get into print during the first quarter of the new century.[2]

Editorial policies varied widely. Isaiah Thomas's *Massachusetts Magazine* (1789-1796) contained the best examples of the developing short story, while the *American Register* (1806-1810) purveyed political and scientific information. Some quickly became specialty magazines, emphasizing agriculture, theology, medicine or the drama.[3] Others, appealing to a particular region, featured events of local interest. A few, like Charles Brockden Brown's *American Review and Literary Journal* (1801) and Robert Walsh's *American Review of History and Politics* (1811-1817), attempted the critical appraisal of letters, but none deserved to rank with the great British quarterlies until Boston's *Monthly Anthology* was revived as the *North American Review* (1815). Particularly outstanding as an editor was

[1] The journals devoting most space to art were the *Port Folio, Analectic Magazine* and the *American Museum* in Philadelphia; the *American Monthly Magazine and Critical Review* and the *Monthly Magazine and American Review* in New York; the *Athenaeum* and the *North American Review* in Boston.

[2] Probably 12 magazines were being issued regularly in 1800; 40 in 1810 and 100 in 1825. F. L. Mott, *A History of American Magazines, 1741-1850* (N. Y., 1930), 120-121.

[3] For the numerous religious journals, see earlier, 255.

Joseph Dennie, who enlisted the support of the literary junto in Philadelphia. His forthright Federalism seemed incongruous in the capital of Jeffersonianism, but the *Port Folio* prospered as its list of contributors lengthened to include such political figures as Richard Rush, Alexander J. Dallas, Gouverneur Morris and John Quincy Adams.[1]

If the literary magazines had any common purpose, it was to produce an indigenous American culture by hothouse methods. Despite heavy borrowing from English sources their pages thundered proclamations against the prevalent colonial-mindedness in business, in medicine, in art and in literature.[2] Both editors and contributors, with few exceptions, seemed to be irritated by evidence of dependence on European countries, especially Great Britain. Poets were reminded that "oak and elm are as good wood to supply poetical fire as cypress and yew," and one commentator proposed that every rimester guilty of importing his ideas from England or France be "exiled from the purlieus of Parnassus as an alien."[3] It was cause for rejoicing that publicists, instead of prattling about "dells and dingles, the Alps and Apennines and the River Po," found their images in that great national "storehouse which was perpetually before them."[4]

Implicit in this crudely phrased campaign for cultural nationalism was recognition of a persistent colonialism

---

[1] A. H. Smyth, *The Philadelphia Magazines and Their Contributors* (Phila., 1892), 93.

[2] For example, see the *Gleaner*, I (1798), 37; *Literary Mag. and Am. Register*, I (1803-1804), 1-2; *Monthly Register*, I (1805), 190; and *Monthly Anthology*, IV (1807), 217. Though Dennie deplored American attempts to rival England, he received the support of many Philadelphians, among them Royall Tyler and Thomas G. Fessenden, who were anxious to promote a distinctively national literature. H. M. Ellis, *Joseph Dennie and His Circle* (Univ. of Texas, *Bull.*, no. 40) ; Smyth, *Philadelphia Magazines*, 93.

[3] *Port Folio*, III (1807), 331; *Tablet*, I (1795), 46.

[4] *Ibid.*, 47.

in literature and the arts.[1] Unfavorable estimates of the young nation's achievements came from American as well as English reviews. Fisher Ames, notoriously pessimistic about his own generation, was not alone in censuring American literature. Magazine editors regretted that fewer than a hundred important books had been published in the United States during the first twenty years of independence, while literary critics poured scorn on a society which could boast of "no epic, tragedy, comedy, elegies, poems — pastoral or amatory." [2] When Joel Barlow's *Columbiad* appeared, some refused to regard the author as a poet and insisted that his "verses" did not merit remembrance.[3] In 1815 William Tudor, surveying the preceding quarter-century from the vantage point of Cambridge and Harvard College, was moved to entitle his commentary "The Literary Delinquency of America." [4] Concerning Massachusetts, Ralph Waldo Emerson was emphatic — surely he did not err on the side of understatement — when he remarked that between 1790 and 1820 "there was not a book, a speech, a conversation or a thought in the State." [5]

But Americans were more willing to criticize their own lack of achievement than to have foreigners do so.

[1] This campaign, which seemed widespread immediately after the Revolution, subsided during the first decade of the nineteenth century only to become more vigorous after 1825. Anne L. Heene, American Opinion Concerning Cultural Nationalism, as Reflected in American Magazines, 1790-1830 (Master's essay. Columbia Univ. Library, 1944).

[2] *Monthly Magazine and American Review*, I (1799), 341; *Monthly Anthology and Boston Review*, III (1806), 579.

[3] *American Review and Literary Journal*, II (1802), 81; *Monthly Register*, III (1807), 177.

[4] *North American Review*, II (1815-1816), 33 ff. Numerous commentators deplored the tendency of Americans to underestimate their own literary efforts and exaggerate European achievements. "The Americans," remarked one critic, "are the only people on earth who uniformly undervalue the affairs of literary genius in their own country." *Monthly Magazine*, I (1799), 19.

[5] R. W. Emerson, *Journals* (Boston, 1909-1914), VIII, 339.

British appraisals, so ran the argument, represented fear and ignorance tinctured with the malice of those who had personal grievances. Depreciation of American life made comforting reading for British industrialists apprehensive over the possible emigration of their workers and the rising competition of American manufacturers. It proved equally pleasant for the upper classes, who disliked the trend toward democracy in the New World. Whatever its basis, the controversy was continuous during the early decades of the nineteenth century. Did the *Quarterly Review* cast animadversions on America's government, society or literature, the *Port Folio* or some other journal leaped to the defense.[1] Stimulated by the War of 1812, the verbal hostilities reached crescendo in Sydney Smith's famous query: "In the four quarters of the globe, who reads an American book? or goes to an American play? or looks at an American picture or statue?"[2]

Thoughtful Americans were still disposed to answer in terms of future prospects rather than present accomplishments. As Joseph Buckminster said in 1809, "The men of letters who are to direct our taste, mold our genius, and inspire our emulation . . . have not yet shown themselves to the world. But . . . the generation which is to succeed us will be formed on better models."[3] Yet his own generation was not devoid of achievement. Literary effort reached fruition in one of several forms: the sentimental lyric, which was highly esteemed, or the occasional poem, seldom as significant in content as the occasion it commemorated; the didactic essay, following English models but rarely attaining equality with its eighteenth-century precedents; and the

[1] *Port Folio*, II (1802), 258; *Monthly Register*, III, 351; J. K. Paulding, *The United States and England: Being a Reply to the Criticism . . . Contained in the Quarterly Review* (N. Y., 1815).

[2] *Edinburgh Review*, XXXIII (1820), 69-80.

[3] Eliza B. Lee, *Memoirs of . . . Buckminster* (Boston, 1851), 388.

elegant oration, liberally sprinkled with classical allusions and faintly bombastic in dealing with patriotic subjects. Political disputation, though spirited, produced little that was comparable to the *Federalist,* or even to the pamphlets of the Revolutionary era.

Fiction struggled rather feebly for recognition in the guise of the romantic novel, sugar-coated with sentimentality.[1] Its beginnings were manifest in such moral tales as *The Power of Sympathy* (1789), probably the first novel by an American,[2] and Susanna H. Rowson's *Charlotte; a Tale of Truth* (1791, known later as *Charlotte Temple*), which proved the most popular American book to the time of *Uncle Tom's Cabin.*[3] Though the familiar formula of English sentimentality was likewise used in Gilbert Imlay's *The Emigrants* (1793), the locale was western Pennsylvania and Kentucky and there were overtones of social reform in the vigorous defense of American institutions and the proposal for an ideal community in the Western wilderness.[4] Hugh Henry Brackenridge obviously found in *Don Quixote* and the great English satirists of the eighteenth century the models for his *Modern Chivalry.* A democrat after the manner of Thomas Jefferson, he took time from political activities and judicial duties to poke fun at lawyers, doctors, clergymen and the political opportunists whom he knew so well; nor did he spare the pseudo-scientists and the pundits of the American Philosophical

---

[1] H. R. Brown, *The Sentimental Novel in America, 1789-1860* (Durham, 1940), chaps. i-vi.

[2] It was published anonymously and its author has never been positively identified as Sarah Wentworth Morton. Milton Ellis, "The Author of the First American Novel," *Am. Lit.,* IV, 356-368.

[3] By 1812, 50,000 copies had been sold. E. L. Bradsher, *Mathew Carey, Editor, Author and Publisher* (N. Y., 1912), 51. By 1933 the various editions of the novel numbered 161. R. W. G. Vail, *Susanna Haswell Rowson, a Bibliographical Study* (Worcester, 1933), 18, 21.

[4] *The Emigrants* was probably written after Imlay left America. R. L. Rusk, "Adventures of Gilbert Imlay," Indiana Univ., *Studies,* X, no. 57, 13-15.

Society. *Modern Chivalry* was aimed at Western pioneers, and in large numbers they read it and liked its humor.[1]

In Europe literature provided a means of livelihood; in the United States at the close of the eighteenth century it was a diversion for one's leisure time. Even Mrs. Rowson's popularity did not permit her to discontinue her school for girls in Boston. It is true that Sally Barrell Wood regarded her writing as something more than an avocation when she published the "wholly American" *Dorval; or, the Speculator* in 1801, but neither in quantity nor quality did her work equal that of Charles Brockden Brown, America's first native professional novelist. In his best romances — *Wieland* (1798), *Edgar Huntley* (1799), *Ormond* (1799) and *Arthur Mervyn* (1800) — Brown strove to "adapt his fiction to all that is genuine and peculiar in the scene before him."[2] It was the sensational rather than the sentimental that interested him. However widely he may have read in English and German literature, his chief inspiration came from his intimate friends: Elihu Hubbard Smith, the New York playwright and physician; the young actor, John Howard Payne; and versatile William Dunlap, who introduced him to the congenial spirits of New York's Friendly Club.[3] Brown's genius burned out quickly. His fiction was practically all written before 1805, and five years later, at the age of thirty-nine, he was dead. His originality in invention, rather than his adaptations of the Gothic novel, won the homage of Hawthorne and Poe.

During the early years of the nineteenth century Phila-

---

[1] *Modern Chivalry* was published serially between 1792 and 1815. See C. M. Newlin, *The Life and Writings of Hugh Henry Brackenridge* (Princeton, 1932), 112-123.

[2] *Weekly Magazine*, I (1798), 202-203.

[3] William Dunlap, *Memoirs of Charles Brockden Brown, the American Novelist* (London, 1822), 43-46.

delphia and New York were rival literary centers. As late as 1811 a resident of Manhattan thought the "metropolis of Pennsylvania" culturally more distinguished than the "commercial emporium" in which he lived.[1] Within the next decade, however, the issue so far as men of letters were concerned was emphatically decided in favor of New York. As Hartford had supplied the background for John Trumbull, Joel Barlow and Dwight, as Philadelphia had nourished a literary tradition from the days of Franklin to those of Brockden Brown, so the noisy port at the mouth of the Hudson provided support for the Knickerbocker group of writers. Young Washington Irving may have erred in comparing the life of his city to that of Addison's London, but he and his associates were eager to make it comparable. The first number of *Salmagundi*, appearing in January, 1807, was avowedly in the style of the *Spectator*. Its gentle satire was but a prelude to the boisterous humor of *Diedrich Knickerbocker's History of New York* (1809), which amused Walter Scott as much as it entertained American Federalists, who were sure they could see the caricature of Thomas Jefferson through the clouds of smoke emanating from the Dutchmen's pipes. Irving spent the seventeen years after 1815 in Europe, publishing *The Sketch Book* (1819) with its Dutch legends of the Hudson Valley, and then *Bracebridge Hall* (1822) and *Tales of a Traveller* (1824), both eloquent of his affection for England.[2] If some Americans were distressed that he had succumbed to European influences, probably more were inspirited by the reports of his increasing reputation wherever great literature was honored.[3]

[1] *Am. Medical and Philos. Register*, II (1811), 236.
[2] S. T. Williams, *The Life of Washington Irving* (N. Y., 1935), I, 208-210, 220-222.
[3] J. D. Ferguson, *American Literature in Spain* (N. Y., 1916), 8-31. *The Sketch Book* was translated into fifteen languages.

The period of Irving's long sojourn abroad was a
lively one in New York's literary circles. The lean years
of the war were over and business depression cast but a
transitory shadow. Prosperous merchants welcomed
their more articulate fellows in their drawing-rooms and
at the dinner table. Clubs were formed, in which there
was much good talk of arts and letters against a merry
social background. But, though there was material as
well as spiritual encouragement for young writers, few
could live wholly by their pens. Joseph Rodman Drake
managed an apothecary's shop that he might write
poetry, while Fitz-Greene Halleck served a long apprenticeship in New York countinghouses. Their business
experiences supplied some background for their satiric
verses in *The Croaker Papers* (1819), but in general it
was a gay city that they celebrated.[1] Its charm held
James Kirke Paulding while he carried on his literary
warfare with Great Britain and composed his first novels
of "rational fiction." [2] It drew William Cullen Bryant
from the Berkshires, where the beauties of Nature had
enchanted him, and started him in 1825 on a long journalistic career in which the poet was quickly lost in the
publicist. Here, too, came James Fenimore Cooper,
blessed with leisure and means for travel, rejoicing in the
success of his novel of Revolutionary days, *The Spy*
(1821), but aspiring to put on paper the spell of the
American frontier which had possessed him since the days
of his up-state boyhood. The author of "Thanatopsis"
and "To a Waterfowl" built his life into the rising city
of New York; the urban mood touched but lightly the
creator of Natty Bumpo.

Like Irving, Cooper quickly gained a large audience

[1] William Dunlap, *Diary* (N. Y., 1930), II, 462, 468.
[2] For example, *The Diverting History of John Bull and Brother Jonathan* (1812), *The United States and England* (1815), *The Backwoodsman* (1818), and *Koningsmarke* (1823). See A. L. Herold, *James
Kirke Paulding, Versatile American* (N. Y., 1926), 46-65.

across the Atlantic. The romantic idealism, dominant in all his novels of adventure, delighted Britons who were devouring each historical romance as it came from the study at Abbotsford on the Tweed. What the border of his native land was to Scott, the American frontier was to Cooper. By 1830 he had completed three of the *Leatherstocking Tales* — *The Pioneers* (1823), *The Last of the Mohicans* (1826) and *The Prairie* (1827) — and had delineated in the frontiersman one of the most picturesque characters in the long gallery of world literature.[1] His Indians may have belonged, as Mark Twain once remarked, to "an extinct tribe which never existed," but at first they seem to have been convincing to most American and all European readers.

Edward Everett, surveying American literature in 1824, was impressed by "an astonishing development of intellectual energy in this country."[2] Probably much that he saw was behind his eyes, for he was under the spell of new forces astir in Boston and Cambridge. It was gratifying to watch the widening influence of the man of letters; to read the essays and reviews of American, English, French and German books in the *North American Review;* to know something of what was in the minds of Richard Henry Dana, the elder, Edward T. Channing, George Bancroft and young John G. Palfrey. Boston, self-centered but world-conscious, seemed to sense already that destiny which Emerson described as a summons "to lead the civilization of North America."[3] But where Everett found cause for rejoicing, William Ellery Channing saw need for renewed effort. With an eloquence surpassing that of others who had sounded a similar warning, he reminded his countrymen that "a

[1] H. W. Boynton, *James Fenimore Cooper* (N. Y., 1931), 106-125.
[2] *An Oration Pronounced at Cambridge before the Society of Phi Beta Kappa* (N. Y., 1824).
[3] *Natural History of Intellect and Other Papers* (Boston, 1894), 79.

William Dunlap's painting of a scene from the drama based on James Fenimore Cooper's novel "The Spy"

Architecture in Rochester, New York, in 1829

people into whose minds the thoughts of foreigners are poured perpetually . . . will become intellectually tame and enslaved." The true sovereigns of any country, he said, are "those who determine its mind." [1]

Americans excused their literary deficiencies by referring to their preoccupation with the practical side of life and by boasting of their literacy.[2] Timothy Dwight, late in the eighteenth century, had reported a large and growing reading public in the Northeastern states; and it was said that the great house on many a plantation had a "book room" and a "respectable library." [3] But those who read regularly — and there is no way of knowing how numerous they were — probably did not read extensively. Either through choice or necessity they learned to know a few books well and to meditate on them. David Ramsay observed that South Carolinians outside Charleston had little available save the Bible and the newspapers, and from these two sources they drew whatever they knew of theology, philosophy, history and science.[4] Where books were more plentiful, John Bunyan's *Pilgrim's Progress* and Richard Baxter's *Saints' Everlasting Rest* were often companion pieces to the Scriptures.[5] Theological works still outnumbered secular in New England, but even that section admired Oliver Goldsmith's poems and Alexander Pope's essays and read the *Spectator* and the *Tatler*. Gentlemen who professed no legal aspirations spoke with knowledge of Blackstone's *Commentaries* and Montesquieu's *Spirit of Laws*. If

[1] "On a National Literature," *Christian Examiner,* VII (1830), 269 ff.
[2] *Literary Mag. and Am. Register,* I, 419-424; Samuel Miller, *Brief Retrospect of the Eighteenth Century* (N. Y., 1803), II, 404-410.
[3] Dwight, *Travels* (New Haven, 1821-1822), IV, 355; Mrs. St. Julien Ravenel, *Charleston* (N. Y., 1906), 389.
[4] David Ramsay, *History of South Carolina* (Charleston, 1806), II, 211-212. If the farmers' almanacs are added, this brief list would be characteristic of many rural districts from Georgia to Maine.
[5] U. P. Hedrick, "What Farmers Read in Western New York, 1800-1850," *N. Y. History,* XVII, 283.

fiction was still suspect at the close of the eighteenth century, *Robinson Crusoe, Don Quixote, The Vicar of Wakefield* and *Gil Blas* passed even clerical censorship in many communities.

Changes in popular literary taste, though not yet fully revealed, were in the making. Even before the opening of the new century Royall Tyler, jurist and playwright, noticed that in New England "some dreary somebody's day of doom" was being supplanted by lighter reading.[1] In 1811 a Pittsburgh book dealer advised Mathew Carey, the Philadelphia publisher, that new novels were "all the rage" in the West. It was creditable to Americans that they quickly recognized the merits of Scott, Irving and Cooper. The earlier *Waverley* novels, in which history seemed both romantic and moralistic, were in great demand long before Sir Walter revealed his authorship; and during the 1820's "bookstands almost creaked" under pirated editions of *Ivanhoe, Quentin Durward, Kenilworth* and *The Heart of Midlothian*.[2] Nowhere were they more influential, then and later, than in the homes of Southern planters.[3]

But if one considers all classes and sections of the country, the vogue of romanticism was more accurately represented in the mediocre works of minor novelists. Maria Edgeworth, in America as in England, was generally regarded as "safe," even for impressionable young women. Of Mrs. Rowson's numerous imitators, probably the ablest was Hannah Webster Foster, whose *Coquette, or the History of Eliza Wharton* (1797) was

[1] Cited in Lillie D. Loshe, *The Early American Novel* (Columbia Univ., *Studies in English*, ser. 2, II, no. 2), 1-2. See T. J. Wertenbaker, *The First Americans, 1607-1690* (*A History of American Life*, II), 243-244, for an explanation of the reference.

[2] Bradsher, *Mathew Carey*, 80-81.

[3] Edward Everett noticed in his tour of the Southern states that many names of stagecoaches, steamboats, etc., were taken from Scott's novels. P. L. Frothingham, *Edward Everett* (Boston, 1925), 119.

republished as late as 1874.[1] Caroline Warren's *The
Gamesters; or Ruins of Innocence* (1805), in which the
seducer's snares never failed, enjoyed an unmerited popularity for several decades.   Somewhat better were novels
based upon American themes: John Neal's *Logan*
(1822), a tale of Indian life in colonial days; James
McHenry's romance of Fort Duquesne, *The Wilderness,
or Braddock's Times* (1823) ; and Timothy Flint's
Francis Berrian (1826), a sentimental story of a New
Englander in the Mexican revolt of 1822, faithfully por-
traying the Southwestern border.

The literary culture of Americans depended in certain
respects on the book trade, which in turn was at the
mercy of inadequate transportation and defective organization.   Distance sometimes established a prohibitive
barrier. Philadelphia, New York, Boston and Baltimore
had almost mutually exclusive hinterlands so far as booksellers were concerned. Convenience of shipment justified the development of smaller publishing centers, such
as Worcester, Hartford, Albany, Lancaster, Richmond
and a score of others.[2] There was little differentiation
of function in the trade, the modern specialties of printing, publishing, distributing and retailing usually being
handled by the same proprietor. The printer-editor-
publisher in the larger towns sometimes maintained a
reading room in conjunction with a circulating library,
where his customers might examine the latest books received. To create a well-balanced wholesale market on
a nation-wide basis Mathew Carey promoted the organization of the American Company of Booksellers, which
managed five literary fairs between 1802 and 1806. But
it quickly aroused the suspicions of small dealers in

---

[1] R. L. Shurter, "Mrs. Hannah Webster Foster and the Early American
Novel," *Am. Lit.*, IV, 306-307.

[2] *N. Y. Daily Advertiser*, May 26, 1802.

regions far from New York and Philadelphia and failed to establish an efficient method of distribution.[1] Energetic publishers of broad vision strove to reach remote customers by sending out special canvassers. Carey, for example, gave particular attention to the South and Southwest, often employing the Reverend Mason L. Weems who used the opportunity to push the sales of his *Life of Washington* until it reached its fortieth edition and fixed for generations the legendary figure of the first President.[2] But most printer-publishers were content to follow the conventional methods of accepting a subsidy from the author or of securing an advance subscription sufficient to meet publication costs. When James and John Harper decided to set up on their own account, James solicited orders from various New York booksellers, agreeing to use their respective imprints if each would take a hundred copies. Thus the House of Harper ran no risk in putting a new edition of John Locke's *Essay on Human Understanding* on the market. By 1825 the firm, only eight years old, had so shrewdly gauged the public demand that it was the largest book manufacturer in the United States.[3]

Most of the books sold in America were not only of British authorship, but also were printed and published in Great Britain. Of some four hundred titles advertised in 1801 by Joseph Nancrede of Boston about two hundred and fifty bore a London imprint, while fewer than a hundred had emanated from the United States. Samuel G. Goodrich estimated that in 1820 approximately seventy per cent of the volumes bought by Ameri-

---

[1] Carey had hoped that "many a musty volume . . . would find a ready market, when transported to the banks of the Susquehanna, the Potomack, or the Santee." *Ibid.* See also *Gazette of the United States,* July 16, 1802; *Aurora,* June 29, 1803; Bradsher, *Mathew Carey,* 15-22.

[2] E. P. Oberholtzer, *Literary History of Philadelphia* (Phila., 1906), 343-344.

[3] J. H. Harper, *The House of Harper* (N. Y., 1912), 15-18.

cans were of British production. A decade later, however, the proportion had fallen to thirty per cent, a change which he attributed to a combination of factors — the vigorous enforcement of tariff regulations, the increased activity of American printers and publishers and the rising national spirit after the War of 1812.[1] But this does not mean that native authors were coming into their heritage, for they continued to be hampered by the absence of an international copyright. It was cheaper for publishers to pirate English "best-sellers" and ignore aspiring American writers. The situation became acute when Scott and then Dickens swept the country; and it was not soon remedied.[2] Carey, knowing well the uncertainties of a transatlantic voyage, engaged fast sailboats to get him copies of new *Waverley* novels before incoming ships touched quarantine. The brothers Harper established a record by reprinting *Peveril of the Peak* in twenty-one hours.[3]

The mechanics of printing had changed little since Benjamin Franklin's youth. Two "partners," as they were called, were still required to run the wooden hand presses.[4] While one applied the ink with hard-stuffed balls, the other laid on the sheets and did the "pulling." In later years Thurlow Weed recalled how he and James Harper, apprentice lads at a New York shop in 1816, managed each day to do a third of a day's work before breakfast, morning after morning, in order to earn overtime.[5] Harper already had established his own publishing house when iron presses, invented in England, began

[1] S. G. Goodrich, *Recollections of a Lifetime* (N. Y., 1856), II, 388-389.

[2] See Fish, *Rise of the Common Man*, 248-249, and A. M. Schlesinger, *The Rise of the City, 1878-1898* (*A History of American Life*, X), 251-255.

[3] Bradsher, *Mathew Carey*, 80; Harper, *House of Harper*, 23-24.
[4] *Ibid.*, 8-9.
[5] Thurlow Weed, *Autobiography* (Harriet A. Weed, ed., Boston, 1883), 57.

in the 1820's to drive out the wheezy wooden ones
and composition rollers began to replace the familiar
and foul-smelling ink balls.

Though the mechanical improvements in printing
were few and simple, remarkable progress was made in
bringing to America the art of bookmaking. On the eve
of the Revolution, Christopher Sauer had cast enough
pica at Germantown, Pennsylvania, to print a small edition of the Bible, but the early type foundries were generally short-lived.[1] Not until 1796 did Binney and
Ronaldson, two Scotch artisans, establish a considerable
business in Philadelphia; and for several years they had no
competitors save in Hartford and New York.[2] Publishing houses were soon boasting that standards in the
United States were equal to those of Great Britain. In
presenting his first quarto edition of the Bible, Mathew
Carey announced in 1804 that its production had been
"all American."[3] Similarly, when the second volume
of Alexander Wilson's *Ornithology* appeared in 1810,
reviewers did not forget that "the exquisite paper, the
distinct type, the correct engraving," as well as the press-
work and the binding, were all domestic.[4] Illustrations
continued to be costly and were often unsatisfactory.
Copperplate engravings, in which American silversmiths
tried vainly to surpass the English, had to be imported if
superior work was desired. After 1793, when Alexander Anderson, a medical graduate of Columbia, perfected his engravings on wood, magazines were more

---

[1] W. W. Pasko, ed., *American Dictionary of Printing and Bookmaking*
(N. Y., 1894), under type foundries.
[2] T. L. De Vinne, "American Printing." C. M. Depew, ed., *One Hundred Years of American Commerce* (N. Y., 1895), I, 314 ff. In 1813
David and George Bruce, improving on the experiments of the Englishman, Dr. John Watts, were beginning to make use of stereotyping by the
plaster process.
[3] *Literary Mag. and Am. Register*, I, 240.
[4] Only the colored ink had been imported. *Medical Repository*, XIV
(1810-1811), 48.

generously, though still indifferently, illustrated.   In 1819 a lithograph, first developed by French inventors, appeared in the July issue of the *Analectic Magazine*, and book publishers quickly realized the possibilities of this relatively cheap process.[1] By 1820 Philadelphia was regarded as a publishing center second only to London among English-speaking cities.

In the transit of printing from the Old World to the New the contribution of European-trained artisans was constantly supplemented by the work of native-born craftsmen who carried forward much fruitful experimentation.   This was notably true of those who might be called alumni of Isaiah Thomas's school.   Their preceptor, as editor of the *Massachusetts Spy* and the *Massachusetts Magazine*, publisher of English classics, historian of his craft in America and manager of several bookstores, brilliantly exemplified the multiple functionary. In his establishment at Worcester many a master printer learned not only to make fine books but also to study and cherish them.[2]

Between publishers and writers an uncertain liaison was maintained by numerous literary associations.   New York had the Friendly Club (1792), in which Charles Brockden Brown, William Dunlap and James Kent were prominent, and the Belles-Lettres Club (1799) whose members probably inspired the *Salmagundi Papers*.[3] In Boston was the Anthology Society whose meetings were characterized by much good talk and many probing questions as its members criticized manuscripts for their monthly periodical, the magazine which Edward T. Channing, Richard Henry Dana and others later trans-

[1] Mott, *History of American Magazines*, 131-132.
[2] John Russell, *An Address Presented to the Members of the Faustus Association* (Boston, 1808), 21-22; President of the American Antiquarian Society, *Communication to the Members* (Worcester, 1814).
[3] Adolf Growoll, *American Book Clubs* (N. Y., 1897), chap. iv; J. W. Francis, *Old New York* (N. Y., 1858), 338-339.

formed into the *North American Review*.[1] Philadelphians organized an Athenaeum (1814), as if the American Philosophical Society, the Library Company and the Academy of Natural Science were not sufficient, and located their reading rooms above Mathew Carey's bookstore. It was neither the first nor the last such venture in this generation. Baltimore's literary circle found its center in the Delphian Club (1816) which welcomed Francis Scott Key, John Howard Payne, Rembrandt Peale and Samuel Woodworth, whose name is forever associated with "The Old Oaken Bucket."[2]

Many literary groups reached out to include every sort of artistic and scientific interest. In a day when versatility distinguished the man of learning, they grew rapidly, emphasizing, as DeWitt Clinton said with magisterial air, that "the communion of cultivated minds must always have a benign influence on knowledge."[3] The prosperous merchants and political leaders whose names appeared in the membership lists were not always unselfishly motivated, but they gave much needed support to those professionally interested in literature, science and the arts. The societies might have accomplished more if they had not become fair targets for satiric critics amused by the pretentious display of "sodalities of vanity."[4] However ineffectual they may have seemed to censorious observers, they developed two significant by-products: the lecture course, containing the essence of the later Lyceum movement, and the library.

In the cities, likewise, the musical tradition derived

[1] M. A. DeWolfe Howe in introduction to Anthology Society, *Journal of the Proceedings of the Society which Conducts the Monthly Anthology & Boston Review* (Boston, 1910), 11-21.

[2] Lippincott, *Early Philadelphia*, 197-199; J. E. Uhler, "The Delphian Club," *Md. Hist. Mag.*, XX, 305-308.

[3] *Introductory Discourse* (N. Y., 1815), 22.

[4] *N. Y. American*, Nov. 24, 1819; March 18, 1820.

from Europe was vigorously maintained. At the beginning of the nineteenth century foreigners, long resident in America, were yielding leadership to others who had recently arrived. In Charleston the St. Cecilia Society, flourishing since 1762, had outgrown its provincial status, while the Bethlehem Moravians continued to set high standards in their choral work, even if their influence failed to reach other parts of the nation. Germans were active in the Euterpean Society in New York after 1799, and they provided the inspiration for the orchestral concerts of Concordia. For a time James Hewitt and his English friends tried to establish London's musical tastes in New York, but in 1812 he moved to Boston where he found fellowship with the Philharmonic Society, founded in 1810 and led by Gottlieb Graupner, a German who had formerly been oboist in Haydn's London Orchestra. From this small orchestral group developed in 1815 the Handel and Haydn Society, chiefly interested in the interpretation of the oratorios of those two composers. Amateurish their performances may have been, but their example was an inspiration to the rural "singing schools" throughout New England.[1]

Probably the most important developments in American musical art during this period were the growth of choral societies and the widening influence of church music. By 1830 even Calvinistic New England had in large part abandoned its hostility to sacred music adapted from the classic composers. Congregational singing was becoming an important part of Protestant worship, and Lowell Mason, who was to be the national leader in this direction, was winning support in Massachusetts for the

[1] Oscar Handlin, *Boston's Immigrants, 1790-1865* (Harvard Historical Studies, L), 151; O. G. Sonneck, *Early Concert Life in America, 1731-1800* (Leipzig, 1907), 118, 310-325; J. T. Howard, *Our American Music, Three Hundred Years of It* (N. Y., 1939), chaps. v-vi.

founding of collections of sacred music in order to stimulate the writing of great hymns.[1]

Though public collections of literary material were not new, most of them were insignificant. The forty-nine in 1800 probably contained fewer than eighty thousand volumes, though the Library Company of Philadelphia and the New York Society Library had been in existence more than sixty years.[2] Within the next quarter-century small collections were established in rapid succession by colleges and academies as well as by literary clubs and learned societies. A writer in the *North American Review* in 1816 thought the best libraries were at Cambridge, Boston and Philadelphia. The first two were particularly strong in theological treatises, Greek and Latin classics and American history, while the Quaker City was esteemed for its works on natural history.[3] New Yorkers learned in 1826 that, though their city was three times as large as Boston, its ten libraries contained only four fifths as many books. Even Baltimore, with but four libraries open to selected readers, possessed three fourths as many volumes as the nation's metropolis.[4] No New Yorker understood the situation better or regretted it more than DeWitt Clinton. Convinced that the government should come to the aid of private benevolence, he proposed to the legislature in 1827 that each school district be permitted to tax itself to establish and maintain libraries for the free use of all its inhabitants. It marked the beginning of the long campaign to create tax-supported libraries.[5]

[1] S. G. Goodrich, *Recollections* (N. Y., 1856), I, 72-73; Fish, *Rise of the Common Man*, 236.

[2] "Public Libraries in the United States," Bureau of Education, *Special Report* (1876), xvi.

[3] *North American Review*, V (1817), 430-431.

[4] James DeKay, *Anniversary Address . . . before the New York Lyceum of Natural History* (N. Y., 1826), 74.

[5] G. W. Cole, "Early Library Development in New York State, 1800-1900," N. Y. Public Library, *Bull.*, XXX, 854-855.

Singularly insensitive to the trend of the times was the critic who complained in 1818 that "all the libraries in America would not furnish materials for a work like Gibbon's Decline of the Roman Empire." [1] He was right; but his fellow countrymen, so far as they wrote history, were much more concerned with the rise of the American republic than with the decline of the Roman Empire. Fixing their attention on the Revolutionary era and its immediate antecedents, some were already engaged in organized endeavors to gather and collate public and private papers. Thus Jeremy Belknap of Boston, John Pintard of New York and Ebenezer Hazard of Philadelphia, eager to emulate the Society of Antiquarians in London, developed a movement for collecting and preserving American antiquities which finally took form in the Massachusetts Historical Society (1791) and the New York Historical Society (1804). These pioneers, setting an example in the high quality of their publications, inspired similar undertakings in all the New England states and Pennsylvania during the twenties, and in 1830 Indiana established the first enduring society beyond the mountains. More comprehensive in scope was the American Antiquarian Society, chartered in 1812 to recruit members "in every part of our Western continent and its adjacent islands." Though its library and museum were located in Worcester, Massachusetts, where Isaiah Thomas, its founder, believed there would be less danger than in Boston from fire and the "ravages" of the enemy, its councilors represented every section, including the trans-Alleghany West, and its chief concern was the history of the nation. [2]

The same desire to hold the past captive impelled several legislatures to create state libraries. Congress in like

---

[1] *North American Review*, VIII (1818), 199-200.
[2] C. L. Nichols, *Isaiah Thomas, Printer, Writer, and Collector* (Boston, 1912), *passim*.

fashion appropriated five thousand dollars in 1800 for the acquisition of books and for "fitting up a suitable apartment for containing them." There was no protest apparently when the first order went to the famous booksellers, Cadell and Davies of London, but fifteen years later the lawmakers, fearing the effect of irreligious and immoral tomes purveying the doctrines of French philosophers and revolutionaries, wrangled long over Jefferson's offer to sell his six thousand books to the Library of Congress. Thereafter important collections of historical materials were added with some regularity.[1]

The increasing accumulation of public documents, pamphlets, newspapers and personalia only slowly influenced historical writing. John G. Palfrey and George Bancroft began to use the libraries of the East in their zealous researches during the twenties. For the most part, however, Americans read their own history in the rather superficial compilations of David Ramsay, William Gordon and John Marshall, the stilted chronicles of Abiel Holmes and Timothy Pitkin, the biographical sketches of Mercy Warren and the pious platitudes of Benjamin Trumbull and Frederick Butler.[2] More widely known, though not necessarily more influential, were the pamphlets and books of "Parson" Weems, who, writing without fear and without research, appropriated oral tradition wherever he found it and embellished it to suit his fancy. But he was not unlike those who set "truth" as their goal, for they, too, believed that history should instruct as well as entertain, that it should preach to the sinner and inspire the patriot.

[1] Lucy Salamanca, *Fortress of Freedom: the Story of the Library of Congress* (Phila., 1942), chaps. i-ii.
[2] For example, David Ramsay, *History of the United States* (Phila., 1816); Abiel Holmes, *The Annals of America* (rev. edn., Cambridge, 1829); Timothy Pitkin, *A Political and Civil History of the United States* (New Haven, 1828); Benjamin Trumbull, *General History of the United States of America* (Boston, 1810); Frederick Butler, *History of the United States to 1820* (Hartford, 1821).

Such historical effusions amazed, when they did not amuse, a generation of Europeans who still enjoyed the literary artistry of Gibbon and were beginning to appreciate the critical acumen of Ranke. But not all American writing was so lightly dismissed. Though most English reviewers continued to sneer, there were occasional signs of change. In 1824 *Blackwood's* ran a series of respectful articles on "American Writers," prepared by John Neal, who had been born in Maine.[1] "How wonderfully America is rising in the scale of intellect!" wrote Mary Russell Mitford after reading *The Last of the Mohicans*. "Depend on it that America will succeed us as Rome did Athens."[2] The tribute was mildly patronizing, to be sure, but it seemed sincere, a prelude to the long-deferred recognition of America's intellectual independence.

[1] Neal was not modest about the merits of his own works, and English editors may have regarded his boasting as characteristically American. Bradsher, *Mathew Carey*, 66-67.

[2] Mary Russell Mitford, *Life . . . Told by Herself in Letters to Her Friends* (A. G. K. L'Estrange, ed., N. Y., 1870), II, 60.

CHAPTER XIV

URBAN INFLUENCES

IN the broadening and deepening of American culture
the larger centers of population, as we have seen, exerted
a pervasive influence. Cities were growing steadily if
not spectacularly during the first three decades of the
nineteenth century. If one accepts the highly dubious
enumerations of the early United States census reports,
there were four times as many urban communities of
8000 or more in 1830 as there had been in 1790, and
they represented a fifteenth as against a thirtieth of the
nation's inhabitants. The twenty-six cities of 1830,
totaling a population close to 865,000, had experienced
their most rapid growth during the preceding decade.[1]
While none could boast of a status comparable to that of
metropolitan London or Paris or Vienna, each was reaching out along the routes of improved roads and newly
dug canals to enlarge its economic and cultural hinterland. New York and Philadelphia had passed the
150,000 mark, and the other seaports — Baltimore,
Boston, New Orleans and Charleston — followed in that
order. But it was such river towns as Albany, Pittsburgh, Cincinnati and Louisville that had shown the
greatest rate of increase in the fifteen years following the
peace of Ghent.

In this period Americans, despite temporary setbacks,
were finding additional uses for power derived from
waterfalls. Small-scale manufacturing, thriving artifi-
cially behind the protective barriers of embargo, nonin-

[1] *U. S. Tenth Census* (1880), *Manufactures*, xxii; A. F. Weber, *The
Growth of Cities in the Nineteenth Century* (Columbia Univ., *Studies*,
XI), 22-23.

tercourse and war, seemed to shrink with distressing
speed when exposed to the combined pressures of European competition and the declining business cycle.[1] The
tariff of 1816, even with the principle of minimal valuation, did not suffice to keep Rhode Island's cotton mills
open, and Pennsylvania and New York ironmasters reported that bar-iron importations doubled during the
first year the act was in force.[2] Manufacturers everywhere sought governmental aid, but relief actually came
from other quarters. American concern for the practical, which Europeans had often remarked, was happily
attended by an awareness of the opportunities in a
steadily expanding domestic market, thanks to the constantly improving lines of transportation and to the
fewness of governmental regulations. An additional
impetus came from the desire, stimulated by the rising
nationalistic temper, to be free from dependence on foreign producers.

The result was an impressive growth in manufacturing enterprises, first apparent in the 1820's.[3] Ingenious
mechanics, trained in America and abroad, invented new
machines and improved old techniques. Merchants and
landlords turned from wharf and farm to calculate the
possibilities of factory and forge — and were convinced.
Occasionally technical skill and financial resources were
combined with remarkable effectiveness. In 1814 Francis Cabot Lowell, Boston merchant, and Paul Moody, a
mechanic, perfected the power loom and, installing it in
the mills of the Boston Manufacturing Company at
Waltham, established the first cotton factory to perform

[1] *American State Papers* (Wash., 1832-1861), *Finance*, II, 666 ff.;
Adam Seybert, *Statistical Annals of the United States* (Phila., 1818),
8-9; K. W. Rowe, *Mathew Carey, a Study in American Economic Development* (Johns Hopkins Univ., *Studies*, ser. LI, no. 4), 44-46.

[2] F. W. Taussig, *The Tariff History of the United States* (N. Y.,
1923), 17-18, 31, 35.

[3] *U. S. Tenth Census, Manufactures*, 542-544.

every operation necessary to convert the raw fiber into cloth.[1] Just as Samuel Slater's spindles had made deep inroads into household spinning, so mechanized weaving, with its numerous improvements, cast the long shadow of the factory system over the craftsman at the loom. By 1830 probably half the cottons, woolens and linens used in Eastern communities came from domestic factories. Imports, except the finer fabrics and pattern weaving, had sharply declined while household production was steadily retreating toward the frontier.[2]

As long as the machine was harnessed to water power, Nature played a major rôle in locating industries. The Blackstone River between Worcester and Providence, though not a mighty stream, had scores of ironworks, machine shops, woolen and cotton mills along its course by 1830. The best sites for dams were being marked on the Merrimack, where the textile town of Lowell was established in 1826. The Connecticut and the Hudson turned the wheels of mills producing a variety of specialties, such as ironware, firearms, lumber and flour. Factory industry was also extending into Pennsylvania, northern New Jersey and parts of Maryland and Delaware,[3] and already the prongs of industrial activity were jutting westward along the route of the Erie Canal and following the tributaries of the Ohio, from western Pennsylvania to northern Kentucky.[4] Even within these boundaries factory production met with resistance, nowhere more stubborn than in the Philadelphia district

[1] Nathan Appleton, *Introduction of the Power Loom, and Origin of Lowell* (Lowell, 1858), 8-10; Caroline F. Ware, *The Early New England Cotton Manufacture* (N. Y., 1931), 60-63.

[2] The data for such estimates were later compiled in Louis McLane's report for 1832, 22 Cong., 1 sess., *House Exec. Docs.*, no. 308.

[3] V. S. Clark, *History of Manufactures in the United States, 1607-1860* (Carnegie Inst., *Publs.*, no. 215 B), I, 464-466; A. H. Cole, *The American Wool Manufacture* (Cambridge, 1926), II, 281-283.

[4] Isaac Lippincott, *A History of Manufactures in the Ohio Valley to the Year 1860* (N. Y., 1914), 79-127.

with its strong tradition of craftsmanship among hand weavers of woolens and ginghams.

The Americanization of the machine in these years contributed only indirectly to the population of the larger cities. Its influence was most palpable in creating new mill villages and factory towns. Even in the Northeastern states, most workers still lived in the rural environment of the small village. Where children toiled long hours, as in Rhode Island cotton mills, there was a marked preference for the family system of employment rather than the English apprenticeship. Parental control relieved employers of many responsibilities and the family group provided a welcome basis for social stability.[1] In Massachusetts, where young women, drawn into the textile factories from the neighboring countryside, constituted more than sixty per cent of the operatives, owners strove deliberately to make tending a machine seem as honorable as any other form of decent labor. Far more concerned with the moral welfare of their employees than with hours, wages and working conditions, they established strict codes of conduct and supervised carefully the company dormitories or boarding houses in which the young women were expected to live.[2]

The factory's worst features probably were not unlike the evil conditions described in the famous Shaftesbury report to the House of Commons, but what completely differentiated the American from the British scene was the spirit of the workers. Few thought of themselves as perennially dependent on the machine. For the young women, employment meant a small cash income during the years before marriage. The young men hoped it

[1] Ware, *New England Cotton Manufacture*, 63-65.
[2] H. A. Miles, *Lowell as It Was and as It Is* (Boston, 1845), 67-166; J. R. Commons and others, eds., *A Documentary History of American Industrial Society* (Cleveland, 1910-1911), VII, 137.

would be an aid to more remunerative positions or to professional careers in the larger towns; and so it was for many of them.

Such organization as American labor achieved before 1830 was among skilled artisans rather than factory and mill operatives. The unions of printers, cordwainers, carpenters and others in Philadelphia, New York and Boston represented the attempt of skilled craftsmen to protect themselves against the growing power of merchant capitalists. Relying upon the strike or "turnout," as they called it, in their disputes with employers, they encountered widespread hostility to any policy which encouraged violence and public disorder. Press and pulpit inveighed against any who would spread a spirit of discontent and insubordination among thrifty and prosperous native-born mechanics. More effective, however, in curbing the incipient labor organizations was the fact that, under the prevailing construction of the common law, any combination of workingmen for the purpose of raising wages was illegal. Six times between 1805 and 1815 local associations of shoemakers were charged with criminal conspiracy in restraint of trade and four times they were brought to trial.[1]

When the first city central union — the Mechanics' Union of Trade Associations — was formed in Philadelphia, some believed that labor was becoming class conscious. If by this they meant that American workers viewed with dismay the widening gulf between the rich and the poor, they were correct. Yet there was little agreement among skilled craftsmen and unskilled laborers concerning the methods by which that gulf could be bridged. In Philadelphia the Mechanics' Union advocated political action and in the columns of its journal,

[1] J. R. Commons and others, *History of Labour in the United States* (N. Y., 1918), I, chap. iii; Mary R. Beard, *Short History of the American Labor Movement* (N. Y., 1920), 84-89.

the *Mechanics' Free Press,* stated the program of the Workingmen's party. In 1829 they held the balance of power between the two older parties in the city, a success which inspired imitation in New York, Boston, Albany and other Eastern cities.

Assuming that social inequality and economic exploitation could be corrected in part by legislation, the labor parties generally agreed on what was needed. Saying little about wages, hours and working conditions in mill and shop, they stressed the importance of free, democratic education, mechanics' lien laws, abolition of banking monopolies and reform of the judicial system. In New York and elsewhere this program was quickly championed by doctrinaire reformers who knew little about the attitude of American workers and often misjudged the temper of the men and women whose support they desired. Factionalism in New York prevented the party from capitalizing on its local successes. Lacking political experience and baffled by the vigorous counterattacks of conservatives, the trade unionists discovered that their most articulate leaders did not come from the ranks of the workers. They were embarrassed, if not politically injured, by the ardor of Robert Dale Owen, fresh from the coöperative community which his father had established at New Harmony, Indiana, in 1825, and by the vigorous campaigning of Frances Wright, who mingled arguments favoring women's rights and denouncing revealed religion with her pleas for free, public education.[1]

Although these early ventures in politics were local in scope and of brief duration, they brought labor's demands into public discussion. By 1830 a score of publications presented the workers' point of view with fairness. Trade-union membership steadily increased. If

[1] W. R. Waterman, *Frances Wright* (Columbia Univ., *Studies,* CXV, no. 1), chap. iv.

the political strength of the Workingmen's parties fell off, their proposals gradually won the support of both Jacksonians and Whigs, as the strategists in the more conservative parties maneuvered for the vote of enfranchised mechanics in the larger towns.[1]

Expanding industry generally looked to the city for its dollars. Though many a successful lawyer or prosperous farmer or inventive artisan so invested his surplus funds, the chief support came from the merchants of the seaports. Boston canal promoters might fail to link their city with a profitable hinterland, but Boston capital, accumulated in many an adventurous voyage to China and the South Seas, built mill villages on the Merrimack and the Connecticut and controlled the factories of Waltham, Lowell and Haverhill. The Lowells, Lawrences, Jacksons and Lees became much more powerful in the textile mills than they had ever been at the ocean's edge.[2] In a similar fashion Benjamin Marshall, with twenty years' profits from foreign trade, gave new impetus to the weaving of fine cottons in the Hudson and Mohawk valleys.[3] Philadelphia, Baltimore and New York capitalists, unlike those of Boston, found abundant opportunities for industrial investment in their own cities, but in no Atlantic port before 1830 had the speed of machines become more important than the skill of craftsman and mariner.

Factory labor, just becoming significant in the structure of urban society, attracted few foreign-born immigrants. Though the era of reconstruction and repression following the Napoleonic wars sent thousands from Great Britain, Ireland and the south German states

[1] See C. R. Fish, *The Rise of the Common Man* (*A History of American Life*, V), 181 ff.

[2] For Boston capital and industrial enterprise, see Vera Shlakman, *Economic History of a Factory Town* (Smith College, *Studies*, XX), 24-47.

[3] A. C. Flick, ed., *History of the State of New York* (N. Y., 1933-1938), VI, 195-196.

to American shores, most of them represented the substantial middle classes rather than the desperately underprivileged. Merchants and men of professional competence mingled with skilled mechanics and thrifty yeomen
in the holds of westbound ships.[1] Peasants who lacked
both craftsmanship and resources had to start their New
World experience as unskilled laborers, building turnpikes and digging canals. Probably more than two hundred and twenty thousand immigrants arrived in the
period between 1815 and 1830, at least three fourths of
them from the United Kingdom.[2] At times the Irish
equaled the combined English, Scotch and Welsh contingents; but less than half the Irish were Gaelic and
Catholic, for Ulster and other Protestant districts also
lost many of their artisans and farmers in this migration.[3]

Generally the immigrant, if he seemed healthy and
law-abiding, was sure of a cordial welcome from a nation
which assumed that it could never get too many workers
and that social assimilation would easily follow legal
naturalization. Fights occurred occasionally on city
streets, but organized hostility, nourished by political
fear, religious bigotry and economic rivalry, flared up
only where the foreign element, instead of adjusting itself to New World conditions, seemed to be creating an

[1] William Faux, *Memorable Days in America* (London, 1823), 29-
30; M. L. Hansen, *The Atlantic Migration, 1607-1860* (A. M. Schlesinger, ed., Cambridge, 1940), 97-98, 121. It should be noted, however, that there were complaints concerning the poverty of newly arrived
immigrants throughout the decade of the twenties. See J. B. McMaster,
A History of the People of the United States (N. Y., 1883-1913), VI,
82-84.

[2] The peak years were 1817 and 1818, during the decade that followed
the Congress of Vienna. Europeans looked with some disfavor on the
United States for several years after the depression of 1819. Hansen,
Atlantic Migration, 107-119. See also S. C. Johnson, *History of Emi-
gration from the United Kingdom to North America* (London School of
Economics and Politics, *Studies*, no. 34), 16.

[3] W. F. Adams, *Ireland and Irish Emigration to the New World from
1815 to the Famine* (*Yale Hist. Publs. Miscellany*, XXIII), 158.

environment of its own. When the Irish in New York, Baltimore and other cities had grown numerous enough to support their own churches, newspapers, social clubs and political leaders, native Americans became acutely conscious of the alien. Their attempts to handle the problem were often conceived in ignorance and carried out in bitterness — warning signals, even before 1830, of the rising spirit of nativism.[1]

Relatively few immigrants entered this country south of Chesapeake Bay or northeast of the Hudson except those who landed at Charleston or Boston.[2] New York, Philadelphia and Baltimore were the chief distributing centers. Here the newcomer, whatever his nationality, was apt to find a helping hand from those of his own kind. Various "national" societies, primarily concerned with combating nostalgia and promoting conviviality among their members, extended financial relief to indigent compatriots and helped them find employment. In New York, for example, the English had the St. George's Society and the Ancient Britons; the Scots made their contributions through the St. Andrew's Society and the Caledonians; while the German Society enlisted support from John Jacob Astor and Stephen Van Rensselaer. The French Benevolent Society, probably because of widespread sympathy for the early refugees, received funds from the common council until 1817.[3] Most active of all were the organizations that aided Irish arrivals.[4] Baltimore's Hibernian Society, the Irish Emi-

[1] See Fish, *Rise of the Common Man*, 115, and R. A. Billington, *The Protestant Crusade, 1800-1860* (N. Y., 1938), chap. i.

[2] Oscar Handlin, *Boston's Immigrants, 1790-1865* (*Harvard Hist. Studies,* L), 41-42; Mrs. St. Julien Ravenel, *Charleston, the Place and the People* (N. Y., 1906), chap. iv. By 1825 New Orleans was becoming important as a port of entry.

[3] Common Council of the City of New York, *Minutes, 1784-1831* (N. Y., 1917), VII, 256; VIII, 121, 454.

[4] James Hardie, *Description of the City of New York* (N. Y., 1827), 291-292.

grant Association of Philadelphia and similar groups in New York, finding their slender resources for charity unequal to the demand, urged Congress in 1817 to set aside certain sections of public lands for Irish colonization. The lawmakers, however, felt that the problem of the needy immigrant could still be handled by private benevolence, especially when lands in trans-Appalachia were attractive to settlers at prices as high as forty or fifty dollars an acre.[1]

Prudential coöperation also manifested itself in the mutual-benefit societies for native workers. Printers, cordwainers, carpenters and many others thus sought a modicum of insurance against illness, misfortune and untimely death.[2] Such organizations, restricted in their charities by the self-interest of members, were welcomed by the property holders of the community, anxious to promote thrift and reduce the tax burden. Their own sense of social responsibility sometimes went no further than the formation of associations to combat petty crimes and protect property.[3] They were more interested in getting rid of the pauper than in curing poverty. This was not, however, the dominant spirit of the period; and accumulated wealth made it possible for a larger number than ever before in America to translate their benevolent sentiments into action.

The humanitarian movement, thus capturing their financial support, was complex in its motivation and comprehensive in its aims. Such unity as it possessed came from a confident belief in human perfectibility and social progress. Its strength derived from the Enlightenment, from the idealism of English liberals, from the

[1] McMaster, *History*, IV, 390-392; Hansen, *Atlantic Migration*, 93-94.
[2] One of the most successful was the General Society of Mechanics and Tradesmen, incorporated in New York in 1792. Hardie, *Description of New York*, 294.
[3] R. T. Thompson, *Colonel James Neilson* (New Brunswick, 1940), 291-295.

reforming zeal of French humanitarians and their converts in Europe, and from the quiet but effective example of the Society of Friends.[1] Christian charity, as interpreted by Protestant and Catholic, by orthodox and liberal, played its part; yet on most fronts humanistic considerations were becoming ever more powerful.[2] ·Indeed, these early years of the nineteenth century were notable for the advance in the secularization as well as the organization of philanthropic effort.

In America the seaboard cities became centers of humanitarian reform. Increasing population emphasized the need for it, while broadening contacts with Europe brought knowledge of what was going forward in other parts of the world. Charity reached out to every sort — widows and orphans, aged seamen and unfortunate debtors, poor seamstresses and repentant Magdalens, the oppressed in foreign lands and the unemployed at home. Nowhere in the United States did poverty reveal such protean forms as it had displayed in Hogarth's London, but Philadelphia, Baltimore and New York, with a mild dissent from Boston, reported that it was on the increase. Even the most enlightened students of the problem believed that individual faults rather than social conditions

[1] Philanthropic effort also owed much to the humane societies established· in imitation of Dutch and English societies for the purpose of administering aid to "persons who meet with such accidents as to produce in them the appearance of death." In New England this life-saving activity long persisted; elsewhere the humane societies frequently became nuclei for a wide variety of charitable enterprises. William Tudor, *A Discourse Delivered before the Humane Society* (Boston, 1817), 19-64; *Medical Repository*, IX (1805-1806), 328; *Sketch of the Origin and Progress of the Humane Society of the City of New York* (N. Y., 1814); H. M. Lippincott, *Early Philadelphia* (Phila., 1859), 219.

[2] The "charity" sermon, which most congregations expected at some time during the church year, received more attention from the press than any other pulpit pronouncements. For examples, see Abiel Abbott, *A Discourse Delivered . . . on the Lord's Day, August 9, 1807* (Portsmouth, 1807); J. B. Romeyn, *The Good Samaritan* (N. Y., 1810); P. M. Whelpley, *A Sermon Delivered on the Fourth of February, 1816* (N. Y., 1816); John Pierce, *A Discourse Delivered on the Ninth of November, 1817* (Boston, 1818).

explained the plight of the poor. Philadelphia's charitable organizations in 1817 reported that destitution was the result of prolonged idleness, excessive indulgence in intoxicants and extravagant spending for food, fuel and clothing. To this list New York's Society for the Prevention of Pauperism in 1818 added ignorance, imprudent marriages, gambling and incontinence. In both cities the many charitable agencies duplicated one another's efforts to such an extent as to enable "vicious rogues and sturdy beggars" to live off the bounty of the public. There was obvious need for a revision of relief methods.[1]

Reliance on the almshouse temporarily increased, especially after John Van Ness Yates's report of 1824 persuaded New York state to adopt a program of setting up county poor farms.[2] However enlightened the policy seemed at the moment, especially against the background of contemporary British debate over the poor laws, these institutions soon were filled beyond capacity with a motley crowd of unfortunates, young and old, feeble-minded and vicious, crippled and diseased. Since the typical almshouse was an appalling place, humanitarians stressed the need for other and better accommodations. Increasing support was given to hospitals ministering to the poor. The Pennsylvania Hospital in Philadelphia, the New York Hospital, the Charity Hospital in New Orleans and the Massachusetts General in Boston pioneered in applying new methods of caring for the indigent insane, based upon the ideas of Philippe Pinel in France and the work of his English disciples. But little could be accomplished until state appropriations, supple-

[1] Managers of the Society for the Prevention of Pauperism in New York, *First Annual Report* (N. Y., 1818); Massachusetts Temperance Society, *Annual Report* (Boston, 1819); Handlin, *Boston's Immigrants*, 22, 227; McMaster, *History*, IV, 525-529.

[2] The Yates report is reprinted in New York State Board of Charities, *Annual Report for 1900*, I, 937-1145.

menting or replacing private charity, made possible separate institutions which received charity patients. As a result, the majority of the mentally sick continued to be incarcerated in jails and almhouses or kept in solitary confinement in private homes, the victims of ignorance and indifference.[1] The first institution to care for the physically handicapped was the American Asylum at Hartford, where the Reverend Thomas Gallaudet, lately returned from studying English and French methods, began in 1817 to conduct a school for deaf mutes.[2] New York copied his system and in 1820 the Pennsylvania Institution at Philadelphia undertook to care for such unfortunates from New Jersey and Maryland as well as those within the state.[3]

Upon no inmates did the almshouse leave a more disastrous impression than upon children, whose only refuge it was until they could be bound out to some form of service. Public authorities did little to improve conditions until feminine interest was roused to the point of action. The Boston Society for the Care of Girls, of which Abigail Adams was a member, established a Female Asylum in 1803, which became the prototype of many others in New England's seaports. Likewise a group of pious women in New York, who had secured a charter as the Society for the Relief of Poor Widows with Small Children, enlarged their benevolence and created an Orphan Asylum Society in 1806 which followed the plans of Francke's famous asylum at Halle. Such institutions were an inspiration to the various religious sects, and soon Catholic, Hebrew and Protestant

[1] *Medical Repository*, XV (1811-1812), 87-88; New York Academy of Medicine, *Transactions*, I (1847), 2-31; H. B. Shafer, *The American Medical Profession, 1783-1850* (N. Y., 1936), 116-119.

[2] T. H. Gallaudet, *A Discourse Delivered at the Dedication of the American Asylum* (Hartford, 1821), 9-15; H. W. Syle, *A Biographical Sketch of Thomas H. Gallaudet* (Phila., 1887), 16-25.

[3] Emerson Davis, *The Half Century* (N. Y., 1851), 107-111.

churches were making at least partial provision for their own children.

Concern for the underprivileged extended to the criminal. The last two decades of the eighteenth century had witnessed reforms in the penal codes of several states. Not all the barbarous penalties of colonial days were swept away, but the pillory, whipping post and branding iron were less in demand. Moreover, the list of offenses for which one could be hanged was steadily diminishing, while the jail, which had once been merely a house of detention between arrest and punishment, became a house of correction.[1] In 1794 Pennsylvania built a prison at Philadelphia, which may be regarded as the beginning of the penitentiary system in the United States. Within two decades New York, Virginia, Massachusetts, Vermont and Maryland followed this example, each reproducing the worst as well as the best features of the original.[2]

Penal reform, which was but one phase of the humanitarianism of this period, received particular impetus from the societies organized to aid imprisoned debtors. These unfortunates, incarcerated in foul jails and workhouses perhaps for trifling debts, often depended on charitable groups for food, fuel and clothing. Their plight, paraded at times in the press, inspired a long campaign to secure revision of state laws governing debtor-creditor relations and to compel public support of those in prison. It also led to investigations of prison conditions in the larger cities and arguments concerning the methods and purposes of punishment. Boston, Baltimore and New York followed Philadelphia's ex-

[1] H. E. Barnes, *The Repression of Crime* (N. Y., 1926), 86 ff.; J. S. Taylor, *A Comparative View of Punishments Annexed to Crime in the United States of America and in England* (London, 1831).
[2] O. F. Lewis, *The Development of American Prisons and Prison Conditions, 1776-1845* (Albany, 1922), 30; Blake McKelvey, *American Prisons* (Univ. of Chicago, *Social Service Series*, 1936), 5-7.

ample in supporting societies that expanded the relief of distressed debtors into a broad program of penal reform.[1]

No one more strikingly represented the reform spirit than Thomas Eddy. Born into the Society of Friends in Philadelphia, he moved to New York where his success in business enabled him to devote considerable leisure time to public affairs. His particular service was coördination of European theories and the Quaker tradition with the practical benevolence of America's leading merchants. Familiar with the writings of Beccaria, Montesquieu and John Howard, he constantly exchanged views with such contemporaries as Benjamin Rush, Roberts Vaux and DeWitt Clinton. As with most of his colleagues, his humanitarian zeal was not confined within narrow limits, but he gave first place to any program which looked toward reformation of the criminal. By precept and example he was really laying the foundation of a new profession, that of penologist and prison executive.[2]

The reformer's reach constantly tended to exceed his grasp. As warden of Newgate in Greenwich Village, Eddy designed and operated for several years a prison which he later regarded as a caricature of his highest ideals. The Walnut Street jail, built in 1790, was better than any which Philadelphia had previously known, but by 1827 it was described as a place of filth and immorality. Baltimore and Boston reported similar conditions, while New York state with a minimum of foresight was planning the penitentiary later known as Sing Sing. In 1830 the congregate system of confinement was still prevalent, though since 1816 Auburn in

[1] *Am. Medical and Philos. Register*, IV (1813-1814), 632-637; S. L. Mitchill, *The Picture of New-York* (N. Y., 1807), 112 ff.; McMaster, *History*, IV, 532-534.
[2] S. L. Knapp, *Life of Thomas Eddy* (N. Y., 1834), 40-57.

New York had used the single-cell construction except in one wing.[1] The regimen behind bars was a matter of heated argument, even among the reformers; and experimentation produced two schools of thought which long contested the field.[2] Some supported the Pennsylvania system, based on the disciplinary effectiveness of solitary confinement at hard labor, while others supported Auburn's plan of congregate work by day, with silence enforced, and separate cells at night.

It was widely supposed that juvenile delinquency was increasing, and so it was in the cities, though there is no way to determine whether it was increasing more rapidly than the population. Characteristically American were the two most common proposals for reform: imposition of new restrictions on dissolute youth, and more adequate instruction in useful trades. Rarely did anyone survey the social environment which harbored the vagrant, or ask what was happening to apprenticeship in the various crafts, or suggest wholesome recreation as a substitute for rowdyism on the city streets.

In the prisons classification of inmates got little beyond separation of the sexes, but the demand was rising for a logical segregation according to the ages and types of offenders. Brushing aside considerations of cost, philanthropists offered to assist the state, if necessary, in distinguishing between "novices in guilt" and "convicts whose hearts are seared to remorse and penitence."[3] In New York, for instance, the Society for the Prevention of Pauperism, having denounced existing prisons as nurseries of vice and crime, joined forces with the Society for the Reformation of Juvenile Delinquents in establishing a House of Refuge in 1825. This reforma-

[1] Gershom Powers, *Brief Account of the Construction, Management and Discipline of the New York State Prison at Auburn* (N. Y. 1826).

[2] See Fish, *Rise of the Common Man*, 259.

[3] Lewis, *Development of American Prisons*, 16-17.

tory, modeled on a similar London institution, did not long remain alone in America, for Boston's house of refuge opened its doors in 1826 and Philadelphia followed two years later.[1]

If the literature of reform reveals an awareness of the increase of poverty and vagrancy, it also shows a growing concern over how the less privileged classes used their idle time. By the 1820's the tavern as a social center was rapidly disappearing. Its function of providing food and lodging for travelers was being usurped by boarding houses and hotels, while the conviviality of its cheerful taproom was cheaply imitated in grogshops and tippling houses. The more reputable of these latter had become poor men's clubs, where apprentices, mechanics and low-salaried clerks congregated for recreation and refreshment. The lowest elements consorted in dramshops which, neglecting the little formality of securing a license, hid behind the pretense of greengroceries. Every corner grocery was permitted to sell liquor by the penny's worth regardless of the customer's age. In Baltimore and Philadelphia the oystermen, having retreated from the wharves and the street carts into convenient cellars, throve on the patronage of youthful idlers, their establishments becoming rendezvous for pickpockets and other petty thieves. New York's Five Points district, not far from the old Collect Pond, had more than its share of unlicensed rumshops and gaudily decorated halls, where dancing was free to all who bought ale or beer.[2]

The general disapproval of such tawdry pleasures sprang partly from the fact that Americans tended to

1 McKelvey, *American Prisons*, 13-14.
2 Society for the Prevention of Pauperism in the City of New York, *Annual Report for 1822; American Daily Advertiser*, June 5, 12, July 9, 1821, cited in McMaster, *History*, IV, 537-539; W. F. Barnard, *Forty Years at the Five Points* (N. Y., 1893), 1-4.

Low Life in New England

Trap Ball

Fives

Hockey

Shuttlecock

Juvenile Sports

regard any sort of frivolous diversion with suspicion.
Thus, except in certain parts of the South, where the
tradition of gentlemanly leisure flourished, evangelical
Protestants as well as the more pietistic sects frowned
on any profanation of the Sabbath, the one day when
most people could escape the daily grind. Nor were
the actions banned on the Lord's Day necessarily encouraged during the rest of the week, for there was
widespread fear that harmless games might be carried
to excess and that the participants, weary from strenuous
exercise, might temporarily drop their guard in the endless battle against temptation. Amusements, said many,
led to the gambling hall, the tippling house and worse.[1]
As late as 1827 the editor of the *American Farmer* had
to argue that hunting, fishing and other outdoor sports
were beneficial to health and morals, even if they did
afford pleasure in addition.[2]

Nevertheless some Americans coveted the reputation
which sportsmen enjoyed in the Old World. Scorning
the excellent craftsmanship of German-American gun-
makers, they imported "elegant London fowling pieces"
and they were quicker than others to adopt the percus-
sion cap in place of the old flintlock.[3] Although most
persons still considered hunting or fishing a profitable
occupation rather than a sport, there were those in every
large city who took up gun and rod only for recreation.
Occasionally they formed clubs, such as Philadelphia's
exclusive Fishing Company of the State in Schuylkill,
established in 1732, which received Lafayette's praise
in 1825 for its happy combination of exercise and con-

[1] Examples of this attitude may be found in the *New Magazine*, V
(1794), 656-657; *American Museum*, XII (1792), 159; *Massachusetts Missionary Magazine*, I (1803), 465-466; *Christian Examiner*,
VIII (1830), 204-205.

[2] *American Farmer*, IX (1827), 55-56.

[3] *American Shooter's Manual* (Phila., 1827), 103, 233.

viviality.[1] New Yorkers found Long Island a veritable paradise for anglers and hunters.[2] Here, also, they could indulge in fox hunting, though less successfully than in the vicinity of Philadelphia. But nowhere north of Maryland was the chase so important a social event as in the upper South. Planters organized in hunt clubs imitated the English gentry, however much they fell short of the pageantry which surrounded the sport in the older society.[3]

City dwellers unable to seek recreation far afield had nevertheless some opportunity, if they could find time, to test their strength and skill. The English game of fives (similar to modern handball), quoits, ninepins, pitch and toss, battledore and shuttlecock — all these were popular.[4] A Philadelphia archery club, organized in 1828, the first to follow the English rules, set a standard for other devotees of the bow and arrow. Interest in swimming, or rather in salt-water bathing at the public bathhouses, had steadily increased since the day when Benjamin Franklin had first published his famous treatise; but the furor occasioned by Francis Lieber's swimming school, established at Boston in 1827, indicates that not many men and fewer women really knew how to swim. The feats of Lieber's pupils in distance tests, reported widely in the press, amazed readers.[5]

Throughout the North, winter rather than summer was the season when many sought the water's edge.

[1] J. F. Watson, *Annals of Philadelphia* (Phila., 1884), III, 296-297.
[2] R. H. Gabriel, *The Evolution of Long Island* (New Haven, 1921), chap. iii.
[3] *American Farmer*, VII (1825), 271; VIII (1827), 268; J. T. Scharf, *History of Maryland* (Balt., 1879), II, 72; William Elliott, *Carolina Sports* (Columbia, S. C., 1918), 246.
[4] Jennie Holliman, *American Sports, 1785-1835* (Durham, 1931), 72, 78-84.
[5] T. S. Perry, ed., *Life and Letters of Francis Lieber* (Boston, 1882), 77, 95.

Wherever inlet, pond or river offered safe ice, skaters formed a colorful and animated group. Where snow abounded, sleighing attracted even greater numbers. Vehicles of every description were used, from the sleigh with numerous cross seats to the cutter built for two. According to a visitor in New York in 1821,

> Broadway exhibits the gayest scene you can conceive. Painted sleighs, with scarlet cloth and buffalo skins, are dashing along in all directions, at a prodigious speed; some with two horses abreast; some harnessed as tandems, and others with four in hand. Every body seems to make the most of the snow while it lasts, and night does not put an end to the festivity.

It was the one outdoor pastime, all observers agreed, which women universally enjoyed and shared on equal terms with men.

Except for cricket, which still survived in communities where recent English immigrants were numerous, competition in the various participants' sports was generally on an individual basis. Americans had not yet introduced the coöperative effort of team play into their ball games. New England's town ball, developing out of boyhood's one-old-cat and two-old-cat, so reminiscent of English stool ball, and involving the competition of two "sides" or clubs, contained only a slight hint of modern baseball. Like shinny and hockey, it was primarily a boys' game, played with emphasis on individual skill and without benefit of spectators.[2]

In a generation which had not yet given substance to the concept of sportsmanship the spectators' interest in sporting events was apt to center in the wagering of

[1] Adam Hodgson, *Letters from North America* (London, 1824), II, 110.

[2] W. R. Wister, *Some Reminiscences of Cricket in Philadelphia* (Phila., 1904), 4-5; A. G. Spalding, *America's National Game* (N. Y., 1911), 29-39.

money on the outcome. The brutal English amusements of cockfighting and animal baiting, which easily lent themselves to the uses of professional gamblers, persisted in America long after they had lost respectability across the Atlantic. New England sentiment forced the promoters to operate under cover. In the Middle states their activities were condoned but rarely publicized. Only in the South, notably Maryland, Virginia and North Carolina, were these sports publicly conducted and attended by all classes.[1]

By the 1820's Eastern cities reported a remarkable increase of spectators at such events as foot races, walking meets and wrestling bouts. Champion wrestlers usually contented themselves with local conquests, but runners from various sections contested on such well-advertised courses as those at Hoboken, on Long Island and near Philadelphia, where thousands watched races which tested endurance rather than speed.[2] Fashionable society preferred water sports, and boat races, briefly interrupted by the War of 1812, became gala events along the seaboard. Clubs sprang up in all the larger cities to sponsor intersectional as well as local matches. Some, like the Whitehall Aquatic Club of New York or the Savannah Boat Club, gained a national reputation for the graceful lines of their craft and the superiority of their oarsmen.[3]

It was generally believed that anyone who participated regularly in strenuous contests imperiled his health and courted serious injury. Perhaps that explains the fanatical enthusiasm with which the crowds hailed the victors. Particularly in boxing bouts the element of danger was ever present. Tolerant though Americans

[1] *Virginia Argus*, March 20, 1800; *Literary Mag. and Am. Register*, VI (1806), 266; *American Farmer*, IX (1829), 79; *Evening Post*, Feb. 8, 1830.

[2] *Ibid.*, July 6, 1824.

[3] *Ibid.*, Nov. 13, 1820; Dec. 9, 1824.

were of disputes settled by fisticuffs or by gouging in the Western manner, they scorned such commercializing of the fighting instinct as the prize ring represented. Tom Molyneux, the giant freed Negro, who claimed the heavyweight championship of the country at the opening of the century, was more profitable to his promoters in his English fights than in his brief American tour.[1] English pugilists, after encountering the vigorous hostility of the press from Boston to Savannah, frequently abandoned the prize ring to establish "schools" for teaching the "manly science of self-defense." Out of their attempts to encourage amateur boxing arose an interest in systematic exercise at the very moment that several young Germans, Charles Beck, Charles T. Follen and Francis Lieber, were introducing in New England the program of gymnastics advocated by Friedrich Jahn. Thus the least esteemed of spectators' sports was in part responsible for bringing the public, as well as the private, gymnasium to America.[2]

The most socially significant sport was horse racing, with its appeal to all classes and all sections of the country. Its most enthusiastic devotees, as in colonial days, were in the South and in those districts of Kentucky and Tennessee peopled by transplanted Southerners.[3] But there was also a growing interest in Northern communities, especially after New York repealed its prohibition against the sport in 1821. The Union Course, built in that year on Long Island, provided a track which soon became famous for its intersectional races, occasionally attended by as many as

[1] Alexander Johnston, *Ten and Out!* (N. Y., 1927), 18-23.
[2] *Evening Post*, Nov. 27, 1826; June 24, 1830; Friedrich Jahn, *Treatise on Gymnastics* (Charles Beck, tr., Northampton, 1828); J. A. Krout, *Annals of American Sport* (R. H. Gabriel, ed., *The Pageant of America*, New Haven, 1926-1929, XIV), 207.
[3] G. W. Ranck, *History of Lexington, Kentucky* (Cincinnati, 1872), 130.

fifty thousand spectators. Here, in 1823, the Northern champion, American Eclipse, defeated the Southern contender, Sir Henry, in two out of three four-mile heats.[1] None of the metropolitan tracks, however, enjoyed the prestige of the Washington Course at Charleston, where the annual racing week was a gala event in February, or the National Course near Washington, which was a favorite rendezvous for Southern congressmen and at times even lured John Quincy Adams from the presidential desk.[2]

Newspaper and magazine carried wearisome discussions of racing as a means of improving the breed of horses. If sometimes this was designed merely to throw dust in the eyes of those who regarded the jockey clubs as aristocratic promoters of idleness and gambling, the utilitarian considerations were frequently genuine, nowhere more so than in New England and the Middle states, where improved roads and the development of the light wagon or carriage excited interest in the stamina and speed of the trotter. The jockey might still be suspect, but the skilled reinsman was often highly esteemed. Contests on the road were no novelty, and the transfer to the race course came gradually in the early decades of the century. At first trotters and pacers, either under saddle or in harness to high-wheeled sulkies, were driven against time, but formal race meets were soon sponsored by associations of owners and breeders.[3] Probably the most successful were the New York Trotting Club (1825), which built its course near the old Jamaica Turnpike on Long Island, and the Hunting

---

[1] Josiah Quincy, *Figures of the Past* (Boston, 1910), 96-99.

[2] Ravenel, *Charleston*, 129-130; John Quincy Adams, *Memoirs* (C. F. Adams, ed., Phila., 1875), VII, 162.

[3] H. W. Herbert, *Frank Forester's Horse and Horsemanship of the United States and British Provinces of North America* (N. Y., 1857), II, 323-325.

Park Association, organized in Philadelphia in 1828.[1]
The pedigree of Top Gallant, Rob Roy, Tom Thumb
and other winners of the period could usually be traced
back to Messenger, the English thoroughbred imported
in 1788 and owned in New York, or to Justin Morgan,
whose blood strain spread after 1790 from Vermont
into many parts of New England and the Middle states.

If the pleasant excitement of the race track had to be
justified in terms of improving the breed of horses, so
the art and entertainment of the theater were originally
sanctioned by many communities only under the disguise
of "histrionic lectures" or "moral dialogues." The
opposition to stage performances was still numerous and
resourceful. It was complained that plays and players
alike, almost without exception, were from England —
"vile minions from a foreign land." It was further
pointed out that the theater was at times a disorderly
place. The two or three rows of semicircular boxes
might be respectable, but in the gallery above and the
pit below and at the house bar there was plenty of
rowdiness. If the orchestra failed to play a tune demanded by a gallery shout, it was showered with mis-
siles; if the actors failed to please, stale eggs provided
an effective form of dramatic criticism.[2] In some play-
houses a section was set aside for bedizened women of
the town eager to attract attention. Nor could the lives
of the performers always stand scrutiny. The Reverend
John Witherspoon, president of Princeton, declared in
his *Letter Respecting Play Actors* that few of them knew
enough of pure love to depict it on the stage. Perhaps
nothing was so resented by the clergy as the blasphemous

[1] *American Farmer*, VIII (1826), 239-240.
[2] W. W. Clapp, *A Record of the Boston Stage* (Boston, 1853), 11,
23; G. C. D. Odell, *Annals of the New York Stage* (N. Y., 1927-1942),
I, 380.

claim that the theater could join hands with the church as a preacher of good morals and an instructor of youth. In 1790 this seems to have been the dominant religious attitude everywhere except in Charleston, where the church was tolerant of polite amusement and one minister actually wrote a play.[1]

Such antagonism to the stage lingered a long time, but counterinfluences worked against it. For many, the patronage of George Washington settled the propriety of the theater.[2] "It is a concomitant of an independent nation," wrote George Clymer, who had helped to frame the Federal Constitution. Actors and managers strove to reassure the public by promises of circumspect behavior and by insisting that "the stage refin'd, cleansed of its dross," could "charm, instruct mankind."[3] Soon among the emerging playwrights were such persons as Charles Jared Ingersoll and Hugh H. Brackenridge, political leaders in Pennsylvania; Judge Royall Tyler of Massachusetts and Vermont; Colonel David Humphreys, the Connecticut manufacturer; and William Dunlap, New York's genial artist. But it was the rich and fashionable, slowly overcoming the prejudice of many intellectuals, who made possible the naturalization of the theater in America. Mrs. William Bingham's set in Philadelphia accomplished the repeal in 1789 of the prohibitory law. The comparable social group in Boston, led by the Russells, achieved a like result a few years later. In Providence it was the same sort of Federalist coterie which prevented a legal ban.[4]

[1] Oscar Wegelin, Early American Plays, 1714-1830 (N. Y., 1900), 67.
[2] P. L. Ford, Washington and the Theater (N. Y., 1899), 35-44.
[3] William Dunlap, History of the American Theater (London, 1833), II, 360-364; D. R. Fox, "The Development of the American Theater," N. Y. History, XVII, 29.
[4] Charles Blake, An Historical Account of the Providence Stage (Providence, 1868), 79; Clapp, Boston Stage, 5; Dunlap, American Theater, I, 105-109.

So it happened that the young republic welcomed, or at least tolerated, an institution which was frankly maintained by and for the occupants of the boxes, with a glance of respect toward the bachelor critics in the pit. Though the gallery furnished additional income, it was seldom enough to relieve the manager's worries. Prices were so high as to prevent clerks and mechanics from attending regularly. Recurrent epidemics in the Eastern cities, closing theaters with tragic frequency, likewise help to explain the slow growth of a playgoing public.[1]

The American theater bore a provincial relationship to the great center of London. Even the appurtenances of its stagecraft were improved largely through the ingenuity of scenic artists from England. Of English birth and training also were most of the important players, come to the United States to seek a relative distinction on less exacting boards.[2] George Frederick Cooke was the first distinguished actor to arrive, in 1811, but within a decade it had become customary for the greatest of the London stage to make American tours — the Keans, the Mathewses and William Charles Macready. Some like Thomas Wignell in Philadelphia and Thomas A. Cooper in New York settled down to become actor-managers, combining art with business. Others founded theatrical dynasties in America, among them the first Joseph Jefferson, James W. Wallack and Junius Brutus Booth. From England likewise came the talent of the playwright. In the prologue to his comedy, "The Contrast" (1787), Judge Tyler confidently wrote:

> Exult each patriot heart—tonight is shown
> A piece which we may fairly call our own.

[1] At New York's Park Theater in 1798 the scale of prices was: boxes, $2.00; pit, $1.50; gallery, $1.00. Arthur Hornblow, *History of the Theatre in America* (Phila., 1919), I, 246. See also G. O. Willard, *History of the Providence Stage* (Providence, 1891), 38, and Odell, *Annals,* I, 348.

[2] Hornblow, *History of the Theatre,* I, 108-109.

Most Americans, however, distrusted the work of their own countrymen and preferred the foreign play as probably of finer quality.

But here as elsewhere there appeared a growing spirit of independence. London's greatest actors were challenged successfully by Americans — the Canadian-born William B. Wood, whom Philadelphia made one of its own; James H. Hackett, whose business failure in Utica pushed him onto the stage in 1826; and Edwin Forrest of Philadelphia, whose success with Edmund Kean brought his call to stardom in New York and afterward to international fame.[1] Though New York was winning from Philadelphia leadership in the theater, the old capital on the Delaware still retained prestige as the literary center of the drama. The Philadelphia school — James N. Barker, Richard Penn Smith, John A. Stone and Dr. Robert Montgomery Bird — wrote some of the most successful plays of the time, holding their own with their British contemporaries and encouraging younger American aspirants.[2]

Stock characters, destined for long life in the American drama, first trod the boards in these years. There was the British fop, so skillfully caricatured in William Dunlap's "The Father," and the shrewd, sanctimonious, yet good-humored Yankee, first presented in Tyler's "The Contrast" and later developed in Samuel Woodworth's "The Forest Rose." After the success of Stone's "Metamora" in 1829, the stage was attacked by a long line of noble Indians, highly romanticized in the manner of James Fenimore Cooper. The comic Negro also made his debut when Thomas D. ("Daddy") Rice in 1828 began his impersonations of Jim Crow. Not only was he popular in the colorful gallery of distinctively

[1] W. B. Wood, *Personal Recollections of the Stage* (Phila., 1855), 24, 53.
[2] Hornblow, *History of the Theatre*, II, 57-61.

American characters, but he became the dominant figure in the evolution of the minstrel show.[1]

The majority of plays produced were romances and tragedies in the European style rather than portrayals of the American scene.[2] If one desired a glimpse of that high contrast in social conditions still persisting in the Old World, it was to be had across the footlights in New York or Philadelphia. For many of the audience the very sound of intense emotion, nobly expressed in the rhythm of blank verse, offered welcome release. But it was realized that tragedy was too heavy a diet to satisfy everyone. To meet all tastes the main drama was often followed by a farce, interspersed with specialty acts. "Hamlet" might share the boards with some piece like "The What D'ye Call It" and a hornpipe.[3] By 1830 this sort of undifferentiated bill was rapidly passing from the principal theaters, but throughout the nineteenth century the small-town audience expected the villain to appear between the acts and do a turn as a juggler or the ingenue to perform on a slack wire.

The managers discovered one formula that proved highly remunerative: the engagement of a Drury Lane or Covent Garden celebrity to play his most popular rôles with a supporting resident company, usually inferior and invariably ill paid. The starring system, firmly established after George Frederick Cooke's appearances in 1811, may have been discouraging to ambitious American actors, but it attracted an assured business to the box office. Though the New York and Philadelphia managers used this plan with greatest profit,

[1] O. S. Coad, "The Plays of Samuel Woodworth," *Sewanee Rev.*, XXVII (1919), 167-169; Hornblow, *History of the Theatre*, II, 61-62; Carl Wittke, *Tambo and Bones* (Durham, 1930), 20-23.

[2] William Dunlap's sixty-three plays were in large part adaptations from Augustus von Kotzebue, the German dramatist. O. S. Coad, *William Dunlap* (N. Y., 1917), 129-243.

[3] Wood, *Personal Recollections*, 112-113; Odell, *Annals*, I, 324.

Boston succeeded in supporting one playhouse; but a second one, opened in 1827, almost brought disaster to both. Philadelphia regarded Baltimore, Annapolis and even Richmond as part of its theatrical hinterland and often billed its stars with local companies to the uncritical delight of patrons in those cities. Albany enjoyed some reputation as a center of the drama even before 1813 when a permanent playhouse was established. Within a dozen years there was need for a larger building, opened in the year that the Erie Canal was completed.[1]

The most characteristic phenomenon of the American theater was the traveling company, facing hardships along forest trail and primitive woodland roads unknown to its English prototype. But transportation difficulties, however unpleasant, could not keep needy actors from any community where support seemed probable; and after the War of 1812 frontier circuits were organized and supplied with talent, some of it first-rate. In the winter of 1810-1811 residents of Lexington and Frankfort, Kentucky, welcomed their first troupe of professional actors, lately arrived from Montreal and Quebec. Soon actor-managers from Albany, Philadelphia and Charleston competed for patronage along the Ohio and the Mississippi. Samuel Drake and his associates leased theaters in Louisville and Cincinnati as well as Lexington and Frankfort. Noah Miller Ludlow pushed into Tennessee, Alabama and Mississippi as a cultural pioneer, playing wherever he could find some primitive substitute for a stage. In 1818 he audaciously invaded New Orleans, where an excellent French theater held sway, and came away with "no contemptible profit," a measure probably of the growing American population in the city rather than of Ludlow's merit. But it was James Caldwell, English-trained with Charleston

[1] Dunlap, *American Theater*, 149-150.

experience, who laid the foundation of an American theater in New Orleans, extending his interests by 1830 to dominate the entire Mississippi Valley. In the towns where traveling companies stopped en route there was feverish, if not protracted, activity in amateur dramatics. Thespian and Roscian societies, sponsored at times by prominent citizens like Andrew Jackson and Sam Houston, rose and fell in the larger communities from Detroit to Mobile. They did not always overcome a persistent social prejudice, stirred anew by some itinerant revivalist.[1]

The American circus was just beginning to roll out of the cities into the rural villages. It was still in process of evolution. The very word "circus," retaining something of its classical meaning, referred to the building where well-trained performers, usually from England, France or Ireland, gave demonstrations of expert horsemanship. Often the proprietors conducted riding schools in addition. Late in the eighteenth century English equestrian shows, which became the central feature of the American circus, had begun to emphasize mounted clowning and to fill the interludes with tumblers, jugglers and artists on the tight wire. From these exhibitions developed the peripatetic shows, of which in the decade after 1815 probably thirty were moving through the Middle Atlantic states, New England and the upper South. They were small, rarely consisting of more than two or three wagons, six horses and six or eight performers, including an acrobat, a clown and an equestrienne resplendent in unclean satin and spangles and a headdress of slightly bedraggled white plumes. A trumpeter, occasionally assisted by fifers, fiddlers and drummers, performed the function of a band in a rather

[1] N. M. Ludlow, *Dramatic Life as I Found It* (St. Louis, 1880), 96-113, 150-159. Contemporary press notices of the frontier theater are numerous in O. S. Coad and Edwin Mims, jr., *The American Stage* (*Pageant of America*, XIV), 125 ff.

sketchy parade. Not many troupes could boast, as did Buckley and Wick in 1828, that they had forty horses, eight wagons and thirty-five people.[1]

This embryonic circus still lacked a menagerie. Americans, like their European ancestors, were fascinated by exotic animals, but they had not yet brought about the union of the menagerie with the "rolling show."[2] Meanwhile, curiosity was stimulated, but never satisfied, by the exhibition of strange beasts at taverns and country stores, usually with highly embellished explanations from trainers or owners. There were numerous small "zoological gardens" such as Dr. King maintained at 28 Wall Street in New York. He advertised as early as 1789 that he had living specimens of the orangutan, baboon, monkey, ant bear, tiger, porcupine, crocodile and various kinds of snakes.[3] It seems probable that the first elephant was brought from Bengal in 1796 and thereafter in the traveling exhibits quickly surpassed all rivals for popular favor.[4]

The urban dweller in search of entertainment found constant improvement in establishments catering to the multitude. Thousands who could not afford even gallery seats in the theater paid the small admission fee at the waxworks museum. Proprietors might stress the artistic and instructive character of their enterprise, but most of their patrons frankly wanted to be amused. Though humorous subjects gained in favor, Biblical scenes and the figures of military celebrities, church dignitaries, American presidents and British royalty held their places securely.[5] At times waxwork exhibits went on tour

[1] I. J. Greenwood, *The Circus, Its Origins and Growth* (N. Y., 1898), 17, 78, 87, 113-116.

[2] Odell, *Annals,* I, 338.

[3] T. E. V. Smith, *The City of New York in the Year of Washington's Inauguration* (N. Y., 1889), 183; *Columbian Centinel,* April 28, 1810.

[4] Sydney and Marjorie Greenbie, *Gold of Ophir* (N. Y., 1925), 53.

[5] Smith, *New York,* 185-186; J. T. Scharf and Thompson Westcott, *History of Philadelphia* (Phila., 1834), II, 950-951.

or were established as features of the public gardens during the summer.[1] New Yorkers were fond of the Vauxhall Gardens, described in 1807 as two miles out on Bowery Road, where they could listen to band concerts and choral singing or watch displays of fireworks or attend performances by actors from well-known theatrical companies. Other cities had similar amusement parks, but none so nearly reproduced the European *Kursaal* as did Niblo's Columbian Gardens in New York, with its large trees transplanted from distant woods, its flower gardens and exotic plants, and its fountains playing in the sunlight.[2]

Though rural America spent little time and substance on social recreation, the farmer differed only slightly in his outlook from the merchant and the artisan. That urban-rural cleavage, which was to develop into bitter antagonism later in the century, counted as yet for little. Foreign travelers, quick to notice superficial differences based on ethnic or regional customs, felt that these were less significant than an underlying agreement on standards of conduct and moral codes. Perhaps that unity seemed the more striking because wherever they went they encountered manifestations of neo-Puritanism, inspired by the reinvigorated evangelical sects and their pietistic allies. No other force was so potent during these early decades in determining both the urban and the rural outlook in America. As long as the spirit of the city was essentially that of the country village, it retarded the development of a distinctive urbanism.

[1] *Cleaveland Herald*, Oct. 25, 1823.
[2] Mitchill, *New-York*, 156-157; Hornblow, *History of the Theatre*, II, 96-97.

CHAPTER XV

New Sectional Tensions

THE Congress of Vienna, whatever its faults, released Europeans from the grip of war which had continuously held them for more than twenty years. At long last, many of them felt free to seek, in distant lands, the opportunities which had grown almost fantastically alluring during the oppressive years of conflict. For some it seemed imperative to put the Atlantic between them and that Old World system of power politics which had so long bred wars. In individual cases poor harvests, uncertain business prospects, religious discrimination and repressive laws acted as spurs. The pietists of Württemberg and certain near-by Swiss cantons, accepting Czar Alexander's promise of religious freedom, started their wagons and carts eastward toward the Caucasus; artisans from Saxony and Prussia established their crafts in Polish villages; German and Swiss peasants, responding to the inducements of agents from South America, sailed for Brazil. But of those crossing the Atlantic in the fifteen years after the Napoleonic wars only a small minority settled south of Panama. Rio de Janeiro, in spite of efforts of the Brazilian government, enjoyed but a brief rivalry with such ports of entry as Philadelphia and New York.[1] To be sure, the Panic of 1819 and the subsequent depression weakened the faith of Europeans in opportunities in the United States, but both before and after that brief interlude the main stream of migration flowed toward North America.

[1] M. L. Hansen, *The Atlantic Migration, 1607-1860* (A. M. Schlesinger, ed., Cambridge, 1940), 79-81, 113-119.

Hezekiah Niles, trying to achieve an approximately accurate estimate, decided that thirty thousand foreigners had entered the country in 1817 and again in 1818.[1] Probably two thirds came from the British Isles — discouraged farmers from Scotland's marginal lands, English artisans and mill workers fearful of a postwar decline in industry, Irish peasants fleeing from a starvation diet and oppressive leases. French was also heard on the westbound ships, from the lips of Napoleonic veterans, now refugees, and of Alsatian peasants exchanging one uncertainty for another. But the chief Continental groups — those from the German Rhineland or the German-speaking Swiss cantons — were quick to find a new life among the Germans of southeastern Pennsylvania.[2]

The impact of these thousands of Europeans was not fully felt until the depression years after 1819. Prior to that time there seemed to be profitable opportunities for all. The brief postwar boom in Atlantic ports revealed the need for such skills as newly arrived artisans and mechanics possessed.[3] Eastern farmers, now that the victories of Harrison and Jackson had quieted Indian alarms in large sections of the Mississippi Valley, quickened the westward march of population. Many an immigrant, possessed of ready cash, took title to a farm, partially improved by a native American who now saw

[1] *Niles' Wkly. Register*, XIII, 35, 314 (Sept. 13, 1817, Jan. 10, 1818); XVII, 36 (Sept. 18, 1819). In the early twenties the annual immigration fluctuated between six and ten thousand, rising at the close of the decade. Hansen, *Atlantic Migration*, 117-119, cites the official statistics.

[2] The hazardous and unsanitary conditions of ocean travel, high-lighted by stories of suffering among the Germans and by rumors of the spread of pestilence, were responsible for the law of March 4, 1819, which placed immigration under federal supervision and charged customs officers to keep statistics of incoming passengers. *Annals of Congress* (Wash., 1834-1856), XXXIII, 414 ff. (15 Cong., 2 sess.); *U. S. Statutes at Large*, III, 488.

[3] R. G. Albion, *The Rise of New York Port* (N. Y., 1939), 337-338.

larger prospects along the rivers flowing toward the heart of the continent. Those newcomers who arrived high in hope but low in purse could usually sell their labor, however unskilled. In West as well as East there were houses and stores to be built, canals to be dug and roads to be improved.[1] So it happened that in New York, Irish laborers "burrowed across the state" and in the process did more than dig the Erie Canal: they established settlements which later became centers of their religious faith.[2]

But pick and shovel and wheelbarrow were poor substitutes for a farm. In the nineteenth century, as in the seventeenth, the great lodestone was land. What seemed impossible for the individual European unfamiliar with pioneering might be accomplished through coöperative ventures. National groups formulated elaborate projects for colonization, which were usually dependent on some special concession by Congress, permitting purchase and settlement. The French, for example, sponsored an organization known as the Society for the Olive and the Vine, which in 1817 bought four townships in Alabama on easy terms. Morris Birkbeck and his English associates were less generously treated when they negotiated the same year for sixteen thousand acres of public land east of the Wabash in Illinois, where they hoped to reproduce the life of an English rural county.[3] Irish, German and Swiss groups petitioned Congress in vain for grants of land on a long-term credit basis that immigrants might be encouraged to acquire frontier homes. The upshot of these proposals, however, was the state-

---

[1] See earlier, 225.

[2] R. J. Purcell, "Immigration to the Canal Era," A. C. Flick, ed., *History of the State of New York* (N. Y., 1933-1937), VII, 25-27.

[3] Morris Birkbeck, *Letters from Illinois* (Phila., 1818), 149-150. See also P. J. Treat, *The National Land System, 1785-1820* (N. Y., 1910), 309-315, and J. B. McMaster, *A History of the People of the United States* (N. Y., 1883-1913), IV, 392-395.

ment of the nation's immigration policy: the government would neither invite nor bar the foreigner; and if he came, he would be free to find his place in the New World in equal competition with the native-born.[1]

During these postwar years Americans, no less than Europeans, were on the move. To Birkbeck, following the National Road across Pennsylvania in 1817, it seemed that the older parts of the nation were "breaking up and moving westward."[2] The family groups which he saw traveling toward the Ohio in almost endless procession were but a continuation of that great colonizing movement which had never ceased since the early days of Jamestown and Plymouth. By the eve of the Revolution it had pushed through the barrier of the Alleghanies. Rising and falling in response to political and economic conditions in the Eastern states and in Europe, it now swept to the Mississippi and beyond. For many the War of 1812 had both dramatized opportunities in the West and improved the means of getting there; military necessity had compelled the improvement of roads. With the return of peace steamboats began to push against the current on many a Western river. Most of the routes westward converged on the Ohio, usually by way of its numerous tributaries.

New Englanders and New Yorkers, though they might not crave each others' company, could use the Mohawk and Genesee turnpikes, or cross the Hudson south of Albany and take the Catskill road to the headwaters of the Alleghany at Olean. Here in 1818 some three thousand settlers waited for the thaw and then floated down river to their Ohio lands in time to get in a first planting.[3] From New Jersey and eastern Penn-

[1] Hansen, *Atlantic Migration*, 96-97.
[2] Morris Birkbeck, *Notes on a Journey in America from . . . Virginia to . . . Illinois* (Dublin, 1818), 25-26.
[3] *History of Cattaraugus County, New York* (Phila., 1879), 35.

sylvania the main route followed the old military road, cut by Forbes in the French and Indian War, through the well-tilled farms of Lancaster County, over the mountains at Bedford and winding down into Pittsburgh. In many parts it could not compare with the turnpike to Cumberland on the Potomac, where the emigrants' families might join the wagon trains, enjoying the improved surface of the new National Road on the long haul into Wheeling. Numerous tributaries from the Valley of Virginia flowed into the National Road before it reached the Ohio River, where most of the routes out of the Lower South followed the gaps in the Alleghanies that led into the central parts of Tennessee and Kentucky. Here some families, turning south, went down the river to Mississippi and Louisiana. Many more, however, pushed on over the difficult roads that finally gave them access to the river bottoms north of the Ohio.[1] In 1817 it seemed as if Virginia, Tennessee and Kentucky were literally pouring out their people so that Illinois and Missouri, following the example of Indiana a year earlier, might achieve statehood.[2]

Since no central agency compiled the statistics, one can only estimate the number of migrating Americans between 1815 and 1830 from the fragmentary reports of tollgate attendants, innkeepers, ferryboat operators and others who were sensitive to travel on highway and river. Though the census reveals the phenomenal growth of Western towns and villages, it is silent about the men and women who optimistically set out for new and fertile fields only to find themselves, disillusioned and broken in health, compelled to take the long road

---

[1] A. B. Hulbert, *Historic Highways of America* (Cleveland, 1902-1905), X, 17-70; XII, chaps. i-v.

[2] W. C. Howells, *Recollections of Life in Ohio* (Cincinnati, 1895), 8-13; McMaster, *History*, IV, 384-385; T. C. Pease, *The Frontier State, 1818-1848* (C. W. Alvord, ed., *The Centennial History of Illinois*, Springfield, 1918-1920, II), 2-7.

back to the East. Probably such confessions of defeat were rare, for between 1810 and 1820 population north of the Ohio River more than doubled and before the next census Ohio had a greater number of people than Massachusetts and Connecticut combined. Within nine years after 1812 six Western states — Louisiana, Indiana, Mississippi, Illinois, Alabama and Missouri — entered the Union. If the older areas of Kentucky, Tennessee and Ohio are included, these nine states of the "new West" had a population of 3,700,000 in 1830 — more than a quarter of the nation.[1] Since 1790 a new section had risen in power; and its strength extended beyond the fledgling commonwealths into the western counties of New York, Pennsylvania and Virginia.[2]

As late as 1830 Americans still thought of the West as the entire section from the Alleghanies to the Mississippi and from the Great Lakes to the Gulf of Mexico. If signs of cleavage between the northern and southern parts of this great valley had already begun to appear, they were generally overshadowed by certain unifying forces. Perhaps the section's most distinctive characteristic was the fact that its social structure had been created out of the experiences of a relatively brief generation of pioneering. Its geographic variations were minimized by the length of the Mississippi and its tributaries, which carried to New Orleans the surplus products of farm and gristmill, of ropewalk and forge. Though the crews that manned the river boats were drawn from every part of the older Union and from many foreign countries, the population of the interior valley was predominantly composed of yeomen from the uplands of Virginia and North Carolina, with large contingents of

[1] U. S. Fifth Census; or, Enumeration of the Inhabitants of the United States (Wash., 1832), 162-163.
[2] F. J. Turner, Rise of the New West (A. B. Hart, ed., The American Nation: a History, N. Y., 1904-1918, XIV), 70-71.

German and Scotch-Irish pioneers from Pennsylvania and Maryland.[1] By 1830 New Englanders had made good their conquest of the Western Reserve in Ohio and had risen to leadership in many of the river towns north of Kentucky, but theirs was not always the dominant influence even in districts where they had been the first settlers.[2]

Whatever the immediate background of the men and women who built the "new West," they exemplified that "fierce spirit of liberty" which Edmund Burke had attributed to an earlier generation of Americans. Individualists, often in revolt against the laws and conventions of older communities, they learned quickly in their new environment to develop self-reliance. The very abundance of natural resources, especially land, stimulated competition in exploitation and its attendant wastefulness, which in a later day would make governmental regulation imperative.[3] But the restraints of government were not easily borne by the man who felt that his farm had been created with his own ax and plow and could be protected with his own gun. Law offered a convenient method of settling individual disputes and it often had to be taken into one's own hands. It had not yet become an instrument to safeguard one's equality with one's fellows.[4]

[1] James Hall, *Letters from the West* (London, 1828), 48, 91; Timothy Flint, *Recollections of the Last Ten Years* (Boston, 1826), 93-94; F. J. Turner, *The United States, 1830-1850* (N. Y., 1935), 18-19, 31; J. M. Miller, *The Genesis of Western Culture* (*Ohio Hist. Colls.*, IX), 38-45.

[2] Lois K. Mathews, *Expansion of New England* (Boston, 1909), 181. Turner, *Rise of the New West*, 76, points out that in the Ohio legislature of 1822 there were 38 members of Middle-states birth, 33 of Southern (including Kentucky) and only 25 of New England.

[3] See H. U. Faulkner, *The Quest for Social Justice, 1898-1914* (*A History of American Life*, XI), 1-4.

[4] An excellent description of the characteristics of Western communities appears in F. J. Turner, *The Frontier in American History* (N. Y., 1921), chap. xiii.

Such coöperative enterprises as this highly individualistic Western society achieved were generally in the
form of extralegal associations. This was true of its
religious as well as its economic and political activities.
We have already noticed the pervasive influence of the
camp meeting in widely scattered communities, where
there were few social outlets for normal human emo-
tions.[1] Similarly their economic needs were satisfied in
many a plowing contest, stump pulling, barn raising
and husking bee. Such instances revealed the persistence
of that spirit of voluntary association so important in
the evolution of American institutions. At many points
this trait forestalled governmental intervention for decades, but nowhere did it show signs of developing into
genuine collectivism. European observers, accustomed
to the power of social convention and legal compulsion,
agreed with Tocqueville that "in most of the operations
of mind, each American appeals only to the individual
effort of his own understanding."[2] Nowhere was this
more true than in the West.

For over a decade after 1815 these Western traits were
generally characteristic of the people of the trans-
Alleghany area, but within the section numerous regional
differences slowly became evident. By 1830 the discerning eye could see increasing contrasts between the
Northwest — roughly bounded by the Ohio, the Great
Lakes and the Mississippi — and the territory south of
the Ohio lying between the Mississippi and the Appalachian barrier. The variant influences of geography
and climate had been accentuated by the Ordinance of
1787, which denied the slaveholder possession of his
human chattels if he carried them north of the Ohio,
and by the infiltration of New Englanders and New

[1] See earlier, 171.
[2] Alexis de Tocqueville, *Democracy in America* (Henry Reeves, tr.,
N. Y., 1838), II, 2. See also I, 170-172, 175-177.

Yorkers into the larger stream of upland Southerners.[1] In 1830 more than half the people of the Northwest were concentrated in Ohio; most of the others lived behind a frontier line which extended from the vicinity of Detroit through the southern part of Michigan and then cut back across north-central Indiana and central Illinois to the Mississippi. In many Ohio counties no farmer had yet invaded the primeval forest; rumors of the unhealthful character of Indiana's swamp lands held settlers in the Ohio and Wabash valleys; in Illinois the pioneer woodsman, pushing up the tributaries of the Ohio and the Mississippi, was prone to avoid the open prairie, however fertile. He preferred the wooded stream.[2] In some districts clearings already constituted a gigantic swath cut through the better timberlands, but no farmer was very far from extensive tracts of unplowed wilderness.

Only along the Ohio did the villages give much promise of developing into cities. In 1830 the cabins near Fort Dearborn, present site of Chicago, probably sheltered fewer than fifty inhabitants.[3] Detroit, incorporated as a municipality in 1824, was merely a village of twenty-two hundred persons with an unsurpassed harbor. Cleveland, about half as large, was just beginning to feel the effects of the new commerce made possible by the opening of the canal connecting the Cuyahoga and Scioto rivers.[4] Pittsburgh, Cincinnati and St. Louis seemed destined for greatest growth. Of the three, Cincinnati, though the youngest, was already

[1] In Indiana and Illinois the position of the Negro was anomalous during the early years of statehood. What amounted to slavery existed under the guise of indentured servitude. Victory for the antislavery forces was not certain in Illinois until the latter part of the decade of the twenties. B. W. Bond, jr., *The Civilization of the Old Northwest* (N. Y., 1934), 96, 163-171; Pease, *Frontier State*, 77-91.

[2] Thomas Ford, *History of Illinois* (Chicago, 1854), 102-103.

[3] Bessie L. Pierce, *A History of Chicago* (N. Y., 1937-   ), I, 44 n.

[4] *Fifth Census*, 122-123, 152-153.

the largest, second only to New Orleans in the Western country. Its twenty-five thousand residents were busy handling the products of the rich farm lands of southern Ohio and northern Kentucky. If the farmers of the region found it more profitable to fatten hogs than to ship their bulky grain to market, Cincinnati took full advantage of the situation. Not only did its business men steadily expand the packing industry until the city was commonly called "Porkopolis," but they built the steamboats to carry their products into the channels of world trade and bring back the fabrics, furniture and hardware so much in demand in the great interior valley.[1]

Pittsburgh, especially after the use of steam power, likewise built the river boats that carried its imports and domestic manufactures down the Ohio. Long favored by its unique location at the junction of turnpike and river, it gradually lost its preëminent commercial position, but found more than adequate compensation in the profits from blast furnace and rolling mill, engine shop and hardware factory.[2] Louisville and St. Louis, both smaller than Pittsburgh, drew their support from commercial activities. The former, at the Falls of the Ohio, was a port of transshipment, serving large vessels which could not ascend the river beyond the falls. St. Louis's strategic situation, between the points where the Missouri and the Ohio empty into the Mississippi, enabled its six thousand inhabitants to levy toll on the fur trade of the upper Mississippi and lower Missouri and on the commerce of the Illinois country.

The growth of these river towns between 1810 and 1830 was one gauge of the rapidly mounting agricul-

[1] Benjamin Drake and E. D. Mansfield, *Cincinnati in 1826* (Cincinnati, 1827), 70 ff.
[2] C. H. Ambler, *A History of Transportation in the Ohio Valley* (Glendale, Calif., 1932), 149-160.

tural surplus which within another two decades would help to transform the Northwest. Already the beginnings were noticeable in an increasing concern over transportation and markets, over credits and currency. The Panic of 1819, with the subsequent depression, sharply defined the Westerner's dependent position in a debtor section. It quickened his desire to achieve economic independence, not only from Europe but from older America. To get his surplus goods to market more quickly and more cheaply seemed to him the most important consideration, making him willing to borrow heavily for the construction of roads and canals. The added debt, he felt, was but one step on the path to a larger freedom.[1]

Western roads and canals in the 1820's still ran toward the Mississippi and its tributaries. Not until the closing years of the decade did the Erie Canal begin to make inroads on the river traffic. By 1830 the Ohio canals were turning some commerce toward the Erie to the great advantage of the port of New York.[2] At the same time the steamboat was revolutionizing trade on the Mississippi. It made the round trip from Louisville to New Orleans in one sixth the time of the keel boat and at a third the cost per ton. As a result, the pork, grain, flour and whisky of the Ohio Valley were shipped downstream in ever increasing volume. In 1830 New Orleans reported it handled twenty-six million dollars' worth of produce from upriver farms and plantations. Its wharves afforded abundant evidence that the produce of the simple agrarian economy of the West was becoming greater in quantity and more varied in character.

While the settlers north of the Ohio were clearing

[1] Turner, *Rise of the New West*, 98-99.
[2] C. P. McClelland and C. C. Huntington, *History of the Ohio Canals* (Columbus, 1905), 30-32.

farms for grain and livestock and building towns for small-scale industries, others from the uplands of the old South or from Kentucky and Tennessee were carrying cotton into the Gulf region. By 1830 certain regional differences could be clearly distinguished. Kentucky's Blue Grass basin was safely in the hands of slaveholding planters, who had far more in common with the tidewater aristocracy of Virginia than with the pioneer farmers in less fertile districts of the state. They had monopolized not only most of the good land, but also most of the tobacco and hemp production; but for a time they derived more satisfaction and profit from the sale of their thoroughbred horses and their mules to the planters of the seaboard South.[1] Tennessee, also, had its limestone basin in the Cumberland Valley, where Nashville merchants prospered from the cotton and tobacco which they handled for the planters. In 1825 they loaded more than a million dollars' worth of cotton on steamboats for New Orleans. A few years later Nashville had become the metropolis of western Tennessee, its hinterland controlled by wealthy landlords who tried, with some measure of success, to maintain the social standards of South Carolina and Virginia. Their slave-operated plantations, often secured through adroit speculation from less fortunate frontiersmen, formed an economic basis for social gradations, which were less obvious among the small farmers of the eastern counties.[2]

South of the Tennessee boundary cotton was creating a new kingdom in the years after the War of 1812. Those who rushed in to occupy the fertile river valleys were generally aggressive and adventurous small farmers. But they were followed quickly by great and lesser

[1] E. G. Swem, ed., *Letters on the Condition of Kentucky in 1825* (N. Y., 1916), 68-74.
[2] T. P. Abernethy, *From Frontier to Plantation in Tennessee* (Chapel Hill, 1932), 277-284.

planters, some of whom counted their slaves by scores. If reluctant to do their own "pioneering," they bought out others' improvements and thus built up their estates. It was a process of land aggrandizement, already well developed in the piedmont, which pushed many a non-slaveholder onto inferior land.[1] So rapidly did settlement proceed that an English traveler in 1821 could describe a plantation in northern Alabama with one hundred acres in cotton and one hundred and ten acres in corn, where less than two years earlier there had been nothing but wilderness.[2] A few years later, even when cotton prices were sharply declining as a result of sensational increases in production, Timothy Flint decided that "no planters in the United States have better incomes, in proportion to their capital and hands," than those in Mississippi.[3]

Prior to 1830 the incoming settlers preferred the rich bottom lands of Alabama and Mississippi, the alluvial soils on both banks of the Mississippi and the fertile valleys of the Red and Arkansas rivers. In two areas — near Natchez and in the Louisiana parishes—they overran fields which had been under cultivation since the days of the French, but in most districts they were exploiting virgin soil. In general they prospered. The entire region had produced only five million pounds of cotton in 1811; a decade later it harvested sixty million; and by 1826 the yield had risen to two and a half times that figure. In 1830 both Alabama and Mississippi were picking almost as large a crop as either South Carolina or Georgia.[4]

With such remarkable increases in production it is not

[1] U. B. Phillips, *American Negro Slavery* (N. Y., 1918), 173-174.
[2] Adam Hodgson, *Letters from North America* (London, 1824), I, 269.
[3] Timothy Flint, *History and Geography of the Mississippi Valley* (Cincinnati, 1832), I, 229.
[4] Turner, *Rise of the New West*, statistical table on p. 47.

surprising that cotton and Negroes became a constant theme, "the ever harped upon, never worn out subject of conversation among all classes." [1] A traveler from Charleston to St. Louis reported in 1827 that the fields adjoined one another in close order for fourteen miles along the road out of Montgomery; cotton land speculators were "thicker than locusts in Egypt"; Mobile's wharves, stores and press houses foamed with white bales; half the steamers and barges on the Mississippi were carrying the crop of the Tennessee and Red River valleys to New Orleans. [2] It was cotton that kept the ties strong between the old South of the Atlantic Seaboard and the newer Southwest. The men who waited expectantly for the bolls to ripen in Alabama, Mississippi, Louisiana and Arkansas Territory had come from the piedmont and, in smaller numbers, from the tidewater. There was evidence of regional preferences. Georgians, for instance, were most numerous in eastern Alabama; Virginians and Carolinians usually sought out the bottom lands of southwestern Alabama and southeastern Mississippi; Tennesseeans congregated in the northern counties of both states. [3]

The entire Mississippi Valley, except for a few districts where French or Spanish influence persisted, was youthful in a double sense — in years of settlement and in the age of its settlers. Ingraham, always a careful observer, remarked in 1830 that one could travel through most of the villages of the Southwest without seeing "an old man or a gray hair." High-spirited young gentlemen set the tone, at least for a time, in many a new

[1] [J. H. Ingraham], *The Southwest* (N. Y., 1835), II, 86.
[2] *Georgia Courier* (Augusta), Oct. 11, 1827, reprinted in U. B. Phillips, *Plantation and Frontier* (J. R. Commons and others, eds., *A Documentary History of American Industrial Society*, N. Y., 1910-1911, I), 283-289.
[3] Flint, *History and Geography of the Mississippi Valley*, II, 217; T. P. Abernethy, *The Formative Period in Alabama, 1815-1828* (Montgomery, 1922), 24-32.

village. They congregated at the tavern bar, lounged on the counters in the general store, met for conversation and cigars in some young lawyer's office. It seemed as if the countinghouses of Eastern cities had poured their clerks into the villages of the West. They were not so much "expectant capitalists" as adventurous youth in a highly speculative mood. Unhampered by family obligations, they moved easily in search of that "lucky hit" which might bring fame or fortune, or happily both. They, and their less fortunate fellows who manned the river boats, were largely responsible for the gambling, profanity, brawling and licentiousness which seemed to be prevalent from Pittsburgh and Louisville to New Orleans and Mobile. Their activities often convinced observers, especially the ill-disposed, that westward migration in America was not the course of empire but a process of social decay.[1]

Many travelers, to be sure, gave an entirely different picture. If the Louisiana sugar planter's home with its elegant furnishings and excellent cuisine seemed to Timothy Flint to be something wholly exotic, in districts farther north along the Mississippi a pioneer society was already settling down to a routine of gracious living.[2] The outward symbols were lacking, for dwellings were generally little more than improved log houses; but inside, a graceful sideboard concealing a crudely whitewashed wall, or a Brussels carpet on a rough planked floor, indicated that rising income was bringing comforts which few had dreamed of in the first years of settlement.[3] Adam Hodgson described the "plain planters"

[1] [Ingraham], *Southwest*, II, 167-168; H. B. Fearon, *Sketches of America* (London, 1818), 279-281; Bernard, Duke of Saxe-Weimar, *Travels* (Phila., 1828), II, 50-51; U. B. Phillips, *Life and Labor in the Old South* (Boston, 1929), 109-111.

[2] Flint, *Recollections*, 335-338; Estwick Evans, *A Pedestrious Tour* (1817), in R. G. Thwaites, ed., *Early Western Travels* (Cleveland, 1904-1907, VIII), 325-326.

[3] [Ingraham], *Southwest*, II, 50-51.

of western Mississippi as enjoying a standard of living comparable to that of "second-rate country gentlemen" in England at the middle of the eighteenth century. When he tarried for a few days with the wealthy and well-established families in the vicinity of Natchez, he admitted he could have easily imagined himself on "the banks of the Mersey rather than on those of the Mississippi." [1]

The cotton and sugar planters of the Southwest built few such thriving towns as lined the banks of the Ohio. Between St. Louis and New Orleans on the Mississippi a community such as Natchez was exceptional. Established by the French early in the eighteenth century, it had been occupied by both British and Spanish before it came under the control of the United States in 1798. By 1830 it was a cosmopolitan river port, the market center of one of the best cotton districts in the Southwest. On its streets one might see descendants of French officials and Spanish dons, younger sons of the first families of Virginia and the Carolinas, lawyers from New York and New England eagerly seeking their first clients among the commission merchants and wealthier planters.

What Natchez meant to its countryside up and down the river was characteristic of villages throughout the Southwest. None were large, but some gained prestige as county-seat towns. Each was the social capital of a surrounding district occasionally twenty-five or thirty miles in radius. Its economic life was supported by the plantations, great and small, and it rendered corresponding services to the planter. If it was primarily the market place for his crops, it also helped him to overcome the isolation of widely separated farms and plantations. Here he found the social influence of lawyer, doctor, editor and teacher, however inadequately repre-

[1] Hodgson, *Letters*, I, 184-186.

sented; here were books and lectures and discussions.
Recreation, especially for the women, often meant riding
into town in a "showy carriage" to meet friends or to
dine at the best tavern or to attend the gala dancing
assembly of the season.[1] Where Georgians and Carolinians were numerous, society endeavored to reproduce
on a small scale the pleasant hospitality of Savannah and
Charleston. Life in the newer Southwest steadily moved
toward the stereotype of life in the older South.

Prior to 1830, as we have seen, the South, either
directly or indirectly, contributed as much as any other
section to the colonization of the new West. Many of
these migrants were discouraged over their economic
prospects, or disgusted by the political hegemony of the
tidewater counties, but their departure did not improve
conditions in their native districts. A committee of the
North Carolina legislature reported in November, 1815,
that within twenty-five years "more than two hundred
thousand of our inhabitants have removed to the waters
of the Ohio, Tennessee and Mobile; and it is mortifying
to witness the fact that thousands of our wealthy citizens . . . are annually moving to the West." A year
later a legislative committee in Virginia somewhat exaggerated the facts in its rhetorical phrases. "The
fathers of the land are gone," ran this gloomy complaint, "where another outlet to the ocean turns their
thoughts from the place of their nativity, and their affec-
tions from the haunts of their youth."[2] During the
twenties westward migration was already slowing down
population growth in the South Atlantic section.
Georgia, opening up some of its Indian lands, showed
rapid increase, but the other seaboard states gained fewer
than five hundred thousand, less than the growth of

[1] Hodgson, *Letters*, I, 186; [Ingraham], *Southwest*, II, 204-208.
[2] The reports are abstracted in *Niles' Weekly Register*, IX, supplement,
149-150, 165-166.

New York state.   A prominent Virginian explained
"the whole secret."   New York, he argued, had retained
its Genesee Valley while Virginia had ceded its Kentucky
lands to form a new state.[1]

The South felt the adverse effect of the Western settlements in other ways than those revealed in statistics
of population.   In competition with the fertile low-
priced lands of the Gulf states, its acres lost in value and
its slaves would have been worth three or four times as
much on plantations along the Mississippi.   Cotton declined in price on the New York market — in 1816 it
was thirty cents, but by 1827 it had dropped to nine —
and at the same time the price of slaves in certain areas
rose.   Many a planter in the old South discovered that
he had to secure more working capital, since his operating expenses increased as he grew more dependent on
Western and Northern farms for his livestock and foodstuffs.   His difficulties were further complicated by the
fact that his competitors in Western cotton fields had
generally better transportation routes, notably along the
rivers that flowed to the Gulf.   New Orleans and Mobile
were drawing this commerce to their noisy wharves.
By 1830 both ports had more than doubled their foreign
exports on the basis of 1820 values, while Savannah
and Charleston were shipping products of slightly less
value than a decade earlier.   Many planters in the older
South who had placed their faith in cotton were bitterly
disappointed.   They blamed their plight on the policies
of the federal government, especially the protective
tariff; and the Charleston district was ready to lead the
revolt.[2]

But no sectional unity existed sufficient to justify the

---

[1] Turner, *Rise of the New West*, 30-31, citing Virginia Constitutional
Convention, *Debates* (1829-1830), 405.

[2] L. C. Gray, *History of Agriculture in the Southern United States to
1860* (Carnegie Inst., *Publs.*, no. 430), II, chap. xxxvii.

term "solid South." In 1830 antagonism between seaboard and interior counties was still lively, though South
Carolina had tried to quiet it in 1808 by giving the
uplands control of one house, while the tidewater retained the other. This compromise, however, left political power in the hands of slave owners. The minority
in some interior counties, where slave labor was not
only rare but unpopular, seldom had a chance to speak
in the legislature.[1] Virginia's concession to its under-
represented western regions was postponed until the constitutional convention of 1829, when acrimonious debate resulted in a reapportionment shifting political
power into the piedmont and the Valley. The trans-
montane counties, where slavery was never to gain a
firm foothold, belonged with the West rather than with
the South. All along the western border of the states
from northeastern Georgia to the rolling hills of Maryland there were settlers of Scotch and German ancestry,
who continued a regimen of diversified farming, sometimes working side by side with their Negroes. Quakers
and Baptists in the same regions, especially in North
Carolina, refused to accept slave labor and, watching
their fellows leave for Ohio, Indiana and Illinois, remained as a rather inarticulate group of nonconformists.[2]

The pattern of conformity in the South was being
broadly sketched, even if many details would be accentuated later. By 1830 it was unmistakably clear
that, wherever cotton moved, slavery would quickly
follow. As pioneer farming steadily receded before the
small and larger plantation, Negroes spread into every
area except the mountainous districts. Nothing more
clearly indicated the economic revolution under way

[1] W. A. Schaper, "Sectionalism and Representation in South Carolina,"
Am. Hist. Assoc., Ann. Rep. for 1900, I, 433-438.
[2] J. S. Bassett, Slavery in the State of North Carolina (Johns Hopkins
Univ., Studies, XVII, nos. 7-8), 324-325, 399.

Harbor View of

ew Orleans

than the changing attitude of the section toward its colored inhabitants. That reluctance to accept slavery as a permanent institution which marked the states of the upper South at the close of the eighteenth century was gradually disappearing. To be sure, most of the antislavery societies in 1825 were located south of the Mason and Dixon line, but eighty per cent of the Southern ones were in western North Carolina and eastern Tennessee. Elsewhere in the slaveholding states hostility to the system was being diverted into the American Colonization Society, with the object of sending free Negroes to Africa.[1]

Colonization was but one evidence of concern over the presence of the free black. Though his status everywhere deteriorated in the decade after 1820, legislation was naturally stricter in the slave states. Virginia enforced more vigorously the law of 1806, which provided that any Negro must leave the state within a year after becoming a freedman. Maryland in 1825 reaffirmed its legislation banishing free persons of color who could not give proper security for good behavior. In both states the number of manumissions declined during the decade.[2] South Carolina's alarm over an abortive slave insurrection in 1822 brought increased limitations on the movement and occupations of free Negroes and a more scrupulous enforcement of the prohibition against their instruction in groups. Opposition grew stronger to the custom of "hiring out" a slave's time for work as a craftsman or as a plantation laborer. In the larger towns white toilers protested the competition, while in

[1] E. L. Fox, *The American Colonization Society, 1817-1840* (Johns Hopkins Univ., *Studies*, XXXVII, no. 3), 46-124.

[2] William Jay, *An Inquiry into the Character and Tendency of the American Colonization and American Anti-Slavery Societies* (N. Y., 1835), 22-24; J. H. Russell, *The Free Negro in Virginia* (Balt., 1913), 74-82; C. G. Woodson, *Free Negro Heads of Families in the U. S. in 1830* (Wash., 1925), xxiii-xxvii. See also J. H. Franklin, *The Free Negro in North Carolina, 1790-1860* (Durham, 1943), *passim*.

the rural districts there was fear that once the custom became well established it might carry the Negro far along the road to emancipation.[1]

No systematic proslavery argument had yet been formulated, but the critics of the institution, resting their case on the Jeffersonian doctrines of liberty and equality, were slowly yielding to those who found a justification in necessity. As late as 1824 Benjamin Lundy won a hearty response for his *Genius of Universal Emancipation* in Maryland, where antislavery sentiment seemed strong. Within four years, however, his subscriptions had so fallen off that he was combing New York and New England for support. In 1829, the very year the *Genius* was temporarily suspended, antislavery forces met a decisive rebuff in the Virginia constitutional convention. At the College of William and Mary, where Chancellor George Wythe had once indoctrinated "young abolitionists," Thomas R. Dew was penning the opening chapters of his defense of slavery on historic and moral grounds.

As the South moved slowly toward an understanding of its own unity, it prepared to protect its interests in a rivalry, not always friendly, with other sections. The growth of the West and its rising power in national affairs threw into bold relief the hopes and fears of other parts of the Union. Missouri's application for statehood, for example, started a debate which raged beyond the halls of Congress and revealed sharp sectional cleavages that discreet politicians would fain have concealed. The bitterness of the controversy filled Jefferson with terror and the compromise seemed to him but a temporary reprieve. "A geographical line," he wrote, "coinciding with a marked principle . . . held up to the angry passions of men, will never be obliter-

---

[1] H. M. Henry, *The Police Control of the Slave in South Carolina* (Emory, Va., 1914), 97-98, 101.

ated, and every new irritation will mark it deeper and deeper." [1] Calhoun and John Quincy Adams, alarmed by the heated arguments, discussed the probable fate of Americans if a dissolution of the Union should occur. Even Henry Clay admitted that the emergence of several confederacies in North America was not impossible. [2]

Quite apart from the far-reaching consequences of the Missouri question, there were more immediate effects in both South and West. Southerners began to reconsider their attitude toward slavery. If they were not yet ready to accept it as "the foundation of southern social and economic life," they became less willing, even in the border states, to support the work of the emancipationists. [3] Furthermore, the South thought it detected firm ground for common action in the West's distrust of the Northeast. There was much to be made of the frank avowal by Rufus King of New York, one-time leader of the Federalists, that the older states of the North were as hostile as they had been at the time of the Louisiana purchase to the rapid settlement of the West and the admission of new states into the Union. [4] The *Missouri Intelligencer* of May 17, 1819, emphasized the fact that the attempt to bar slavery from Missouri was almost exclusively the work of congressmen from Eastern states: "They view with a jealous eye the march of power westward . . . therefore they have combined against us; but let them pause before they proceed further, or the grave they are preparing for us, may be their own sepulchre." [5] An analysis of the final vote

[1] Thomas Jefferson, *Writings* (P. L. Ford, ed., N. Y., 1892-1899), X, 157.

[2] John Quincy Adams, *Memoirs* (C. F. Adams, ed., Phila., 1875), IV, 526, 530-531.

[3] Turner, *Rise of the New West*, 170-171.

[4] Rufus King, *Life and Correspondence* (C. R. King, ed., N. Y., 1894-1900), VI, 267, 279, 339-344.

[5] Quoted in F. H. Hodder, "Sidelights on the Missouri Compromise," Am. Hist. Assoc., *Ann. Rep. for 1909*, 153.

which rejected the prohibition against slavery in Missouri showed that the 58 Southerners had been supported by 17 of the 25 Westerners and by only 15 of the 94 congressmen from New England and the Middle Atlantic states. Obviously, there might be a chance for some sort of political alliance between the seaboard South and certain districts in the West.[1]

Few decades in the history of the United States offer more varied data for the laboratory work of the political scientist than the years between 1820 and 1830. Superficially described as an "era of good feelings," because only one negative vote had been cast in the electoral college when James Monroe was reëlected, the period was really marked by the frantic attempts of leading politicians to guide economic and sectional forces in ways that would permit each of them to use his local supporters as the founders of a new party national in scope. Calhoun, anxious over the temper of his countrymen as they slowly recovered from the Panic of 1819, believed there was "a general mass of disaffection to the government." Though unable to discern its particular direction, he suspected that it was "ready to seize upon any event and looking out anywhere for a leader."[2] There was no lack of hopeful aspirants for leadership. William H. Crawford of Georgia, Monroe's secretary of the treasury, captured the congressional caucus, which had functioned smoothly for two decades in maintaining the "Virginia Dynasty" in the White House. But he was an ill man and, in the face of popular disgust with congressional domination, his victory was an empty one. For a time it seemed that John Quincy Adams and Henry Clay, forgetting personal differences, had found a happy combination of sectional interests and economic principles that gave them a political program of wide appeal. Its

---

[1] Turner, *Rise of the New West*, 165.
[2] The comment is in Adams, *Memoirs*, V, 128.

broad outlines were reminiscent of the Hamiltonian proposals of an earlier generation; but, like Hamilton, its proponents failed to sense the mood of their countrymen. That triumph was reserved for Andrew Jackson and his friends.

The balanced economy, which Clay coveted for his country, had much popular support.[1] Many who rejoiced in the economic nationalism inherent in the "American system" felt misgivings only when they tried to settle tariff schedules, make federal appropriations for internal improvements, or regulate the sale of Western lands. Then local jealousies, constitutional scruples, sectional rivalries — or a combination of all — rose to confound legislator and administrator alike. In general, the economic nationalists found their support in the Middle Atlantic states — New York, New Jersey and Pennsylvania — and the Northwest and Kentucky, with some aid from the manufacturing districts of New England.[2] Throughout the twenties this combination was fairly constant on the issue of protection of American manufactures. It gained strength in New England as that section increased its textile mills, and it lost slightly in the West when particular tariff schedules did not suit Western producers.

The Ohio Valley, however, was not wedded to the Northeast, either economically or politically, prior to 1830. On specific appropriations for internal improvements it often found it had as many supporters in the South and Southwest as in the Middle Atlantic states. The Western demand for lower prices on public lands

[1] Its popularity was in part a result of the work of such versatile propagandists as Mathew Carey and Hezekiah Niles. They were as nationalistic in their exposition of economic theory as was William Ellery Channing in his plea for a truly national literature. See earlier, chap. xiii; also R. G. Stone, *Hezekiah Niles as an Economist* (Balt., 1933), 44, 130-131.

[2] *Niles' Wkly. Register*, XXVI, 113-114 (April 24, 1824).

irritated, if it did not alarm, Eastern manufacturers and financiers. After 1824 Congress was perennially busy with bills providing for distribution of land sales, graduation of prices, donations to needy settlers and preëmption rights for squatters, almost all advanced by the West with growing Southern support.[1]

The South indeed was beginning to realize its opportunity. As Calhoun reluctantly accepted the fact that his section was a minority in the expanding Union and formulated the doctrine of nullification for its defense, Thomas H. Benton of Missouri directed his verbal attack against New England and all other opponents of Western land policies. Southerners looking northward saw the citadels of protectionism; Westerners looking eastward saw the strongholds of those who favored high prices for public lands. A political alliance seemed indicated. It had its first formal test in 1828 when the old South accepted the West's hero, Andrew Jackson, and helped him into the White House.[2]

But the dramatic revelation of the character of the West-South alliance came in the Senate of the United States in the early months of 1830. New England's fear that her laboring population would be drawn westward, and that her interests generally would be jeopardized by the rapidly growing Western states, was revealed in the resolution of Senator Samuel Foot of

[1] R. M. Robbins, *Our Landed Heritage* (Princeton, 1942), 42-45.

[2] For the meaning of Jackson's election, see C. R. Fish, *The Rise of the Common Man, 1830-1850* (*A History of American Life*, VI), chaps. i-ii. Turner, in *United States, 1830-1850*, 30, believed that "an agricultural society . . . had triumphed, for a time, over the conservative, industrial, commercial, and manufacturing society of the New England type." But the Jacksonians, like the Jeffersonians, failed to develop a positive program for American agrarianism. They had no real sympathy for the confiscatory features of Thomas Skidmore's land policy and little understanding of George Henry Evans's campaign against land monopoly. Cf. Commons and others, *Documentary History of American Industrial Society*, V, 43-44; Fish, *Rise of the Common Man*, 273; and F. T. Carlton, "The Workingmen's Party of New York City," *Polit. Sci. Quar.*, XXII, 401-415.

Connecticut, looking toward the limitation of the sale of public lands, especially in areas where large amounts remained unsold. In the intimacy of the little Senate chamber sectional views were stated with a forthrightness that alarmed the more discreet. Benton of Missouri, ever fertile in proposals for liberalizing federal land policies, bitterly accused New England of hostility to the West. When Hayne of South Carolina enthusiastically supported the Westerner's accusations, there were some who could see a scheme to "break down the union of the Eastern and Western sections" and effect an enduring alliance between the West and the South.[1]

Hayne's elaboration of the right of nullification, already sketched in South Carolina's Exposition of 1828 as a safeguard against the tyranny of the majority, gave New Englanders a chance to take the offensive. Webster, with bland disregard of the state-rights attitude of New England Federalism twenty years earlier, not only defended his own section from the charge of particularism, but attacked any who dared selfishly to calculate the value of the Union.[2] His "Reply to Hayne" became a classic, oft repeated by American schoolboys; but the nationalism which it apostrophized bore little relation to the circumstances of the moment. Beneath its rhetorical eloquence was much substantial food for the cynic.

By 1830 the American people seemed to have traveled a long way from the nationalism of 1815. Then they had talked confidently of national preparedness and economic self-sufficiency. Congress had reorganized the army, chartered the Second Bank and passed the protec-

---

[1] Adams, *Memoirs*, VIII, 190 ff.

[2] Webster, conferring more frequently with Lowell factory owners than with Salem merchants, had been converted to support of a protective tariff. His attitude toward the West may have been affected by his close friendship with Abbott Lawrence, who was deeply alarmed by the Western drain on New England's population. R. G. Wellington, *Political and Sectional Influence of Public Lands* (Cambridge, 1914), 27-28.

tive tariff of 1816. Under Calhoun's whip the "Bonus Bill" for setting up a systematic survey of transportation needs would have become law save for Madison's veto on constitutional grounds. From the Supreme Court came a series of decisions which not only gladdened the hearts of merchants and manufacturers, but also encouraged those who were working to exalt the power of the federal government. Yet beneath the surface old sectional antagonisms revived and new ones appeared. Particularism seemed more rampant as Jackson took office than it had in the days of Thomas Jefferson. The state rights of the Kentucky and Virginia resolutions, or of the Hartford Convention type, had sounded less dangerous than that which Hayne expounded on Capitol Hill. Symbolic was the position of Calhoun. Once the champion of the nation's unity, he now hesitated, torn between his devotion to his state and section and his desire to play a commanding rôle in national affairs.

Meanwhile, in the valley of the Sangamon in Illinois, a young man came of age. He was more sensitive than Jackson to the moods of the West and more catholic than Benton in his intellectual interests. In his thinking there was something of Calhoun's early concern for the preservation of the nation's unity, of Webster's conception of the nature of the federal government, of Clay's enthusiasm for the balanced economy of the American system. When he first announced his political principles, they seemed to stem from the Hamiltonian rather than the Jeffersonian tradition. "My politics," he said, "are short and sweet, like the old woman's dance. I am in favor of a national bank. I am in favor of the internal improvement system, and a high protective tariff." [1] Within thirty-five years, in one of

[1] Abraham Lincoln, *Early Speeches, 1832-1856* (W. C. Whitney, ed., N. Y., 1907), 1.

the greatest crises of the nation's history, Abraham Lincoln watched his principles take the form of law. It was in a sense the triumph of Hamilton, but modified, so Lincoln hoped, by the spirit of Thomas Jefferson.

CHAPTER XVI

CRITICAL ESSAY ON AUTHORITIES

PHYSICAL SURVIVALS

THE nonliterary remains of the generation with which this volume is concerned have generally been neglected by historical societies and museums. The buildings were rapidly destroyed, especially those which marked the transition from log cabins to frame or brick dwellings. But Spring Mill Village at Mitchell, Indiana, is a careful restoration of a score of houses and stores dating from 1814 to 1830; and Dayton, Ohio, has preserved as an historic museum a log cabin built in 1796. On the Atlantic Seaboard may be seen notable examples of the better architecture. The state house in Boston, as well as that in Hartford, was built in the last decade of the eighteenth century. Some of New England's most distinguished churches, including Ithiel Town's Center Church in New Haven, belong to this period. New York's City Hall, begun in 1803, represents the work of the Frenchman, Joseph Mangin, and the American, John McComb. In Philadelphia the central pavilion of the Pennsylvania Hospital reveals the "late colonial" designers at their best. The central portions of the Capitol and the White House in Washington were planned and constructed before 1830, while across the Potomac stands Arlington, its Doric columns supporting Roman capitals. Within Virginia the influence of Thomas Jefferson still lives. At Monticello, on the grounds of the University of Virginia, at Montpelier, which was James Madison's home, and in the state capitol at Richmond one is constantly reminded of the lines of the Maison Carrée in southern France. A valuable, though by no means complete, directory of historic houses appears in L. V. Coleman, comp., *Historic House Museums* (Wash., 1933). These museums usually contain furnishings of the period.   Similar exhibits can be found in the American Wings of the Boston Museum of Fine Arts and New York's Metropolitan Museum of Art.

The life and work of the "plain folk of the soil" may be most vividly recalled in special agricultural museums, notably the one maintained by the Bucks County Historical Society at Doylestown, Pennsylvania; the Farm Museum at Hadley, Massachusetts; and the Farmers' Museum of the New York State Historical Association at Cooperstown, appropriately housed in a huge stone barn on the shore of Otsego Lake.   Agricultural apparatus constitutes but one feature of the constantly expanding Ford Museum at Dearborn, Michigan, and of Chicago's Museum of Science and Industry.   A helpful guide to exhibits of farm implements and household industries is E. E. Edwards, ed., *References on Agricultural Museums* (U. S. Dept. of Agr., *Bibliographical Contribs.*, no. 29, 1933).   The most extensive collections of land and inland-waterways transport may be seen in the Ford Museum and in the United States National Museum at Washington, D. C.   Excellent contemporaneous drawings of river craft are available in the Missouri Historical Society at St. Louis and in the New York Historical Society.   The Carnegie Institute at Pittsburgh and the Chicago Historical Society have Conestoga wagons used in the first decade of the nineteenth century.   The maritime history of New England is well portrayed by the collections of ship models, nautical instruments, drawings and maps in the Peabody Museum and the Essex Institute at Salem, Massachusetts.   Similarly the Old Dartmouth Historical Society Museum in New Bedford renders visual some of the stirring experiences of whaling days.

The best examples of graphic arts may be found in the Metropolitan Museum of Art, the New York Public Library and the New York Historical Society.   An invaluable guide to this interesting subject is *American Graphic Art* (rev. edn., N. Y., 1924) by Frank Weitenkampf.   Though there were few genre painters, the Museum of Fine Arts in Boston has several excellent examples of scenes from the common life.   The portraiture and the historical paintings of the early republic are to be found in most large galleries. Uniquely interesting is the collection of portraits in the Yale School of the Fine Arts.

DOCUMENTARY SOURCES

Official documents for the years when federal and state governments were establishing precedents are voluminous and valuable. Reports of the various federal departments, supplemented by pertinent correspondence, may be found in *American State Papers* (Wash. 1832-1861) in several series and 38 volumes. Two indices are particularly helpful in locating the more important House and Senate reports and executive communications: *House Document,* no. 163 (18 Cong., 1 sess., 1824), and T. H. McKee, comp., *Index to Reports of the Senate* (Wash., 1887). The Congressional debates were inadequately, and often inaccurately, recorded in *Annals of Congress, 1789-1824* (42 vols., Wash., 1834-1856), and in *Register of Debates* (14 vols., Wash., 1824-1837). There is an *Abridgment of the Debates of Congress, 1789-1856* by T. H. Benton (16 vols., Wash., 1857-1861). Because of the legislation dealing with commerce, finance and land the *Statutes at Large* contain significant materials for the student of social history. A convenient guide is *Index Analysis of the Federal Statutes . . . 1789-1907* (Wash., 1908), prepared by G. W. Scott and M. G. Beaman. The first five census reports are not satisfactory; enumeration was faulty and the published compilations omitted much information that could have been secured from the manuscript data. *A Century of Population Growth, 1790-1900* (Wash., 1909), compiled by W. S. Rossiter, contains useful maps and descriptions based on the first census. Since the publication of C. H. Van Tyne and W. G. Leland, comps., *Guide to the Archives of the Government of the United States in Washington* (Carnegie Inst., *Publs.,* no. 92, 1907), some of the manuscripts therein described have appeared in print, but the unpublished data for the period before 1830 are still impressive. In 1934 the National Archives assumed responsibility for such documents; its accessions are described in *Guide to the Material in the National Archives* (Wash., 1940) and in the annual reports of the Archivist of the United States.

For social life the state, town and village records are more essential than those of the national government. The condition of the state archives has changed considerably since it was described some forty years ago in the reports of the Public Archives Commission of the American Historical Association, which appeared in the *Annual Reports* of that organization. Valuable information concerning public documents has come from the work of the Historical Records Survey (1936-1942), which is described in G. W. Roach, "Historical Records Survey: Final Report," *N. Y. History*, XXIV, 39-55. Unfortunately, none of the various programs was completed for the entire nation. Every state has issued fragmentary inventories of county archives, but only North Carolina has as yet published a state-wide guide to county records. Useful in finding state sources are Adelaide R. Hasse's successive indices (by states) to *Economic Material in Documents of the States* (Carnegie Inst., *Publs.*, no. 85, 1907-1922); R. R. Bowker, comp., *State Publications* (4 pts., N. Y., 1899-1908); and A. F. Kuhlman, comp., *Official Publications Relating to American State Constitutional Conventions* (N. Y., 1936). The *Journals* of the various state legislatures are disappointing because of the inadequate reporting of debates, but the messages and papers of the governors are often far more significant than the presidential papers which have been collected in J. D. Richardson, comp., *Messages and Papers of the Presidents, 1789-1908* (11 vols., Wash., 1909).

GENERAL ACCOUNTS

Of the comprehensive histories which cover this period the most rewarding for the student of American society is J. B. McMaster, *A History of the People of the United States* (8 vols., N. Y., 1883-1913), which is rich in data obtained from contemporary newspapers, pamphlets and magazines, some no longer easily available. Volumes ii-v deal with the years from 1790 to 1829. Edward Channing, *A History of the United States* (6 vols., N. Y., 1905-1925), devotes several chapters in the fifth volume, covering the period 1815-1848, to a fuller discussion of social and economic factors than appeared in his earlier volumes. Less detailed than McMaster's treatment, but more penetrating in analysis, is Henry Adams, *History of the United States . . . 1801-1817* (9 vols., N. Y., 1889-1891), especially in the discriminating descriptions in the first and last volumes. Of *The American Nation: a History* (28 vols., N. Y., 1904-1918), edited by A. B. Hart, the volumes by K. C. Babcock and F. J. Turner are most successful in treating politics as a social concern. Social trends of this era are discussed in Allen Johnson, ed., *The Chronicles of America Series* (50 vols., New Haven, 1918-1921), especially in the volumes by F. A. Ogg (XIX), Constance L. Skinner (XVIII), Allen Johnson (XV), E. S. Corwin (XVI) and A. B. Hulbert (XXI). Among older surveys which are still valuable, the following contain information on religious, humanitarian, educational and scientific developments: T. D. Woolsey, F. A. P. Barnard, D. A. Wells and others, *The First Century of the Republic: a Review of American Progress* (N. Y., 1876), and Emerson Davis, *The Half Century* (Boston, 1850).

PERIODICALS

The best introduction to magazine literature is F. L. Mott, *A History of American Magazines, 1741-1850* (N. Y., 1930), which contains information concerning editors as well as their journals. General magazines were numerous, but most of them were of brief duration. The trend toward specialized journals, so marked in the next generation, had already begun. As a compendium of news and commentary *Niles' Weekly Register* (76 vols., Balt., 1811-1849) was widely read, and is now a veritable source book. Two literary journals gained distinction: the *Port Folio* (44 vols., Phila., 1801-1815) and the *North American Review* (Boston, 1815-1877; N. Y., 1878-1940). The newspaper had

not yet become the mirror of social conduct. Its columns of
foreign intelligence and official documents occupied space now
given to local news. A comprehensive list for the period
before 1820 is C. S. Brigham, ed., "Bibliography of American Newspapers," Am. Antiquarian Soc., *Proceeds.*, n.s.,
XXIII-XXXVII, *passim.* For interesting appraisals of influential papers, see F. L. Mott, *American Journalism*
(N. Y., 1941). Little investigation has been carried forward in the field of rural journalism, but M. W. Hamilton,
The Country Printer, New York State, 1785-1830 (*N. Y.
State Hist. Assoc. Ser.*, no. 4, 1936), is a pioneer study,
Other monographs along similar lines are needed.

TRAVEL ACCOUNTS

In this, as in all periods of American history, the comments of literary travelers should be used with caution.
Some, like Charles Janson, Richard Parkinson and Thomas
Ashe, were genuinely hostile; while others, among them
Jonathan Carver and William Bartram, saw people and
institutions through a romantic haze. W. P. Trent and
others, eds., *The Cambridge History of American Lit-
erature* (4 vols., N. Y., 1917-1921), I, 468-490, contains
a general list of travelers for the years 1763 to 1846.
Bibliographies of English accounts are included in Allan
Nevins, ed., *American Social History as Recorded by British
Travellers* (rev. edn., N. Y., 1931), and Jane L. Mesick,
The English Traveller in America, 1785-1835 (Columbia
Univ., *Studies in English and Comparative Literature;* N. Y.,
1922). The French travelers are listed by Frank Monaghan,
comp., *French Travellers in the United States, 1765-1932*
(N. Y., 1933). Among the accounts by British visitors the
following are important: John Davis, *Travels of Four Years
and a Half in the United States of America* (London, 1803);
H. B. Fearon, *Sketches of America* (London, 1828); Basil
Hall, *Travels in North America in the Years 1827 and
1828* (2 vols., Phila., 1829); Mrs. Basil Hall, *The Aristocratic Journey* (N. Y., 1931); John Lambert, *Travels
through Lower Canada and the United States of North*

America (2 vols., London, 1816); John Melish, *Travels in the United States of America, in the Years 1806-1811* (Phila., 1812); William Priest, *Travels in the United States of America* (London, 1802); Henry Wansey, *An Excursion to the United States . . . in 1794* (Salisbury, Eng., 1798). Most of the French accounts have been translated, including Duke de La Rochefoucauld-Liancourt, *Travels through the United States of North America* (4 vols., London, 1799), and C. F. Volney, *A View of the Soil and Climate of the United States* (C. B. Brown, tr., Phila., 1804). An excellent collection of works by visitors to the trans-Alleghany regions is available in R. G. Thwaites, ed., *Early Western Travels, 1748-1846* (32 vols., Cleveland, 1904-1907).

THE GEOGRAPHIC BASE

A discriminating study, describing the physical environment of the Eastern seaboard as portrayed in contemporary accounts, is R. H. Brown, *Mirror for Americans: Likeness of the Eastern Seaboard, 1810* (Am. Geog. Soc., *Special Publ.*, no. 27, 1943). Indispensable for the student of regionalism, especially as it became manifest in this period, are J. R. Smith, *North America* (N. Y., 1925), and Isaiah Bowman, *Forest Physiography* (N. Y., 1911). A regional survey, which should serve as a model for other studies, is Rupert Vance, *Human Geography of the South* (Chapel Hill, 1935). The best cartographic material appears in C. O. Paullin, comp., *Atlas of the Historical Geography of the United States* (J. K. Wright, ed., N. Y., 1932), and C. L. and Elizabeth H. Lord, comps., *Historical Atlas of the United States* (N. Y., 1944). Because of its map studies, D. R. Fox, ed., *Harper's Atlas of American History* (N. Y., 1920), is still useful for this period.

STATE AND LOCAL HISTORIES

Several coöperative state histories set a high standard: A. B. Hart, ed., *The Commonwealth History of Massachusetts* (5 vols., N. Y., 1928-1930); A. C. Flick, ed.,

History of the State of New York (10 vols., N. Y., 1933-1937); I. S. Kull, ed., *New Jersey, a History* (6 vols., N. Y., 1930-1932); and C. W. Alvord, ed., *Centennial History of Illinois* (6 vols., Chicago, 1918-1924). Of the last work the following volumes are important for the period: C. W. Alvord, *The Illinois Country, 1673-1818;* S. J. Buck, *Illinois in 1818;* and T. C. Pease, *The Frontier, 1818-1848.* Other regional or state studies which stress social and intellectual forces are J. T. Adams, *New England in the Republic* (Boston, 1926); W. F. Dunaway, *A History of Pennsylvania* (Carl Wittke, ed., *Prentice-Hall History Series;* Pittsburgh, 1935); C. H. Ambler, *Sectionalism in Virginia, 1776-1861* (Chicago, 1910); T. P. Abernethy, *The Formative Period in Alabama, 1815-1828* (Montgomery, 1922); C. H. Ambler, *A History of West Virginia (Prentice-Hall History Series;* N. Y., 1933); T. P. Abernethy, *From Frontier to Plantation in Tennessee* (Chapel Hill, 1932); Charles Kerr, ed., *History of Kentucky* (5 vols., Chicago, 1922); and B. W. Bond, jr., *The Civilization of the Old Northwest* (N. Y., 1934).

The larger towns of the Atlantic Seaboard are described in Justin Winsor, ed., *Memorial History of Boston, 1630-1880* (4 vols., Boston, 1880-1881); M. A. DeW. Howe, *Boston, the Place and the People* (N. Y., 1903); William Kirk, ed., *A Modern City: Providence, Rhode Island* (Chicago, 1909); I. N. P. Stokes, ed., *Iconography of Manhattan Island* (6 vols., N. Y., 1915-1928), which contains some source material for this period; S. I. Pomerantz, *New York, an American City* (Columbia Univ., *Studies,* no. 442, 1938), based upon wide use of municipal records from 1783 to 1803; J. T. Scharf and Thompson Westcott, *History of Philadelphia* (3 vols., Phila., 1884); L. P. Powell, ed., *Historic Towns of the Southern States* (N. Y., 1900); T. J. Wertenbaker, *Norfolk, Historic Southern Port* (Durham, 1931); Mrs. St. Julien Ravenel, *Charleston: the Place and the People* (N. Y., 1906); and J. S. Kendall, *History of New Orleans* (3 vols., Chicago, 1922). Examination of scores of county histories, many of which are badly organized and carelessly written, also reveals a wealth of data for social history. These works are too numerous to list here. There is need for more bibliographies comparable to A. C. Bining, comp., *Pennsylvania History: a Selected Bibliography of Secondary Works* (reprinted from *Pa. Library Notes*, Oct. 1933).

PERSONAL MATERIAL

As in the Revolutionary Generation, diaries, autobiographies and reminiscent writings often disclose reasons for social attitudes. Particularly useful in this respect are John Quincy Adams, *Memoirs* (C. F. Adams, ed., 12 vols., Phila., 1874-1877); Charles Warren, ed., *Jacobin and Junto* (Cambridge, 1931), containing extracts from the diaries of Nathaniel Ames; Lyman Beecher, *Autobiography* (Charles Beecher, ed., 2 vols., N. Y., 1864); William Bentley, *Diary* (Salem, 1905-1914); Charles Biddle, *Autobiography, 1745-1821* (Phila., 1883); Levi Beardsley, *Reminiscences* (N. Y., 1852); Samuel Breck, *Recollections* (Phila., 1877); S. G. Goodrich, *Recollections of a Lifetime* (2 vols., N. Y., 1857); Philip Hone, *Diary, 1828-1851* (Allan Nevins, ed., 2 vols., N. Y., 1927); Edward Hooker, "Diary," Am. Hist. Assoc., *Ann. Rep. for 1896*, I; Alexander Graydon, *Memoirs* (Harrisburg, 1811); C. H. Haswell, *Reminiscences of an Octogenarian, 1816 to 1860* (N. Y., 1896); William Maclay, *Journal* (E. S. Maclay, ed., rev. edn., N. Y., 1927); E. S. Thomas, *Reminiscences of the Last Sixty-Five Years* (Hartford, 1840); and Thurlow Weed, *Autobiography* (Harriet A. Weed, ed., Boston, 1884).

A few editions of the collected works of public men will indicate the voluminous nature of the materials: George Washington, *Writings from the Original Manuscript Sources* (J. C. Fitzpatrick, ed., 33 vols., Wash., 1931-1941), the most comprehensive edition; John Adams, *Works* (C. F. Adams, ed., 10 vols., Boston, 1856); Alexander Hamilton, *Works* (H. C. Lodge, ed., 12 vols., N. Y., 1904); Thomas Jefferson, *Works* (P. L. Ford, ed., 12 vols., N. Y., 1904-1905); John Jay, *Correspondence and Public Papers* (H. P. Johnston, ed., 4 vols., N. Y., 1890-1893); James Madison,

Writings (Gaillard Hunt, ed., 9 vols., N. Y., 1900-1910) ; James Monroe, *Writings* (S. M. Hamilton, ed., 7 vols., N. Y., 1900) ; Albert Gallatin, *Writings* (Henry Adams, ed., 3 vols., Phila., 1879) ; S. E. Morison, *Life and Letters of Harrison Gray Otis* (2 vols., Boston, 1913) ; C. R. King, *Life and Correspondence of Rufus King* (6 vols., N. Y., 1894) ; and H. C. Lodge, *Life and Letters of George Cabot* (Boston, 1877). An indispensable guide to biographical data is Allen Johnson and Dumas Malone, eds., *Dictionary of American Biography* (21 vols., including index, N. Y., 1928-1937), a work which underscores the fact that the careers of little-known, sometimes obscure, men and women are significant factors in the evolution of American civilization. But much that would shed light on social and intellectual attitudes remains in manuscript form. Access to it has been made easier by the compilation of guides and indices, particularly H. P. Beers, comp., *Bibliographies in American History: Guide to Materials for Research* (rev. edn., N. Y., 1942). C. W. Garrison has prepared a *List of Manuscript Collections in the Library of Congress to July 1931* (Wash., 1932, reprinted from Am. Hist. Assoc., *Ann. Rep. for 1932*, 123-249).

AGRICULTURE AND COUNTRY LIFE

Numerous references to this period appear in E. E. Edwards, comp., *A Bibliography of the History of Agriculture in the United States* (U. S. Dept. of Agr., *Misc. Publ.*, no. 84, 1930). Comprehensive surveys are P. W. Bidwell and J. I. Falconer, *History of Agriculture in the Northern United States, 1620-1860* (Carnegie Inst., *Publs.*, no. 358, 1925), and L. C. Gray, *History of Agriculture in the Southern United States to 1860* (*ibid.*, no. 430, 1933). L. H. Bailey, ed., *Cyclopedia of American Agriculture* (N. Y., 1911), is still very useful. Farming in New England early in the nineteenth century is discussed in H. F. Wilson, *The Hill Country of Northern New England* (Columbia Univ., *Studies in the History of American Agriculture*, III, 1936), and P. W. Bidwell, "The Agricultural Revolution in New

England," *Am. Hist. Rev.*, XXVI, 693 ff. An excellent state survey is U. P. Hedrick, *History of Agriculture in the State of New York* (N. Y., 1933). Various aspects of rural life in the North are described in A. D. Mellick, *The Story of an Old Farm* (Somerville, N. J., 1889); and in R. H. Gabriel, *Toilers of Land and Sea* (R. H. Gabriel, ed., *The Pageant of America*, 15 vols., New Haven, 1926-1929, III), which contains the best pictorial material. Contemporary discussions include J. B. Bordley, *Essays and Notes on Husbandry and Rural Affairs* (Phila., 1799); R. R. Livingston, *Essay on Sheep* (N. Y., 1809); William Strickland, *Observations on the Agriculture of the United States* (London, 1801), which is too critical of agricultural achievement; John Taylor, *Arator* (Georgetown, 1813), a philosophic essay; and Timothy Dwight, *Travels in New-England and New-York* (New Haven, 1821-1822), which contains some excellent descriptions of rural communities.

The outstanding study of farm journals, A. L. Demaree, *The American Agricultural Press, 1819-1860* (Columbia Univ., *Studies in the History of American Agriculture*, no. 8, 1941), is especially valuable for its bibliography and for extracts from publications. Among the more important journals are the *American Farmer* (Balt., 1819-1834); the *New England Farmer* (Boston, 1822-1846); the *Plough Boy* (Albany, 1819-1823); and the *Southern Agriculturist* (Charleston, 1828-1846). For agricultural societies and fairs, see Elkanah Watson, *History of Agricultural Societies on the Modern Berkshire System* (Albany, 1820), and W. C. Neely, *The Agricultural Fair* (N. Y., 1935). The standard works on the plantation system are U. B. Phillips, *American Negro Slavery* (Wash., 1918), and *Life and Labor in the Old South* (Boston, 1929). A. O. Craven's *Soil Exhaustion as a Factor in the Agricultural History of Virginia and Maryland, 1606-1860* (Univ. of Ill., *Studies*, XIII, no. 1, 1926) is particularly important for the post-Revolutionary generation. An excellent portrait of the gentleman farmer of the upper South is presented in P. L. Haworth, *George Washington, Country Gentleman* (N. Y., 1925). For descriptions of the Southwest, consult J. H.

Ingraham, *The Southwest* (N. Y., 1835). References on Negro labor, cited later, contain material on the Southern plantation.

THE MERCHANT AND COMMERCIAL ACTIVITY

FOREIGN AND DOMESTIC COMMERCE: A general introduction to various phases of business enterprise is available in ʻE. R. Johnson and others, *History of Domestic and Foreign Commerce of the United States* (2 vols., Carnegie Inst., *Publs.*, no. 215 A, 1915). Its extensive list of sources needs to be supplemented for this period by the bibliography in R. G. Albion's admirable study, *The Rise of New York Port, 1815-1860* (N. Y., 1939). The statistical basis for descriptions of American commerce appears in *American State Papers* (already cited), the two series on *Commerce and Navigation* and *Finance*. I. D. Andrews, *Report . . . on the Trade and Commerce of the British American Colonies and upon the Trade of the Great Lakes and Rivers* (32 Cong., 1 sess., *Senate Exec. Doc.*, no. 112, 1853), contains many data not included in such contemporary accounts as Adam Seybert, *Statistical Annals* (Phila., 1818), and Timothy Pitkin, *A Statistical View of the Commerce of the United States* (New Haven, 1835). A secondary work of a general nature is C. M. Depew, ed., *One Hundred Years of American Commerce, 1795-1895* (2 vols., N. Y., 1895). Of the regional studies the best is S. E. Morison, *Maritime History of Massachusetts, 1783-1860* (Boston, 1921). Special phases of foreign commerce are treated in W. F. Galpin, *The Grain Supply of England during the Napoleonic Period* (Univ. of Mich., *Publs.*, VI, 1925); F. L. Benns, *The American Struggle for the British West India Carrying-Trade, 1815-1830* (Indiana Univ., *Studies*, X, no. 56, 1923); and F. R. Rutter, *The South American Trade of Baltimore* (Johns Hopkins Univ., *Studies*, XV, 1897). On the trade with the Orient, consult Tyler Dennett, *Americans in Eastern Asia* (N. Y., 1922), and F. R. Dulles, *The Old China Trade* (Boston, 1930). Other interesting accounts are Gertrude S. Kimball, *The East India Trade of Providence,*

1787-1807 (Providence, 1896); R. E. Peabody, *Merchant Venturers of Old Salem* (Boston, 1912); and K. S. Latourette, "The History of Early Relations between the United States and China," Conn. Acad. of Arts and Sciences, *Trans.*, XXII, 1-209.

THE RÔLE OF THE MERCHANT: No general work on American mercantile enterprise deals with the significant part played by the individual merchant. Several recent studies indicate that the material for such a synthesis is both abundant and not confined to the prominent merchants of the great commercial centers. See, for example, R. T. Thompson, *Colonel James Neilson, a Business Man . . . in New Jersey* (New Brunswick, 1940); H. B. Howe, *Jedediah Barber* (N. Y., 1939); and Sister Marietta Jennings, *A Pioneer Merchant of St. Louis, 1810-1820* (Columbia Univ., Studies, XXI, no. 3, 1939). In similar vein Lewis Atherton (in his "Services of the Frontier Merchant," *Miss. Valley Hist. Rev.*, XXIV, 153-171) has stressed the influence on Western development of those who controlled the channels of trade. Of the numerous biographies of "merchant princes" several deserve mention because of their revelation of various phases of the social process in America: K. W. Porter, *John Jacob Astor, Business Man* (2 vols., *Harvard Studies in Business History*, I, 1931); J. B. McMaster, *Life and Times of Stephen Girard* (Phila., 1918); C. W. Bowen, *Lewis and Arthur Tappan* (N. Y., 1883); W. H. Hillyer, *James Talcott, Merchant, and His Times* (N. Y., 1937); Edward Gray, *William Gray of Salem, Merchant* (Boston, 1914); K. W. Porter, ed., *The Jacksons and the Lees* (2 vols., *Harvard Studies in Business History*, III, 1937); C. E. Trow, *The Old Shipmasters of Salem* (N. Y., 1905); and Amos Lawrence, *Extracts from Diary and Correspondence* (W. R. Lawrence, ed., Boston, 1855).

ORGANIZATION OF MERCANTILE ENTERPRISE: There is no adequate treatment of the organization of foreign commerce, but N. S. Buck, *The Development of the Organisation of Anglo-American Trade, 1800-1850* (New Haven, 1925), throws light on an intricate problem. On the domestic side the most complete discussion is F. M. Jones, *Middlemen in the Domestic Trade of the United States (Ill. Studies in the Social Sciences,* XXI, no. 3, 1937). The story of financial policies and their impact on American business has not been fully told, but the following works are helpful: Margaret G. Myers, *The New York Money Market* (4 vols., N. Y., 1931-1932); J. T. Holdsworth, *The First Bank of the United States* (Wash., 1910), which must be supplemented by numerous articles that J. O. Wettereau has published since 1930; R. C. H. Catterall, *The Second Bank of the United States* (Univ. of Chicago, *Decennial Publs.,* ser. 2, II, 1903); D. R. Dewey, *State Banking before the Civil War* (N. Y., 1910); and J. C. Brown, *A Hundred Years of Merchant Banking, a History of Brown Bros. & Co.* (N. Y., 1909). The general course of business trends is traced in W. B. Smith and A. H. Cole, *Fluctuations in American Business, 1790-1860 (Harvard Econ. Studies,* I, 1935). There is great need for a complete list of the collections of papers of individual business firms now rapidly accumulating in various libraries.

TRANSPORTATION AND COMMUNICATION

While there is no lack of material dealing with transportation, even in general accounts, it has not so far been presented in effective form. Seymour Dunbar, *History of Travel in America* (4 vols., N. Y., 1915), and B. H. Meyer, Caroline E. MacGill and others, *History of Transportation in the United States before 1860* (Carnegie Inst., *Publs.,* no. 215 C, 1917), are faulty in organization, and the second is far from complete. A. B. Hulbert, *The Paths of Inland Commerce (Chronicles of America,* XXI), is admirable for the early national period. Of the regional studies, two are outstanding: U. B. Phillips, *A History of Transportation in the Eastern Cotton Belt to 1860* (N. Y., 1908), and W. J. Lane, *From Indian Trail to Iron Horse: Travel and Transportation in New Jersey, 1620 to 1860 (Princeton History of New Jersey,* I; Princeton, 1939).

A. B. Hulbert, *Historic Highways of America* (16 vols., Cleveland, 1902-1905), devotes a volume to each of the more important turnpikes. Two regional studies are systematic and thorough: F. J. Wood, *Turnpikes of New England* (Boston, 1919), and J. A. Durrenberger, *Turnpikes, a Study of the Toll Road Movement in the Middle Atlantic States and Maryland* (N. Y., 1931). For the engineering problems in the construction of roads and bridges, see N. C. Rockwood, *One Hundred and Fifty Years of Road Building in America* (N. Y., 1914), and H. G. Tyrrell, *History of Bridge Engineering* (Chicago, 1911). From his studies of the stagecoach business, O. W. Holmes has published "Levi Pease, the Father of New England Stage-Coaching," *Journ. of Econ. and Business History,* III, 241-263, and "The Stage-Coach Business in the Hudson Valley," N. Y. State Hist. Assoc., *Quar. Journ.,* XII, 231-256. Good pictures of life along the roads may be gained from T. B. Searight, *The Old Pike* (Uniontown, Pa., 1894), a picturesque account of the Cumberland Road; Richardson Wright, *Hawkers and Walkers in Early America* (Phila., 1927), which describes various phases of the peddler's career; Alice M. Earle, *Stage-Coach and Tavern Days* (N. Y., 1902) ; and Elsie Lathrop, *Early American Inns and Taverns* (N. Y., 1926).

On the canal era the most comprehensive work is A. F. Harlow's popular account, *Old Towpaths* (N. Y., 1926). Albert Gallatin's famous report on roads and canals is in *American State Papers, Miscellaneous,* I, 724-921. Other contemporary summaries are S. A. Mitchell, *Mitchell's Compendium of the Internal Improvements of the United States* (Phila., 1835), and H. S. Tanner, *A Description of the Canals and Railroads of the United States* (N. Y., 1840). N. E. Whitford, *History of the Canal System of the State of New York* (2 vols., N. Y., 1906), the most complete treatment of the Erie Canal, corrects some of the inaccuracies in Elkanah Watson's *History of the Western Canals in the State of New York* (Albany, 1820). Julius Winden, *The Influence of the Erie Canal upon the Population along Its Course* (Madison, 1901), places more emphasis on politics than the title suggests. For detailed discussion of other canal systems, see T. B. Klein, *The Canals of Pennsylvania and the System of Internal Improvements* (Harrisburg, 1901) ;

W. F. Dunaway, *History of the James River and Kanawha Company* (N. Y., 1922); and G. W. Ward, *The Early Development of the Chesapeake and Ohio Canal Project* (N. Y., 1899).

No general account treats all phases of river transportation. For the years before the steamboat two books are accurate and readable: L. D. Baldwin, *The Keelboat Age on Western Waters* (Pittsburgh, 1941); and C. H. Ambler, *History of Transportation in the Ohio Valley* (Glendale, Calif., 1932). F. H. Dixon, *A Traffic History of the Mississippi River System* (Natl. Waterways Comn., *Docs.*, no. 11, 1909), devotes considerable attention to the beginnings of steam navigation. There are interesting sidelights in F. E. Dayton, *Steamboat Days* (N. Y., 1925); D. L. Buckman, *Old Steamboat Days on the Hudson River* (N. Y., 1903); and A. B. Hulbert, *Waterways of Western Expansion* (*Historic Highways*, IX, 1903). Most of the literature on railroads deals with the evolution of separate lines or technical problems of engineering. T. W. Van Metre, *Early Opposition to the Steam Railroad* (N. Y., 1924), is an interesting compilation of contemporary comments from newspapers and pamphlets. The conflict between the canal interests and the railroad promoters is well portrayed in Lane, *From Indian Trail to Iron Horse* (already cited). A careful analysis of the possibilities of the railroad appears in William Strickland, *Report on Canals, Railways, Roads and Other Subjects* (Phila., 1826). For the early locomotives, see W. H. Brown, *History of the First Locomotives in America* (N. Y., 1871). The first chapters of Edward Hungerford, *The Story of the Baltimore and Ohio Railroad, 1827-1927* (2 vols., N. Y., 1928), are important for the student of social conditions.

Much significant material appears in the biographies of inventors whose work was closely associated with transportation changes. See especially A. D. Turnbull, *John Stevens: an American Record* (N. Y., 1928); H. W. Dickinson, *Robert Fulton* (N. Y., 1913); Thompson Westcott, *The Life of John Fitch* (Phila., 1857); and Allan Nevins, *Abram S. Hewitt, with Some Account of Peter Cooper* (N. Y., 1935), which gives an excellent picture of Cooper's early interest in railroads. The record of the social effects of improved transportation and communication is to be found in the travel literature of the period (which has already been listed) and in the story of expanding postal facilities. On the latter, see W. E. Rich, *History of the United States Post Office to the Year 1828* (*Harvard Econ. Studies*, XXVII, 1924), and A. F. Harlow, *The Old Post Bags* (N. Y., 1928).

INDUSTRY AND LABOR

MANUFACTURES: The best general survey of manufacturing during the period is V. S. Clark, *History of Manufactures in the United States, 1607-1928* (Carnegie Inst., *Contribs. to Am. Econ. History*, rev. edn., 3 vols., N. Y., 1929). In conjunction with R. M. Tryon, *Household Manufactures in the United States, 1640-1860* (N. Y., 1917), it gives an adequate picture of secondary industries. Two regional surveys deserve attention: Isaac Lippincott, *A History of Manufactures in the Ohio Valley to the Year 1860* (N. Y., 1914), which describes handicraft and small-mill production; and Grace P. Fuller, *An Introduction to the History of Connecticut as a Manufacturing State* (Smith College, *Studies*, I, no. 1, 1915). Relatively few good monographs on particular industries deal with this period. Caroline F. Ware, *The Early New England Cotton Manufacture* (N. Y., 1931), emphasizes the region north of Boston. Other industries that have been carefully studied include A. H. Cole, *The American Wool Manufacture* (2 vols., Cambridge, 1926); C. B. Kuhlmann, *The Development of the Flour-Milling Industry of the United States* (N. Y., 1929); and Blanche E. Hazard, *The Organization of the Boot and Shoe Industry in Massachusetts before 1875* (*Harvard Econ. Studies*, XXIII, 1921). Kathleen Bruce, *Virginia Iron Manufacture in the Slave Era* (N. Y., 1930), provides a model for a survey of the entire industry. Contemporary data may be obtained from a wide variety of sources, most important of which are certain government documents. *American State Papers* contains Hamilton's report on manufacturing (*Finance*, I, 123 ff.), Gallatin's report of 1810 (*Finance*, II, 425 ff.), and Tench Coxe's digest of manufactures for 1814 (*Finance*, II, 666 ff.). The most reliable survey for this period, however, is Secretary Louis McLane's report in 1832-1833 which appears in *Executive Document*, no. 308 (22 Cong., 1 sess.). Other documents are readily available in J. R. Commons and others, eds., *A Documentary History of American Industrial Society* (10 vols., N. Y., 1910-1911), and Alexander Hamilton, *Industrial and Commercial Correspondence* (A. H. Cole, ed., *Business Historical Studies*, I, 1928). There are interesting items on the social effects of industrial changes in Tench Coxe, *View of the United States . . . between 1787 and 1794* (Phila., 1794); F. L. Humphreys, *Life and Times of David Humphreys* (2 vols., N. Y., 1917); G. S. White, *Memoir of Samuel Slater* (N. Y., 1836); Nathan Appleton, *Introduction of the Power Loom* (Boston, 1858); and Samuel Batchelder, *Introduction and Early Progress of the Cotton Manufacture of the United States* (Boston, 1863).

LABOR: The story of the wage-earner is told in J. R. Commons and others, *History of Labour [Labor] in the United States* (4 vols., N. Y., 1918-1935), with emphasis on developing organization. Edith Abbott, *Women in Industry, with an Appendix on Child Labor before 1870* (N. Y., 1870), W. R. Waterman, *Frances Wright* (Columbia Univ., *Studies*, CXV, no. 1, 1924), and Helen L. Sumner, *History of Women in Industry in the United States* (61 Cong., 2 sess., *Senate Doc.*, no. 645), shed light on working conditions. H. A. Miles, *Lowell as It Was and Is* (Boston, 1845), presents a more favorable view than the facts warrant. For labor organizations, see Ethelbert Stewart, *A Documentary History of the Early Organizations of Printers* (58 Cong., 3 sess., *House Doc.*, no. 386), and F. T. Carlton, *History and Problems of Organized Labor* (N. Y., 1920). In addition to previous references on Southern agriculture, the following are important for servile labor: J. C. Ballagh, *A History of Slavery in Virginia* (Johns Hopkins Univ., *Studies*, extra vol. XXIV, 1902); H. A. Trexler, *Slavery in Missouri, 1804-1865* (*ibid.*, XXXII, no. 2,

1914) ; E. I. McCormac, *White Servitude in Maryland, 1634-1820* (ibid., XXII, nos. 3-4, 1904) ; R. H. Taylor, *Slaveholding in North Carolina* (*James Sprunt Hist. Publs.,* XVIII, nos. 1-2, 1926) ; I. E. McDougle, *Slavery in Kentucky, 1772-1865* (Wash., 1918) ; and C. A. Herrick, *White Servitude in Pennsylvania* (Phila., 1926).

IMMIGRATION

The most satisfactory general account of American immigration during this period is M. L. Hansen, *The Atlantic Migration, 1607-1860* (A. M. Schlesinger, ed., Cambridge, 1940). Several of the essays in his *The Immigrant in American History* (A. M. Schlesinger, ed., Cambridge, 1940), also touch upon the early nineteenth-century migration. Special studies need to be consulted, especially W. F. Adams, *Ireland and Irish Emigration to the New World from 1815 to the Famine* (*Yale Hist. Publs. Miscellany,* XXIII, 1932) ; A. B. Faust, *The German Element in the United States* (2 vols., N. Y., 1927) ; S. C. Johnson, *A History of Emigration from the United Kingdom to North America* (London School of Econs. and Polit. Sci., *Studies,* no. 34, 1913) ; and M. L. Hansen, *The Mingling of the Canadian and American Peoples* (*The Relations of Canada and the United States;* J. B. Brebner, ed., New Haven, 1940). Oscar Handlin, *Boston's Immigrants, 1790-1865* (*Harvard Hist. Studies,* L, 1941), which should serve as a model for studies of other cities, emphasizes the years after 1830. For the French, see J. G. Rosengarten, *French Colonists and Exiles in the United States* (London, 1905), an early work now supplemented where it is not superseded by Frances S. Childs, *French Refugee Life in the United States, 1790-1800* (Balt., 1940). L. F. Ruskowski, *French Emigré Priests in the United States, 1791-1815* (Catholic Univ. of Am., *Studies,* XXXII, 1940), brings together the information in many scattered accounts. The travel literature (already cited) contains interesting observations on the immigrant in America. Thomas Cooper, *Some Information Respecting America* (London, 1794), was really a superior guidebook for those contemplating migration.   Other immigrant manuals were Gilbert Imlay, *A Description of the Western Territory of North America* (Dublin, 1793), unreliable because of its attempt to promote real-estate sales; John Bristed, *America and Her Resources* (London, 1818); S. H. Collins, *Emigrant's Guide . . . to the United States* (4th edn., Hull, 1830); and Martin Doyle, *Hints on Emigration* (Dublin, 1831).   Documentary materials, dealing chiefly with legislation, have been collected by Edith Abbott in *Immigration; Select Documents* (Univ. of Chicago, *Social Service Series,* 1924) and *Historical Aspects of the Immigration Problem* (*ibid.*, 1926).

THE PROFESSIONS

LAW: The status of the legal profession is well described in Charles Warren, *History of the American Bar* (Boston, 1911), though it should be supplemented at some points by the penetrating observations of Roscoe Pound in *The Formative Era of American Law* (Boston, 1938).   For legal education, consult A. Z. Reed, *Training for the Public Profession of Law* (N. Y., 1921); Charles Warren, *History of the Harvard Law School* (3 vols., N. Y., 1908); anon., *The Litchfield Law School, 1784-1833* (Litchfield, Conn., 1900); H. C. Van Schaack, *Life of Peter Van Schaack* (N. Y., 1842); James Kent, *Dissertations: Being the Preliminary Part of a Course of Law Lectures* (N. Y., 1795); and David Hoffman, *Syllabus of a Course of Lectures on Law* (Balt., 1821).   The numerous biographies of distinguished practitioners add information on the training and changing status of the profession, notably A. J. Beveridge, *The Life of John Marshall* (4 vols., Boston, 1916-1919); C. B. Swisher, *Roger B. Taney* (N. Y., 1935); C. M. Fuess, *Daniel Webster* (2 vols., Boston, 1930); J. T. Horton, *James Kent* (N. Y., 1939); William Kent, *Memoirs and Letters of James Kent* (Boston, 1898); W. W. Story, *Life and Letters of Joseph Story* (2 vols., Boston, 1851); F. H. Chase, *Life of Lemuel Shaw* (Boston, 1918); E. S. Delaplaine, *Life of Thomas Johnson* (N. Y., 1927); C. M.

Fuess, *Life of Caleb Cushing* (2 vols., N. Y., 1923); W. B. Hatcher, *Edward Livingston* (University, La., 1940); J. P. Kennedy, *Memoirs of the Life of William Wirt* (2 vols., Phila., 1849); Raymond Walters, jr., *Alexander James Dallas* (Phila., 1944); W. M. Meigs, *The Life of Thomas Hart Benton* (Phila., 1904); and J. E. D. Shipp, *Giant Days; or the Life and Times of William H. Crawford* (Americus, Ga., 1909). The judicial reports of the various states constitute a library of information on social conditions, the importance of which has been admirably stressed in J. G. Randall, "The Interrelation of Social and Constitutional History," *Am. Hist. Rev.*, XXXV, 1-13. Much can also be gleaned from the files of the *American Law Journal* (Phila., 1807-1817); the *American Jurist* (Boston, 1829-1843); and the *United States Law Journal* (New Haven and N. Y., 1822-1826). Other contemporary writings of value are Nathan Dane, ed., *General Abridgment and Digest of American Law* (9 vols., Boston, 1823-1829); James Kent, *Commentaries on American Law* (4 vols., N. Y., 1826-1830); and Edward Livingston, *System of Penal Laws, Prepared for the State of Louisiana* (New Orleans, 1824), *Commercial Code* (New Orleans, 1825) and *Civil Code of the State of Louisiana* (New Orleans, 1825).

MEDICINE: Three general surveys of medical history devote some attention to this period: F. H. Garrison, *Introduction to the History of Medicine* (rev. edn., Phila., 1929); F. R. Packard, *History of Medicine in the United States* (rev. edn., 2 vols., N. Y., 1931); and R. H. Shryock, *The Development of Modern Medicine* (Phila., 1936). The most important work on the early history of American medicine is now being done by Professor Shryock, whose articles have appeared in many learned journals. H. B. Shafer, *The American Medical Profession, 1783 to 1850* (N. Y., 1936), emphasizes formal instruction and presents an excellent introduction to the textbooks used in courses and the periodicals published by medical societies. Educational facilities may also be traced in N. S. Davis, *Contributions to the History of Medical Education and Medical Institutions in the United States, 1776-1876* (Wash., 1877); E. H. Clarke and others, *A Century of American Medicine, 1776-1876* (Phila., 1876); T. F. Harrington, *The Harvard Medical School . . . 1782-1905* (3 vols., N. Y., 1905); Joseph Carson, *A History of the Medical Department of the University of Pennsylvania* (Phila., 1869); and E. F. Cordell, *An Historical Sketch of the University of Maryland School of Medicine, 1807-1890* (Balt., 1891). Local studies include J. J. Walsh, *History of Medicine in New York* (5 vols., N. Y., 1919), and W. L. Burrage, *A History of the Massachusetts Medical Society, 1781-1922* (Boston, 1923).

The careers of individual practitioners are conveniently summarized in S. D. Gross, ed., *Lives of Eminent American Physicians and Surgeons of the 19th Century* (Phila., 1861). The most important biographies are Nathan Goodman, *Benjamin Rush* (Phila., 1934); J. A. Spalding, *Dr. Lyman Spalding* (Boston, 1916); E. D. Mansfield, *Memoir of Daniel Drake* (Cincinnati, 1855); and S. D. Gross, *Memoir of Valentine Mott* (Phila., 1868). For folk medicine and quackery, consult Samuel Thomson, *New Guide to Health* (Boston, 1825); Lewis Merlin, tr., *The Treasure of Health* (Phila., 1819); R. H. Shryock, "Public Relations of the Medical Profession in Great Britain and the United States, 1600-1870," *Annals of Medical History*, n.s., II, 308-339; Morris Fishbein, *Medical Follies* (N. Y., 1925); and H. W. Haggard, *Devils, Drugs, and Doctors* (N. Y., 1929), a popular account. The most significant contemporary material is found in the medical journals: *American Medical Recorder* (6 vols., Phila., 1818-1823); *Medical Repository* (24 vols., N. Y., 1797-1824); *Boston Medical Intelligencer* (5 vols., Boston, 1822-1826); *New England Journal of Medicine and Surgery* (15 vols., Boston, 1812-1826); *Philadelphia Medical Museum* (6 vols., Phila., 1804-1811); and *New York Medical and Physical Journal* (9 vols., N. Y., 1822-1830).

RELIGIOUS TRENDS

GENERAL: There is no satisfactory comprehensive account of religious development in this period. Pertinent chapters in W. W. Sweet, *The Story of Religion in America* (rev. edn., N. Y., 1939), are factual rather than interpretative. P. G. Mode, ed., *Source Book and Bibliographical Guide for American Church History* (Menasha, Wis., 1921), is a good introduction to the earlier literature. For the relations between church and state the best analysis is E. B. Greene, *Religion and the State* (N. Y., 1941). A convenient summary of the legal aspects of church-state relations appears in Carl Zollmann, *American Church Law* (St. Paul, 1933). The denominational histories include J. G. Shea, *History of the Catholic Church in the United States* (4 vols., N. Y., 1886); Peter Guilday, *Life and Times of John Carroll* (2 vols., N. Y., 1922); W. S. Perry, *History of the American Episcopal Church* (2 vols., Boston, 1885); C. A. Briggs, *American Presbyterianism* (N. Y., 1885); W. W. Sweet, *Methodism in American History* (N. Y., 1933); Williston Walker, *A History of the Congregational Churches in the United States* (*American Church History Series*, 13 vols., N. Y., 1893-1897, III); and David Benedict, *A General History of the Baptist Denomination in America* (2 vols., Boston, 1813).

LIBERAL RELIGION: Unorthodox tendencies are dealt with in G. A. Koch, *Republican Religion* (*Studies in Religion and Culture*, VII, 1933); H. M. Morais, *Deism in Eighteenth Century America* (Columbia Univ., *Studies*, no. 397, 1934); John Pell, *Ethan Allen* (Boston, 1929); Thomas Paine, *Writings* (M. D. Conway, ed., 4 vols., N. Y., 1894-1896); Gilbert Chinard, *Jefferson et les Idéologues* (Balt., 1925); Dumas Malone, *The Public Life of Thomas Cooper* (*Yale Hist. Publs. Miscellany*, XVI, 1926); Adrienne Koch, *The Philosophy of Thomas Jefferson* (N. Y., 1943); G. W. Cooke, *Unitarianism in America* (Boston, 1902); and Richard Eddy, *Universalism in America* (Boston, 1884).

RELIGION ON THE FRONTIER: For this subject, see P. G. Mode, *The Frontier Spirit in American Christianity* (N. Y., 1923); W. W. Sweet, ed., *The Baptists* (same ed., *Religion on the American Frontier*, N. Y. and Chicago, 1931-1939, I), and *The Presbyterians* (*ibid.*, II); W. B. Posey, *The Development of Methodism in the Old Southwest* (Tuscaloosa, Ala., 1933); Catherine C. Cleveland, *The Great Revival in the West, 1797-1805* (Chicago, 1916); N. H. Sonne, *Liberal Kentucky, 1780-1828 (Columbia Studies in Am. Culture,* no. 3, 1939); T. T. McAvoy, *The Catholic Church in Indiana, 1789-1834* (Columbia Univ., *Studies,* no. 471, 1940); W. H. Milburn, *The Pioneers, Preachers and People of the Mississippi Valley* (N. Y., 1860); Peter Cartwright, *Autobiography* (W. P. Strickland, ed., N. Y., 1857); J. B. Finley, *Sketches of Western Methodism* (W. P. Strickland, ed., Cincinnati, 1854); John Rogers, *The Biography of Elder Barton Warren Stone* (Cincinnati, 1847); and Alexander Campbell, *Memoirs* (Robert Richardson, ed., 2 vols., N. Y., 1868).

THE PROTESTANT COUNTER-REFORMATION: E. B. Greene, "A Puritan Counter-Reformation," Am. Antiquarian Soc., *Proceeds.,* n.s., XLII, 17-46, is a stimulating essay. See also C. R. Keller, *The Second Great Awakening in Connecticut (Yale Hist. Publs. Miscellany,* XL, 1942); J. K. Morse, *Jedidiah Morse, a Champion of New England Orthodoxy (Columbia Studies in Am. Culture,* no. 2, 1939); R. J. Purcell, *Connecticut in Transition* (Wash., 1918); Leonard Woods, *History of Andover Theological Seminary* (Boston, 1885); Lyman Beecher, *Autobiography* (Charles Beecher, ed., 2 vols., N. Y., 1865); Francis Eddy, *The Sabbath School Century* (Hamilton, Ohio, 1882); and C. E. Cuningham, *Timothy Dwight* (N. Y., 1942).

MISSIONARY ENTERPRISE: Various aspects are treated in the following works: O. W. Elsbree, *The Rise of the Missionary Spirit in America, 1790-1815* (Williamsport, Pa., 1928); C. B. Goodykoontz, *Home Missions on the American Frontier* (Caldwell, Idaho, 1939); J. B. Clark, *Leavening the Nation* (N. Y., 1903); Rufus Anderson, ed., *Memorial Volume of the First Fifty Years of the American Board of Commissioners for Foreign Missions* (Boston, 1862); J. O. Choules and Thomas Smith, *The Origin and History of Missions* (2 vols., Boston, 1837); W. E. Strong, *The Story of the American Board* (Boston, 1901); R. H. Gabriel, *Elias Boudinot, Cherokee* (Norman, Okla., 1941); Francis Wayland, *The Moral Dignity of the Missionary En-*

terprise (Boston, 1824); S. J. Mills and Daniel Smith, *Report of a Missionary Tour* (Andover, 1815); and W. A. Hallock, *A Sketch of the Life and Labors of Justin Edwards* (N. Y., 1855).

PHILANTHROPY AND REFORM

HUMANITARIANISM: Early efforts to combat poverty and vice in the larger towns are discussed in McMaster, *History* (cited earlier), IV, chap. xxxvii, and R. T. Thompson, *Colonel James Neilson* (New Brunswick, 1940). Contemporary data are available in the documents of the various societies for the prevention of pauperism. Particularly important are the annual reports (1818-1830) of the Society for the Prevention of Pauperism in the City of New York and the *Sketch of the Origin and Progress of the Humane Society of the City of New York* (N. Y., 1814). The rôle of the churches in charitable undertakings is emphasized by the annual "charity sermon" which became traditional in most denominations. James Hardie, *Description of the City of New York* (N. Y., 1827), suggests the wide range of the benevolence of the wealthier classes.

TEMPERANCE REFORM: For a general survey, see J. A. Krout, *The Origins of Prohibition* (N. Y., 1925). Other works are Lebbeus Armstrong, *History of the Temperance Reformation* (N. Y., 1868); G. F. Clark, *History of the Temperance Reform in Massachusetts, 1813-1883* (Boston, 1888); H. A. Scomp, *King Alcohol in the Realm of King Cotton* (Oxford, Ga., 1888); William Dunlap, *Thirty Years Ago, or Memoirs of a Water Drinker* (N. Y., 1837); and Lyman Beecher, *Six Sermons on the Nature . . . of Intemperance* (Boston, 1827).

PRISON DISCIPLINE AND PENAL CODES: This subject is dealt with in O. F. Lewis, *The Development of American Prisons and Prison Conditions, 1776-1845* (Albany, 1922); H. E. Barnes, *The Repression of Crime* (N. Y., 1926); Blake McKelvey, *American Prisons* (Univ. of Chicago, Social Service Series, 1936); J. S. Taylor, *A Comparative View of Punishments Annexed to Crime in the*

United States of America and in England (London, 1831); and S. L. Knapp, *Life of Thomas Eddy* (N. Y., 1834). The annual reports (Boston, 1820-1830) of the Prison Discipline Society are indispensable.

EDUCATION

HIGHER EDUCATION: The standard work on the colleges is C. F. Thwing, *History of Higher Education in America* (N. Y., 1907), though it must be supplemented at many points. D. G. Tewksbury deals with the expansion of facilities in *The Founding of American Colleges and Universities before the Civil War* (Teachers College, Columbia Univ., *Contribs.*, no. 543, 1932), while G. P. Schmidt, *The Old Time College President* (Columbia Univ., *Studies*, no. 317, 1930), discusses various phases of instruction and administration. For changes in the curriculum, see L. F. Snow, *The College Curriculum in the United States* (N. Y., 1907); R. F. Butts, *The College Charts Its Course* (N. Y., 1939); C. H. Handschin, *The Teaching of Modern Languages in the United States* (U. S. Bur. of Educ., *Bull.*, no. 3, 1913); and Anna Haddow, *Political Science in American Colleges and Universities, 1636-1900* (F. A. Ogg, ed., *The Century Political Science Series;* N. Y., 1939). The most valuable of the institutional histories is S. E. Morison, *Three Centuries of Harvard* (Boston, 1936), but the following should also be consulted: V. L. Collins, *Princeton* (N. Y., 1914); Ebenezer Baldwin, *Annals of Yale College* (New Haven, 1831); W. C. Bronson, *The History of Brown University, 1764-1914* (Providence, 1914); W. H. S. Demarest, *A History of Rutgers College, 1766-1924* (New Brunswick, 1924); L. B. Richardson, *History of Dartmouth College* (2 vols., Hanover,, 1932); and E. M. Coulter, *College Life in the Old South* (N. Y., 1928).

LOWER SCHOOLS: The literature is voluminous. A select list would include E. P. Cubberley, *Public Education in the United States* (rev. edn., Boston, 1934); F. H. Swift, *A History of Public Permanent Common School Funds in the United States from 1795 to 1905* (Wash. 1906); Clifton

Johnson, *Old Time Schools and School-books* (N. Y., 1904); W. O. Bourne, *History of the Public School Society of the City of New York* (N. Y., 1870); G. F. Miller, *The Academy System of the State of New York* (Albany, 1920); W. A. Maddox, *The Free School Idea in Virginia* (N. Y., 1918); C. L. Coon, *North Carolina Schools and Academies* (Raleigh, 1915); J. F. Reigart, *The Lancasterian System of Instruction in the Schools of New York City* (N. Y., 1916); and J. J. McCadden, *Education in Pennsylvania, 1801-1835* (Phila., 1937).

THEORY: Educational theories, particularly as they related to the popularization of knowledge, may be studied in A. O. Hansen, *Liberalism and American Education in the Eighteenth Century* (N.Y., 1926); Merle Curti, *The Social Ideas of American Educators* (Comn. on Social Studies, *Rep.,* X, 1935); F. T. Carlton, *Economic Influences upon Educational Progress in the United States, 1820-1850* (Univ. of Wis., *Bull.,* no. 221, 1908); H. R. Warfel, *Noah Webster, School Master to America* (N.Y., 1936); E. A. Fitzpatrick, *The Educational Views and Influence of DeWitt Clinton* (N.Y., 1911); and R. J. Honeywell, *The Educational Work of Thomas Jefferson* (*Harvard Studies in Educ.,* XVI, 1931). Significant contemporary writings are Noah Webster, *A Collection of Essays and Fugitive Writings* (Boston, 1790); Robert Coram, *Political Inquiries* (Wilmington, 1791); S. H. Smith, *Remarks on Education* (Phila., 1798); Samuel Knox, *Essay on the Best System of Education* (Phila., 1799); Benjamin Rush, *Essays, Literary, Moral & Philosophical* (Phila., 1798); Nathaniel Chipman, *Sketches of the Principles of Government* (Rutland, Vt., 1793); and Jesse Torrey, jr., *The Intellectual Torch* (Ballston Spa, 1817).

SCIENCE

As a guide to the scientific literature of the period W. M. and Mabel S. C. Smallwood, *Natural History and the American Mind* (*Columbia Studies in American Culture,* no. 8,

1941), is helpful, though the emphasis is on the early naturalists. For specific subjects, see G. P. Merrill, *The First One Hundred Years of American Geology* (New Haven, 1924); Jacob Bigelow, "Botany of the United States," *N. Am. Rev.*, XIII (1821), 100-134; R. A. Proctor, "Astronomy in America," *Pop. Sci. Mo.*, X (1877), 75-86; Florian Cajori, *The Teaching and History of Mathematics in the United States* (U. S. Bur. of Educ., *Circular of Information*, 1890, no. 3); and T. C. Johnson, jr., *Scientific Interests in the Old South* (Univ. of Va., *Institute Monograph*, XXIII, 1936). On individual scientists, see W. J. Youmans, *Pioneers of Science in America* (N. Y., 1896); J. W. Harshberger, *The Botanists of Philadelphia and Their Work* (Phila., 1899); F. H. Herrick, *Audubon the Naturalist* (2 vols., N.Y., 1917); Ethel M. McAllister, *Amos Eaton, Scientist and Educator, 1776-1842* (Phila., 1941); E. F. Smith, *Priestley in America, 1794-1804* (Phila., 1920); C. R. Hall, *A Scientist in the Early Republic; Samuel Latham Mitchill, 1764-1831* (N.Y., 1934); E. F. Smith, *James Woodhouse* (Phila., 1918); and Alexander Young, *Discourse on the Life and Character of Nathaniel Bowditch* (Boston, 1838). For the slowly developing profession of engineering, see P. C. Ricketts, *History of the Rensselaer Polytechnic Institute, 1824-1934* (N. Y., 1934); E. C. Boynton, *History of West Point* (N. Y., 1864), part ii; J. K. Finch, *Early Columbia Engineers* (N. Y., 1929); Greville Bathe, *Oliver Evans* (Phila., 1935); A. H. Waters, *Biographical Sketch of Thomas Blanchard and His Inventions* (Boston, 1878); G. L. Vose, *Sketch of the Life and Works of Loammi Baldwin, Civil Engineer* (Boston, 1885); and C. B. Stuart, *Lives and Works of Civil and Military Engineers of America* (N. Y., 1871).

THOUGHT AND CULTURE

The most recent general survey, with penetrating and provocative discussion of intellectual crosscurrents, is Merle Curti, *The Growth of American Thought* (N. Y., 1943).

V. L. Parrington, *Main Currents in American Thought*: *the Romantic Revolution* (N. Y., 1927), stresses the social implications of American literature during the period. The most extensive bibliographies are in Trent and others, *Cambridge History of American Literature* (cited earlier). Excellent regional studies are Clement Eaton, *Freedom of Thought in the Old South* (Durham, 1940); R. L. Rusk, *The Literature of the Middle Western Frontier* (2 vols., N. Y., 1925); and Van Wyck Brooks, *The Flowering of New England, 1815-1865* (N. Y., 1938). Representative men of letters are portrayed in D. L. Clark, *Charles Brockden Brown, a Critical Study* (N. Y., 1923); T. A. Zunder, *The Early Days of Joel Barlow* (N. Y., 1934); C. M. Newlin, *The Life and Writings of Hugh Henry Brackenridge* (Princeton, 1932); R. B. Davis, *Francis W. Gilmer: Life and Learning in Jefferson's Virginia* (Richmond, 1939); A. L. Herold, *James Kirke Paulding* (N. Y., 1926); J. E. Kirkpatrick, *Timothy Flint, . . . 1780-1840* (Cleveland, 1911); S. T. Williams, *The Life of Washington Irving* (2 vols., N. Y., 1935); and H. W. Boynton, *James Fenimore Cooper* (N. Y., 1931).

Literary and cultural contacts between Europe and America may be traced in O. W. Long, *Literary Pioneers* (Cambridge, 1935); [G. S. Hillard and others], *Life, Letters and Journals of George Ticknor* (2 vols., Boston, 1876); R. E. Spiller, *The American in England during the First Half Century of Independence* (N. Y., 1926); H. M. Jones, "The Influence of European Ideas in Nineteenth-Century America," *Am. Lit.*, VII, 241-273; W. B. Cairns, *British Criticisms of American Writings, 1783-1815* (Univ. of Wis., *Studies in Language and Literature*, no. 1, 1918); W. E. Leonard, *Byron and Byronism in America* (Boston, 1905); G. H. Orians, *The Influence of Walter Scott on America and American Literature before 1860* (Urbana, 1929); H. M. Jones, *America and French Culture* (Chapel Hill, 1927); J. D. Ferguson, *American Literature in Spain* (N. Y., 1916); and J. A. Walz, *German Influence in American Education and Culture* (N. Y., 1936).

THE ARTS

ARCHITECTURE: A. J. Wall, comp., *Books on Architecture Printed in America, 1775-1830* (Cambridge, 1925), affords an introduction to the contemporaneous literature. Of the general historical surveys the most helpful are Fiske Kimball, *American Architecture* (Indianapolis, 1928), and T. F. Hamlin's profusely illustrated *The American Spirit in Architecture* (*Pageant of America*, XIII). Dealing particularly with this period are Howard Major, *The Domestic Architecture of the Early American Republic: the Greek Revival* (Phila., 1926); Aymar Embury II, *Early American Churches* (N. Y., 1914); Fiske Kimball, *Domestic Architecture of the American Colonies and of the Early Republic* (N. Y., 1922); and Talbot Hamlin, *Greek Revival Architecture in America* (N. Y., 1944). Biographical studies include C. A. Place, *Charles Bulfinch, Architect and Citizen* (Boston, 1925); Aymar Embury II, *Asher Benjamin* (N. Y., 1917); Joseph Jackson, *Early Philadelphia Architects and Engineers* (Phila., 1923); Fiske Kimball, *Thomas Jefferson, Architect* (Boston, 1916); and B. H. Latrobe, *The Journal of Latrobe* (N. Y., 1905).

SCULPTURE: This period of hesitant beginnings receives slight attention in such general works as C. H. Caffin, *American Masters of Sculpture* (N. Y., 1903), and Lorado Taft, *History of American Sculpture* (N. Y., 1924). Ethel S. Bolton discusses wax portraiture in *American Wax Portraits* (Boston, 1929), while C. H. Hart describes the work of John H. I. Browere in *Browere's Life Masks of Great Americans* (N. Y., 1899).

PAINTING: William Dunlap's *Rise and Progress of the Arts of Design* (1834) has been issued in a revised edition (2 vols., Boston, 1934). Oskar Hagen, *The Birth of the American Tradition in Art* (N. Y., 1940), provides an excellent background for this period. The preliminary inventory prepared by George C. Groce, jr., lists 1440 names of *Early American Portrait Artists, 1663-1860* (Newark, N. J., 1940). Special studies are Laurence Park, comp. *Gilbert*

Stuart, with an Account of His Life by John Hill Morgan (4 vols, N. Y., 1926) ; Theodore Bolton, *Early American Portrait Painters in Miniature* (N. Y., 1921) ; Archibald Robertson, *Letters and Papers* (Emily Robertson, ed., London, 1895) ; Chester Harding, *My Egotistigraphy* (Cambridge, 1866) ; John Trumbull, *Autobiography, Reminiscences and Letters* (N. Y., 1841) ; and Carleton Mabee, *The American Leonardo, a Life of Samuel F. B. Morse* (N. Y., 1943).

THE THEATER: Several works deal with this period: Arthur Hornblow, *A History of the Theatre in America* (2 vols., Phila., 1919) ; Laurence Hutton, *Curiosities of the American Stage* (N. Y., 1891) ; and A. H. Quinn, *A History of the American Drama, from the Beginning to the Civil War* (N. Y., 1923). A contemporary account is William Dunlap, *History of the American Theatre* (N. Y., 1832). The special works include G. C. D. Odell, *Annals of the New York Stage* (13 vols., N. Y., 1927-1942), esp. II and III; D. O. Willard, *History of the Providence Stage* (Providence, 1891) ; W. W. Clapp, *A Record of the Boston Stage* (Boston, 1853) ; and O. S. Coad, *William Dunlap* (N. Y., 1917). The development of the theater along the frontier is fully treated in N. M. Ludlow, *Dramatic Life as I Found It* (St. Louis, 1880), and O. S. Coad and Edwin Mims, jr., *The American Stage* (*Pageant of America*, XIV), chap. vi. See also I. J. Greenwood, *The Circus* (N. Y., 1898).

MUSIC: The most comprehensive survey is J. T. Howard, *Our American Music* (N. Y., 1931). In addition to the studies cited in E. B. Greene, *The Revolutionary Generation* (*A History of American Life*, IV), the following are valuable: H. C. Lahee, "A Century of Choral Singing in New England," *New England Mag.*, XXVI (1902), 102-117; and W. T. Upton, *Anthony Phillip Heinrich* (N. Y., 1939).

SOCIETY AND LEISURE

Dixon Wecter, *The Saga of American Society: a Record of Social Aspiration, 1607-1937* (N. Y., 1937), provides an excellent general setting. The standards set by the patrician leaders are outlined in R. W. Griswold, *The Republican Court: or American Society in the Days of Washington* (N. Y., 1856); Anne H. Wharton, *Social Life in the Early Republic* (Phila., 1902); Gaillard Hunt, ed., *The First Forty Years of Washington Society, Portrayed by the Family Letters of Margaret Bayard Smith* (N. Y., 1906); and Elizabeth F. Ellet, *The Court Circles of the Republic* (Hartford, 1869). Much incidental information appears in A. W. Calhoun, *A Social History of the American Family* (3 vols., Cleveland, 1917-1919); Martha J. Lamb and Mrs. Burton Harrison, *History of the City of New York* (3 vols., N. Y., 1896); J. W. Francis, *Old New York* (N. Y., 1865); J. T. Scharf and Thompson Westcott, *History of Philadelphia: 1609-1884* (3 vols., Phila., 1884); and Ravenel, *Charleston* (cited earlier).

Popular recreation is discussed in its many phases in F. R. Dulles, *America Learns to Play* (N. Y., 1940). On the fashionable resorts, see G. M. Davison, *The Fashionable Tour* (Saratoga Springs, 1825); F. A. Wilson, *Some Annals of Nahant* (Boston, 1928); Jefferson Williamson, *The American Hotel* (N. Y., 1930); and R. H. Gabriel, *The Evolution of Long Island* (New Haven, 1921). J. A. Krout, *Annals of American Sport* (*Pageant of America*, XV), is a general account. For social attitudes in regard to amusements and games, see Jennie Holliman, *American Sports, 1785-1835* (Durham, 1931). Special developments are described in C. A. Peverelly, *The Book of American Pastimes* (N. Y., 1866); Hiram Woodruff, *The Trotting Horse of America* (N. Y., 1871); H. W. Herbert (Frank Forester, *pseud.*), *Horse and Horsemanship of the U. S.* (2 vols., N. Y., 1857); F. G. Griswold, *Race Horses and Racing* (N. Y., 1926); A. H. Clark, *The History of Yachting, 1600-1815* (N. Y., 1904); and Alexander Johnston, *Ten—and Out* (rev. edn., N. Y., 1936).

THE NEW WEST

Theodore Roosevelt, *The Winning of the West* (4 vols., N. Y., 1889-1896), and Justin Winsor, *The Westward*

Movement (Boston, 1897), are still useful, but the most satisfactory general work on the changing frontier is F. L. Paxson, *History of the American Frontier, 1763-1893* (Boston, 1924). Other surveys of value are R. E. Riegel, *America Moves West* (N. Y., 1930), and Douglas Branch's popular account, *Westward* (N. Y., 1930). Several essays in F. J. Turner, *The Frontier in American History* (N. Y., 1920), deal with this period; and his *Rise of the New West* (*American Nation*, XIV) contains the best discussion of the years 1819-1829. D. R. Fox, *Ideas in Motion* (N. Y., 1935), and B. F. Wright and others, *Sources of Culture in the Middle West* (D. R. Fox, ed., N. Y., 1934), offer suggestions concerning the transit of civilization in America.

For the process of migration, consult Lois K. Mathews, *The Expansion of New England* (Boston, 1909), and P. D. Evans, *The Holland Land Company* (Buffalo, 1924); and, among earlier works, Orsamus Turner, *History of the Pioneer Settlement of Phelps and Gorham's Purchase and Morris' Reserve* (Rochester, 1851); Morris Birkbeck, *Notes on a Journey in America* (Dublin, 1818); James Hall, *Letters from the West* (London, 1828); Adam Hodgson, *Letters from North America* (2 vols., London, 1824); Timothy Flint, *Recollections of the Last Ten Years* (Boston, 1826); Isaac Finch, *Travels in the United States and Canada* (London, 1833); and Ingraham, *The Southwest* (already cited).

Conditions in various frontier communities are well described in S. J. and Elizabeth H. Buck, *The Planting of Civilization in Western Pennsylvania* (*Western Pennsylvania Series;* Pittsburgh, 1939); Bond, *Civilization of the Old Northwest* (cited earlier); T. P. Abernethy, *The Formative Period in Alabama, 1815-1828* (Montgomery, 1922), and *From Frontier to Plantation in Tennessee* (Chapel Hill, 1932); J. M. Miller, *Genesis of Western Culture* (Columbus, 1938); E. G. Swem, ed., *Letters on the Condition of Kentucky in 1825* (N. Y., 1916); J. E. Wright and Doris S. Corbett, *Pioneer Life in Western Pennsylvania* (*Western Pennsylvania Series;* Pittsburgh, 1940); and S. J. Buck, *Illinois in 1818* (C. W. Alvord, ed., *The Centennial History of Illinois*, II, Springfield, 1920).

The history of the public domain may be traced in R. M. Robbins, *Our Landed Heritage: the Public Domain, 1776-1936* (Princeton, 1942); P. J. Treat, *The National Land System, 1785-1820* (N. Y., 1910); and B. H. Hibbard, *A History of the Public Land Policies* (N. Y., 1924). On land companies and speculation, see A. M. Sakolski, *The Great American Land Bubble* (N. Y., 1927); Shaw Livermore, *Early American Land Companies* (Columbia Univ. School of Law, *Publs. of the Foundation for Research in Legal History*, 1938); Ohio Company, *Records of the Original Proceedings* (A. B. Hulbert, ed., 2 vols., Marietta, Ohio, 1917); T. T. Belote, *The Scioto Speculation and the French Settlement at Gallipolis* (Cincinnati, 1907); C. S. Hall, *Benjamin Tallmadge* (N. Y., 1943); and D. R. Fox, *The Decline of Aristocracy in the Politics of New York* (Columbia Univ., *Studies*, LXXXVI, 1919).

INDEX

Ministers, support Federalists, 162-
163; waning importance of,
163; attacked, 164; embrace
Unitarianism, 168; on frontier,
171-172, 174, 253; training of,
248-250; as educators, 265-
266; scientific interests of, 314-
315; hostile to theater, 393-394.
See also Missions, Religion.
Missions, home, 251-253, 258-
259; foreign, 254-258; bibliography of, 453-454.
Mississippi, theater in, 398; joins
Union, 407; planters of, 414.
Missouri, relief legislation in, 215;
migration to, 406; joins Union,
407; controversy over, 422-
424.
Mitchill, S. L., on gypsum, 115;
as Columbia instructor, 118,
272, 323, 324; on education,
178-179; supervises writing of
pharmacopœia, 302; recom-
mends yellow-fever treatment,
305; as editor, 310; other scientific interests of, 317-318, 319.
Mitford, Mary R., on American
writing, 369.
Mobile, trade of, 221-223, 415,
419.
Monroe, James, dress of, 35; re-
elected, 209, 424; as President,
211; home of, 337.
Moody, Paul, perfects power loom,
371.
Moore, Thomas, on agriculture,
114.
Morals, frontier, 171, 416; influence of camp meetings on, 174;
taught, 183-184; Indian, 195;
of army in War of 1812, 204;
of country merchant, 244-245;
attempts to reform, 261-265;
professional, 292-296; art and,
345; among factory workers,
373; theater and, 393-394. *See
also* Corruption, Crime.
Moravians, as innkeepers, 89; as
missionaries, 251; as musicians,
365.
More, Hannah, initiates tract societies, 259.
Morris, Gouverneur, buys land, 55;
as author, 349.

Morris, Robert, land promoter, 53,
55-56.
Morse, Jedidiah, on recreations,
108, 109, 134; supports Federalism, 163; opposes Unitarianism, 169, 247-248; as geogra-
pher, 183-184, 207; and War
of 1812, 201; on college equipment, 276.
Morse, S. F. B., artistic interests of,
341-342.
Muhlenberg, Henry, scientific interests of, 315, 319 n.
Murray, John, Universalist, 167.
Museums, marine, 65-66, 431;
natural-history, 316-317, 322;
art, 347, 431; waxwork, 400-
401; historical, 430-431; agricultural, 431.
Music, international influences on,
38, 364-365; as social diversion, 110, 119, 133, 155, 401;
patriotic, 207; development of,
364-366; bibliography of, 460.

NAPOLEON, and Louisiana, 189-
190; and embargo of 1807-
1809, 198.
Nashville, growth of, 413.
Natchez, post office at, 86; trade
of, 189, 417.
National Gazette, political controversy in, 158.
National Road, immigrants use,
405, 406.
Nationalism, in education, 176-
179, 207; sectionalism hinders,
185; the capital a symbol of,
185-188; and expansion, 188-
192; expressions of, 206-207,
209-210; preached, 207-208;
economic, 208-209, 371, 425,
427-428; European influence
on, 210-211; cultural, 318-
319, 349-351, 356-357. *See
also* War of 1812.
Natural sciences, taught, 301, 322-
325; amateur interest in, 313-
321; societies promote, 321-
322; applied, 326-331.
Navy, in War of 1812, 205-206.
Neal, John, as novelist, 359; on
American writers, 369.
Negroes, in South, 7, 122, 131; in